Walking Macao, Reading the Baroque

Walking MACAO, Reading the Baroque

Jeremy Tambling and Louis Lo

Published in conjunction with

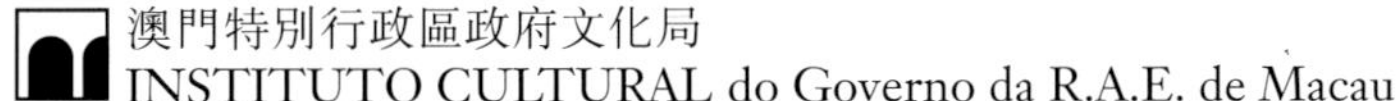

澳門特別行政區政府文化局
INSTITUTO CULTURAL do Governo da R.A.E. de Macau

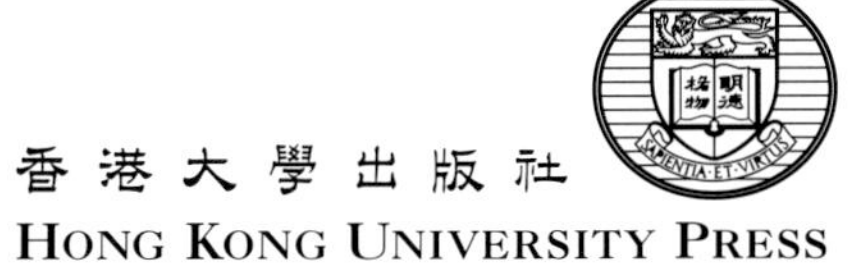

香港大學出版社
HONG KONG UNIVERSITY PRESS

Hong Kong University Press
14/F Hing Wai Centre
7 Tin Wan Praya Road
Aberdeen
Hong Kong

© Jeremy Tambling and Louis Lo 2009

ISBN 978-962-209-937-1 Hardback
ISBN 978-962-209-938-8 Paperback

Secure On-line Ordering
http://www.hkupress.org

British Library Cataloguing-in-Publication Data
A catalogue copy for this book is available from the British Library.

Printed and bound by United League Graphic & Binding Co. Ltd. in Hong Kong, China

Table of Contents

Illustrations

Preface

This short study complete with new photographs of Macao does four things. It is a guide-book to parts of Macao, spelled here with the old Portuguese usage, rather than as 'Macau'. It discusses Macao as a colonial city, as having a history of baroque art and architecture, and as being fascinating in its own right. It thinks about what is meant by 'baroque' when this term is used in contemporary literary and critical theory. So, the book is for readers interested in Macao and others who want to discover theory because they are working in cultural studies. Those who live in Hong Kong particularly will be surprised at how much theory of the baroque — which also includes a theory of allegory, deconstruction, postmodernism, colonialism, globalisation, and the phenomenology of perception — can be learned from Macao. The book also gives a very elementary introduction to the work of Walter Benjamin — in fact, we once thought of calling the book *Macao, Capital of the Sixteenth-Century*. Finally, we hope it will be of interest to anyone who wants to 'read' cities, whether baroque or global.

Armed with a digital camera, we have walked the length and breadth of Macao, looking at its architecture. Photographs were all taken by Louis Lo and the text was written jointly, in Hong Kong, Manchester and Macao.

We have read everything we can on Macao, some material very informational; this book uses much information gleaned in this way, but the reader should be warned that the selection of material here is more personal than comprehensive, and that one of its keynotes is to discover, and write about, what is 'baroque' in Macao. A number of terms from architecture, art criticism and cultural theory have been used, and where terms are technical, they have been explained in the course of writing, and in more detail in a glossary which appears at the end. But there are also gaps in the information we could obtain. There are frustrating differences in the attitude taken towards visitors coming to Macao in comparison to historical sites in Europe. Macao deserves a more discerning attitude towards its past; if it had had that, there might not have been such destruction of its past. Visitors are kept from making discoveries by the unhelpful information that we, for example, have sometimes received while walking the city. (No one would take responsibility for helping us, and seemed surprised that we were interested in places which, in any other context, would have crowds of tourists visiting.) Sites which are listed as 'popular' and 'world heritage' are only interested in attracting consumption rather than understanding, not to mention places which are not in the list, but which are equally interesting. We have been struck by the paucity of information about the sites. We have looked at books, talked to people at the various sites, consulted websites, for information that was ultimately unattributable, uncertain in quality, poor in quantity. Even finding decent maps has been a problem. Much information found, especially on websites, has merely repeated or recycled other pieces of information, much of it inaccurate. Those doing cultural studies often discuss the difficulties of 'reading the city'. To those theoretical issues which they face — the complexity of signs in the city, and their several meanings — can be added the practical issue of being able to read Macao as a text where interpretative keys seem to fail, partly because of a lack of basic informative detail about the city, and partly because that detail may be taken in so many ways, with differing implications for Chinese and Portuguese readers. Much of what follows is tentative. It needs more detailed research, which will only come when art historians and archaeologists turn on Macao the detailed attention that it needs and deserves.

In spite of frustrations, we also encountered wonderful helpfulness from people who let us photograph from their houses or shops, and each visit to Macao produced kindness: the Ho Tung librarians; Pedro Ascenção, the head teacher at Dom José da Costa Nunes kindergarten; the Institute for Tourism; Professor Mao Sihui; the clergy of São José and of the St Joseph the Workers' Church; the Instituto Salesiano, Macao; and César Guillén Nuñez and Eric Sautede and the Ricci Institute, where Jeremy Tambling gave a paper on Macao on 11 May 2005 entitled 'Chinese Urban Culture and the Ruins of Macau' (Macau Ricci Institute Forum 13). The Ricci Institute has also provided invaluable library assistance. Thanks to Bernhard Klein for a sight of his chapter on Camões; to Jonathan Hall for comments on the manuscript; to the Universities of Manchester, and Hong Kong, and Shue Yan University for their help and hospitality; and to

Isaac Hui Ting Yan and Ian Fong Ho Yin for help with footnoting.

Last, a note on how to use the book. Chapter 1 introduces the topics we are interested in: walking the city, reading baroque. Chapters 3, 4 and 5 are mainly dedicated to single sites, and match discussion of them with theories of the baroque. They have a guide-book format. Chapter 10 is a little similar to these. Chapter 2 gives an easy lead-in to the subject of the baroque, and to some interesting sites in Macao; this chapter and later ones move around different but comparable areas and artworks, analysing them, sometimes returning to individual places for a second look. Chapters 2, 6, 7, 8 and 9 are arranged thematically, and though they could each be read using the sites as an itinerary, we do require the reader to visit, at least imaginatively, very disparate parts of Macao, so that quite a lot of dotting about is needed. Unlike other places, however, such going backwards and forwards is possible; Macao is not big, and as one resident of the city said, it is not difficult to be on time for appointments in it. The index should be used to see what has been discussed (and there are things not discussed: our principle of selection appears in chapter 1). Throughout, there is a slow build-up of a reading of a history of colonial Macao, so that chapters 11 and 12 reach the present in discussing modern architecture, though there are examples of this interest in earlier chapters too; all the while baroque art and architecture are never really left behind.

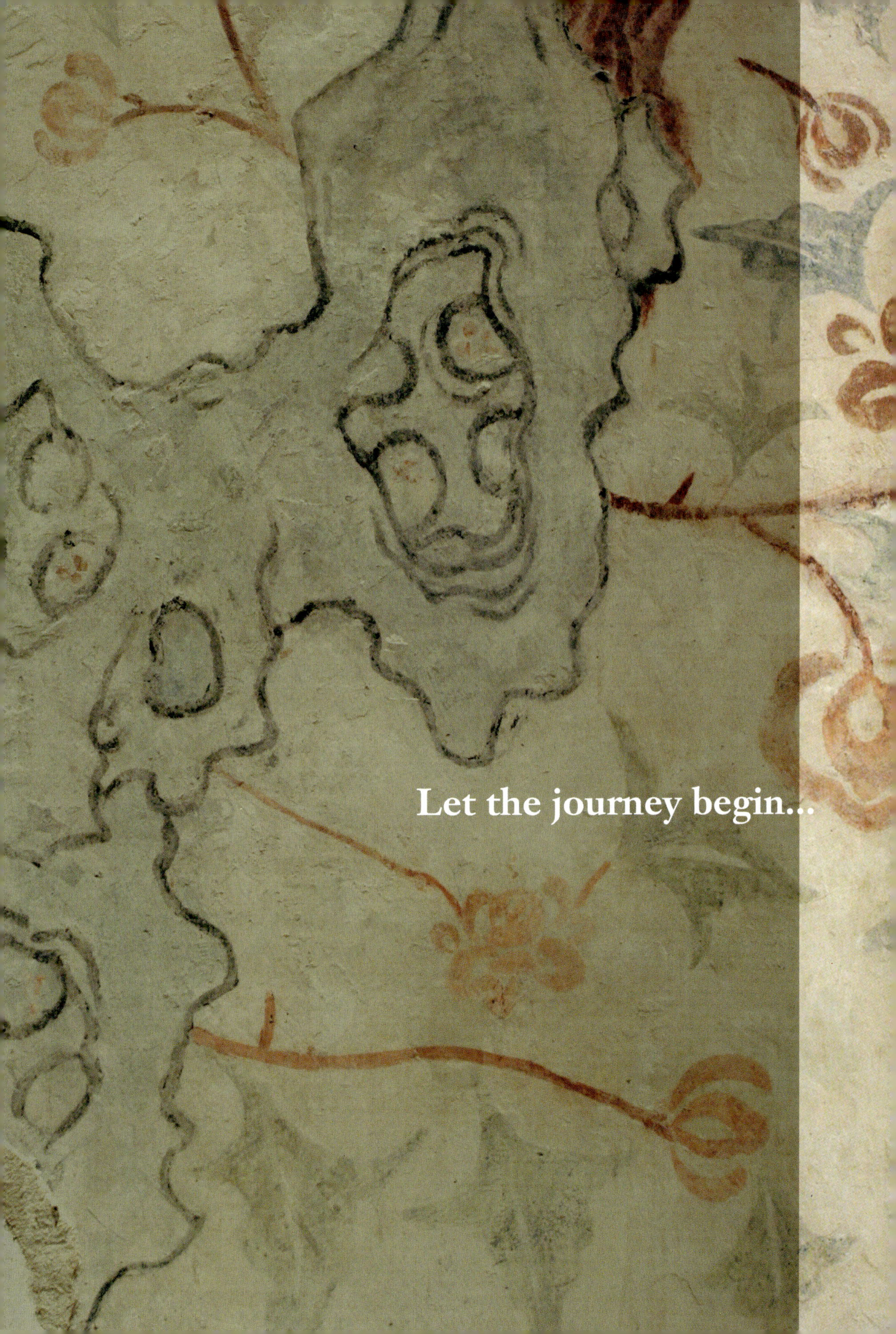
Let the journey begin...

Learning from Macao:
An Introduction

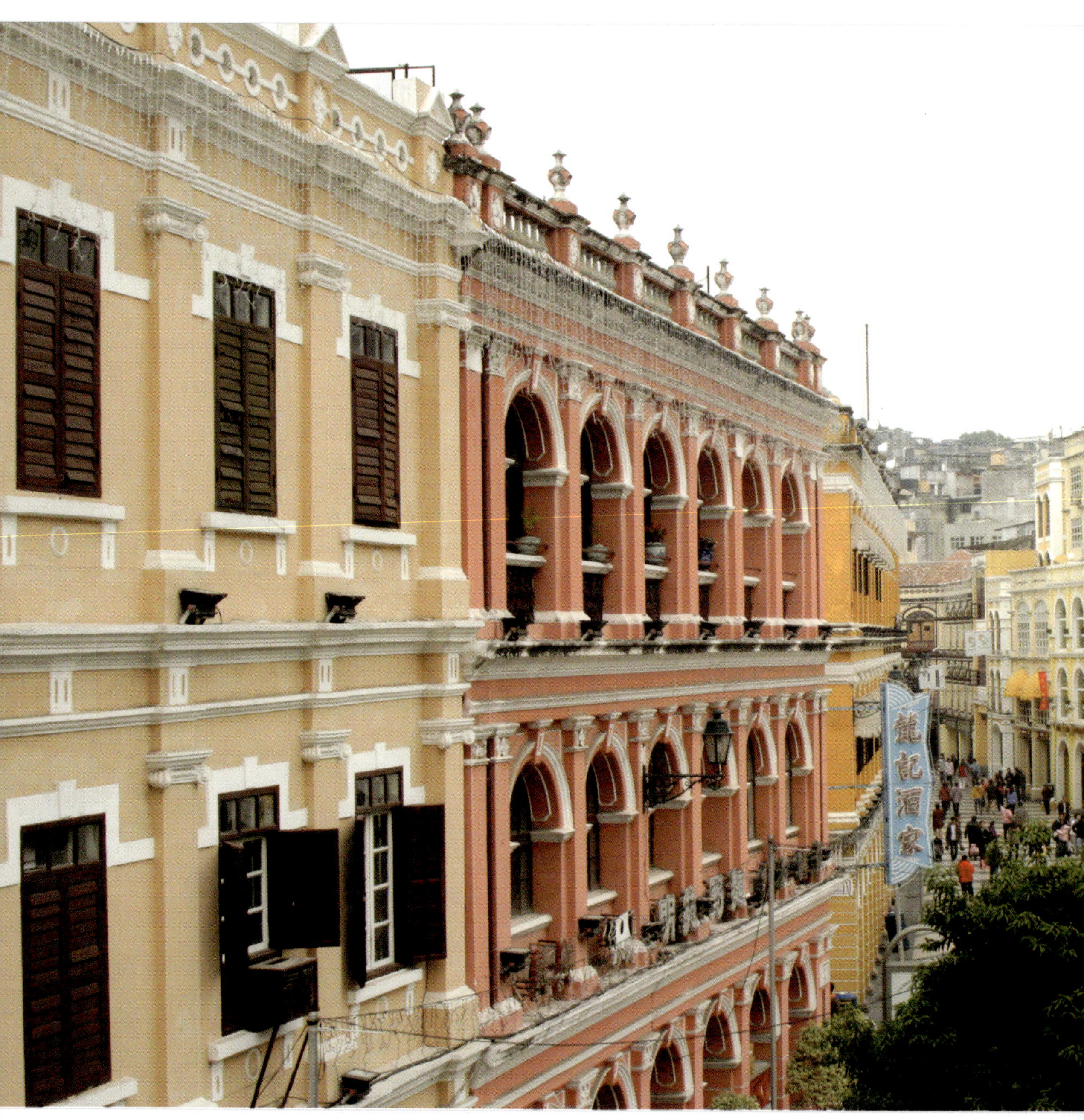

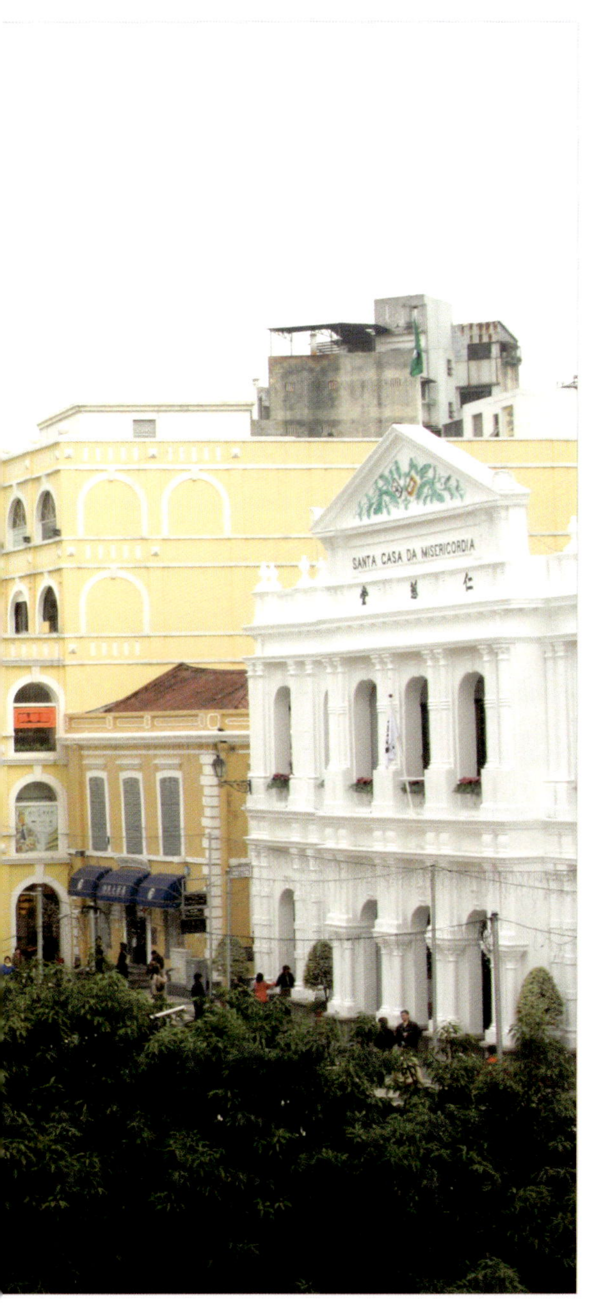

1. Senado Square

The impression visitors who do not penetrate the city of Macao to its old heart will get is of a capital of consumption, full of high-rise buildings, brightly coloured neon lights, and casinos. It is hard to link the two: the older colonised space and this new reclaimed land. Our chapter-title refers to Robert Venturi's 1977 book on the postmodern, *Learning from Las Vegas*. As Macao is often called the Las Vegas of Asia, and has a bigger turnover and better architecture than Las Vegas (though Las Vegas has also reached it in the form of the Venetian Resort on Cotai Strip), it seems particularly suggestive.

The photograph shows Macao's old centre, with buildings with porticos right and left hurrying away towards the vanishing-point of the photograph. A city, like its people, on the move, with buildings, like train-carriages, disappearing away from the spectator. Those famous wavy lines in the pavement look like stairs carrying people away. The angle of buildings on the left changes, begins to fold, and creates a sense of a space we cannot see. This is a guide-book to those obscure spaces in Macao, and to some of Macao's architecture, colonial history, its present and its past. Like Venturi who subtitles his book *The Forgotten Symbolism of Architectural Form*, this book is interested in what is forgotten, in the symbolism still partly readable in Macao, and in architecture. The difference from most other books on Macao is that this book particularly explores baroque elements in Macao.

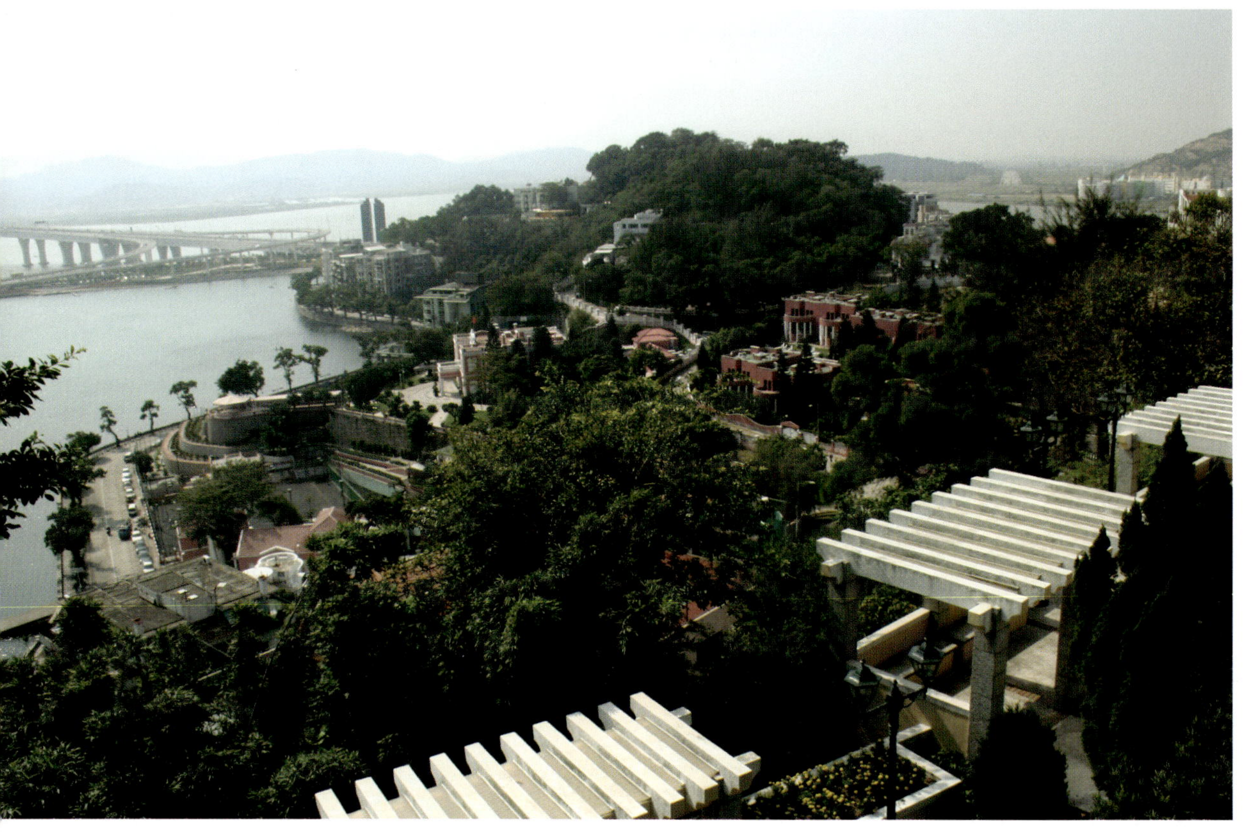

2. Southwest Macao including Santa Sancha

Macao is known more for its gambling and Grand Prix (the 53rd in 2006) than for the baroque; it is on a hilly tip of southeast China, at the mouth of the Pearl River, forty miles from Hong Kong. It was once a Portuguese enclave, reverting to Chinese rule in 1999, two years after Hong Kong, and its rapid new developments are partly financed by its casinos.

The photograph looks towards the southwest part of Macao, so that the Inner Harbour is seen at the right. It was taken from the site of a Portuguese fort on Penha Hill, and looks towards the area that had to be defended: in the centre may be seen the nineteenth-century Santa Sancha Palace (1846), which became the governor's residence in 1937. The palace was on the Praya Grande, which folds round towards the Inner Harbour; behind that is mainland China. The site is no longer a fort, but the courtyard in front of the church of Nossa Senhora da Penha, one of the highest points in Macao (sixty-three metres above sea level), looks towards the islands of Taipa and Coloane, now virtually indistinguishably connected. The new architecture of Macao proceeds apace in land reclamations that have turned the Praya Grande from a sea shore to a lake side, and in the bridges and the Macao tourist sight-seeing tower, not photographed. Designed by Gordon Moller of Craig, Craig, Moller & Associates, it is 388 metres high, and suitable for bungee-jumping. This new architecture, which offsets some very Mediterranean-looking villas in the hills below Penha, contrasts with the architecture of the church of Nossa Senhora da Penha, built in 1935, but replacing a church of 1622. The modern Madonna and child at the summit of the church rises into the air in contrast to the Macao Tower, standing on an older, perhaps seventeenth-century, plinth (see photograph 65).

Macao became a colonial city under Portuguese rule in the 1550s. Any visitor will see its self-confidence as a Chinese city, in its postmodern architecture and airport, in its quasi-Disneyland developments, and in such events as the hosting of the Fourth East Asian Games, and the awarding of twenty-year licences to Stanley Ho's Sociedade de Jogos de Macau (SJM). Then there is the opening of the Las Vegas–style Wynn Resorts and the Galaxy Consortium, the Venetian Resort's split from Galaxy, the opening of the Sands Casino, and the hosting of conferences, such as the 54th PATA (Pacific Asia Travel Association) Annual Conference at the Convention and Entertainment centre at the Macao Tower.[1]

But a visitor will discover old buildings, many of which are, loosely, baroque in style. Some are hidden away, though as Macao has become more conscious of itself as a heritage and tourist site, they are being cleaned up and made more accessible. There are twenty-five buildings and sites in it which belong to UNESCO world heritage, and these, all together comprise just one of thirty-one such sites throughout China.[2]

In the following list of heritage sites, the first three comprise fortifications, whose character is mainly pre-baroque:
1. The old city walls, which date back to the 1560s,
2. Monte Fort (Mount Fortress) (1617–1626),
3. Guia Fortress (1622–1638).

Others may be loosely considered as baroque:
4. Senado Square,
5. Santa Casa da Misericórdia (The Holy House of

Mercy) (founded 1569, built 1700s, renovated 1905),

6. Igreja de São Domingos (St Dominic's Church),
7. The Ruins of St Paul (1640),
8. Dom Pedro V Theatre (1860–1873),
9. Igreja de Santo Agostinho (St Augustine's Church) (1874),
10. Igreja de São Lorenzo (St Lawrence's Church),
11. Igreja e Seminário de São José (St Joseph's Seminary and Church) (1758),
12. The Moorish Barracks (1841),
13. Largo do Lilau (Lilau Square),
14. Sir Robert Ho Tung Library (1894), originally belonged to D. Carolina Cunha, and bought by Sir Robert Ho Tung (1862–1956) in 1918; after his death the building was passed to the Macao government to be a public library.

In addition to these, there are neo-classical buildings, which have a complex relationship to the baroque:

15. Leal Senado (founded 1583, renovated 1783 and 1940),
16. Igreja de Santo António (St Anthony's Church),
17. Igreja de São Lázaro (St Lazarus' Church) (1954),
18. Igreja da Sé (The Cathedral) (1844, rebuilt 1938).

This book discusses these, and also those Chinese buildings which have become part of the UNESCO heritage:

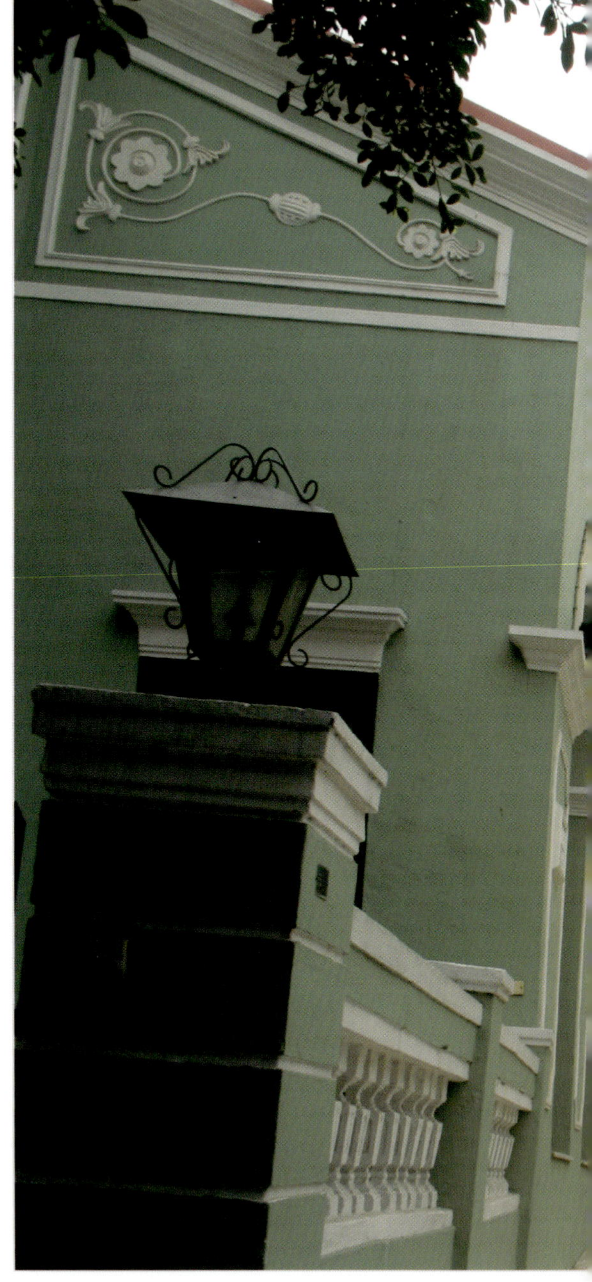

3. Dom Pedro V Theatre and St Augustine's Church and a distant view of the Sir Robert Ho Tung Library

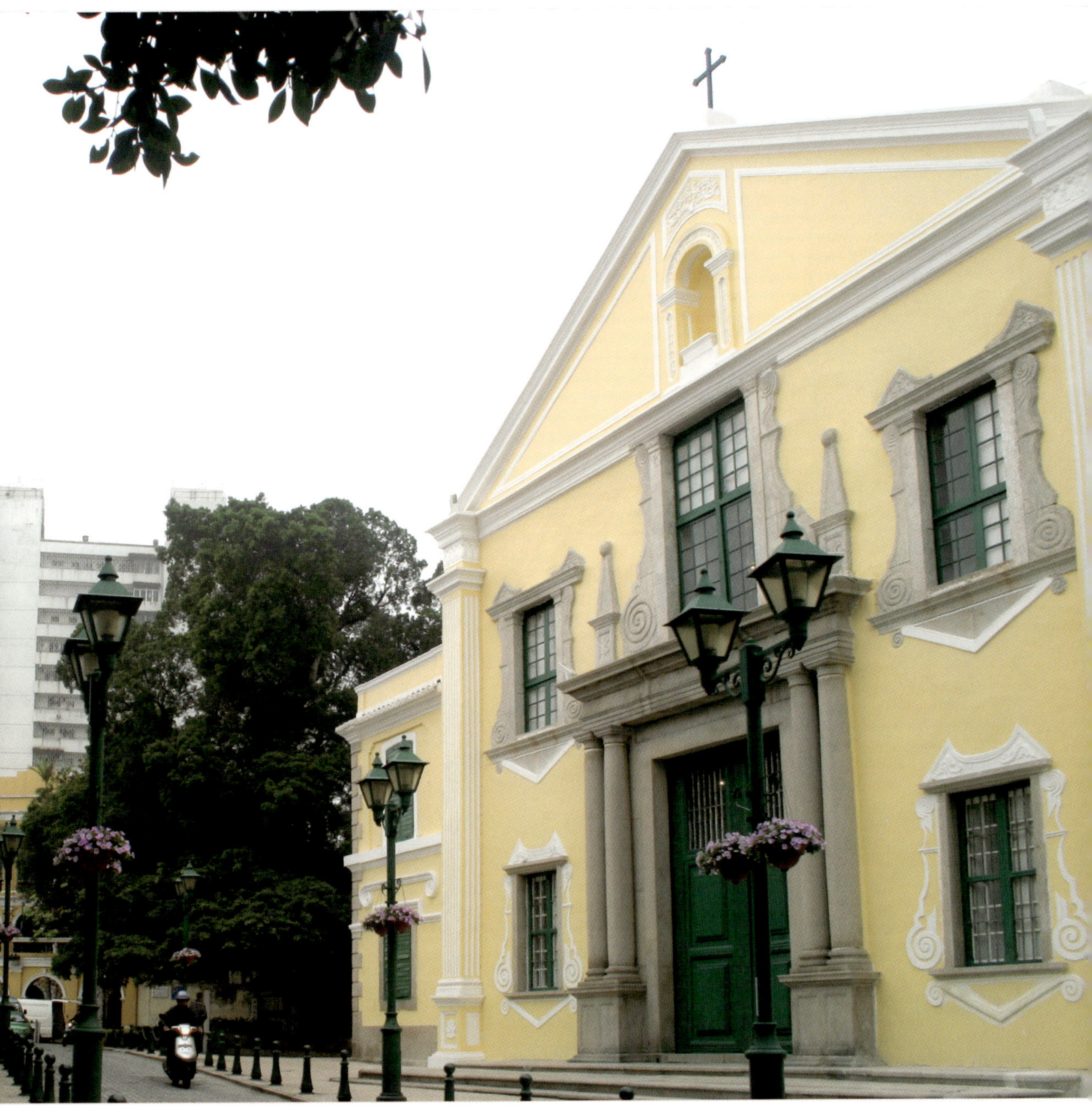

19. A-Ma temple (before 1555),
20. Sam Kai Vui Kun temple (after 1720s),
21. Lou Kau mansion (1889),
22. Na Tcha temple (1888–1901).

As the Chinese garden in formal terms may also relate to the baroque, three open spaces are discussed, two of which are memorials of colonialism:

23. Jardim de Luís de Camões (The Camões Garden) (eighteenth century), always in legend associated with Camões. The tradition says that he wrote his epic poem *Os Lusíadas* (*The*

4. Moongate, Mandarin's House

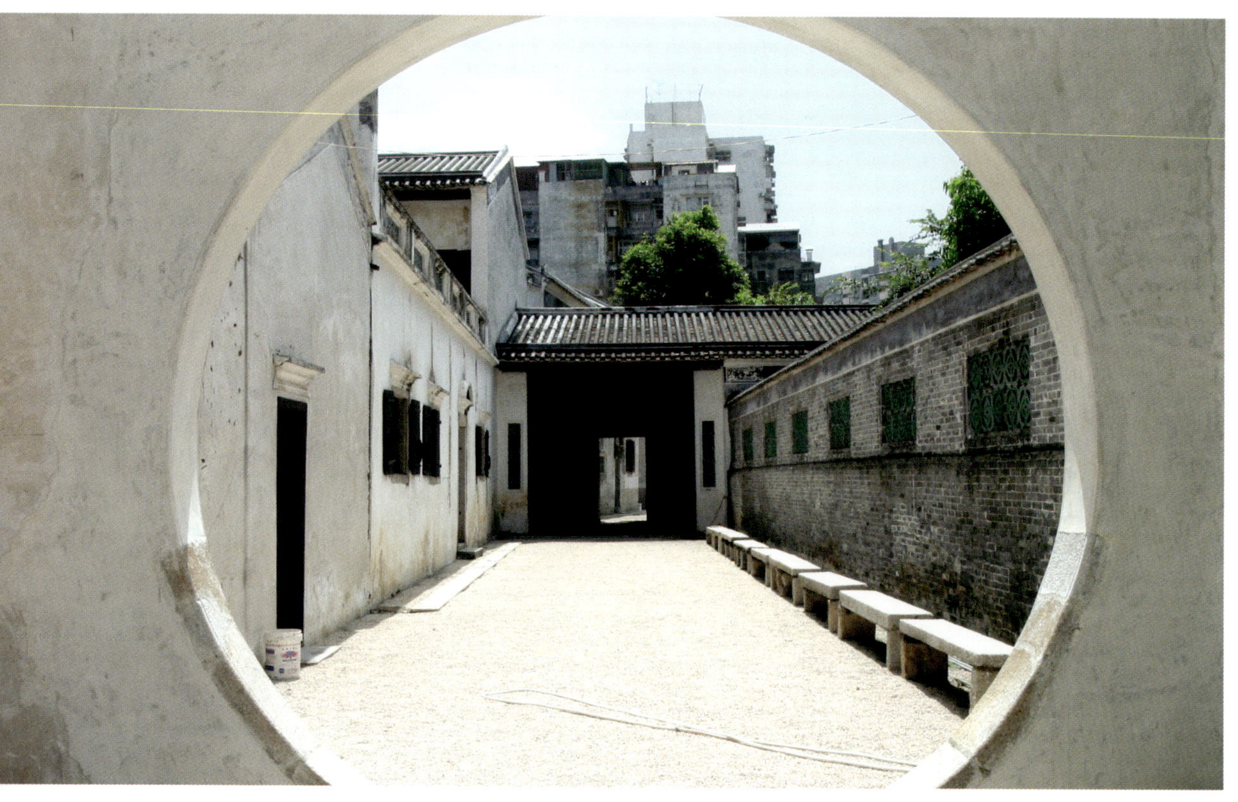

Lusiads) here, immediately after Macao became a Portuguese colony in 1557. A bronze bust of Camões was set up in the mid-nineteenth-century colonial Macao, thus making a claim to being the home of the national poet.

24. The Protestant cemetery (1814), originally part of the Casa Garden; a house built in the 1770s, and occupied by the British East Indian company.

25. The Lou Lim Ioc Chinese Garden (built by Lou Kau 1837–1906) and named for his son who invited an architect, Liu Jiliu, from Zhongshan, to create a garden in the style of Suzhou.

Included here is the Mandarin's House, which was owned by Zheng Guanying and his father Zheng Wenrui, and which was built around 1881. Running to about four thousand square metres at the corner of Barra Street and António da Silva Lane, it is a traditional Chinese-style compound, for master and servants, containing a number of buildings of traditional grey Chinese bricks. The orientation of the building is towards the northwest. In 2001, the Cultural Affairs Bureau of the Macao S.A.R. government bought it, and the house was, in 2007, under renovation.

Many of the buildings named are both baroque *and* colonial, which gives an added complexity, even a contradiction, to be worked out throughout this book. And Macao has many new buildings. Can these be called baroque? Does it make sense to think of baroque as a term applicable to postmodern architecture, or as having any relationship to it? The question may be more relevant since it was in the moment of the postmodern that the baroque became highlighted as the object of some kinds of critical theory. This gives an incentive to think about contemporary, 'postcolonial' Macao as also constructed by the inspiration of the baroque, making Macao radically different from Hong Kong, which has virtually no European architectural heritage, and very few buildings older than 1900.[3] Fisherman's Wharf as a modern commercial development could hardly exist in Hong Kong; its guiding spirit which sees European and American history as material for a 'theme-park' could only come from a culture which had been subjected to such European influences, which had them within its very grain and lived in them, knowing them in a way that Hong Kong quite simply neither did, nor does. This colonial history, which makes Macao as old as many European cities in terms of the artefacts it preserves, brands what is 'postmodern' within Macao as different from Hong Kong, which has little sense of being able to draw on or play with a European architecture which has now become 'heritage'. Perhaps the 'postmodern' does not apply to one set of concepts only; Hong Kong postmodern and Macao postmodern may be different in the degree of playfulness in the architecture.[4] The difference between Hong Kong and Macao is this: Hong Kong has never had a colonial history which left interesting buildings for it to react against; Macao has, and its new buildings are consistently more interesting than Hong Kong's.

Explaining Terms —
1: Postmodernism

Walking Macao, Reading the Baroque studies all of the heritage, non-postmodern buildings listed above and some not listed. It also discusses some modern architecture, to see if there is anything 'baroque' in it. The concept of the 'baroque' is explored in the context of colonialism, postcolonialism and postmodernism, using terms derived from modern critical theory. Readers could treat this as a guide-book — both to Macao as a city (so that readers should bring the book with them to walk Macao's streets) and to baroque as a concept. It is for readers on foot and in armchairs, since Macao is a library in which to read the baroque. Walking through Macao and reading the baroque can be done together. This book responds to Macao's rich historical and visual culture and asks for readers who need a guide-book, one like Ruskin's *Stones of Venice*, with its enthusiasm for Gothic architecture.

What is 'postmodern'? It can apply to the art of the historical period which comes after modernism, a style which reacts against the functionalist and minimalist characteristics of modernism, and which tries to be popular.[5] But it could also be defined, as by the art critic Hal Foster, as a drive or tendency which 'destructures the order of representations'.[6] Here, postmodernism breaks with the idea that art should represent, or reproduce, existing reality. At its limits, it toys with the idea that art represents reality, as with Fisherman's Wharf, which makes a 'pastiche' of the architectural styles it reproduces (pastiche imitates something without having any sense of criticism, as opposed to parodying it).[7] When critics call postmodern styles decorative, superficial, refusing the concept of 'depth', saying that they are 'kitsch', it can be replied that postmodernism is refusing to refer to some reality that it feels it should reproduce. In doing so, it questions the authority implied in saying that other works of art have 'depth of meaning' and 'essential truth'.

2: Baroque

There is a third form of postmodernism which relates to these two forms. The philosopher Alain Badiou (born 1937) has characterised the ideas of the polymath theorist Gilles Deleuze (1925–1995), who may be provisionally thought of as postmodernist, in this way:

> Deleuze is ... the inventor of a contemporary baroque, in which our desire for the multiple, intermixtures, and the co-existence of universes free of any common rule — in sum, our planetary democratism — is able to recognise itself and unfurl. In short, we end up with Deleuze as the joyous thinker of the world's confusion.[8]

Deleuze sees the baroque in terms of 'the fold', so that depth and surface, and the intricacies of what is pleated and wavy (like the wavy black lines in so many of Macao's pavements), and what exists in light and shadow together, are part of both baroque and the postmodern. What Deleuze means by 'the fold' will become clearer in the next two chapters, after the historical baroque has been defined, but provisionally, contemporary baroque is a form of the postmodern. Some elementary definitions of the historical meanings of baroque — a Portuguese word — can be offered:

1. It is the name for an artistic movement, variously applied to art, sculpture, architecture, music, and even literature. It was broadly identified with Europe from the sixteenth to eighteenth centuries, coming out of mannerism and turning into rococo, and it is sometimes seen as Catholic in tendency.

2. The term often serves to describe a particularly complicated way of thinking and feeling. It has been said 'what characterises baroque poetry is the repetition of conceit'.[9] (A 'conceit' is a clever expression, or trick of language.) In baroque literature, playing and punning with language is pluralised and repeated.

3. Some discussions of baroque use it to describe a 'top-down', authoritarian culture which is both commanding and manipulating.

4. The baroque has been seen as a style which is also 'heterogeneous', containing things which cannot be categorised or generalised into a whole system. There is a contradiction here with definition 3, which will be discussed later. As the art of the heterogeneous, the baroque becomes associated with micro-narratives. This has made 'baroque' a significant term in recent criticism and cultural studies.

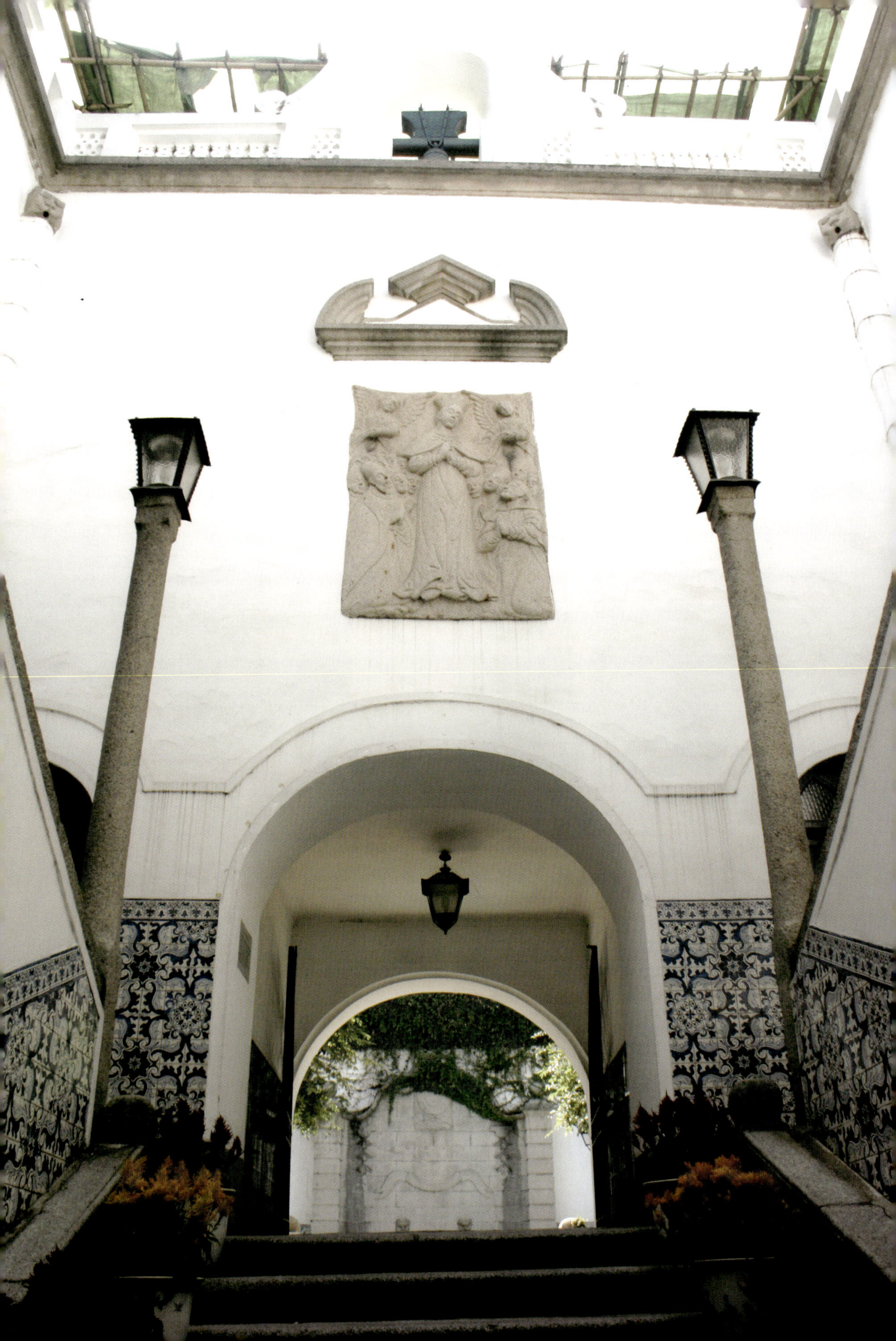

Photographing Spaces

Photographs in this book look at Macao's different spaces, as here, inside the Leal Senado: going up steps towards an arch on the other side of which is a garden.[10] The steps are inside a virtual well enclosed by walls, and overlooked by balconies. The visitor has entered the well and is climbing up stairs lined by plants and *azulejos* [blue and white tiles]; at the landing, two sets of stairs will return to go on up further, framing the photograph like two coulisses. At the top of the wall, set into the balustrade, is a bell, a reminder of an older way of telling time and giving warning in the walled city. Embedded in the wall are only half-decipherable images: here, granite stone-work of Mary, Our Lady of Mercy, dispensing mercy to all, including the Pope. Above that is an architrave-cornice, whose design, common in Macao, is baroque. The street lamps are a reminder that this inside space is also an outside space. The drainpipes, bamboo-like and fluted, each have at the top two gargoyles, grotesque masks, with mouths open as water-spouts. Whenever they were made, they recall a Gothic tradition in the European middle ages which made such pagan, Dionysian figures and thought nothing of putting them next to sacred Christian images.[11] Other gargoyles can be seen in Macao, for instance, on the façade of St Paul's. The view at the foot of the stairs can be seen in photograph 57.

5. Leal Senado

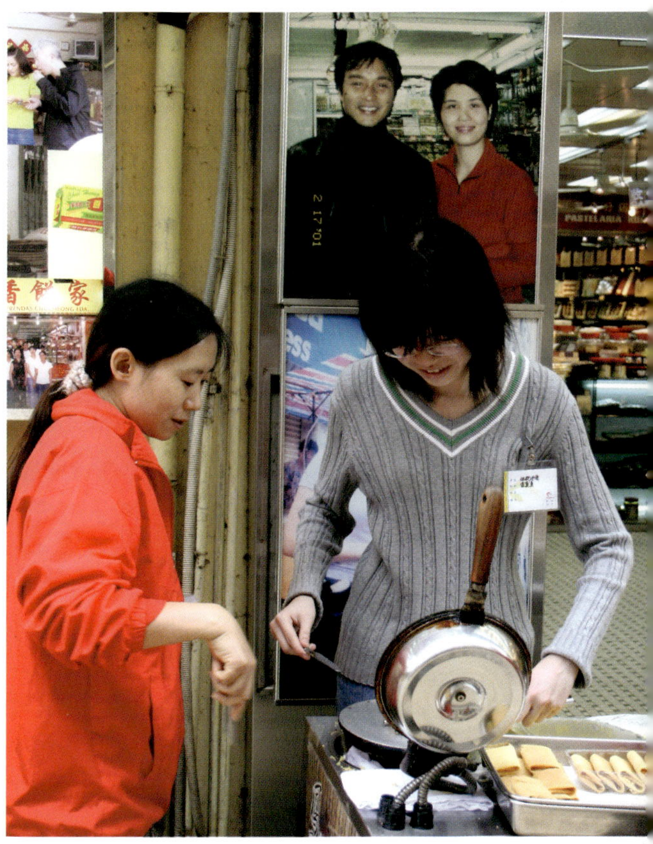

6. Leslie Cheung

Photographs also illuminate the city as cinematic, not static but changing behind the apparent solidity of its buildings.[12] (Some of its squares are like film-sets; this artificiality needs exploring.) How the city relates to film appears in the photograph of Leslie Cheung, the famous Hong Kong singer and film star (e.g. *Happy Together* [1997]), who, on the evidence of photograph 6, visited Macao on

17 February 2001, and is pictured next to the boss of the souvenir shop, in a photograph of the shop which appears behind the two women. Another photograph is below them, which gives a reason for cropping the photograph of the star: in city-culture, nothing is seen whole, everyone has, as Andy Warhol says, but fifteen minutes of fame. The photographs, and those to the left, which have been cropped (the lower one showing the staff of the souvenir shop, whose work is selling cakes), give some of the several levels of reality in the photograph, which shows two women folding phoenix rolls, little pancakes, in the street. The shop is near the façade of St Paul's, and it suggests how many lives are rolled together into one moment, which holds the past and the present within it.

In this book photographs and text are equally important. Critical points are made with reference to one sole source of evidence: photographs (we have no reproductions of Chinnery, for instance). But there are problems associated with attempting to capture the city on camera (taking photographs that escape from being 'mere' tourist photography). Taking photographs is easy, especially with a digital camera which facilitates night-time photography, but it does not mean that the city is thereby fairly

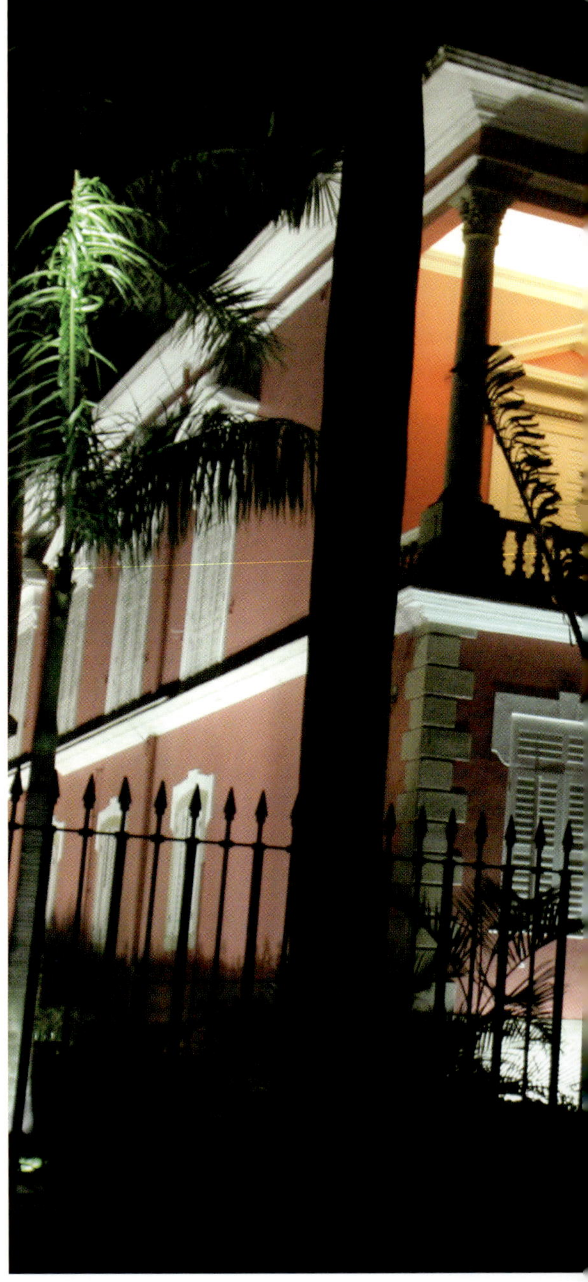

7. *Government House by night*

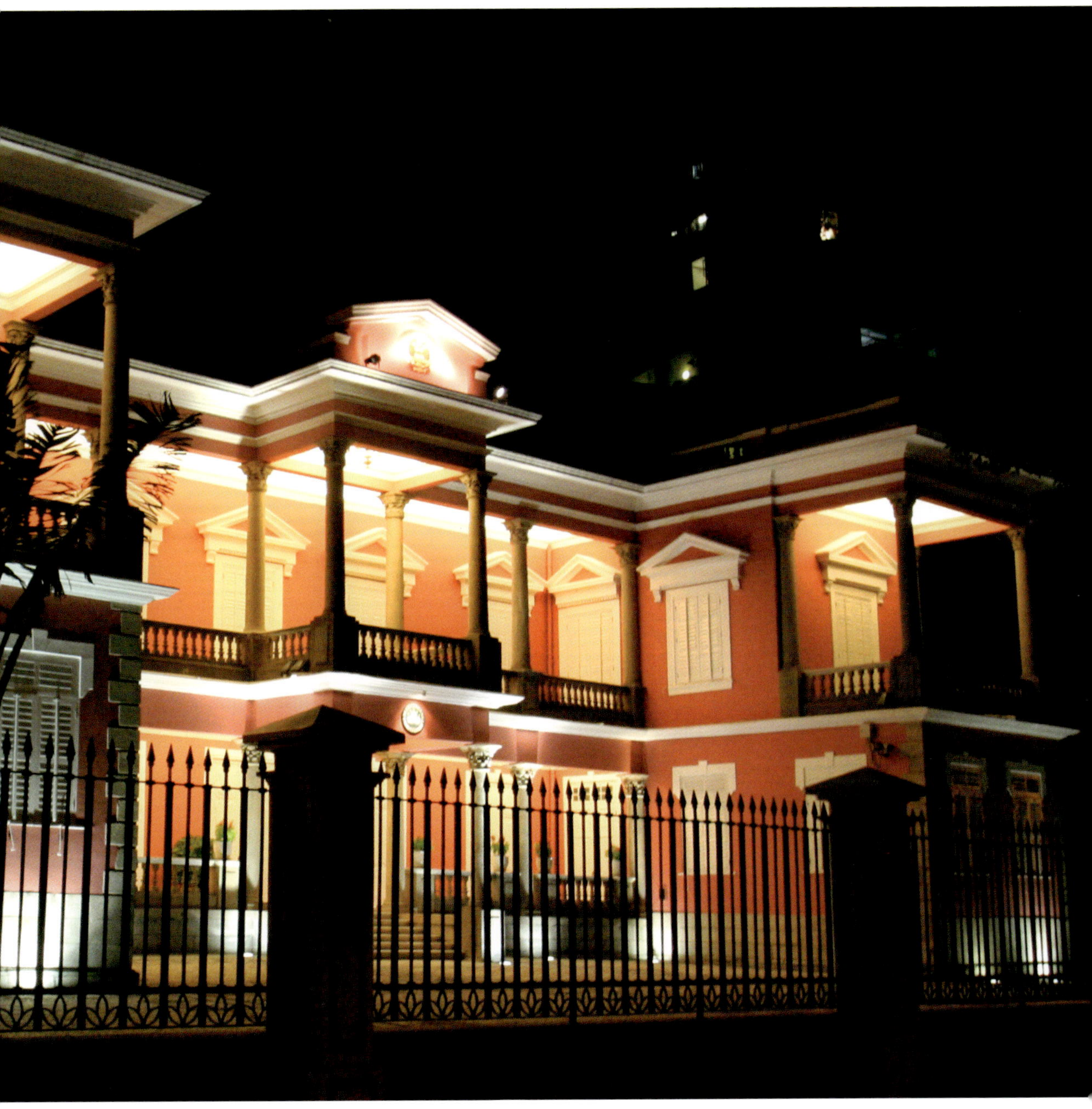

'represented'. Something escapes, since how a photograph is taken is framed and influenced by what we understand as photography, and by people's pre-conceptions of what the city is like. A photograph says something about what is consciously considered significant in culture, but the danger here is that a photograph is always a cliché, and not to be looked at. Why do tourists photograph themselves in front of a historical building? Is it to remind ourselves that we have indeed been there? As if saying if we had not taken a photograph, we could not prove it, as if we no longer have memory. We need souvenirs, and photograph ourselves before we have truly seen the building: the copy (the photograph) precedes the original in the importance ascribed to it.

This is more ironic with Macao since colonial architecture is the art of the copy, reproducing the vernacular architecture of the colonising country. The photograph becomes the copy of the copy, what the postmodern theorist Jean Baudrillard called the 'simulacrum'.[13] Simulacral, pastiche architecture gets photographed in its turn by tourists: here photography does not respect authenticity, or difference: everything circulates as a photographic image. And the colonial building, while beautiful, may look like a pastiche of the original European design. Take for example, Government House, (1849) designed by José Agostinho Tomás d' Aquino (1804–1852), Macanese-born, but who studied in Lisbon, and returned to Macao in 1825. As a government building, it is stately, but it was built as a private palace for a Portuguese aristocrat, Alexandrino Antonio de Melo, Viscount of Cercal, after d'Aquino had completed Santa Sanchaz for him. As such, the central portico and the pediment above the flat roof are in excess, like the Corinthian columns. It is as if the colonial style wanted to exceed the Portuguese; the tendency towards excess is part of the 'baroque' but the pastiche element curiously anticipates Fisherman's Wharf.

To photograph Macao becomes impossible because any photograph circulates in the realm of images which have become no more than clichés. That is why the city is unrepresentable. In a way, the task is to photograph an 'invisible city', or, by using photography, to find what photography cannot represent. The points raised in this paragraph are especially pertinent to Macao: while researching for this book, we could hardly find any images of the places that were not aimed at tourists. The ideal is to go beyond the conventional memory people have of Macao, by photographing it as baroque, so that behind the flat surface of the photograph on the computer screen or as printed out, there are depths, folds and pleats, baroque characteristics, not noticed in conventional photography where images have been looked at to the point of saturation.

What gets photographed seals our relationship to what is thought of as culturally important. When buildings are used as backdrops for photographs of tourists, they are seen in what the Marxist theorist Walter Benjamin (1892–1941) called a state of 'distraction'.[14] People's reaction to architecture is to take photographs of it, and perhaps to add themselves in the photographs, but not to concentrate on it. A photograph of a building is almost certainly not to be looked at; its fate is to be treated like any other photograph. But the photograph has the task of showing the city as that which cannot be represented, because of the multiplicity of images that circulate about it, destined to be consumed in a state of distraction.

Another problem of representation is that all its forms (including literature and photography, which is thought of as its most 'realistic' mode) turn the 'otherness' (or 'strangeness') of what is there to be seen into the language or imagery of the person who has the power of representation. To be able to represent is to control, but the controlling power of that person (e.g. the photographer) is concealed. The power of representation appears as objective. To give an example: the realist and romantic paintings of Macao by George Chinnery (1774–1852), discussed in chapter 9, are truly admirable. But there is a sense in which he patronises the Chinese fisherfolk he represents and looks on them with a colonial eye that miniaturises them. To represent or 'capture' something in photography is to kill it, when what is expected in photography is that it will show everything and put everything on display.

Unsurprisingly, modern photographs of Macao tend to duplicate each other. But the modern city, like Macao, challenges the photographer to do otherwise than reproduce a cliché. The city is always in change, always in process, its buildings always under scaffolding or modification. It was impossible to photograph the Senado Square without some exceptional event taking place in it: it has no normal state. It would be good to say that the photographs are a creation, not a mere 'record' of the 'real' Macao, so making the city live in a way which gives detail where the eye could only see an impression, thereby doubling its existence. Digital technology adds something to the picture, but something still escapes the eye. Something in the picture, as in what is to be seen, resists being domesticated into full revelation to the eye. There is something missing to the viewer's vision in what is commonly called 'the picture'. A commonplace statement in art history is that anything we look at must be discussed in terms which assume that it is a 'picture', or a 'landscape' — a word itself deriving from art history. Because of this sense that there is something missing in every photograph, one trick played here is to not have necessarily matched up the description with the 'right' photograph, preferring a 'montage' effect, with a diverse text and picture.

Theorising the Baroque

Beginnings of modern attention to the baroque came with Heinrich Wölfflin's *Renaissance and Baroque* (1888), which focused attention on churches in Rome, such as the Jesuit church, the Gesù, which was the work of Vignola (1580), or Santa Susanna, the work of Maderno (1603).[15] The Society of Jesus had been approved by Pope Paul III in 1540: baroque meant, for the French, *le style jésuite*.[16] For Wölfflin, baroque architecture is 'painterly', striving after the effects of art, and he thought of it in terms of *movement* in contrast to the severe, static, style of the classical:

If the beauty of a building is judged by the enticing effects of moving masses, the restless jumping forms or violently swaying ones which seem constantly on the point of change, and not by balance and solidity of structure, then the strictly architectonic conception of architecture is depreciated. In short, the severe style of architecture makes its effect by what it *is*, by its corporeal substance, while painterly architecture [baroque] acts through what it *appears* to be, that is, an illusion of movement.[17]

Since Wölfflin, the concept of the 'baroque' has been taken over for modern critical theory, and so becomes crucial for 'modernism' and 'postmodernism'. In part, this is because of its use in the work of Walter Benjamin (1892–1940) in *The Origin of German Tragic Drama* (1928), a text discussed in this book. Much of what has appeared on allegory and more specifically the baroque has been influenced by Benjamin's study.

The postmodern cannot be spoken of as though it was simply the opposite of the baroque, since *Baroque Poetry* defines the baroque as repeating images, as artificial, as echoing things through what the editors call the baroque's favourite topics, 'the echo and the mirror' (xvi). It seems then that the early modern baroque responded to, and created in, the absence of a norm. *Baroque Poetry* argues that 'modern man … like his baroque predecessor, faces a fragmented and puzzling world with no guidelines save those of his own making' (xvii). The baroque is echoed in the postmodern, which is its mirror. If Macao is trying to become modern or postmodern in its architecture, it is not necessarily ceasing to be baroque.

French critical theory from the 1960s onwards used the baroque as a critical tool or concept. This applies to Roland Barthes (1915–1982),[18] Deleuze, Jacques Derrida (1930–2004), Michel Foucault (1926–1984)[19] and Jacques Lacan (1900–1981), whose writings are often called baroque, and who also discusses baroque art and architecture. Another theorist who uses Benjamin and the baroque is Christine Buci-Glucksmann, writing on modernity in France. Another take comes from Latin America, from such writers as Jorge Luis Borges (1899–1986), Alejo Carpentier (1904–1980),[20] the Cuban writer Severo Sarduy (1937–1993) in *Barroco* (1974), and Octavio Paz (1914–1998) who discusses baroque 'novelty and surprise'.[21] Other writers drawn on for this book are the Spanish historian José Antonio

Maravall, Roberto Echevarría for Spanish and Latin American literature, the Italian critic Mario Perniola, and art critics such as Robert Harbison, whose recent study of the subject includes a chapter on colonial baroque, with examples taken mainly from Latin America.[22] 'Baroque' has been used in many contexts: art, architecture, literature, and in relationship to modernity and the postmodern. The opportunity to focus on its diverse meanings through looking at it in both its vitality and its vestiges, in a colonial and postcolonial city which can be explored easily in a day, is irresistible.[23]

Seven Libraries

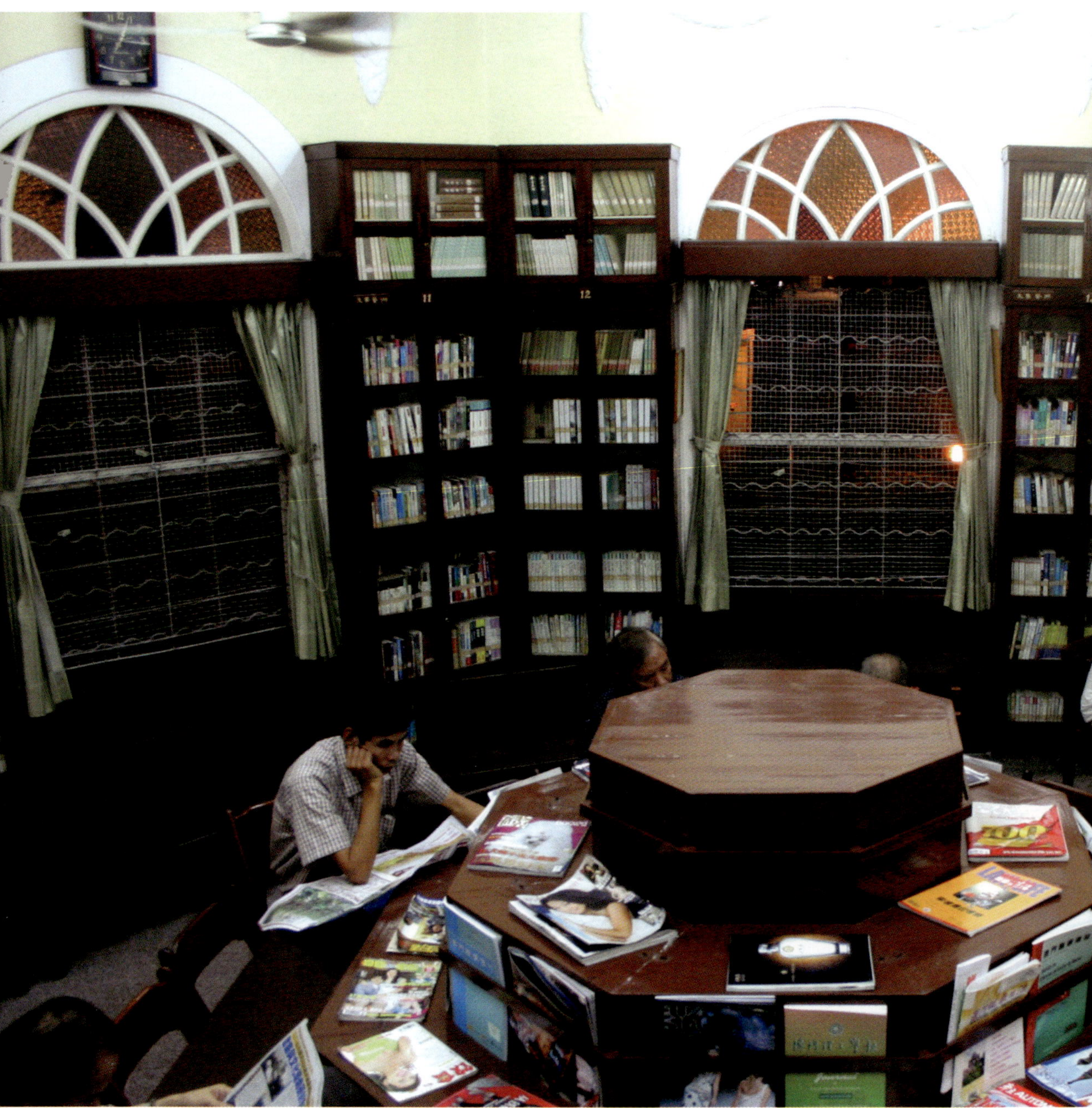

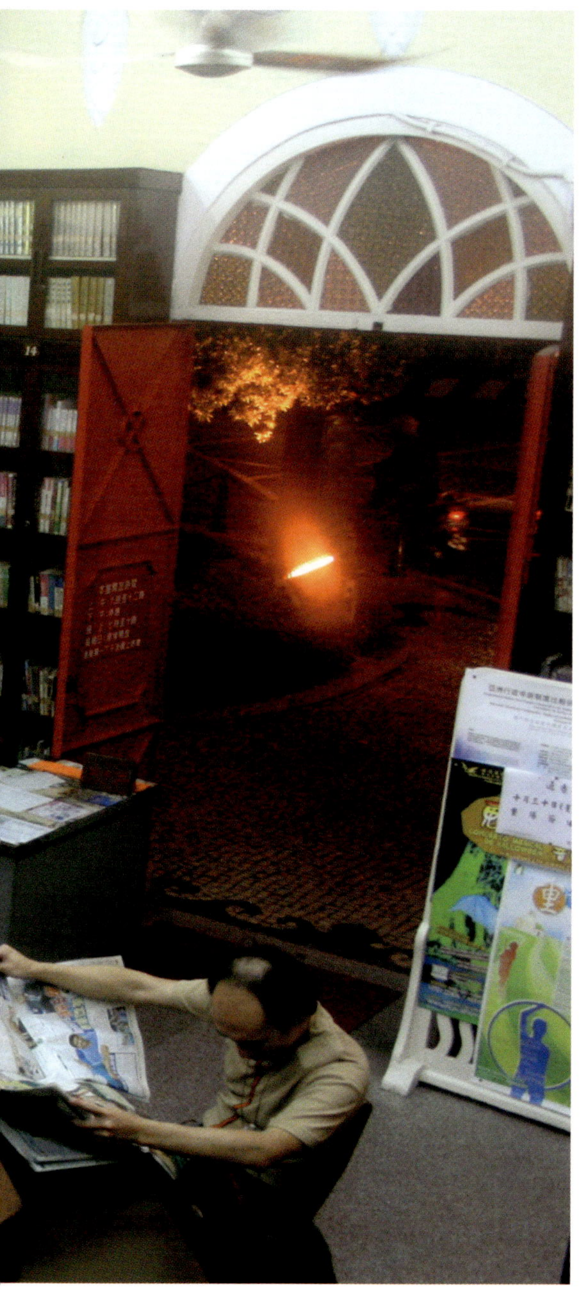

8. *Interior of library,
Jardim de São Francisco*

The Renaissance explores the universe, the baroque explores libraries. Its meditations are devoted to books.

—Walter Benjamin[1]

The classic of Portuguese literature which celebrates Portuguese colonialism is Luís Vaz de Camões' (1524–1580) *The Lusiads* (*Os Lusíadas*). It is both Renaissance and baroque. Discussed more fully in chapter 10, it is complete with Roman classical gods, who are partly allegorical, and it is also a history of Portugal and the Portuguese seaborne empire. Macao was colonised by the Portuguese from Goa in India, which itself had been colonised by 1510. (Goa has crucial examples of colonial baroque.)[2] Portuguese vessels sailed out from Goa to reach Chinese territory on their way to Japan where the Spanish St Francis Xavier (1506–1552) preached in 1549. He was one of the founders of the Society of Jesus (in 1540), and, working under Portuguese auspices, had gone to Goa; he was also to visit Canton (Guangzhou). Goa had been first reached in 1498, by the Portuguese Vasco Da Gama (1460–1524). He returned to Portugal in 1499, and his voyage is the subject of *The Lusiads*.

If we adopt the first half of Benjamin's statement, quoted as the epigraph to this chapter, comparison becomes irresistible with Camões and *The Lusiads*. The Renaissance goes outwards into the world, as with the Portuguese seaborne empire. The baroque corresponds to that part of the poem which has an inward tendency, being melancholic, introspective. The antithesis between the Renaissance and the baroque is stated in Benjamin's *The Origin of German Tragic Drama*, which is a study of the plays of lamentation, tragedies, plays whose theme is mourning (*Trauerspiel*), which were written in baroque Germany in the seventeenth century, some of them in the context of the Thirty Years' War (1618–1648). Benjamin links the baroque with a melancholia which perceives the world as in ruins, and he thinks of allegory as the art form best fitted to discuss this. So allegory, the art form for using one thing to describe another, becomes that which suits the baroque. For Benjamin it is

> characteristic of seventeenth-century trends that the representation of the emotions is emphasised increasingly at the expense of a firmly defined action, such as is never absent from the drama of the Renaissance. The tempo of the emotional life is accelerated to such an extent that calm actions, considered decisions occur more and more infrequently. The conflict between sensibility and will in the human form, which [Alois] Riegl [a Viennese art historian] has demonstrated so beautifully in the discord between the attitude of head and body in the figures of Giuliano and Night on the Medici tombs [in Florence], is not confined to the manifestations of this norm in the plastic arts, but also extends to the drama. (99)

The melancholic belongs, according to Benjamin, to the library, the site of reflection on disjunctions between the self and the exterior world. The library, like the city, is an archive: the city archives memories through its street names: Portuguese, Chinese, English; 'through its street names, the city is a linguistic cosmos', Benjamin writes.[3] If the library is baroque, Macao is a library of the baroque as well as containing libraries in itself. It certainly has libraries for the most melancholic.

At its simplest, Benjamin's aphorism about the Renaissance and the baroque suggests one way of thinking about Macao's baroque: its libraries. Macao's richness can be suggested by looking at one of its unusual aspects: its libraries. This chapter explores seven.

The Leal Senado library is an adaptation of the eighteenth-century library in the Convento de Mafra outside Lisbon (built 1717–1730), for which the architect was the southern German Fredrico Ludovice (1670–1752).[4] The library there, built for João V (ruled 1706–1750) was modelled on inspirations from Germany and Italy. João's library occupies a space like a church, with a crossing and

*9. Library in the
Leal Senado*

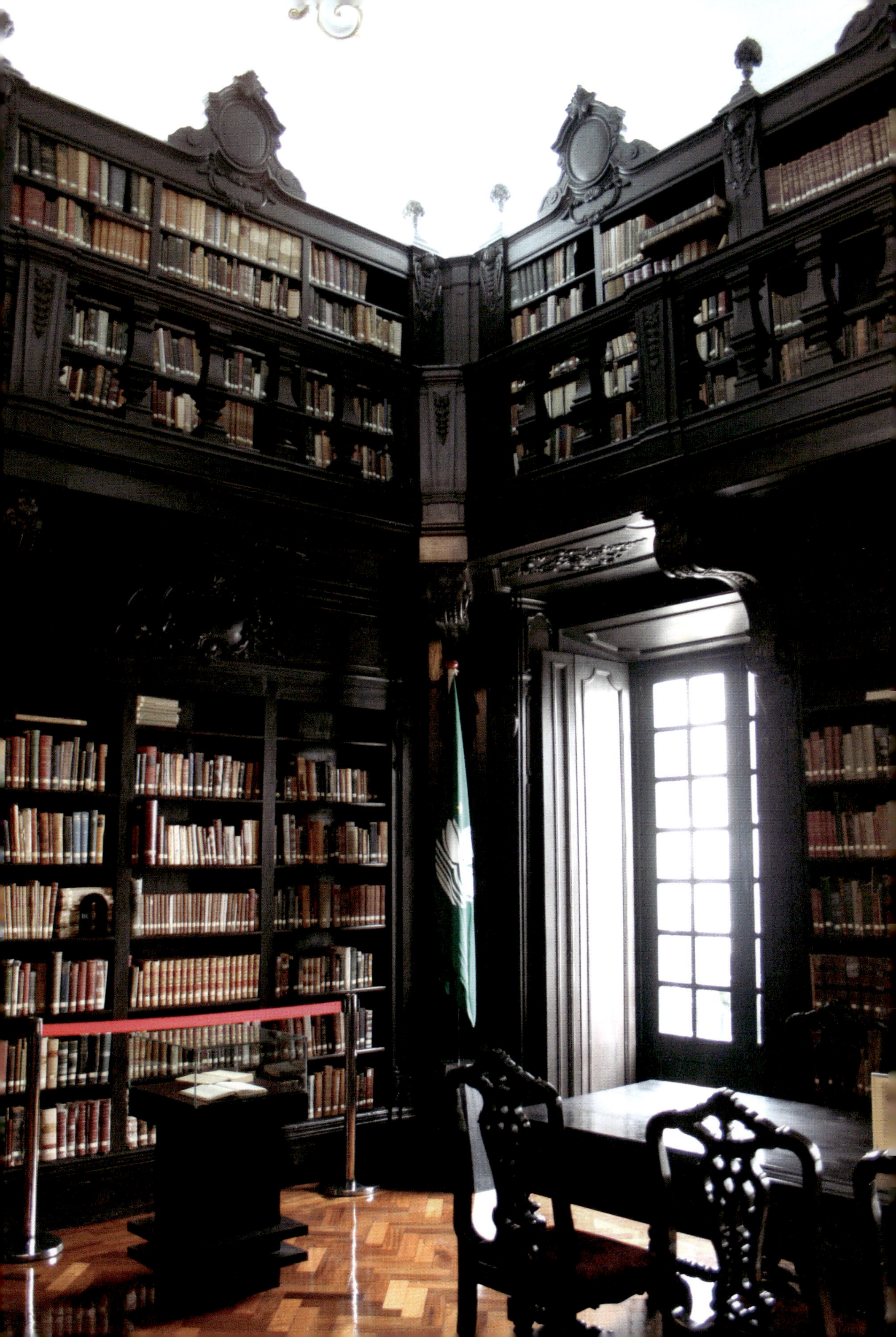

a cupola.[5] The library in Macao, obviously much smaller, two rooms only, shows its baroque character in the scrolling on its ceiling, the cartouches which surmount the dark wood book cases and in the graceful wavelike projections in its first-floor balcony, just visible to the left in photograph 9.

Libraries distinguish Macao from Hong Kong; the library on Coloane island (1915), for example, which looks straight onto the waterfront, is a little classical structure with a façade of six fluted pillars whose capitals are an imitation of the classical Ionic order, giving straight onto the street (no steps), and a purely ornamental pediment which is completely unadorned save for the simple words, in Chinese and Portuguese: Library. The pediment, or gable, contrasts with the gable of the fisherman's cottage which is to the right of the library, and it can be seen how the cottage has pushed itself right up against it, as if impatient with its symmetry. The cottage itself has a primitive balcony: one interesting feature of Macao is its balconies (prime attraction in the novels of Henry James, who distinguishes between balconies which go out over the street, and those which are set back): their presence means that walking through the city, the eye must be aware of the first-floor level.

Taipa Library compares with that on Coloane, neo-classical and temple-like, but with no gable. It stands in a square in old Taipa village, above the Taipa Praya, and opposite Our Lady of Carmel Church. Its six columns have Ionic capitals, of a

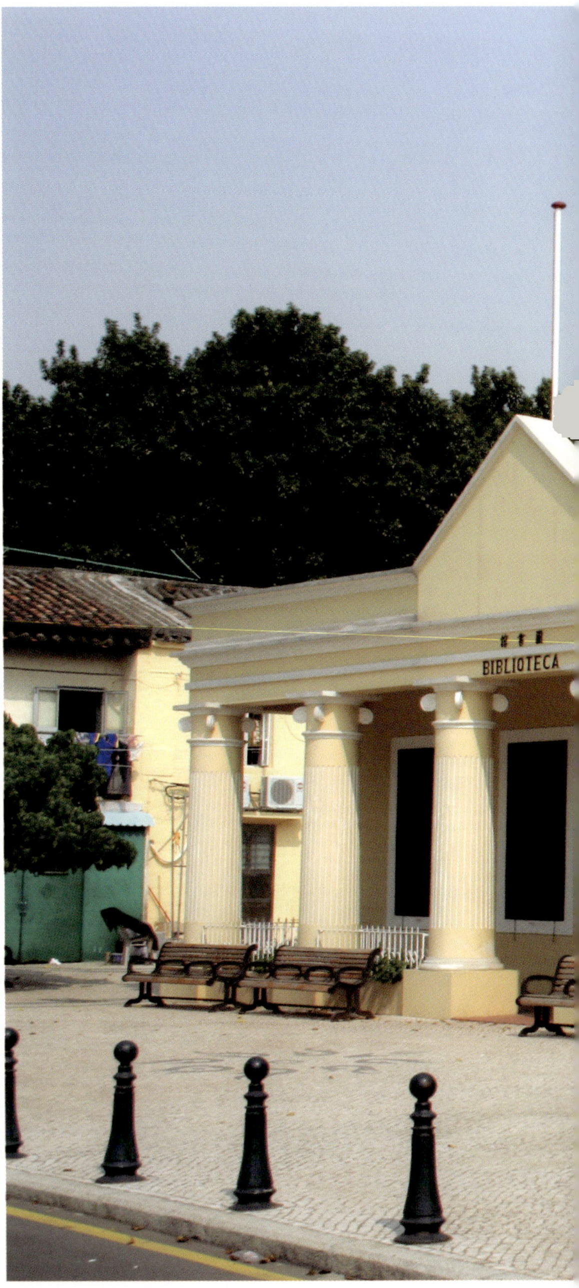

10. Library at Coloane

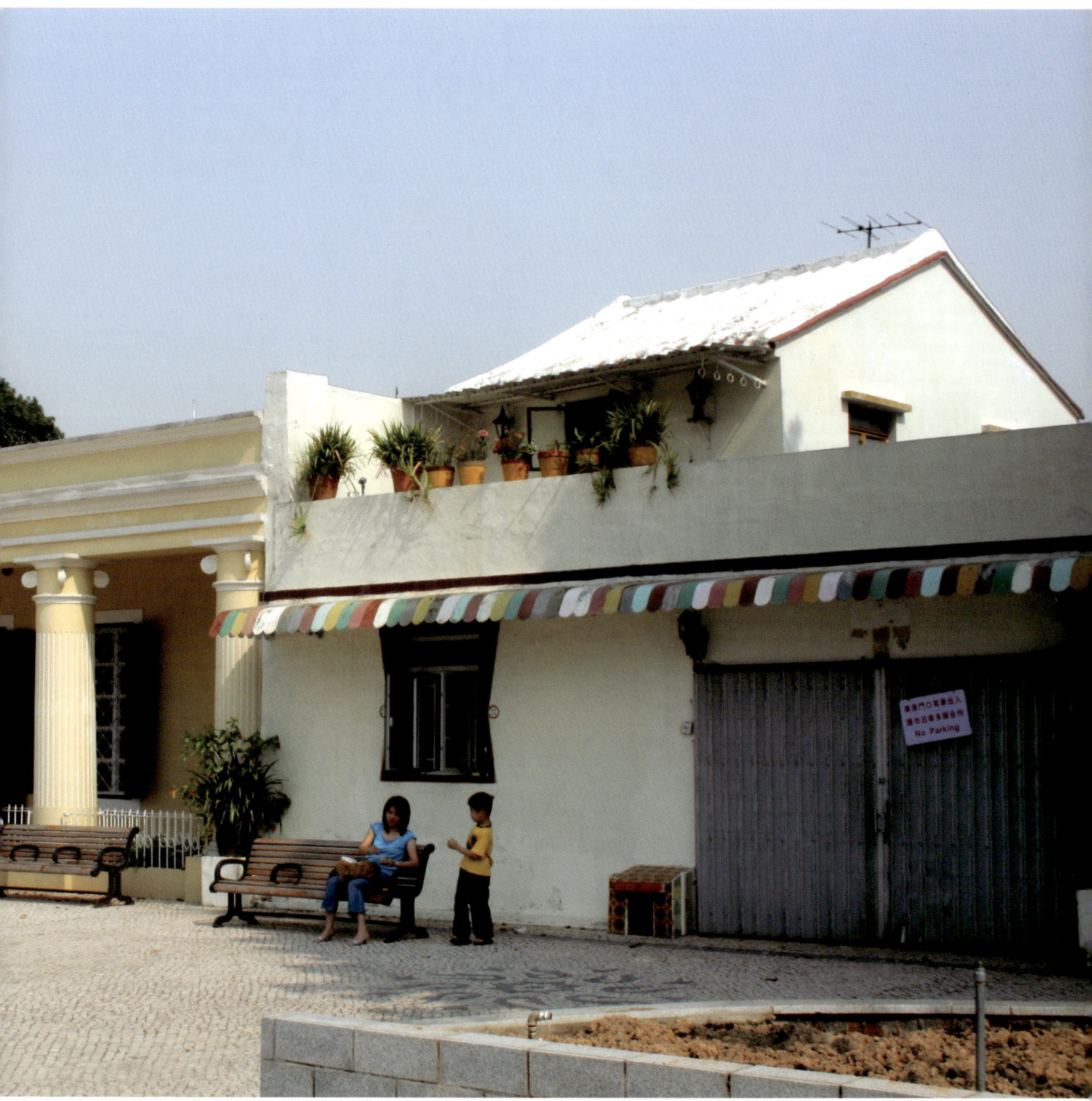
No Parking

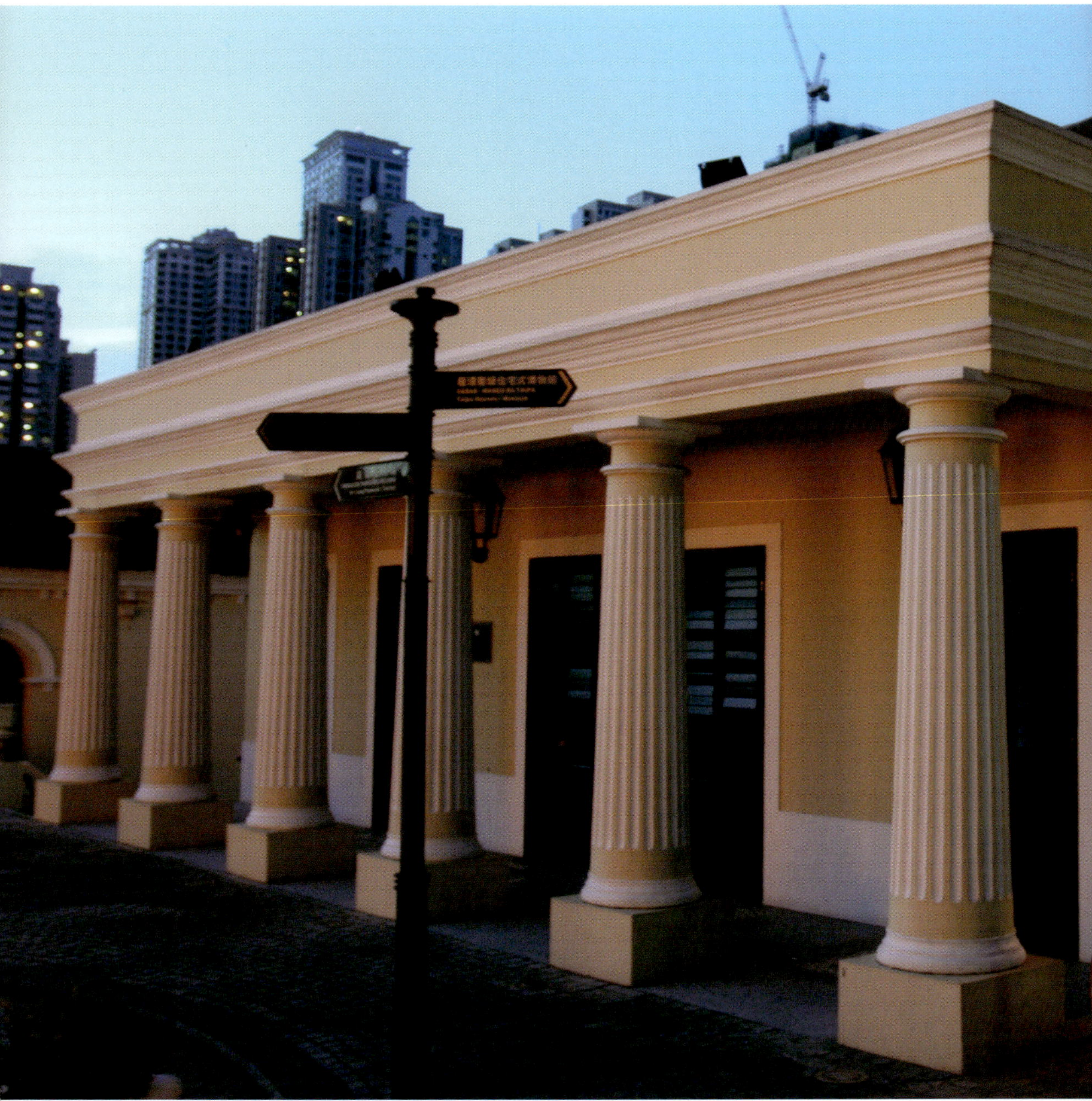

sort, and there is even less inscription than the library at Coloane.

The link of church and library across a square seems characteristic in Macao, as in the new square which has been created (2007) by the architect Carlos Marreiros, which brings the main libraries for Macao's archives, and the city's Cultural Affairs Bureau, in houses built in 1926, onto one side of the newly designed Tap Seac Square, intending to move the centre of Macao a little away from the Leal Senado Square to this new space.

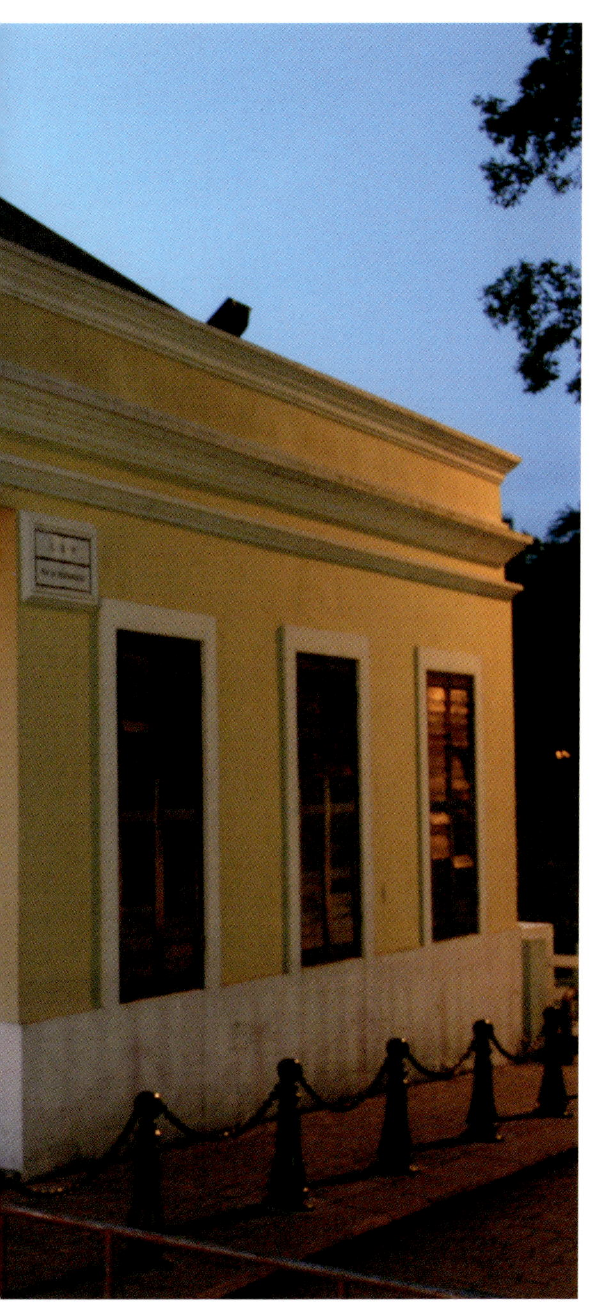

11. Taipa Library

This new space, where the traffic goes underground, like a subterranean river, in a tunnel visible to the right, makes the most of fragments of Macao's architecture, as photograph 28 shows. The 1920s buildings framing the square on the right are just visible; in the centre at the back of the photograph is a 1928 house with Rua Filipe O' Costa behind it; behind the camera is a new building, and the square itself, as a non-regular, sloping space, recalls baroque motifs since it tilts from left to right, and contains circles, with a pavement design which

12. Tap Seac Square

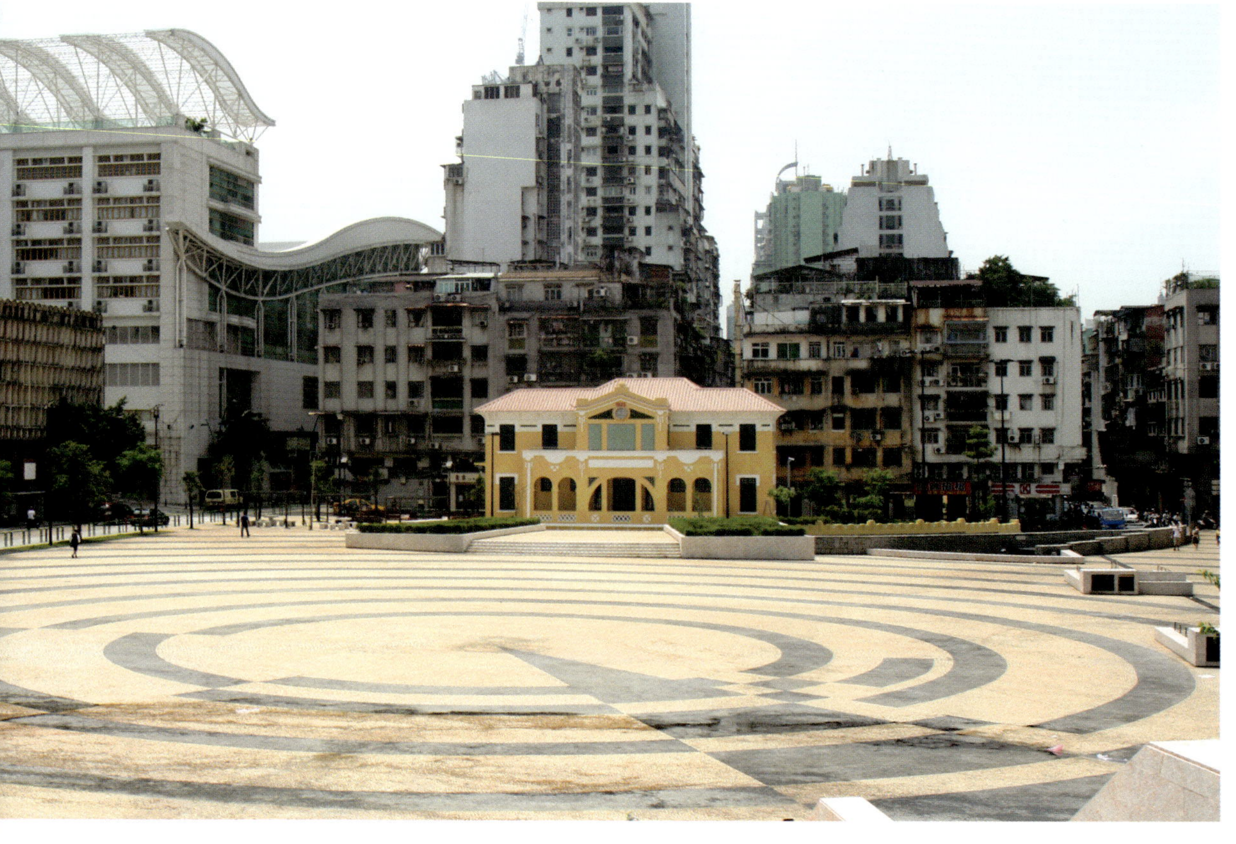

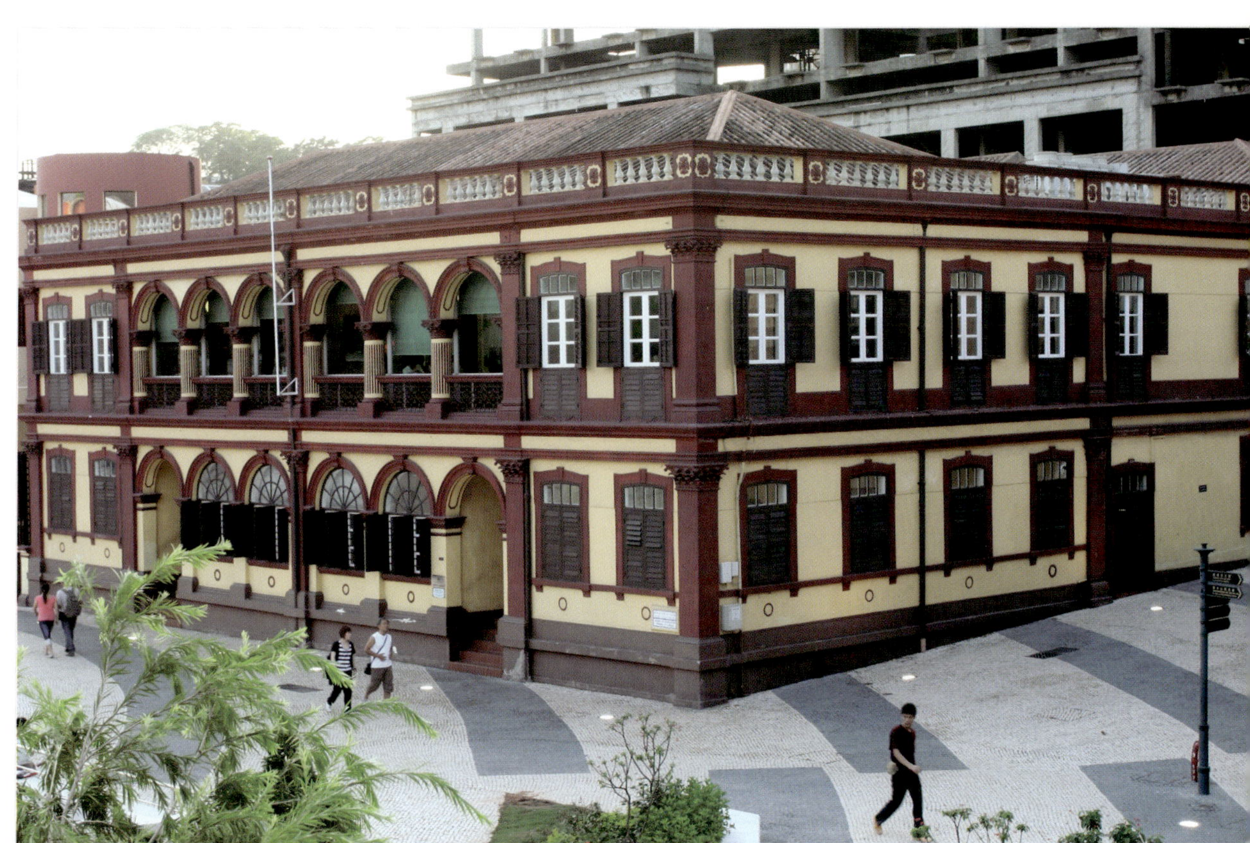

13. Library for Macao archives

looks like a sundial and is off-centre to the new building behind.[6] A new square, easily equivalent in size to the baroque Piazza Navona in Rome, has been produced. It seems an allegory of modernity since so few historic buildings could be found to line it, and yet there is a courage involved which is apparent in making the most of what is left of the city.

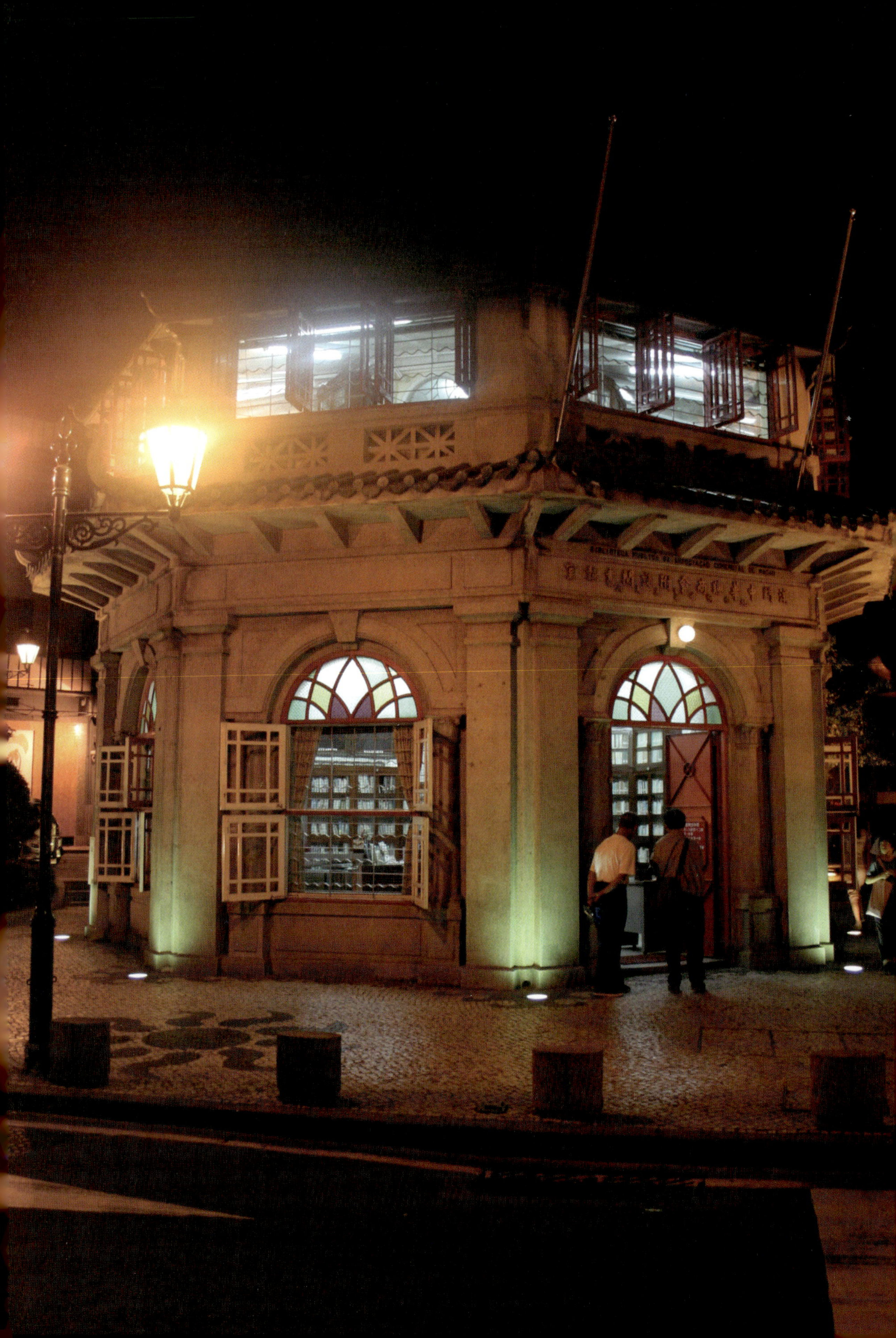

Macao places libraries in the middle of crowded spaces, as in photograph 14, which is located at a road junction, and in the midst of a tiny garden, Jardim de São Francisco, where it was once a booth for selling drinks. The library, or reading-room, built in 1926 in reinforced concrete (which means that it follows an international style in architecture), is octagonal (it is called 'Octagonal Pavilion' in Chinese). It has bright red windows and doors, and grey walls, and despite the international style, it remains a mixture of European classical styles (in the window-arches) and Chinese motifs (in the tiled roofing and projecting dragon-heads). It became a privately owned library in 1948, belonging to the Chinese merchants' association, and given in memory of the donor's grandmother. Even in such a small way, the library becomes associated with death. Like much else in Macao, it makes best use of its tiny proportions, for the reading room has two storeys, with a staircase curling up to the first floor inside the building.

This library, whose interior appeared in photograph 8, gives a refuge from the hurry of the street, from the motorcyclist who can be glimpsed outside. Characteristic Portuguese pavement-tiling marks the inside/outside boundary, but the inside and the outside in Macao are co-present in a way which allows for little islands to be created in the middle of the world outside where the news is being made and read about slowly inside, in an atmosphere free of the speed of new technology. The exterior of the library, photographed at night, brings out something baroque: delight in the night. As with Caravaggio (1571–1610), the baroque paints the blackness of night: it is fascinated by what cannot be seen, what resists science and knowledge.[7] Libraries are islands of light within a blackness which connotes what cannot be known.

An interesting, tiny, once private library, also Chinese, appears in the Camões Garden, site of so much that is recreational: here the building has been squeezed into a space between a rock and three arches of a banyan tree; the rock pushes into the interior reading-space, and the front door had to be framed by the trees.

Yet another library design appears in the Sir Robert Ho Tung House, built in 1895 and occupied by him as a country retreat. Glimpsed at in photograph 3, it is set in the square of Santo Agostinho, with the Dom Pedro V Theatre in front of it, the Igreja de Santo Agostinho to its left, and the entrance to St Joseph's Seminary to its right. The library's front garden is accessed through a front structure of arcades framed by pilasters in front of the entrance patio. The garden, which contains to the left,

14. Exterior of library, Jardim de São Francisco

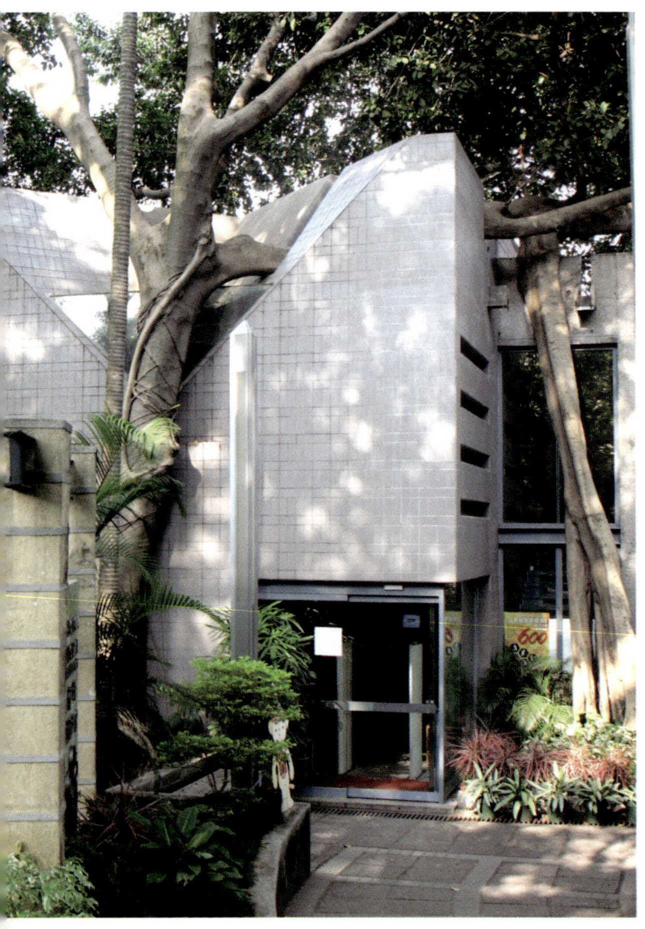

*15. Biblioteca Municipal
Sr. Wong Ieng Kuan*

tucked into a fold, another miniature Chinese-style garden, is delightful for its curves and its stairs (see photograph 80). Its rocaille features, which are of course Chinese, suggest a link between the baroque, or rococo (which supplies the word 'rocaille') cult of rock-like ornamentations within baroque buildings. It implies that Chinese gardens should be thought of as having baroque features themselves (so much so that rocaille was thought of in the west as 'chinoiserie').[8] Rocaille and rococo are baroque, and delicate forms; the rock that protrudes into the Sr. Wong Ieng Kuan Library is also, therefore, baroque or rococo-like, and much less miniature.

The front of the Sir Robert Ho Tung House seems ordinary, with its classical form, and glassed verandah and pediment which show the influence of art deco more than classical art. But there is a surprise for the visitor, nonetheless, a *trompe l'oeil* effect, for the back has been transformed by the addition of a new glass and steel structure on three storeys, designed by the architect Joy Choi Tin Tin. It opened in mid 2006, giving a greatly enriched space.

*16. Intersection between
new and old library*

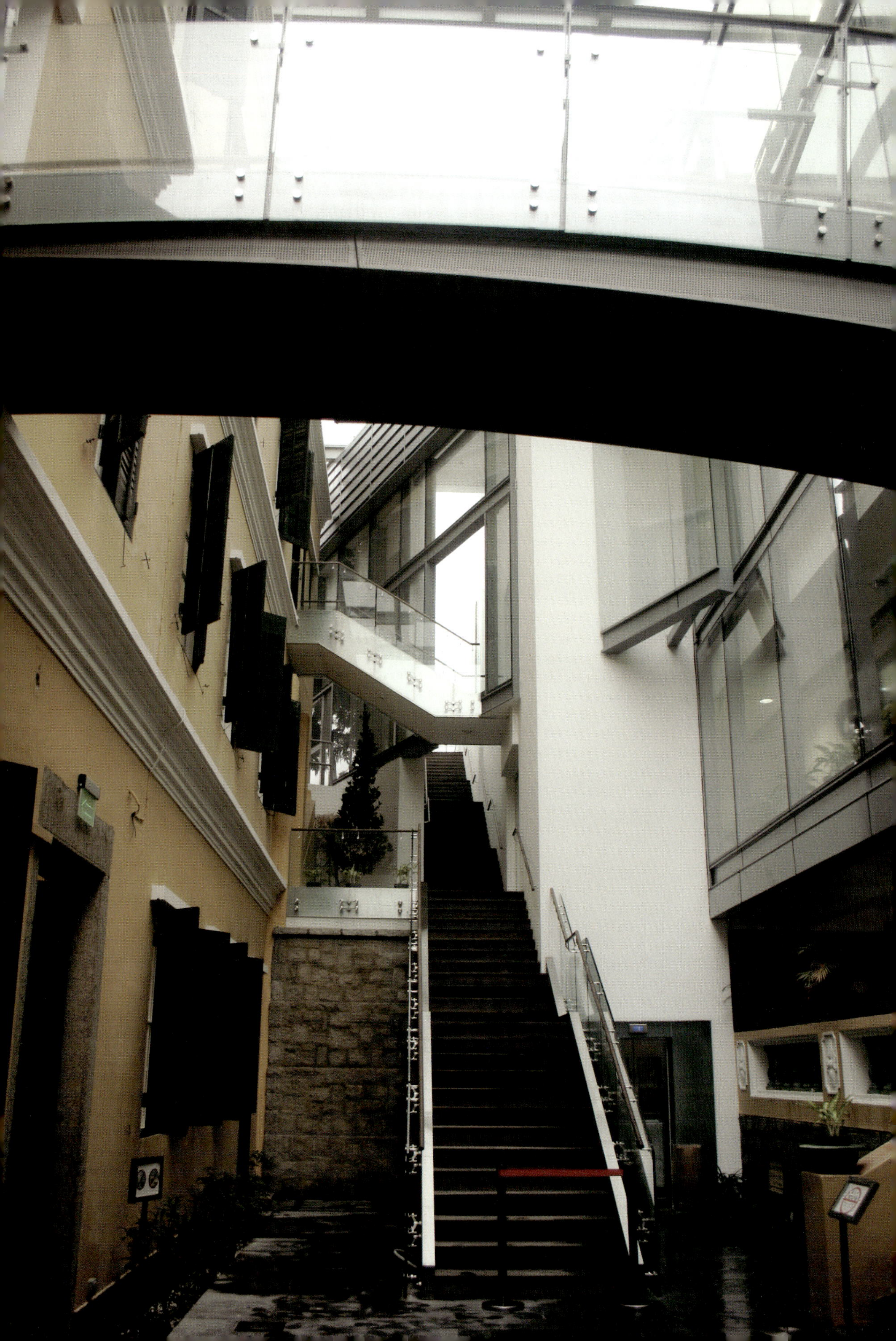

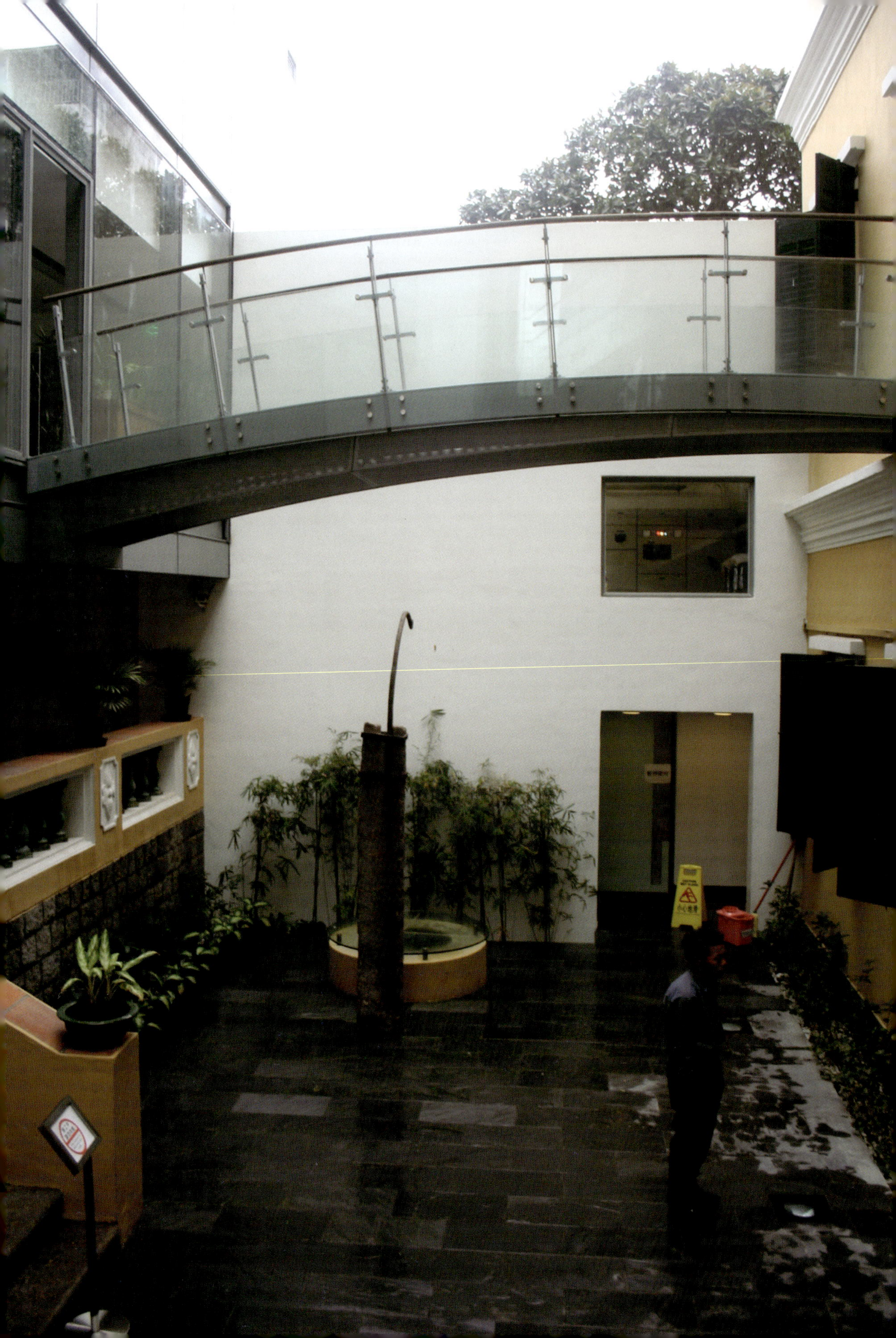

The extension rises above the European garden (containing Chinese curving paths) at the back of the house. The preservation of the old library makes the entire building a library, indexing both an old colonial and a new baroque style of asymmetrical stairs and girders and Piranesi-like walkways, which shoot off at right angles to each other and where glass reflects glass. (If it was a purer form of baroque, the angles would be curved.) The space behind the rear wall of the nineteenth-century house, between that and the new building, is covered by a glass roof, like an atrium, so that windows give out into further interiors, which are, however, also exteriors because of the pervasive sense of the garden subtending the structure. There is even a well in the garden — one of several we will notice in Macao — in the in-between space of the old and new libraries.

Here, surface slides under surface, garden under structure. The extension's design is postmodern and non-minimalist within a miniature space. These libraries exist in buildings interesting in their own right; the library therefore extends both inside and outside, destroying, or shaking, the distinction between these two concepts.

This questioning of the idea of a discrete inside and outside space is at the heart of both the baroque and deconstruction, which, as with Derrida, critiques any philosophy which makes a firm separation between 'inside' and 'outside'. What is interior belongs to the subject and to private space and to the natural; what is exterior belongs to culture. The inside is the privileged term of these two. In Derrida, however, there is a stress on the inner as filled by the outer, so that what is inside is not one thing: there is no single inner space. Derrida stresses both the difference that exists within the inner space (because it contains the outer) as well as the articulation of the inner and the outer, by using the word *'brisure'* which may be translated as 'joint', 'break', 'fault', 'split', 'fragment', or, to use a term which applies to building, 'hinge'.[9]

Deconstruction and architecture relate to each other in such architects as Peter Eisenman and Bernard Tschumi; punning, it could be said that deconstruction is the study of the hinge, and also the 'unhinged', the mad. The Spanish historian Maravall stresses that the baroque is the art of *furor* (madness), bringing out '*furor* and ecstasy' (214);

17. Well in the in-between space

quoting from the baroque writer Luis Alfonso de Carballo:

> *Furor* draws one forth as if out of oneself and transforms one into another nobler, more subtle and delicate mode of thinking; one is elevated and enthralled in it to such an extent that it is possible to say that one is outside of oneself and has no knowledge of the self.

Maravall comments on this idea of ecstasy as an 'alienating state'. (The *OED* defines ecstasy as 'the state of being "beside oneself", thrown into a frenzy or a stupor, with anxiety, astonishment, fear, or passion'.) These points may be brought together by seeing deconstruction as questioning what it means to be 'outside the self' by asking what 'the self' is that is so constituted as private. Interest in the hinged and the unhinged is in what joins and forms a 'fold'.

Derrida on the inside and outside may be compared with Deleuze's statement in his book *The Fold* (*Le Pli*: the French word 'pli' is found in such English words as 'implicate', 'complicate', and 'replicate'), that the baroque 'endlessly produces folds [...]. The baroque trait twists and turns its folds, pushing them to infinity, fold over fold, one upon the other. The Baroque fold unfurls all the way to infinity' (3).[10] This can be taken in three ways. First, folds mean that everything inside is simultaneously on the outside. Second, folding associates with the labyrinth: baroque architecture is often said to be labyrinthine. Deleuze says: 'a labyrinth is said, etymologically, to be multiple because it contains many folds. The multiple is not only what has many parts but also what is folded in many ways' (3). The labyrinth is at the heart of Walter Benjamin's meditations on the city and he discusses how important it is to get lost within it (despite its tiny size, it happens very easily in Macao!).[11] Study of Macao draws attention to the fold, the hinge, and the labyrinth.

But third, the statement 'the Baroque fold unfurls all the way to infinity' is a quotation from Leibniz (1646–1716) who says that

> the division of the continuous must not be taken as of sand dividing into grains, but as that of a sheet of paper or of a tunic in folds, in such a way that an infinite number of folds can be produced, some smaller than others, but without the body ever dissolving

into points or minima. (quoted in Deleuze 6)

This, which recalls that Borges, in his short story 'Death and the Compass' sees a straight line as a labyrinth, implies that the baroque is the art that goes on for ever.[12] It folds endlessly (creating secrets, and enigmas, another name for which is allegories) and unfolds (denuding, revealing, removing clothes). Even a fountain of water becomes a series of folds: there are many fountains to be noticed in Macao, while every tiny corner becomes a series of folds to be understood better through the trope of the baroque. The straight line is favoured by classicism and the fold, within a straight line, by the baroque. Michel Conan suggests that 'classical art could be seen as the epitome of a civilizing thrust of reason, and the baroque understood as the emergence of an unconscious protest against the demands exerted by reason in the name of civilized progress'.[13] The point brings out the contradiction within the baroque: that it is both authoritarian and heterogeneous, playful, disseminating any authoritarian control. The authoritarian aspects tie in with classicism. The interplay of classicism and the baroque appears in many of the buildings discussed and photographed, but for now it can

be said that it seems as if the baroque brings out what is not perceived, or negated, or denied, in the classical.

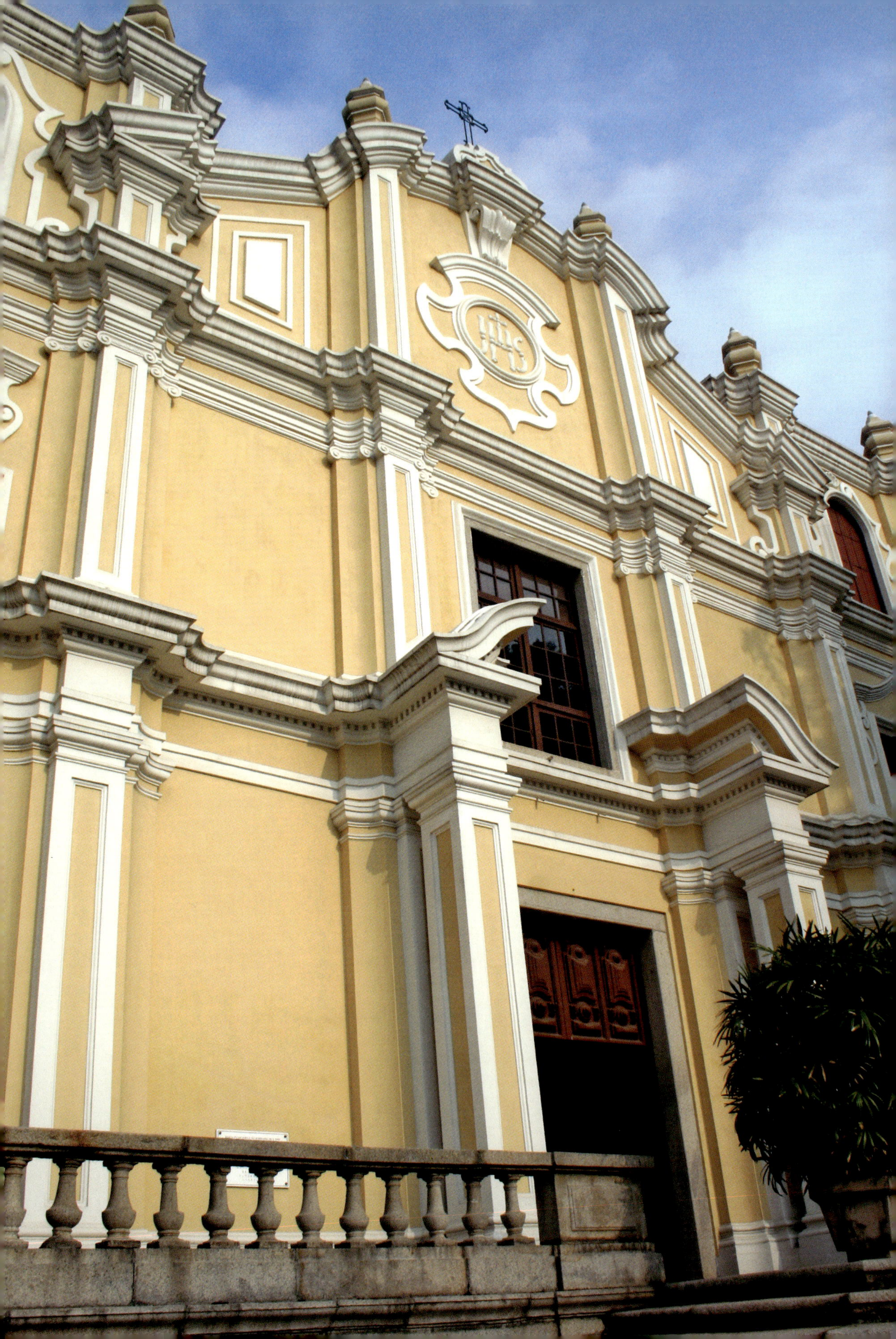

Chapter 3

Igreja e Seminário São José
(St Joseph's Seminary and Church)

Macao becomes a library of the baroque in St Joseph's Seminary and Church, which is the main place visited in this chapter (there is also a discussion of Santo Agostinho). It was constructed from 1728 to 1758 for the Society of Jesus, who was expelled from Macao in 1762: the Seminary was then passed to the Lazarists (1784). São José is one of Macao's most beautiful buildings, and because it has the advantage of being outside the places which tourists are encouraged to visit, it allows people to linger. The church's upper part is visible on walking down the sloping street (Rua da Prata) that leads down to the main entrance, but disappears from the gaze when the visitor walks through the entrance under the canopy, at the foot of the small hill where the church sits.

The photograph shows a basic elegance in Macao; things work on high and low levels simultaneously. The church is on a hill, as Macau, 'City of the Name of God in China' as the colony was first called, was a missionary 'city set on a hill' (Matthew 5:14). It is approached from street level; the entrance was rendered as a pen-and-ink with watercolours in *Gateway to the Seminary of São José, Macao* by George Chinnery.[1] Chinnery shows a baroque archway, seen at an angle, and with its European distinctiveness contrasted by a small Chinese figure near it, but no Europeans; the archway seems a baroque ruin, out of date. The gateway's canopy with a scallop-shell design

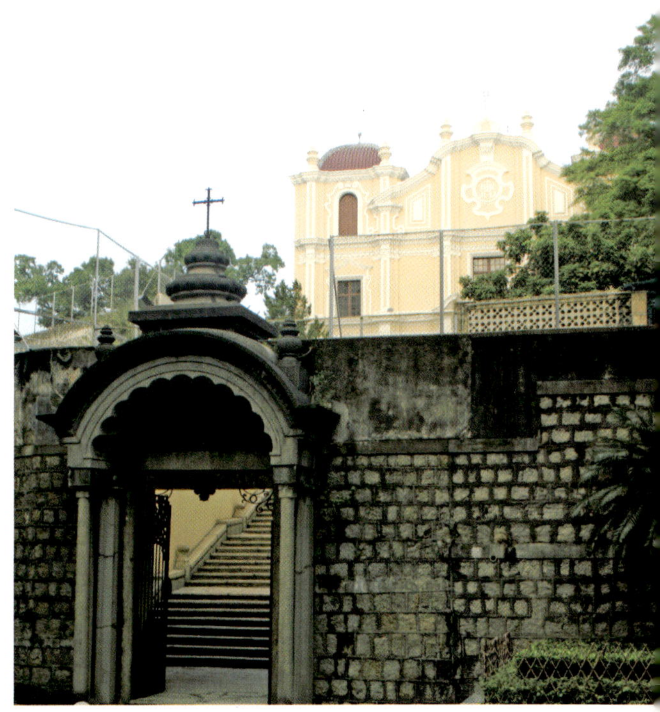

19. Distant view of São José

18. Side view of façade

overhanging the pavement has hardly changed since Chinnery.

This shell's significance was both medieval and baroque, implying initiation via baptism, for the scallop appeared in art, as used for the baptism of Christ, while, worn on the hat, it denoted a medieval pilgrim coming from the shrine of St James at Compostela. Venus comes ashore on a scallop-shell in Botticelli (1445–1510)'s painting *The Birth of Venus* (1484), as an allegory of the baptism of Christ.[2] Ornamented shell-work, within rocaille and other forms of decoration, appears within the baroque, suggesting what unfolds. Shell formations unfold a history which has always been in place, what is already there. The shell as a series of folds implies virginity (including Mary's virginity: the shell is symbolic of Mary because it creates a pearl without external intervention). The baptismal significance is remembered in an example of the baptism of Christ which may be seen in the artwork in another church, São Domingos, in a painting by V. Pacia of 1928.

To look at Pacia's painting, perhaps inconsiderable in itself, helps to focus on some details of colonial baroque. Four women look on to see a dark-robed John the Baptist, his body forming an S-shape from the right foot to the right hand, pouring water from a shell onto Christ, clad in a white loincloth, his head and knees bent, hands open, passive and vulnerable-looking, the posture and clothing both suggestive

of the crucifixion, just as his body shows signs of emaciation, the ribs visible. Behind Jesus and the Baptist, heavenly liquid (as in Botticelli's painting) rains down like a waterfall in the form of light, while Christ stands with feet in water. The women take up the position of the viewer in the picture; their emotions are stirred by the power of excess. The facial expression of John the Baptist is not seen, even by the women. One characteristic difference between the Renaissance and the baroque appears in the lightness and brightness of Botticelli, and the heaviness in the *chiaroscuro* of Pacia's admittedly much later painting. Jesus would presumably have been baptised in the daytime, but the scene is night, with only the bright rays descending behind the central figures. The painting's date makes it anachronistic baroque.

More could be said about the dark background, following from discussions in chapter 2. Deleuze writes that essential to the baroque and Leibnizian conception of the 'monad' is its 'dark background' (27). (The monad is an object which cannot be known, as there is no way to get into the interior.) He makes the baroque suggest something secret, unknowable (like the monad, which as Leibniz discusses, has no windows that give out onto the outside). In the baroque things are contained within darkness. The emphasis on the baroque as giving what is hidden, or secret, or encrypted, will be pervasive for reading Macao.

*20. Baptism of Christ, painting
kept at São Domingos*

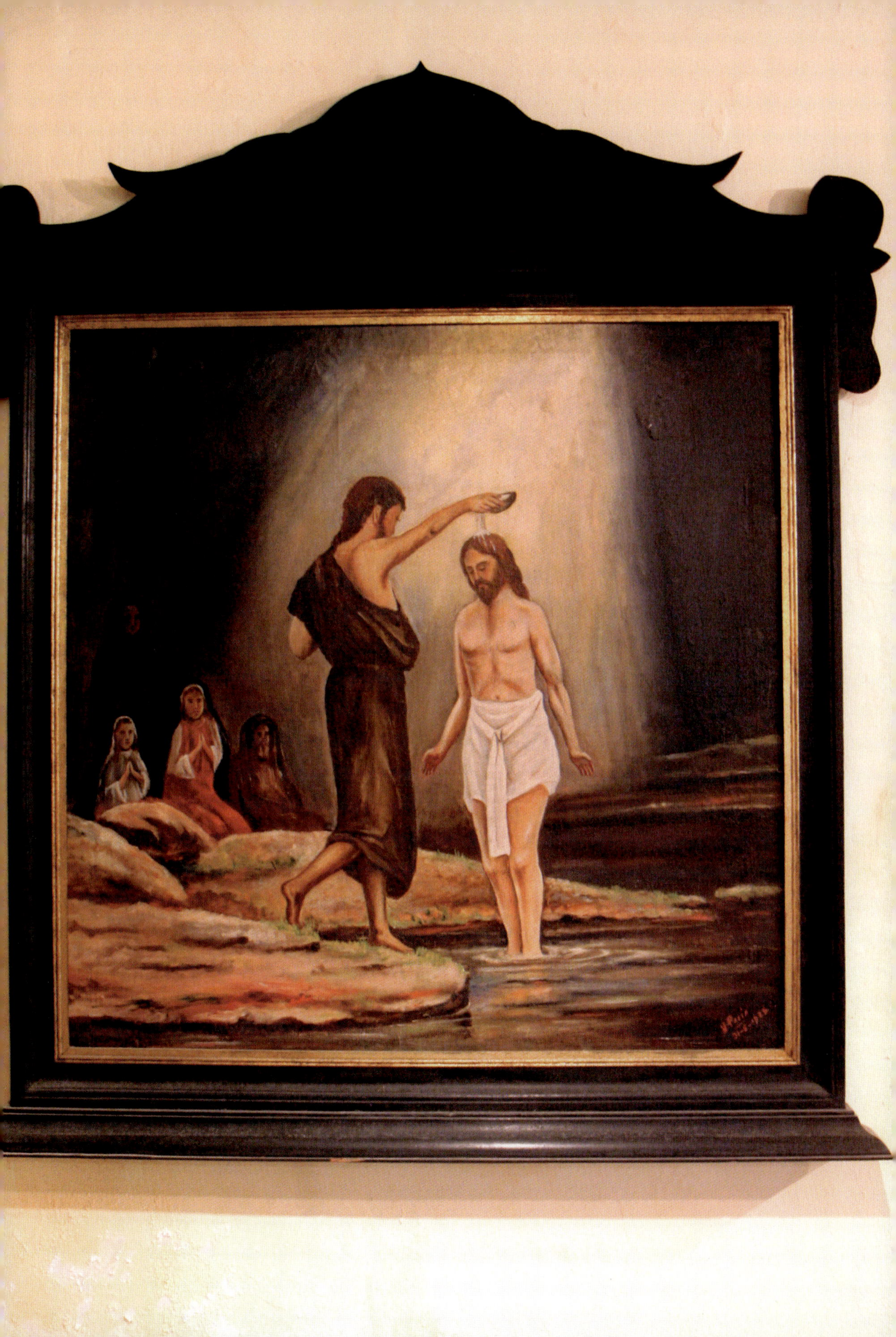

The white and yellow façade of the recognisable baroque building, combining bareness in the yellow walls, and white wavy lines in the stucco-work which decorates that bareness wherever they can, reappears after the gate has been entered. The lower part of the building reveals itself as fifty-two steps are climbed. The church is set, geographically and architecturally, to attract the eye of the arrival, like a theatre set. The eye first sees the top of the façade and then the lower part comes into view in an increasing revelation, which by magnifying the church's height, diminishes the viewer's.

Here is an example of what has been called, 'by means of the façade the conquest of exterior space'.[3] The façade, which conceals the building's roof and dome, has three storeys, and five different vertical spaces, divided by columns, none of which has any load-bearing function, apart from those supporting the broken pediment above the front door. In the first and fifth bays, there are two towers, pierced by doors at ground level, windows at the first floor, and rounded arches at the second. Coming in from there, the second and fourth bays are virtually bare, except for some decoration at the second-floor level, under the diagonal of the overarching pediment. The central bay, leading into the nave, has a door, larger than those in the first and fifth bays, and a window above. And above that, in the frieze, appears a cartouche, which leads the eye up to virtually the only Christian symbolism on the façade: a cross.

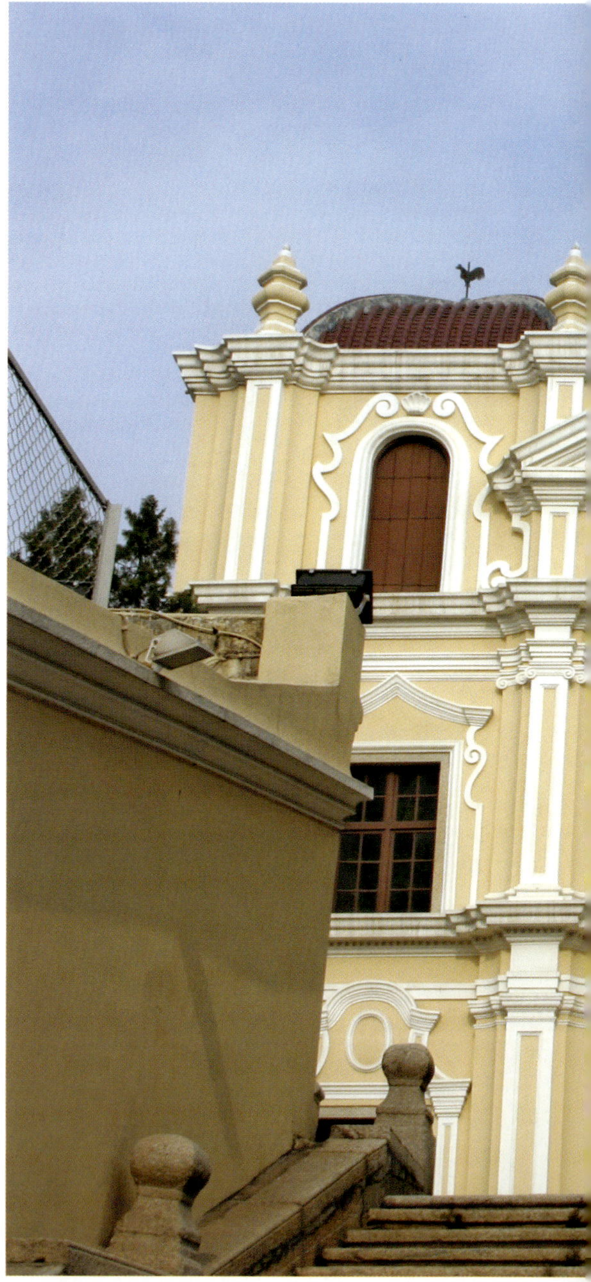

21. Façade of São José

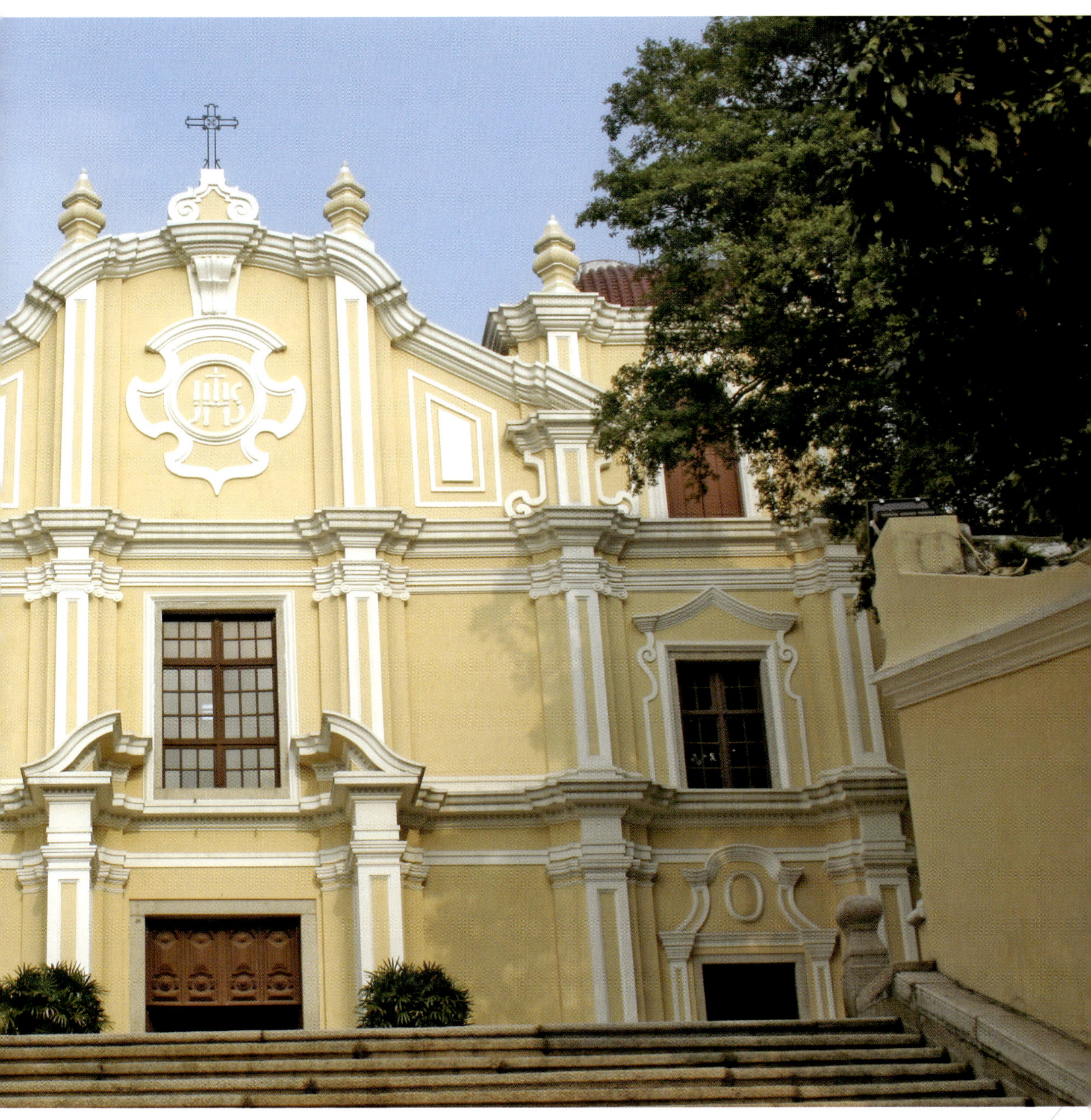

The cartouche contains writing recognisable as IHS (the first three letters of Jesus' name in Greek) in a flower-like design where the rhythm of the pillars along the façade comprises folds. The cartouche frame connects to what looks like a keystone structure which is a base for the summit of the crest of the roof which, constructed six-fold deep, forms the top of the pediment. Each frame (which should define an inside space) becomes a *parergon*, part of another work, so that the artwork cannot be divided into separate spaces.[4] This keystone is a support in the shape of a scroll which also suggests horns: this ornamentation, like the volutes of Ionic columns, or the acanthus-leaves of Corinthian columns, so often seen in these buildings, comprises folds and spirals and rocaille formations which resist being pulled into a definite form. The pediment is surmounted by a metal cross, containing a St Andrew's cross within a central circle and supported at the side by reversed S-shapes, giving the appearance of the cross bursting out like a flower budding.[5]

At first-floor level, there is a broken pediment above the front door of the building, and this pediment and its support have been brought forward so that the façade appears folded or to bend, like a wave on a sea surface as seen from above. There are further empty cartouches above the doors on the sides. The pediment at second-floor level, recognisably an adaptation of a classical pediment like the Parthenon in Greece, has had its triangular size bent, made wavy and it starts halfway up the height of the second-floor storey making a broken baseline which is curved outwards and supported by pilasters. Above the six vertical columns by which the façade is articulated there are altogether six double pyramidal obelisks, which do not reach the height of the central cross. In a European church these structures would be replaced by statues of saints, but here the stress falls on decoration for its own sake, ornateness without meaning.

What is baroque here? A beginning point would be the brokenness of the pediment. The Portuguese *barroco* implies a rough, or imperfect pearl, and the *OED* cites 1765 for its first use in English. The passage runs: 'this style in decorations got the epithet of *Barroque* taste, derived from a word signifying pearls and teeth of unequal size'. Baroque architecture is irregular, eccentric, the art of brokenness. Classical formal symmetry is replaced by something which draws attention to excess and lack of completeness.

Inside, the floor plan of the church is like a cross, enclosed in a square. Above the central crossing is a shallow dome, which lights the church from above in two circles of windows. A dome suggests the Renaissance (as with Michelangelo's St Peter's in Rome), or the baroque as in Wren's St Paul's Cathedral in London.

The dome, swelling above the roof-line, and finished in 1758, is seen from outside and from

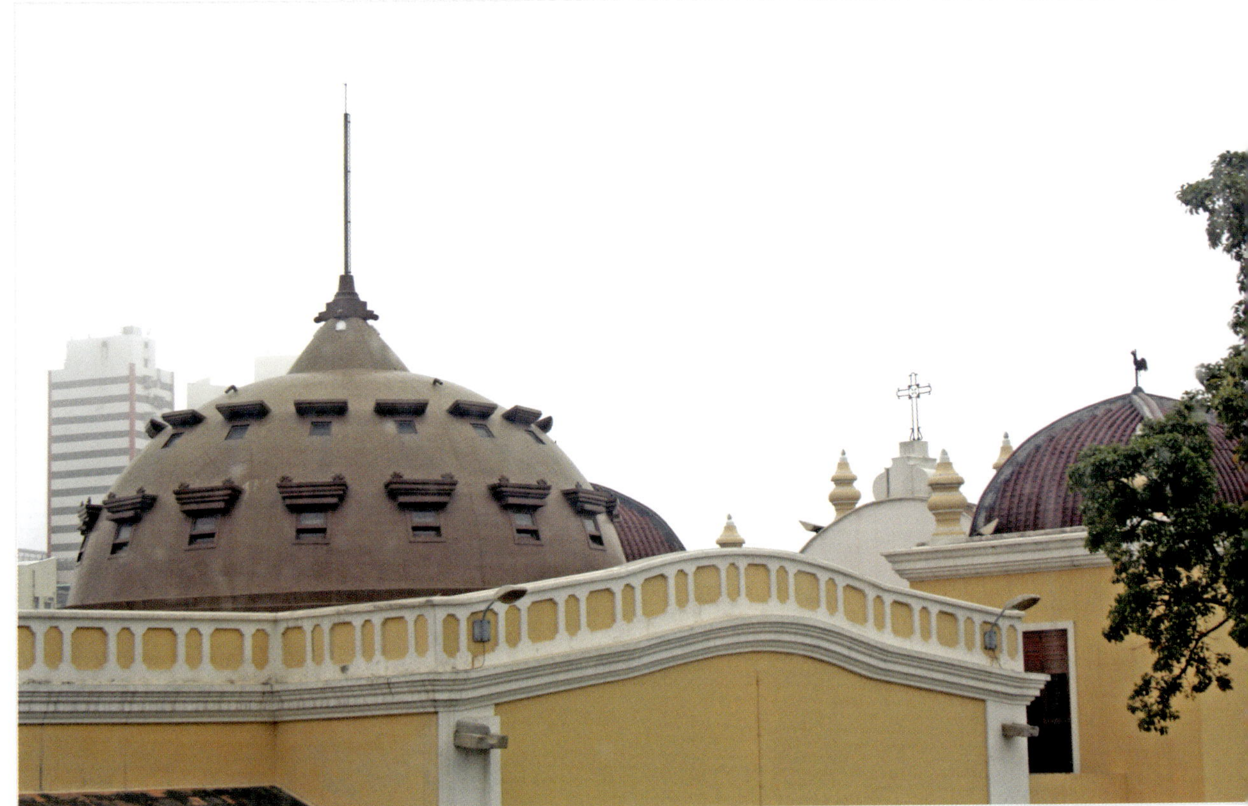

22. Dome and skyline

behind: the viewer will take in the elegant curve of the fake balustrade above the wall of the church, the rear of the façade with the metal cross on it, more visible now than from the front, and the roofs of the twin towers, one surmounted by a weathercock. This dome is small, but it is miraculous that it is there at all; it appeared much earlier than the concrete dome above Hong Kong's legislative assembly building, (c.1910, architect Sir Aston Webb [1849–1930]) for instance.

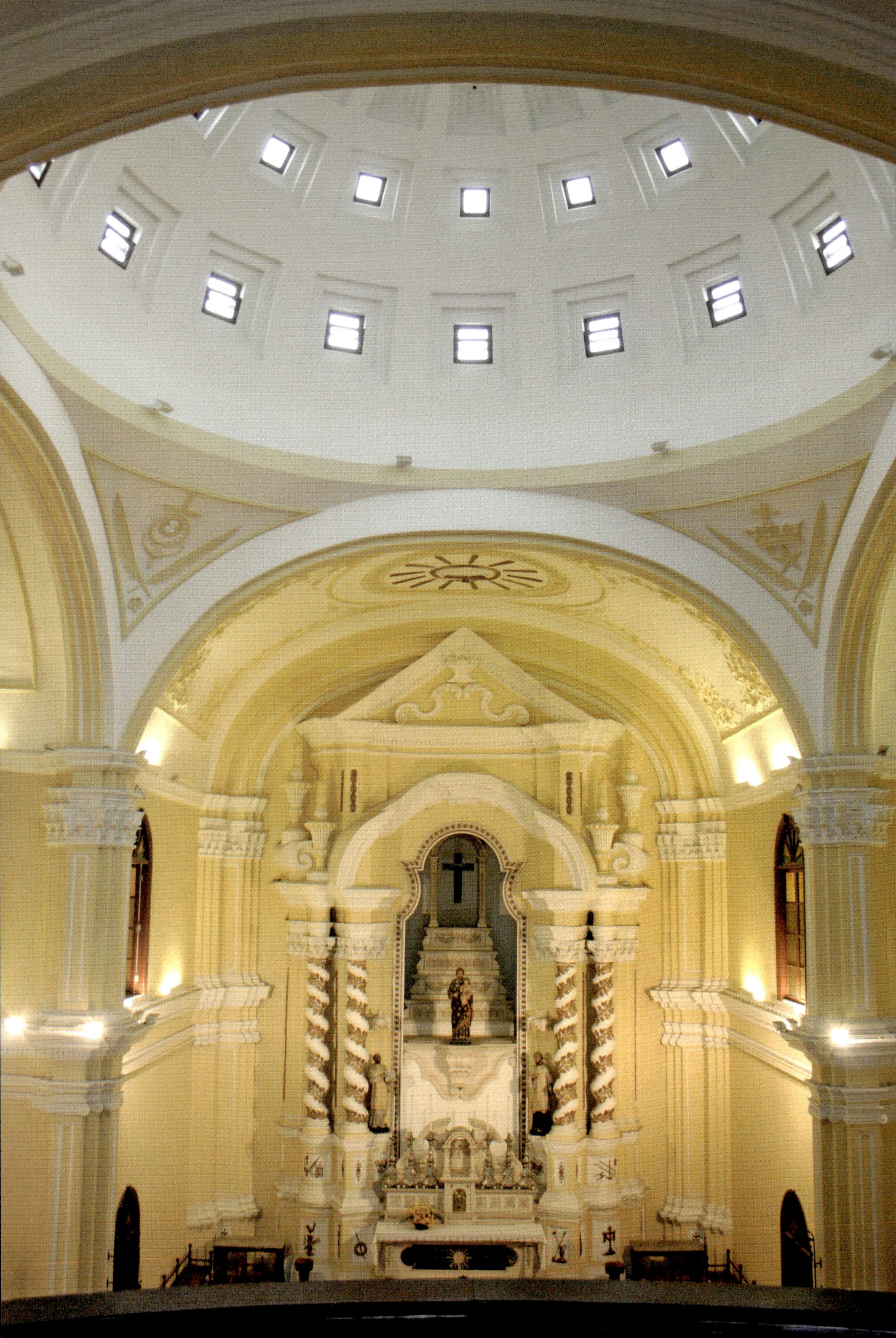

Inside São José

The eye is taken toward the high altar which, because it is at the east end of the church, captures the afternoon light. The eye is led up towards the cupola, seen from the outside already, and another source of light, which is an outstanding symbol in the baroque, and beyond the cupola to the altar at the east end. The roofing over the altar is barrel-shaped, and set into the space is a baldacchino, a word which the *OED* gives, for etymology, as deriving from Bagdad in Iraq (non-colonial (Italian) architecture derives from colonial sources).

Prominent here are the Solomonic (twisted) double columns which are decorated with twining branches and leaves. The eye rises from seeing the altar towards the retable, with a ledge with six candles and above that to a virgin and child on another ledge while to the sides but below the level of the virgin there are statues of the founder of the Jesuits, St Ignatius of Loyola (1491–1556) and St Francis Xavier (1506–1552). Behind the virgin and child, four ledges reminiscent of sarcophagi, and a reminder of the link between the baroque and lamentation (*Trauer*), rise in a cavernous, perhaps feminine space towards a cross, which is framed within a shrine, which itself is held within a larger frame formed by the Solomonic columns. This is theatre within theatre.

The Solomonic columns which produce a broken pediment above them lead the eye upwards towards an uncanny sense, which comes partly from a *trompe l'oeil* effect — that the pediment has been turned inwards, so that what is missing is the segment of the oval which should be in front of the baldacchino, as if that segment has been taken away, or unhinged, to reveal the secret of a woman within, like an egg which has been opened up, to show the mystery of birth and death. The contrast of this pediment with that of the façade, which has no curve, should be noticed (see photograph 19). It contrasts with the baroque in Europe, for instance, with the baldacchino which enshrines Bernini's statue of St Teresa in Maderno's church, St Maria della Vittoria (architect Maderno, 1612) in Rome. There, the pediment of the baldacchino thrusts forward, forming a convex arc, pushing forward the statues inside the shrine. It makes them more visible, more on display, as though the shrine was bursting out, in a process that Derrida calls 'dehiscence'.[6] In contrast, in Macao, the baldacchino turns inward, as if sexually timid.

The artwork here is amateurish and fails to fill space, leaving empty large sections of the support upon which the virgin stands. It is as if in this colonial baroque everything is only done half way. Nor do the symbolic figures in the supports to the columns fill those spaces. They remain schematic

23. View of interior of São José

and merely gestural. The baldacchino does not quite fit the space as our photograph of the east end and the south transept together brings out.

The hinge or fold which unites these walls at a right angle comes forward, unlike the corner of the library in photograph 9 above. The library is the space of interiority — heavy, dark, melancholic. The baroque church attempts to create new spaces to the right and left, but our analysis and photography attempt to bring out something else — that the cavernous space of the interior has an emptiness within it, which, as an image, suggests the inability of the baroque subject to complete itself as a unity.

A similar point may be made about the shrines in the transepts; the white wall behind the Saviour in the south transept emphasises how much the space cannot be filled up, how much this art records absence, how much it cannot be inscribed, because there is no authentic history here: the history that commands and manipulates comes from elsewhere — from Portugal, not from China. The rhythms created by the tiers of folds of the receding pilasters at each of the right-angled corners of the church (in the photograph, up to five of these can be counted) try to bring to the space, which is however too large as a theatrical display, a sense of enclosure. That the baldacchino is like a stage set, movable, with props which are not integrated into the architecture makes it look out of place, showing the poverty of colonial baroque.

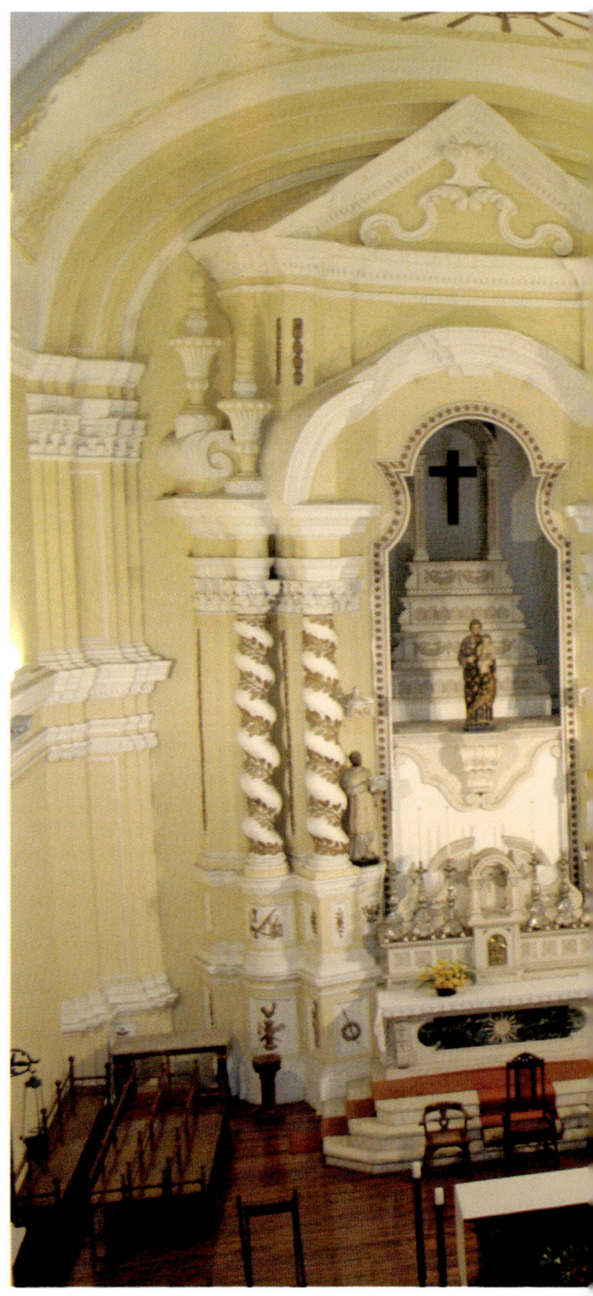

24. Overview of the interior of São José — from the right

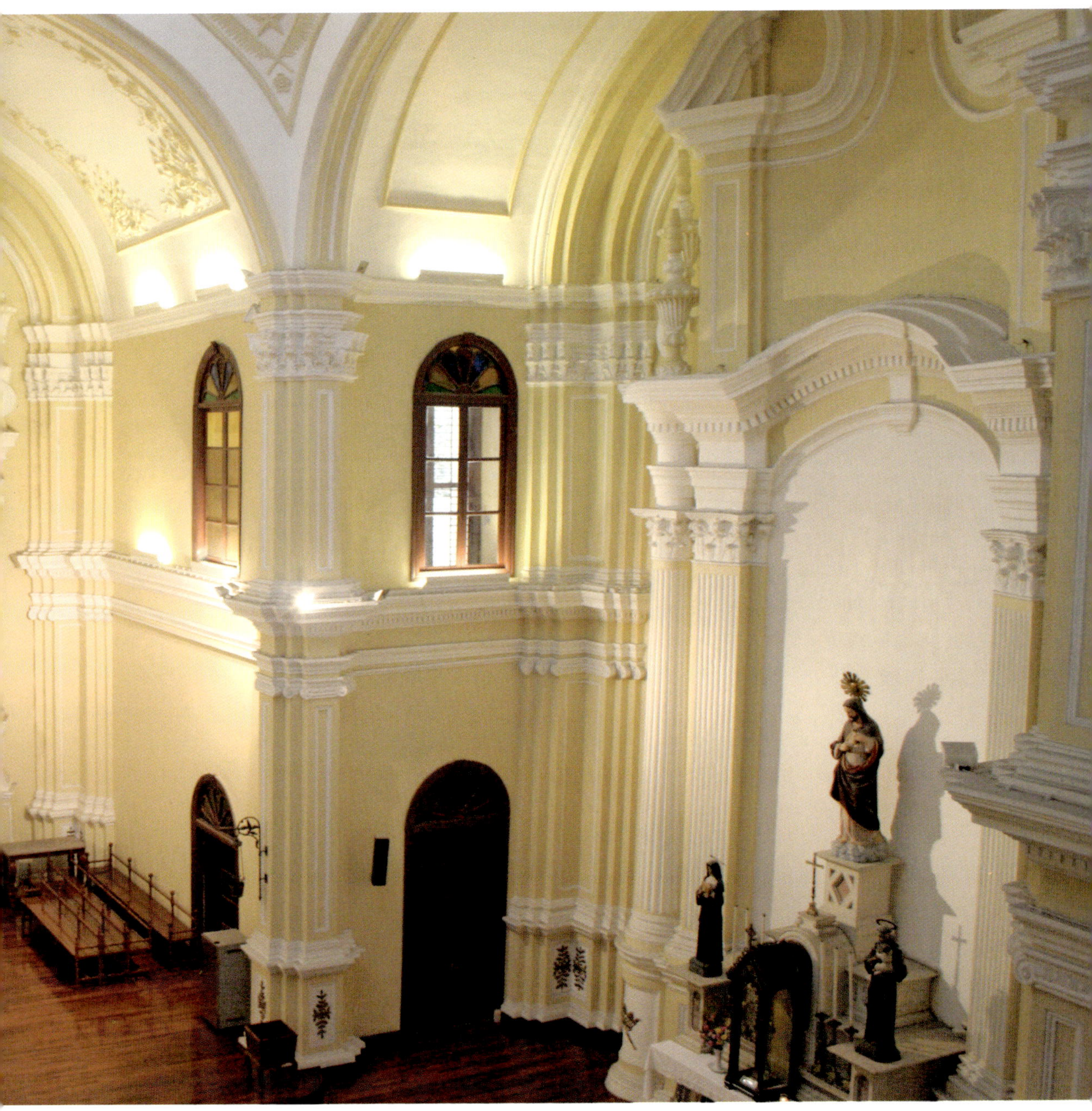

The church is like a theatre, just as the Dom Pedro V Theatre (1859) seating 250 people (façade designed by d'Aquino, Baron Cercal, added in 1879) is constructed like a classical temple or church. The theatre is set between São José and St Augustine's Church, seen in photograph 3. St Augustine's, which contrasts well with São José, and is therefore discussed here, began from Spanish Augustinians setting up a seminary in Macao in the late 1570s: later, it became Jesuit. Its seminary and the church in the present square date from 1591, and its local name, 'Dragon Beard Temple' apparently recalls that, when first built, its roof was of leaves, not wood, as it is now.

Comparison with São José shows St Augustine's to be simpler, and though it has columns which give it side aisles, its form is not that of a cross. The altar has a baldacchino, its columns folding inwards and outwards, concave and convex together, with an affecting red-robed Christ bearing the cross inserted in the theatrical space below; and with, as background, two empty crosses on stage-like hills, against a blue background. A picture of St Augustine as Bishop, has been placed above in the frieze.

Benjamin sees the supreme form of European theatre in the drama of Spain 'a land of Catholic culture in which [...] baroque features unfold [...] brilliantly, clearly and successfully' (81). The equation is between (a) 'life as a dream', (b) the world as theatre, and (c) the baroque, for:

in the [baroque] drama the play-element was demonstratively emphasised and transcendence was allowed its final word in the worldly disguise of a play within a play. (82)

In São José, the various shrines are theatrical props which, because of the inadequate size of the setting (though the whole church is like a stage set), leave to either side bare walls, while the pediment of the central baldacchino fits uneasily with the shallow curve of the roof. The wall behind the baldacchino is also left bare.

Benjamin emphasises that the plays of the German seventeenth century were travelling theatre: 'the stage is not strictly fixable, not an actual place' (119). The baroque then is temporary space, improvised, part of 'life as a dream' (*La vida es sueño*), the title of Calderón's play of 1631. It is this sense of temporality that accentuates baroque melancholia. The theatrical images are ready to disappear. As Prospero the colonialist says in Shakespeare's *The Tempest*, after making, creating, and sending away a baroque masque:

Our revels now are ended. These our actors,
As I foretold you, were all spirits, and
Are melted into air, into thin air;
And like the baseless fabric of this vision,
The cloud-capped towers, the gorgeous palaces,

25. Interior of St Augustine

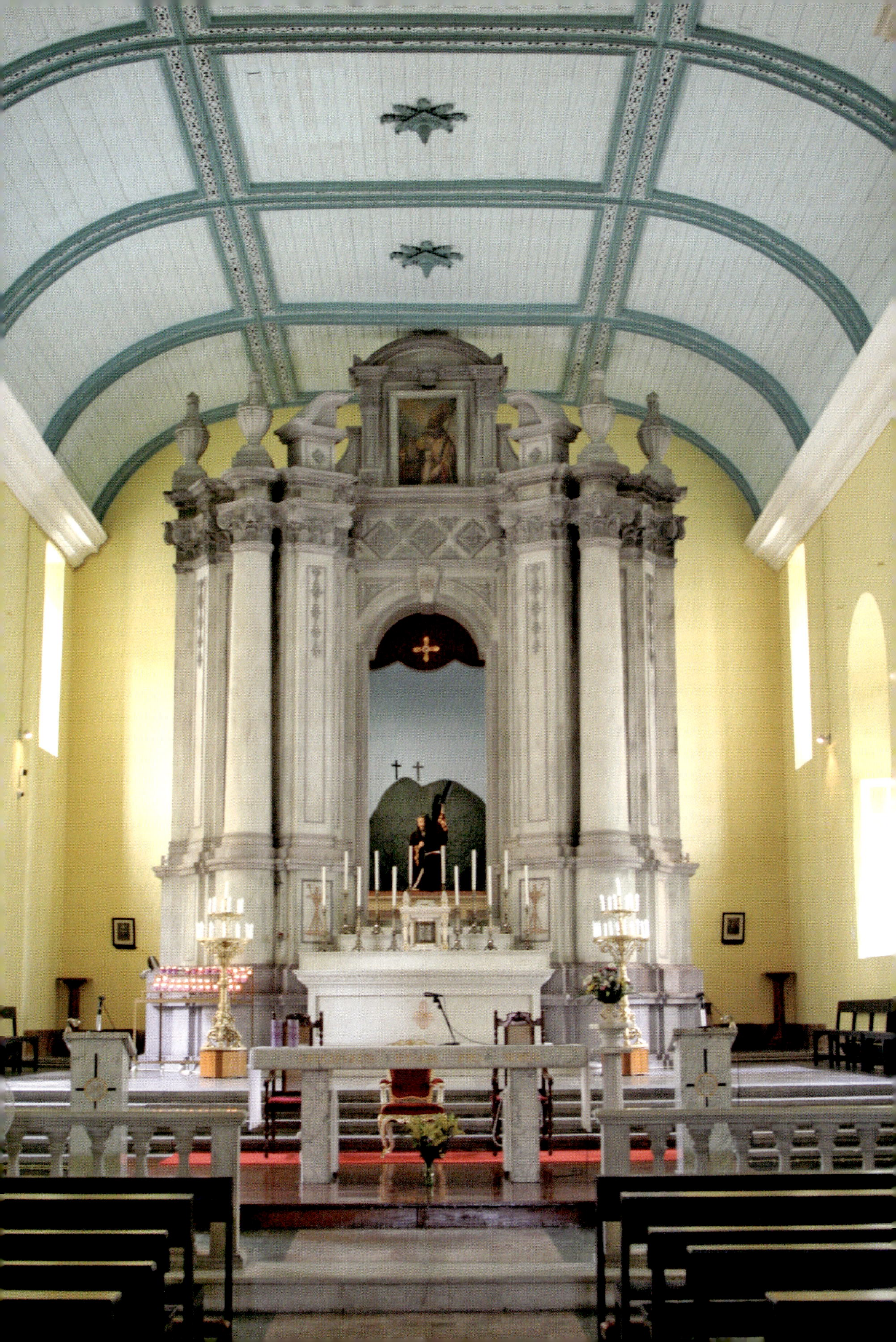

The solemn temples, the great globe itself,
Yea, all which it inherit, shall dissolve;
And, like this insubstantial pageant faded,
Leave not a rack behind. We are such stuff
As dreams are made on, and our little life
Is rounded with a sleep.

(IV.i.148–58)[7]

To complete the theatricality of the baldacchino, at the summit of the Solomonic columns there are mock urns with the fire of sacrifice ascending straight up to the heavens in sculpted smoke. The repetition of scrolls within the entablature which are at the same time horns, and the keystone structure at the top but within the pediment, echoing the keystone on the pediment of the façade, should also be noticed for the absence of specifically Christian references. The repetition amplifies what Borges says: 'I would define the baroque as the style that deliberately exhausts (or tries to exhaust) its own possibilities, and that borders on self-caricature'.[8] Motifs are exhausted by repetition throughout the building.

This theatrical nature evokes a further characteristic of the baroque: Maravall, quoted before, in the context of Spain, calls the baroque a 'guided culture', a 'kitsch culture', and a manipulating culture. Ecstasy and *furor* are not 'natural'; they are produced, manipulated. Within the paranoid structure of absolutist Spain which expelled Jews and Muslims in 1492, while possessing as much of the rest of the world as it could, the counter-Reformation expressed itself as a culture of control which worked by mass images. In sixteenth- and seventeenth-century Spain, Philip II, and those kings who followed him — who also occupied Portugal for a time — made Christianity, the state religion, a reaction to Spain's colonisation of the world. There was a need to appeal to the 'mass', and at the same time for the monarchy to conceal its absolutism, most signified within El Escorial, the palace and mausoleum which answered to the royal archive at Simancas in Spain, begun by Charles V, but completed by Philip II.[9] For Maravall,

The baroque attempted to guide human beings who were grouped together in masses, acting upon their will, psychologically motivating [*moviendo con resortes*] them by means of a technique of attraction that, as such, effectively exhibited a mass character.[10]

The excess within the baroque, such as the Solomonic columns and the wavy façade, are all features intended to bring about 'amazement' (75)

which is the due response to a 'guided culture' (the title of Maravall's second chapter). The Mexican writer Octavio Paz only confirms this in saying about baroque literature, 'The conceits, metaphors, and other verbal devices of the baroque poem are designed to amaze: what is new is new if it is unexpected'.[11] In architecture, the amazement comes through the eye, which evokes the power of affect. Maravall writes:

> Distinct from the serenity sought by the Renaissance, the Baroque set out to stir and impress, directly and immediately, by effectively intervening in the motivation [*resortes*] of the passions. Wölfflin already observed this, recalling that many baroque artists manifested neuroses — Bernini, Borromini [...] Along with [its] contemporary, Descartes, baroque thought considered that human judgements are based 'on passions by means of which the will lets itself be convinced and seduced beforehand'. (75)

Bernini (1598–1680) and Borromini (1599–1667) were Italian architects, the latter a suicide. For Maravall, 'there is scarcely a baroque work of high quality — from Bernini's Santa Teresa to Poussin's Pastoral, to Calderón's *La vida es sueño* — that escapes being touched by kitsch. Everything that belongs to the baroque emerges from the necessities of manipulating opinions and feelings on a broad public scale' (90). 'Kitsch' is a nineteenth-century term, and in this context, implies a sentimental religiosity. Maravall's baroque culture is an allegory of the modern.

Memento Mori: Baroque and the Allegorical Image

Turning from the large structures in São José to the smaller examples of monuments, we see two marble slabs facing each other, set into the walls at eye level, near the church's west end.

The first, to the left, has a heavy dark frame enclosing words in Latin which memorialise the person who died in 1855. To the right and to the left of the writing inside the frame hover angels, one with a wreath, which is also a crown of life, the other holding out a branch, like a palm tree for a pilgrim (a palmer), while in her right hand she holds a tree of life. These angels have their garments hanging and blowing behind them in graceful folds. Above the frame, and resting on its top, appears a baroque allegorical design in low relief, characteristically wavy and comprising folds:

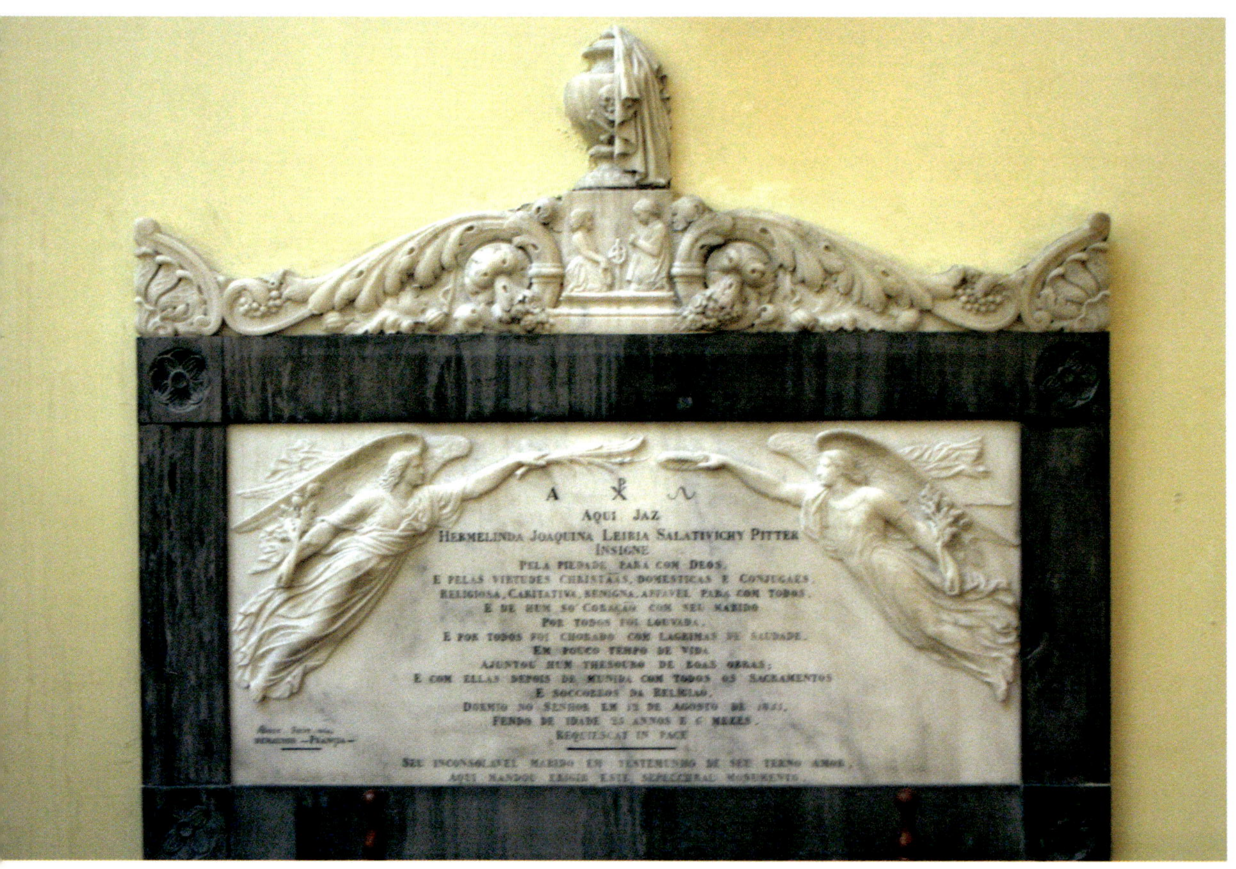

26. 'Angels and skull'
(tablet on the left)

a design of fruits and leaves with, in the centre, a slab which supports an urn. Inside the slab are two children kneeling in prayer with a wreathed cross between them; the girl also has a wreath in her hand, which repeats the wreath held by the angel below her. They express vulnerability, and complement the angels who are below them. Since the children are young, their non-sexual nature repeats the androgyny of the angels. Above the slab of stone which frames them is a large urn partly veiled, but leaving visible half a death's head and beneath it a pair of crossed bones.

The slab opposite shows also two vignettes within a frame which carries writing in Latin memorialising the dead. To the left a mother and a child sit beneath a tree; to the right the same mother is under the tree, her right hand supporting her drooping head. Her knees are brought up towards her chin, and her left hand held behind her right

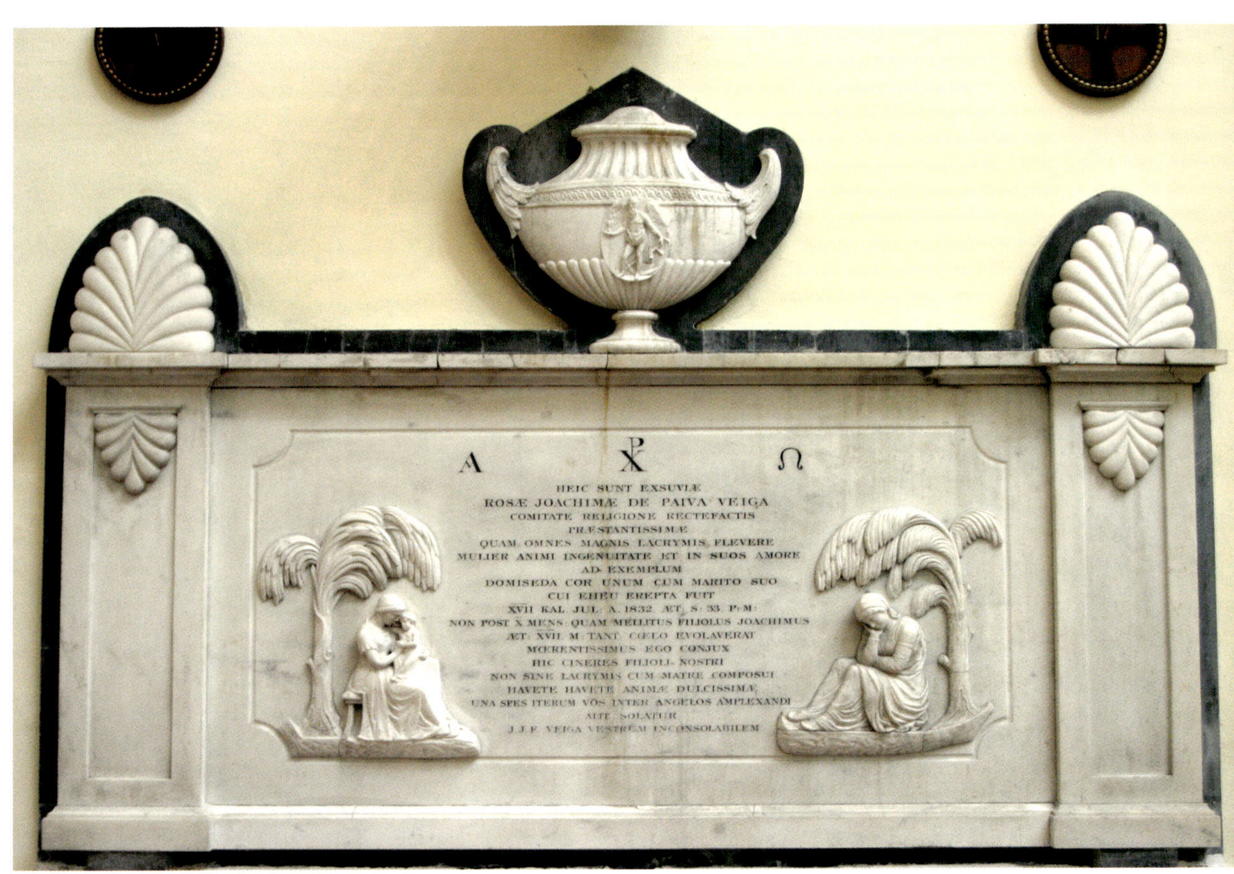

27. 'Mourning mother'
(tablet on the right)

elbow. Her death-like posture approaches a foetal position, image of a depressed state. Cradle and grave come together, the womb and the tomb: these baroque commonplaces make the intervening space (represented by the writing, that which implies the Law of the Father) nothing but an illusion.[12] She also repeats something of the character of Dürer's figure of *Melencolia I* (1513), as a figure of melancholy. The child on the left, seen in a typical Madonna-and-child relationship, has died and the grieving mother in the foetal position now replaces it as it is issued from the womb: that she can replace it suggests death as desexualisation. A repetition has taken place: from the newly born child to the mother who is as if in the womb.

The writing in the frame, both epitaph and the unmoving law, appears within the representation of a sarcophagus which is surmounted by shell-like leaves to the right and left, and by an urn in the centre. Set as a cartouche on the front of the urn appears the figure of Time, an old man, bald save for his forelock, winged, naked save for a loincloth, because 'naked I came from my mother's womb and naked I shall return' (Job 1:21). He holds in his extended right hand an hourglass, and in his left, which is held behind him, a scythe as a reminder that 'all flesh is as grass' (Isaiah 40:6).

His forelock brings out the classical saying expressing the need to 'take time by the forelock', so the allegorical image is a rebus, interpretable as an inscription. These allegorical images of death and time can be discussed in the light of Benjamin's linking of the concepts of allegory and melancholy. He says that baroque drama made much use of emblems, and in baroque drama, 'the corpse becomes quite simply the pre-eminent emblematic property'.[13] Hamlet holding the skull of Yorick (*Hamlet* V.i) is an example of what Benjamin meant. Hamlet is a baroque figure, in the same way as this fragment of a wooden statue (photograph 27) collected among the relics in the museum attached to the Igreja de São Domingos.

Here, a skull is in the hand of the saint, as a relic for him to look at and contemplate as a reminder of death, a *memento mori*.

Benjamin contrasts the idea of the symbol with the allegorical image, and prefers the latter. As opposed to the symbol which the Romantic poets saw as an ideal, he shows that allegory responds to mourning and to history as the record of ruin, history as disaster. The symbol says, implicitly, that ruin can be redeemed, made whole, restored, because it celebrates a complete relationship between the idea

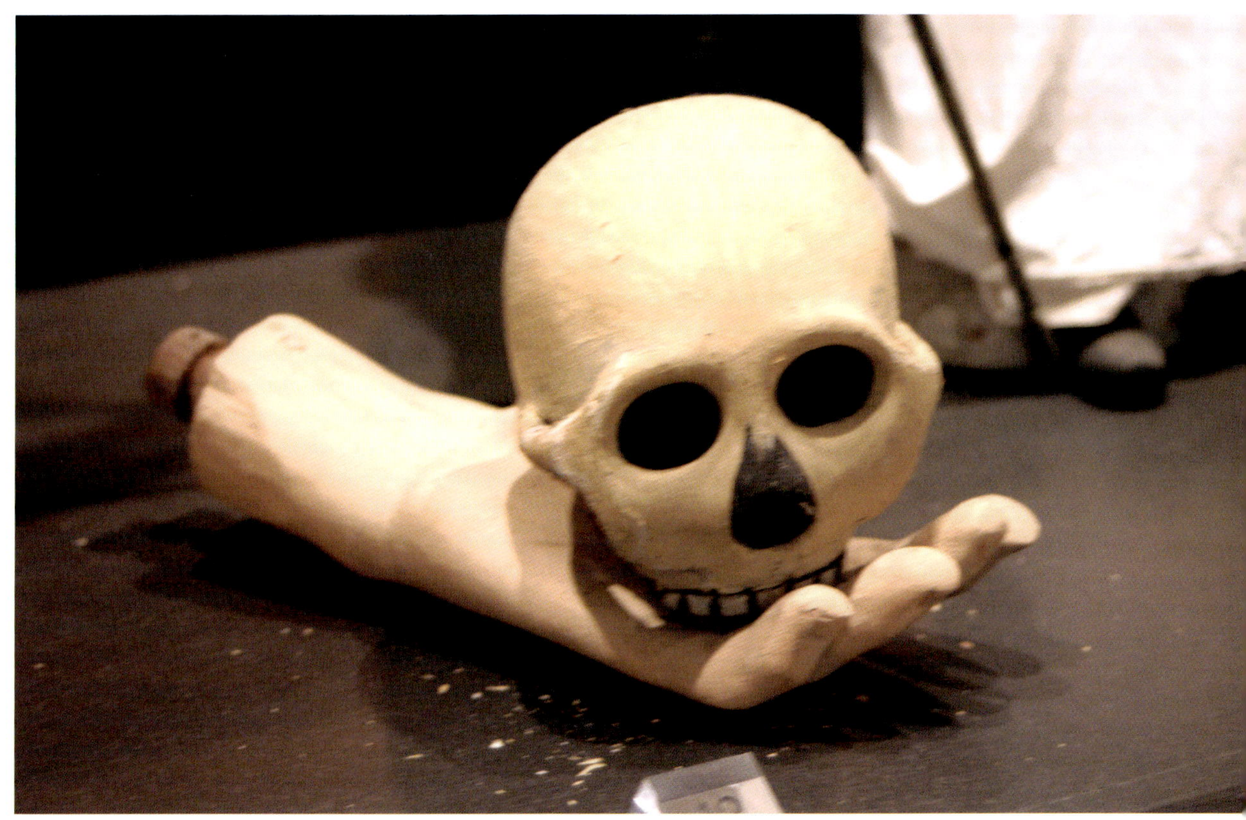

*27. Fragment of hand and skull,
relic kept at São Domingos*

being symbolised and the image. Allegory, however, does not try to idealise suffering. The difference between symbolism (which is not baroque) and allegory (which, for Benjamin, is baroque) shows itself when symbolism tries to assert a 'natural' relationship between an object and its meaning. In symbolism, the link between the signifier and what is signified is timeless, because it is natural. Allegory, however, shows that all such relationships are in the service of a false means of consolation. Symbolism, in short, does not take account of the gaps left by tragic events, by what is 'untimely, sorrowful, unsuccessful'. Allegory shows that there is something hollow and empty and illusionistic within any representation, that any expression is inadequate. The emptiness within the allegorical image finds its most complete expression in the empty skull. What has been said paraphrases the following quotation from Benjamin:

> Whereas in the symbol destruction is idealized and the transfigured face of nature is fleetingly revealed in the light of redemption, in allegory the observer is confronted with the *facies hippocratica* [the death's head, or more accurately, the face seen at the point of death] of history as a petrified, primordial landscape. Everything about history that, from the very beginning, has been untimely, sorrowful, unsuccessful, is expressed in a face — or rather in a death's head.[14]

Allegory, then, is at the heart of the baroque, and the two images to be discussed are the veiled

skull on the urn (photograph 26) and the figure of Time (photograph 27). The first of these brings out another aspect of allegory, that it works by veiling, folding: meaning is always partly concealed, never open. The other figure, Time, has the usual iconographic features to identify him, with unfolded wings and the folds of his loincloth and of his beard, but the arbitrariness of the emblems he bears (e.g. the hourglass, the bald head, and the scythe) shows that there is no 'natural' way of representing time. All representations show up their own inadequacy and are in turn victims of time which takes away — or veils — the possibility of reading such images. The allegorical image of Time shows itself to be the victim of time's folding and unfolding; the baroque is the image of temporality. Temporality of meaning implies that there can be no fixed meaning, even for the figure of Time. Hence Benjamin associates allegory with the baroque and with the fragment (of which the skull, like Time, a ruined figure because he is an old man, is a good example).

For Benjamin, the baroque is the art of the ruin, which includes the loss of meaning, or the point that meaning is already ruined:

> Allegories are in the realm of thoughts,
> what ruins are in the realm of things.

> This explains the baroque cult of the
> ruin. [...] That which lies here in ruins,
> the highly significant fragment, the
> remnant, is, in fact, the finest material
> in baroque creation. For it is common
> practice in the literature of the baroque
> to pile up fragments ceaselessly, without
> any strict idea of the goal, and [...] to
> take the repetition of stereotypes for a
> process of intensification. (178)

This passage illuminates the art of São José,
whose repetition of stereotypes has been analysed,
with the façade and the baldacchino, as a desire
for intensification. Similarly the images of
fragmentation on the monuments to the dead are
multiple. An allegorical figure of Time holds the
hourglass, as an allegory of time (another repetition
of stereotypes), so imaging the emptiness of life. A
ruined and faded figure of Time points to Macao
as decayed in a threefold way: because it indicates
death as the ruin of everything; because it exists
as an old and battered emblem in an old church;
and because the church itself is part of a ruin since
so much of baroque Macao has been bulldozed to
let new developments take place. What remains is
almost accidental.

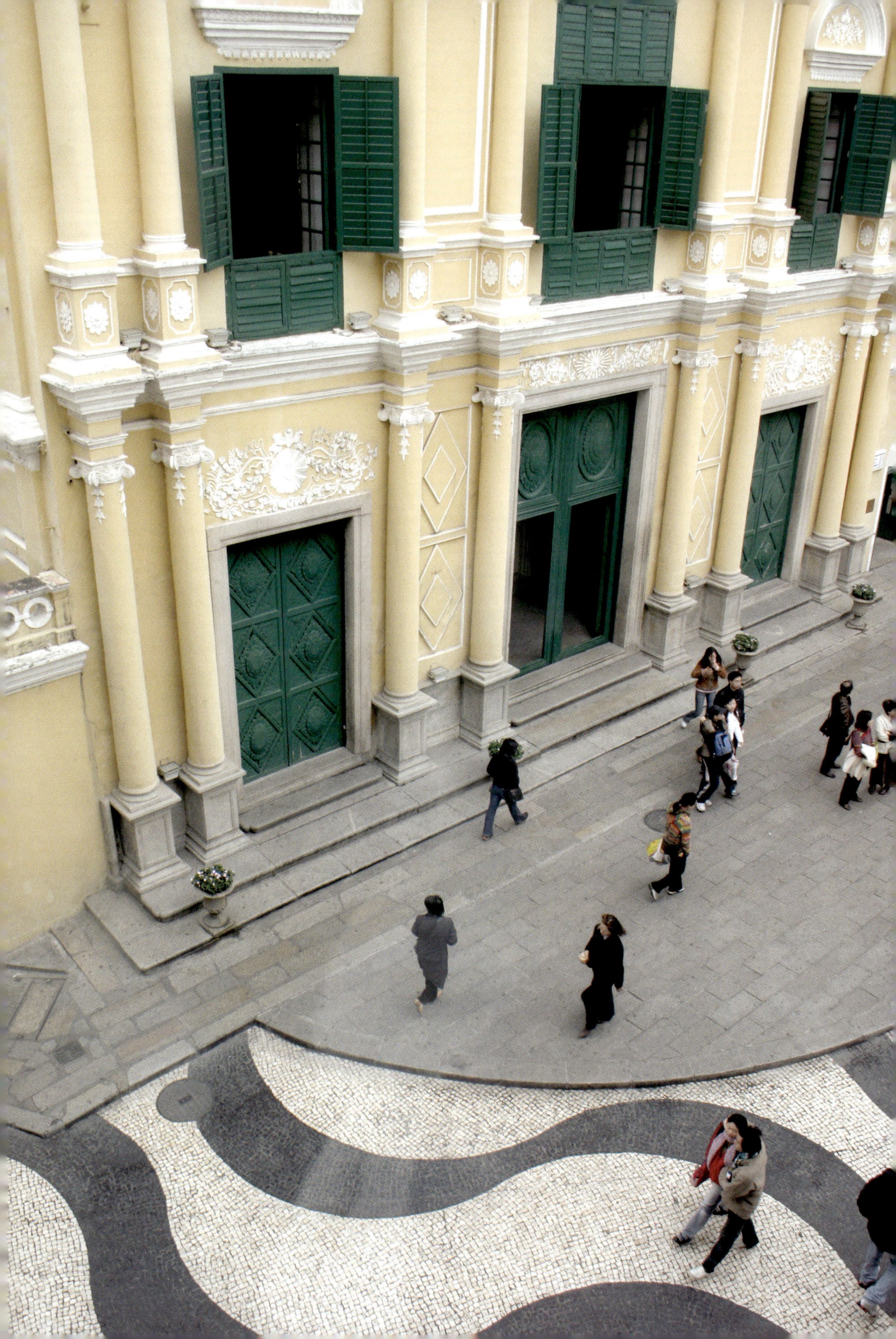

Chapter 4

Igreja de São Domingos
(Church of St Dominic)

After São José, a different example of the baroque can be visited: the Igreja de São Domingos. This chapter approaches it from the Senado Square through a detour, to see how it relates to the city space that has produced it, and how it has created space around it. São Domingos stands in its own small square (*largo*) at the other end of the Senado Square, which itself has its miniature aspects. Many things in Macao seem like miniatures of European forms. Perhaps it is a peculiarity of colonial architecture and colonial space, to make things small and sometimes doll-like for economic reasons.

The Senado Square is situated in front of the classically built Leal Senado, and in photograph 30, embodies Macao at its most carnival with the decoration for the Chinese New Year of the Dog (2006), where the mock-ups of the dog show that miniaturisation — which here looks like Disneyfication — takes many forms, and does not necessarily mean making the model of the dog look smaller!

And behind the Leal Senado in a little side street, as the road begins to make an ascent, there may be seen a distant glimpse of one of those crumbling neo-classical buildings whose colour, size, and sheer existence make Macao attractive, even though the meaning of the building remains only partially legible (photograph 31). The inscription suggests that it

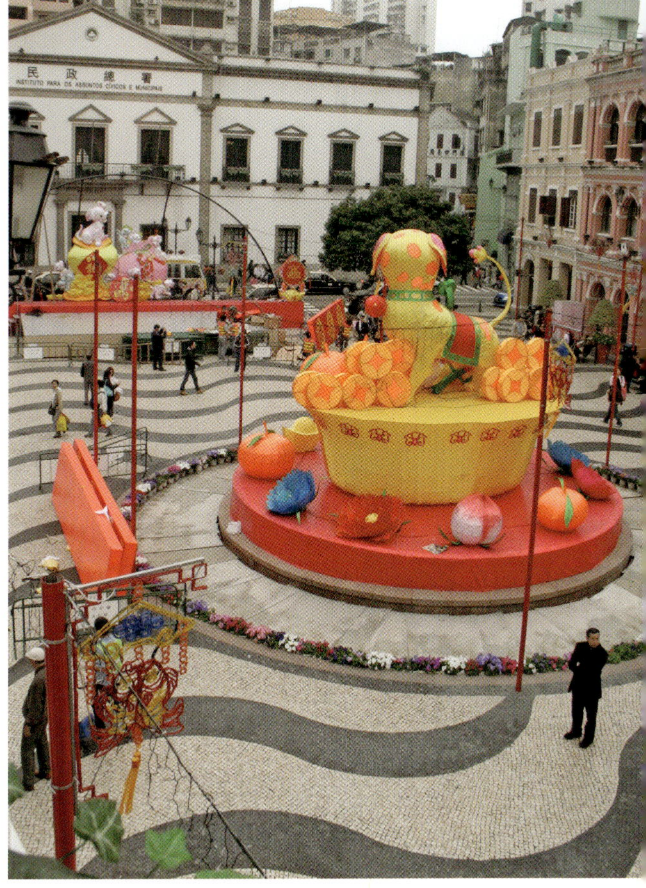

30. View of Leal Senado

29. Igreja de São Domingos

was once a place of association for people from four cities (Siyi), or five, in Guangdong province (Enping, Taishan, Xinhui, Kaiping, and Heshan, in the Pearl delta, all part of Jiangmen); now disused, the title, like the house, remains as a palimpsest, testimony to several unreadable histories.

As the building is seen in closer detail, it will be noticed how it lacks symmetry. The cartouches within the pediment are, as so often, empty: the building has not received any European inscription, only a Chinese one below, as if in a refusal of the cartouche-space. Why the left wing lacks a window in the upper storey is part of the forgotten history of Macao. The balcony on the return wall of the right wing only adds to the asymmetry of the whole. There is an empty space to the left of the building, climbing the hill.

The Senado Square, actually more a triangular shape, narrows towards a funnel shape as it approaches the *largo* São Domingos (as could be seen in photograph 1). But a detour can be taken by turning down the street Rua Sul do Mercado de São Domingos, to the left of the square facing away from the Leal Senado. This street is full of traders, with markets to the left and right. To the left there suddenly appears Sam Kai Vui Kun temple, which was a place of business, the Chinese complement to the colonial administration in the Senado. The road continues down to the Rua dos Mercadores.

31. Associação de Beneficência dos Naturais de Sei Iap de Macau

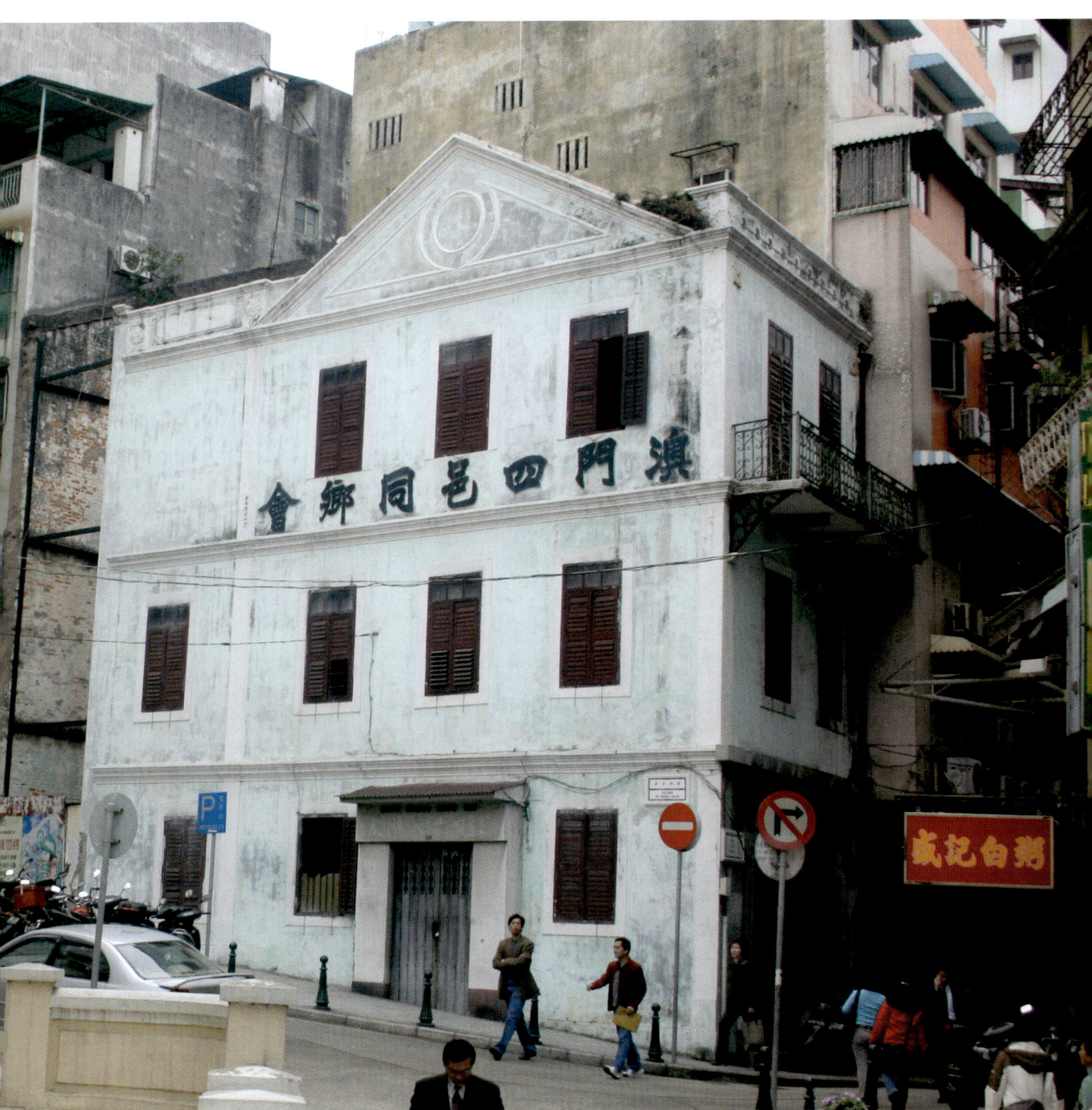

澳門四邑同鄉會
粥白記

Photograph 32 shows the three streets governed by Sam Kai Vui Kun temple, which means 'Three Streets Conference Committee'. At the rear of the photograph the Leal Senado square can just be seen, with the 1929 neo-classical Post Office (architect: Chen Kwen Pei) behind it. The second street runs down the extent of the photograph, and the temple is just visible, behind a high-rise building of 1928, renovated in 1988. The third street is where we stand. As we look into this temple, it is worth contrasting the business and fullness of its shrine with the much emptier colonial baroque model in São José, commented on before.

Having arrived at Rua dos Mercadores, there is a right turn into the Travessa do Soriano, following the graceful curve made by the now run-down 1920s colonial and Chinese building (which formerly housed a bank), with graceful ironwork balconies, and a rhythm of double pilasters with double doors between them, opening onto the street. This view permits in the distance a view of the rear of São

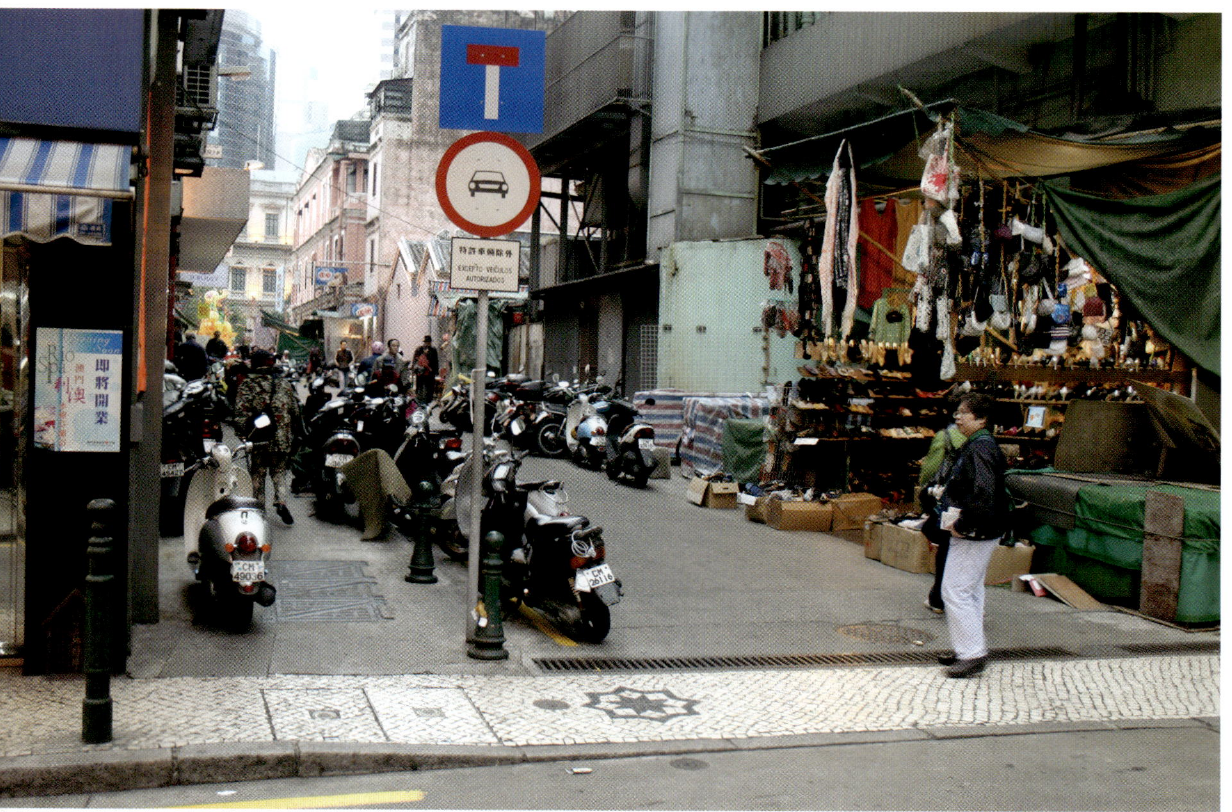

▲ *32. Three streets*

33. Shrine in Sam Kai ▶

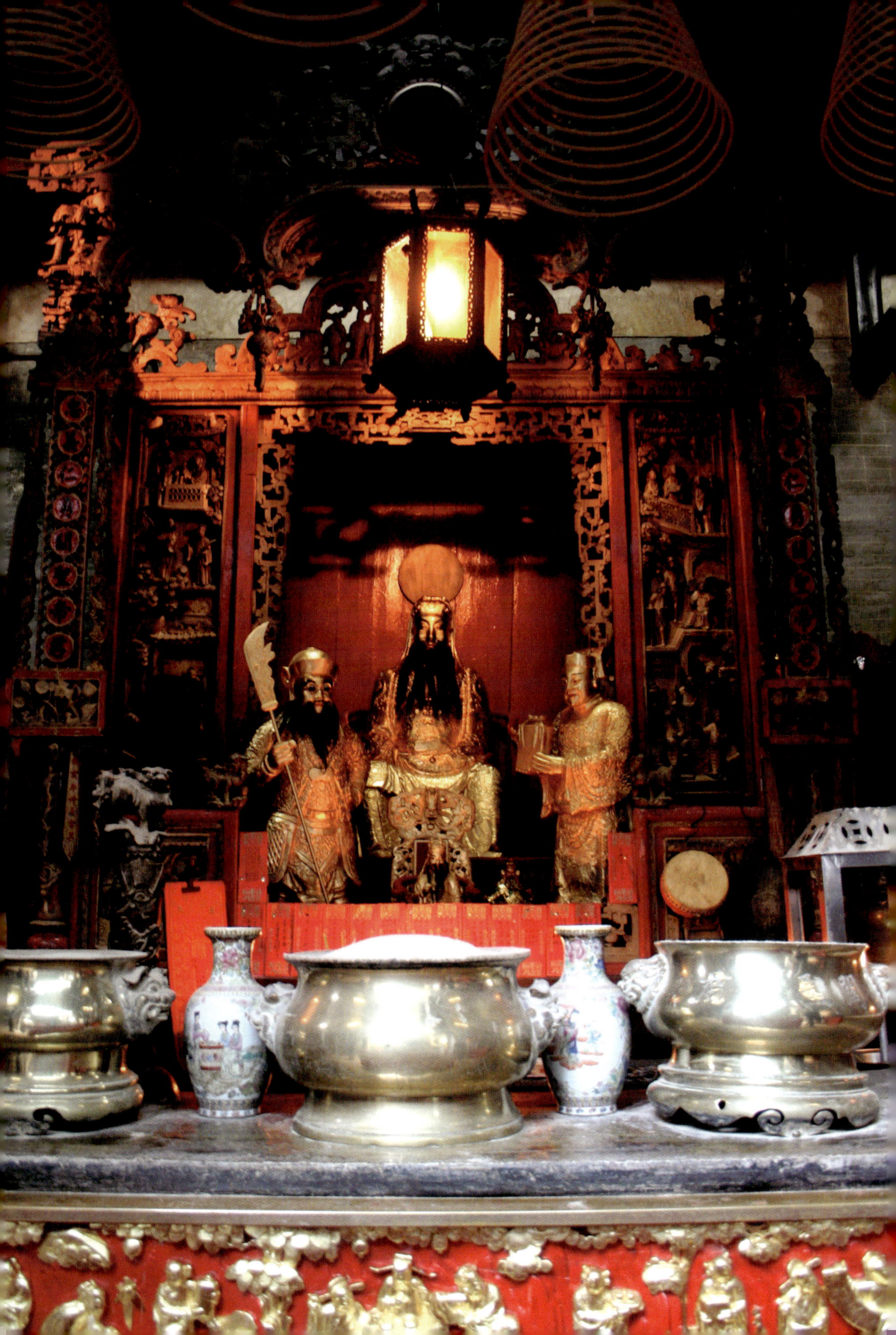

Domingos' façade (what should never be seen in the baroque).

The colonial buildings, which recede into the distance (see photograph 1 for comparison) are succeeded by a row of early twentieth-century shop houses on two floors, with pitched Chinese roofs and Mediterranean balconies. Their end-gable is wedged right up against São Domingos: they were not there when Chinnery painted the scene outside the church in the 1820s. It is as if the shops are trying to look through the green shutters into the church, as if there cannot be any waste of space; and as they look from the first-floor level, there forms a graceful, irregular cross.

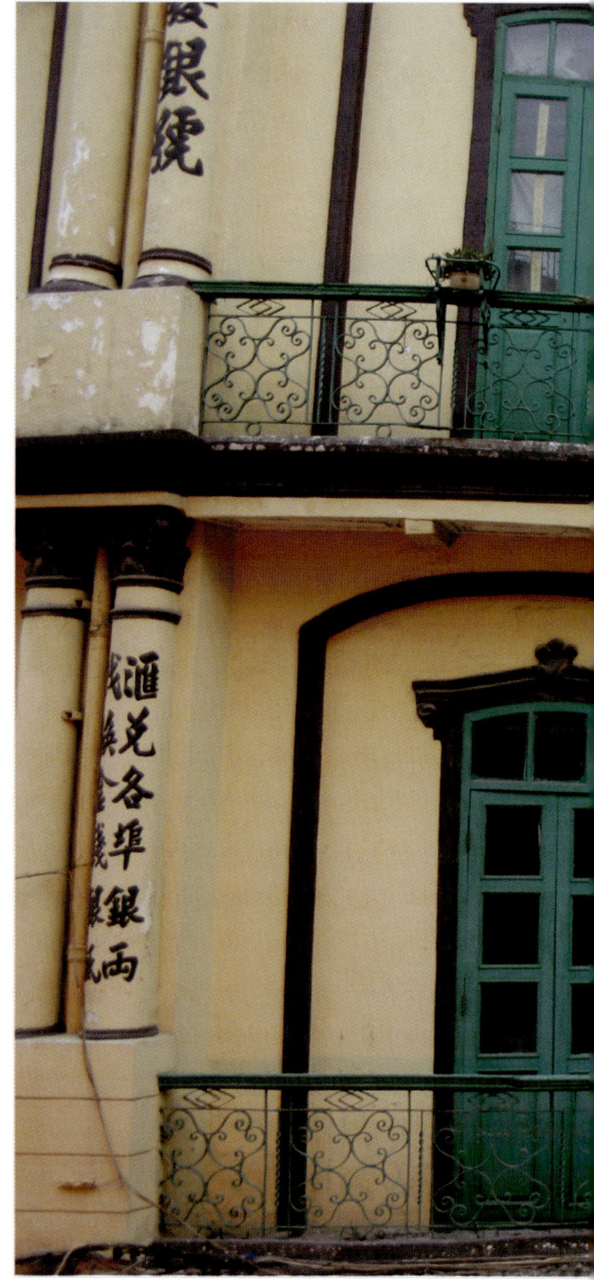

34. Former bank behind São Domingos

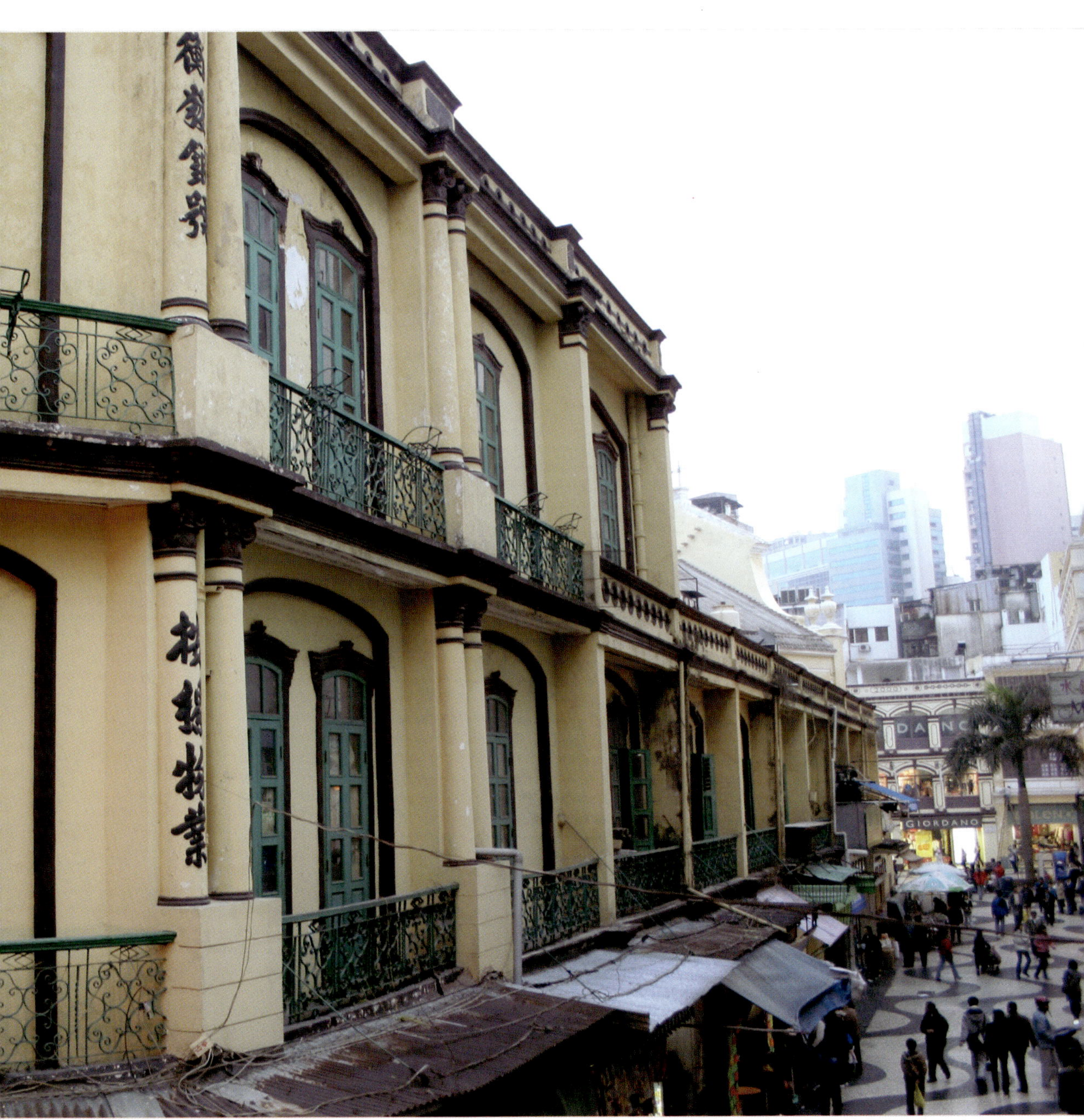

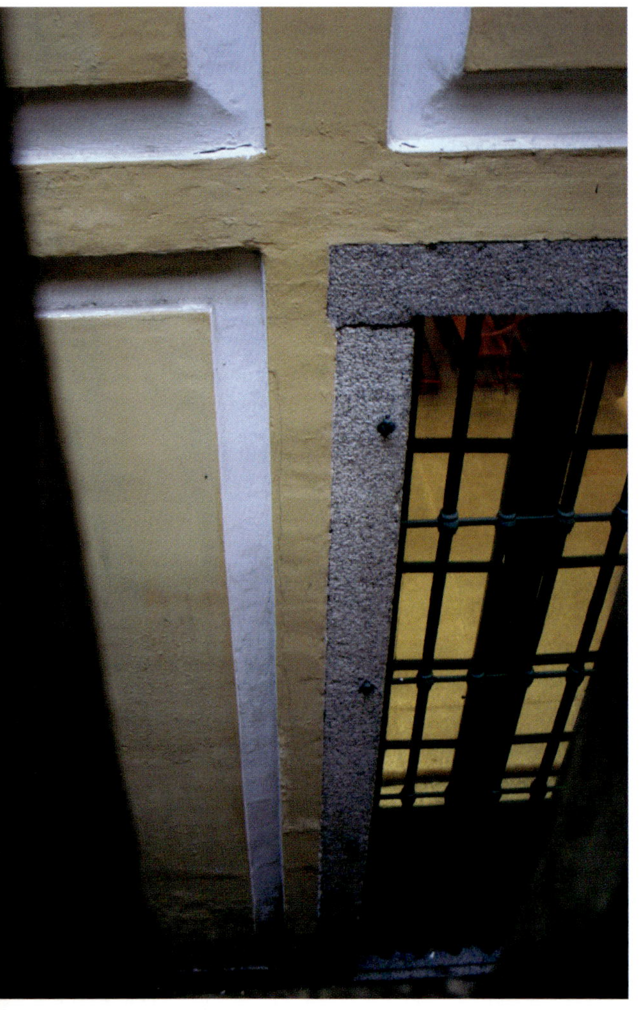

35. Cross formed by walls

Photograph 35 from the back of the shop, Mercearia Tong Fong, follows the gaze into the body of the church, and just captures the narrow floor space in-between. An alternative cross is formed by the front view from the shop's first floor where the Travessa do Soriano is visible, and looking down the street (Rua Leste do Mercado de São Domingos) to a distant sight of the temple (in the third street) (photograph 36).

The cat occupies an equally narrow ledge on the balcony, the space in between.

The viewer walks down the Travessa do Soriano and turns into the São Domingos square to see the church. This is framed on the other side by modern architecture, and stands in a space where the pavings fall into the graceful wavy patterns associated with the Senado Square.

Within this curve, which is echoed by another broad one made by the lip of the paving that forms the spacious entry into São Domingos, there is a combination of business, commerce and a baroque structure which seems to be pushed into this city-space, as though there is no place for it, which adds to the sense of miniaturisation. The colonial space of the Senado Square and everything within São Domingos is reduced in size.

36. Cat looking back

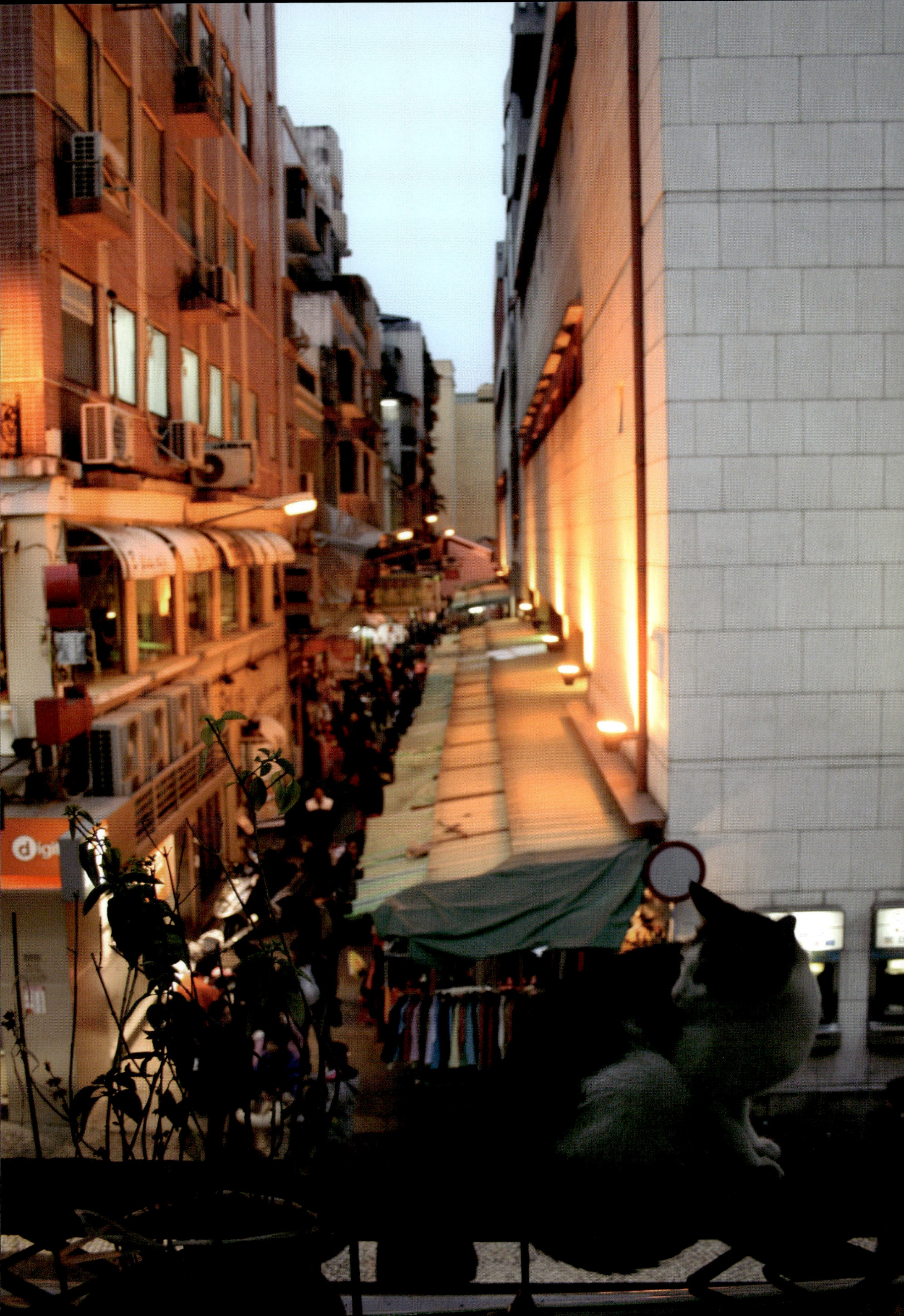

Inside São Domingos

São Domingos is basically a nineteenth-century church with older elements in it, which go back to its founding as a convent in 1587 by Spanish Dominicans (the teaching order of Friars established in the thirteenth century). These Dominicans came from the Philippines, which were colonised by the Spanish in 1565. The convent was to be taken over by Portuguese Dominicans a year later, in 1588. The exterior of this church in white and yellow is classical with three bays and two storeys, and a pediment rising above (photograph 29). Baroque appears in the white decorations which are like lace work, adorning particularly the columns, the pediment above the windows and the three doors in the three bays, and comprising the cartouche, which dominates the centre of the pediment, and the four urns which rest upon the top of the façade like bookends for it. Inside, the church (a little grander than Santo Agostinho) keeps its three bays with two rows of arches running down to the east end.

This photograph shows the view toward the north aisle of the church (facing the front door), with pictures on the walls displaying the last few of the fourteen 'Stations of the Cross', which were fixed as meditation points for the Christian in the time of the baroque, and it also shows the graceful curve of the balconies with the light shining through from the windows behind. These light wooden balconies, and the wide-open windows pouring light in are

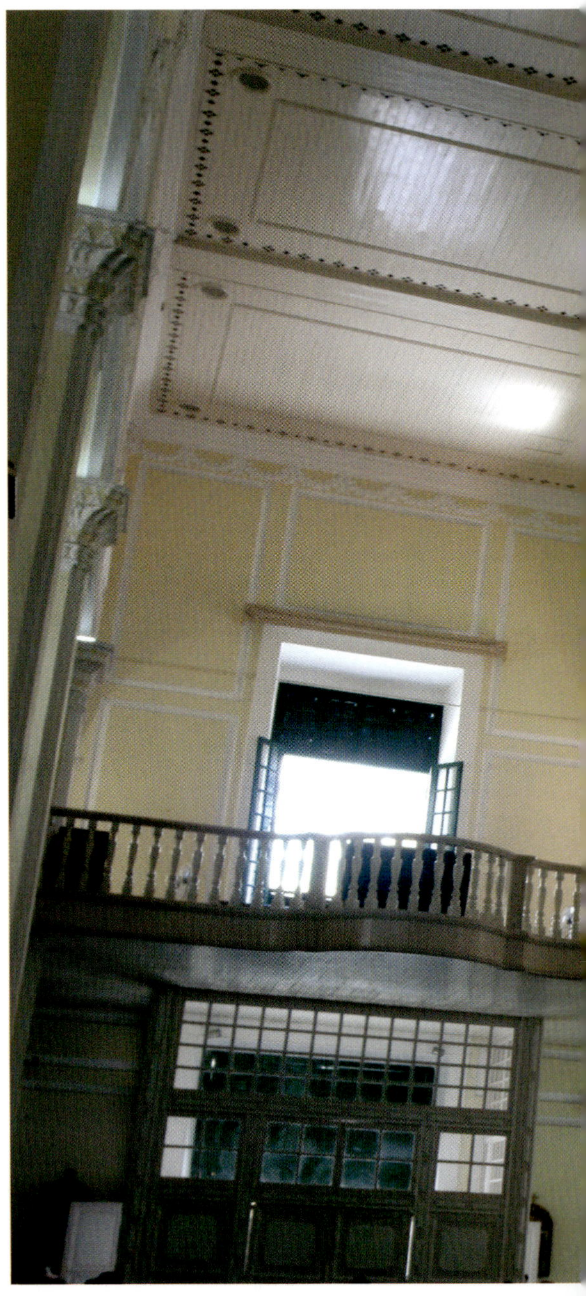

37. View of north aisle in São Domingos

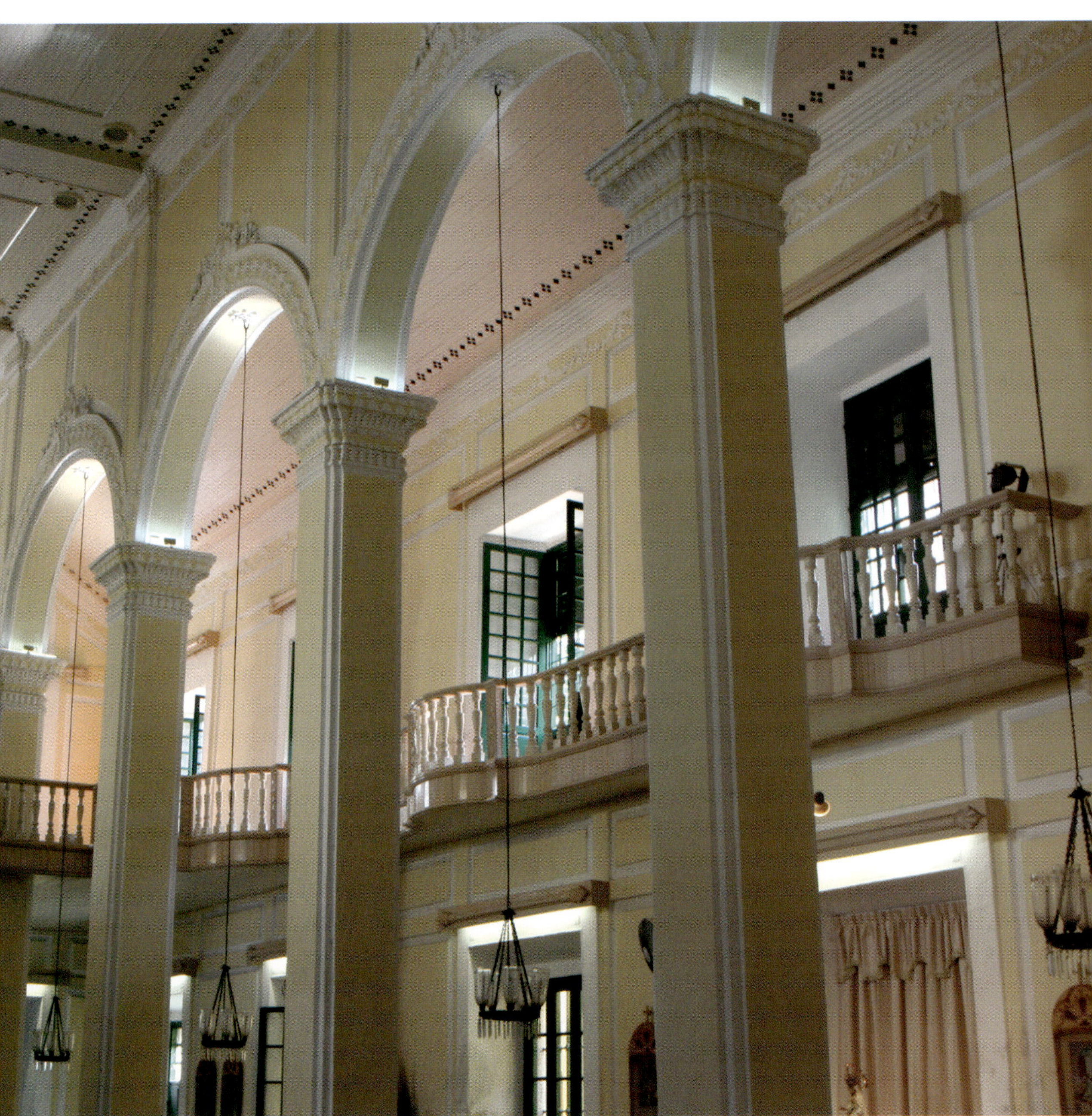

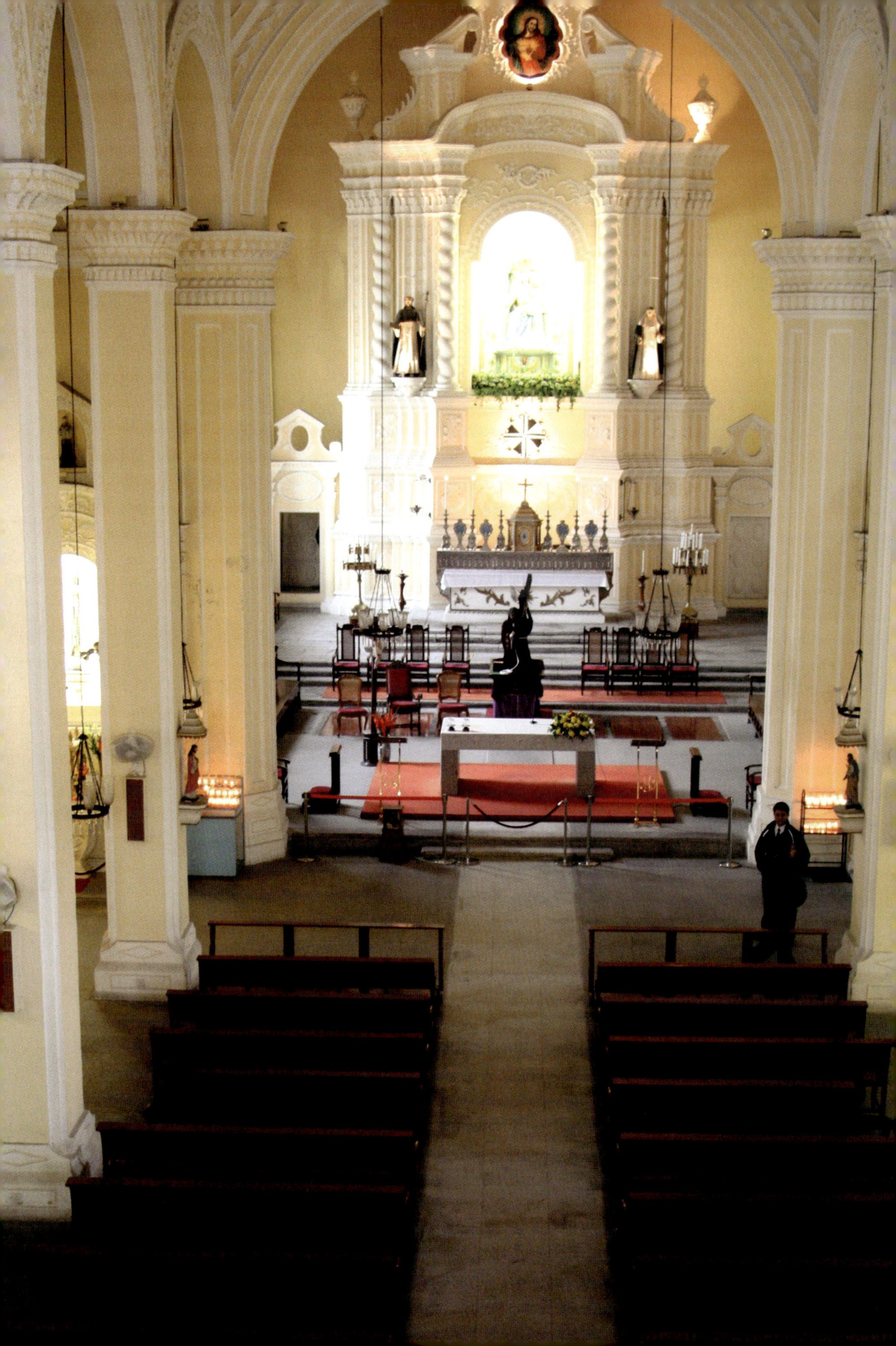

features of a hot climate. High up in the summit of the baldacchino at the east end is an illuminated cartouche, like a red seal, showing Christ as if looking through an open window into the church from heaven, surveying the faithful, with his right hand displaying theatrically his burning heart which is held in his left. The heart, like a large strawberry, encircled by a green garland, is surmounted by the crucifix, while the burning light repeats that seen in the burning halo: head and heart, mind and passion, are equally aflame; no Cartesian separation of mind and body is intended here.[1]

Above Christ the sacred dove soars away into the wooden ceiling. One object within Christ's all-seeing view is himself bearing the cross, a figure seen within the chancel. The spatiality is important — Christ above looks down at Christ in humiliation. Such a stress on arousing an affect within the worshipper was not to be found within the central architecture of São José but here it seems more integral. It is an allegorical image.

Such affecting images of Christ may be found in the treasury of São Domingos. Three of these may be distinguished, and may be supplemented by the baptism of Christ discussed in chapter 3 (see photograph 20: Baptism of Christ). Photograph 39 is a wooden statue of Christ tied to the column for flagellation.

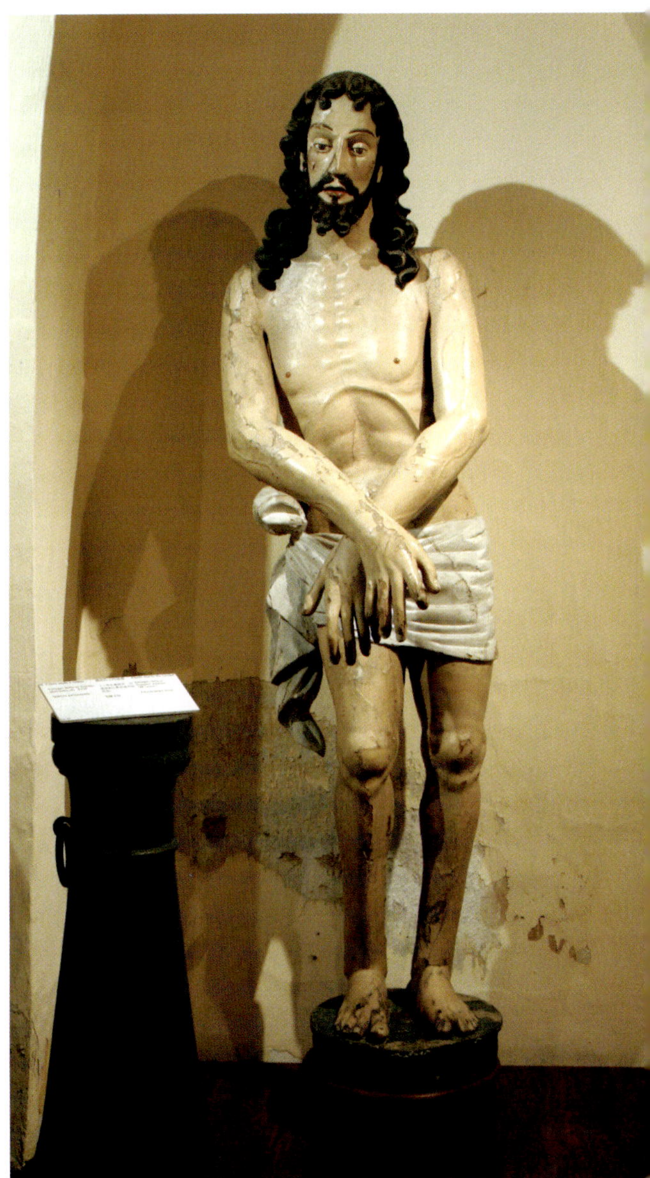

39. Christ tied to a column

*38. View of the baldacchino
in São Domingos*

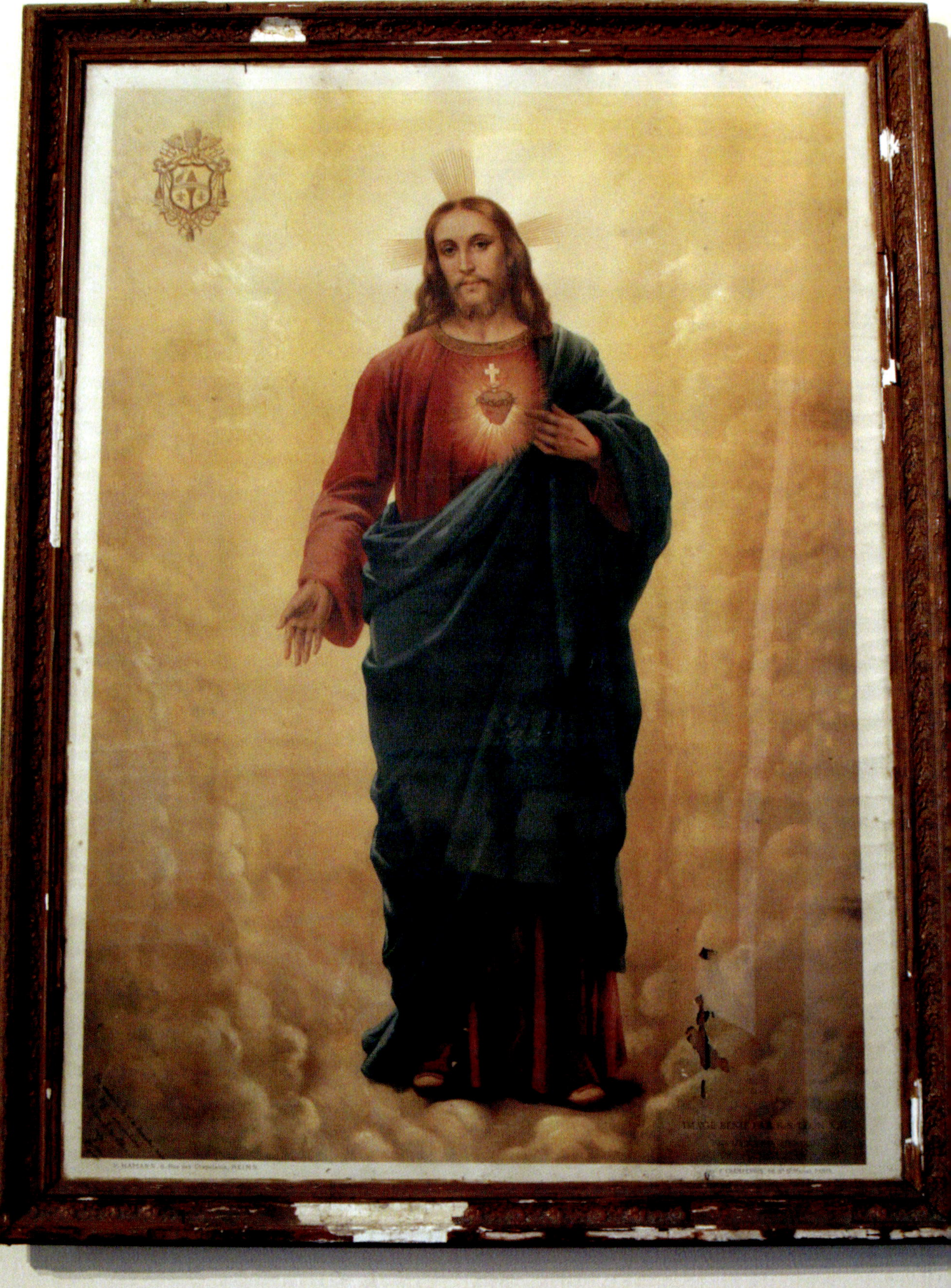

The statue emphasises realism in the protruding veins of Christ's arms and in the projecting ribcage. It comes from Goa in the eighteenth century: it is colonial baroque art which has circulated by sea (hence the bollard) from one colonial space to another, given from one colonial space which is alienated from the European source and meaning of the image to another space. The mass production of images, which is all important not only for the baroque but more so for colonialism, becomes yet more apparent with a particular representation. This is Christ in glory.

The source of glory, however, might be called, following Deleuze, 'any-space-whatever [*espace quelconque*]'[2] because from the inscription at the bottom of photograph 40 seems to have been manufactured in Shanghai from a template authorised in Paris, and marked *Image bénie par S. S. Leon XIII pour les missions Catholiques* (Image blessed by Pope Leo XIII (1878–1903) for Catholic missions), and is dated 1895. Italy, France, Portugal and China have all cooperated with this image for Macao. As in the cartouche in the main church, Christ points with his left hand to his heart, which is girt with a crown of thorns, and surmounted by a cross, shines with rays of fire. His right hand, also with the stigmata, points downward. This Christ is European with fair hair and blue eyes, and he brings out the kitsch aspects of baroque.

The image below is yet more baroque in style, being a late nineteenth- to early twentieth-century sacrarium containing arms and feet from the image of Our Lord of Passion.

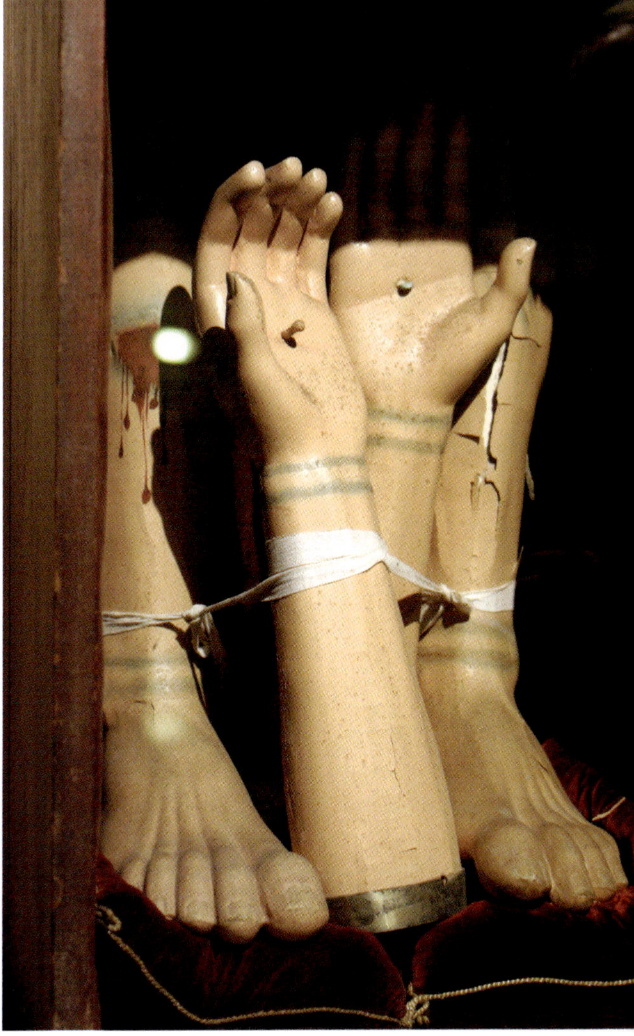

41. Relic: feet and hands

40. Painting of Christ showing burning heart

Many boxes here preserve fragments from the body of Christ, looking like parts of dolls or manikins — miniature forms again, painted hands with the nails still in them, and the legs (still dripping blood) and feet put together on a red cushion as instances of the body in pieces.[3] But since the feet have no marks of the nails, it may be assumed that the hands are Christ's but the legs and feet are not, so that these have been put together in a confusion of identities: Christ's hands mixed up with his saints' feet, where the feet are unattributable, disseminated. Here are allegorical images to which no single signified can be given, a delirium of signs. There are also several heads with heavily rouged lips.

The baroque shows, alongside its interest in fragments, attention to relics, to be discussed here and in the following chapter. Relics are parts of baroque's culture of display, a uniting of the colonial drive which dictates to the Chinese the affective response they should have, and a culture of consumption. The heart on fire is a reminder of St Teresa (1515–1582) and of her experience of the angel with his spear, which became the theme of a quintessentially baroque work of art by Gianlorenzo Bernini. His statue of St Teresa is in the Cornaro Chapel of Santa Maria della Vittoria (1646) in Rome, and was referred to in chapter 3. The art historian Nikolaus Pevsner, describing it, says that:

at the centre of the altar, where one would have expected to find the painting [...] there is a niche with a sculptural group, treated like a picture and giving an illusion of reality that is as startling today as it was three hundred years ago. Everything in the chapel contributes to this *peinture vivante* illusion. [...] Bernini has [also] portrayed in marble, behind balconies, members of the Cornaro family, the donors of the chapel, watching with us the miraculous scene, precisely as though they were in the boxes, and we in the stalls of a theatre.[4]

And what has Bernini represented? St Teresa writes in her *Life* of her mystical and ecstatic experience of being pierced by an angel:

[The angel] was not tall but short, and very beautiful; and his face was so aflame that he appeared to be one of the highest rank of angels, who seem to be all on fire. They must be of the kind called cherubim, but they do not tell me their names. I know very well that there is a great difference between some angels and others, and between these and others still, but I could not possibly explain it. In his hands I saw a great golden spear, and at the iron tip there appeared to be a point of fire. This he plunged into my heart several times so that it penetrated to my entrails. When he pulled it out, I felt that he took them with it, and left me utterly consumed by the great love of God. The pain was so severe that it made me utter several moans. The sweetness caused by this intense pain is so extreme that one cannot possibly wish it to cease, nor is one's soul then content with anything but God. This is not a physical, but a spiritual pain, though the body has some share in it — even a considerable share.[5]

Lacan has often been seen as baroque both in his way of writing and in his cultural interests. He discusses the vision of St Teresa as rendered by Bernini, and says that she is experiencing an extreme wordless sexual pleasure (*jouissance*) which goes beyond heterosexual experience.

You have only to go and look at Bernini's statue in Rome to understand immediately that she is coming, there is no doubt about it. And what is her *jouissance*, her coming from? It is clear that the essential testimony of the mystics, is that they are experiencing it but know nothing about it.[6]

Lacan identifies Bernini's baroque statue with an eroticism which is not only characterised by excess, but is feminine at core; he makes St Teresa a figure whose sexual ecstasy is not produced by the male, and therefore stands outside all codifications of the sexual, all considerations of normative heterosexuality as that which produces pleasure (*jouissance*). Bernini's statue with Lacan's comment thereon can be compared with the St Teresa in Macao, a work of the 1920s.

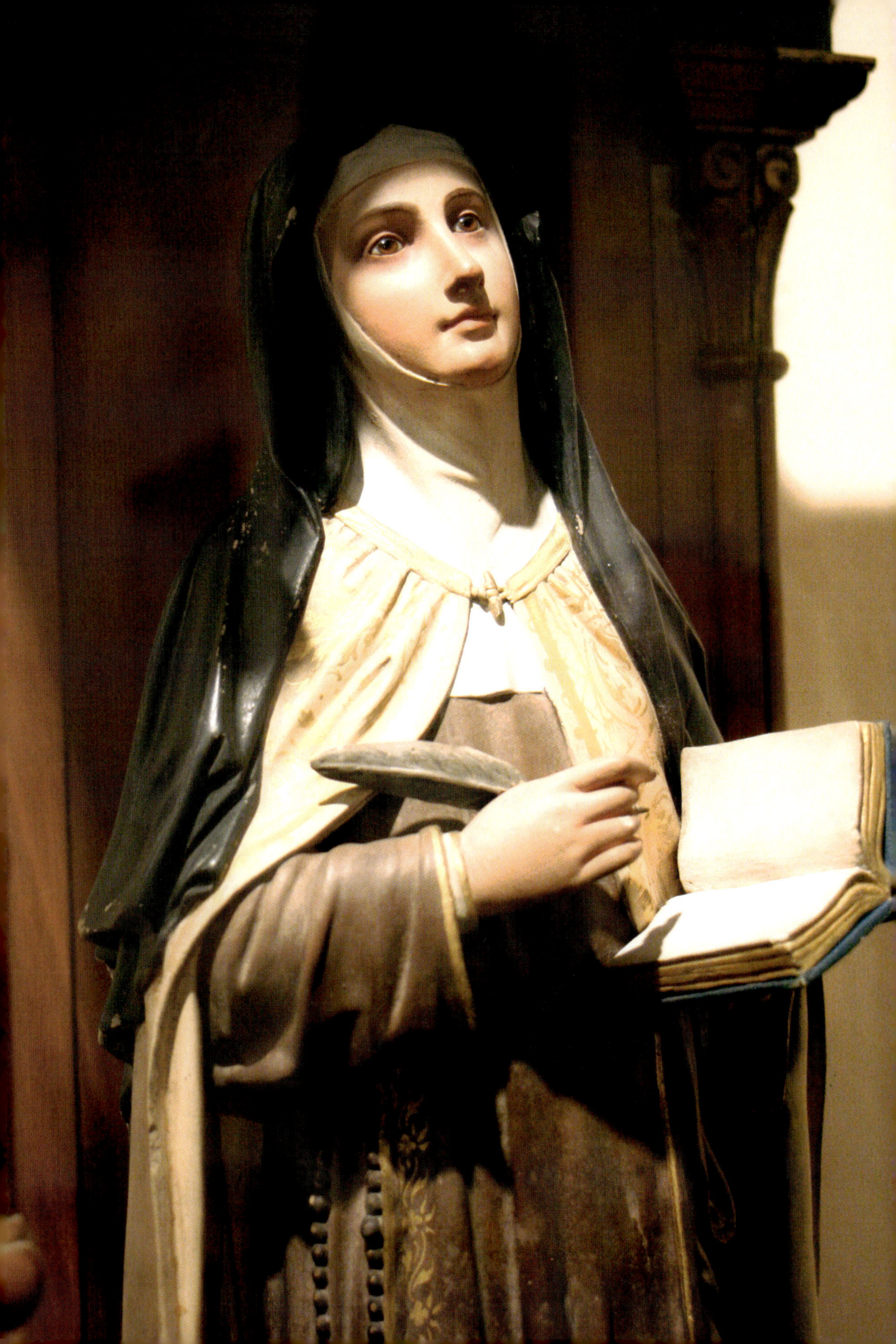

Here the waxy smiling face, almost bare of lines (which means there are only very few folds), looks upwards, while she suspends her writing in a book. Her garments are all ordered, undisturbed. The subject-matter is baroque but the change from Bernini's intensity indicates something of a colonial repression; the baroque and the colonial are here in conflict. Here it is worth returning to the comments made earlier about the baldacchino in São José where the turning inwards of the broken arch of the pediment indicates a certain timidity or retreat in contrast to the exuberance of the baldacchino that frames Bernini's sculpture. The discourse of the baroque seems to mean one thing within Europe and another in the colonial context, where there is a poverty which is inseparable from it being the repressing agency more definitely than in Europe even, and indicating fear of excess. Derrida's essay 'Force and Signification' gives a definition of the baroque as inherently bursting out and breaking rules of structure in moments of historical crisis:

> It is during the epochs of historical dislocation, when we are expelled from the *site*, that this structuralist passion, which is simultaneously a frenzy of experimentation and a proliferation of schematizations, develops for itself. The baroque would only be one example of it. Has not a 'structural poetics' 'founded on a rhetoric' been mentioned in relation to the baroque? But has not a 'burst structure' also been spoken of, a 'rent poem whose structure appears as it bursts apart?'[7]

To summarise from these images, the baroque in Europe is three things: (a) a culture of control through its images; (b) the art of a culture in crisis where things burst out of control; (c) a heterogeneous and feminine culture whose excess attacks masculine control. In Macao, baroque is: (a) a culture for control; (b) an art whose anxieties retreat from dehiscence (splitting), and attempt to impose a unifying order, which is both Chinese and European; (c) an art of heterogeneity and of the feminine, but whose resources are always impoverished, always reduced. Colonialism cannot afford either *furor* or ecstasy.

42. St Teresa at São Domingos

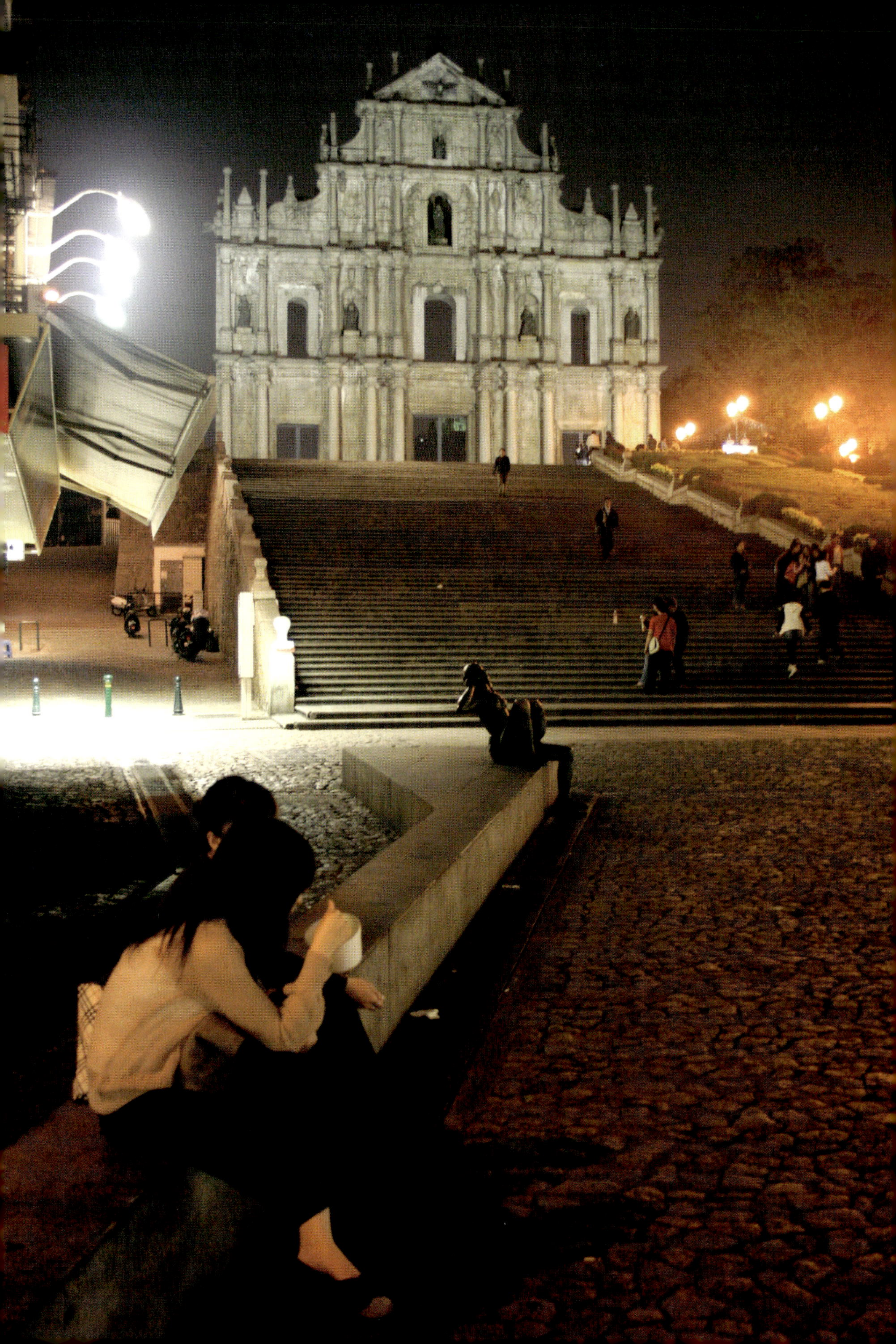

Chapter 5

Ruínas de São Paulo
(Ruins of St Paul's)

The building discussed here is known world-wide, and is visited by every tourist to Macao. The Ruins of St Paul, on a hill twenty-six metres above sea level, must constitute one of the most famous baroque images: every tourist climbs up the steps to see them and is photographed against them. Macao promotional tourism features St Paul's Ruins; they are Macao's Eiffel Tower, its Sydney Opera House.

São Paulo was built by the Jesuits in the first thirty or so years of the seventeenth century and burned down in 1835. It is now approached by six flights of eleven stairs each, divided by landings and with a balustrade running up each side.[1] The stairs climb upward through ten metres. The photograph shows the journey towards the façade up a ramp towards the free flight of stairs which can be seen as a single discrete unit. Nickolaus Pevsner argues that the design of staircases was crucial to the Renaissance and even more to the baroque, which exploited their ability to give a sense of movement.[2] Macao makes attractive use of staircases, both inside and outside, even in the most casual contexts. (Note the staircases in photographs 16 (the Ho Tung Library) and 21 (the São José).) The stairs of São Paulo are disconnected in direction from the façade, being, as the photograph shows, de-centred to the left because earlier on, there were buildings where there is now an elegant floral display running the length of the stairs. A nineteenth-century pen-and-ink sketch by Chinnery illustrates the point: before, there was no overall view of the façade.

Lacan thinks of architecture as 'organised around emptiness'. Hegel considers architecture as masking death, preserving it and superseding it, as Denis Hollier says 'architecture is something appearing in the place of death, to point out its presence and to cover it up: the victory of death and the victory over death'.[3] If it is a cover, its existence is expressed best in the idea of a façade. The granite façade of St Paul's, all that is left, becomes the essence of architecture, because this façade is literally all there is to see: a gate in the middle of the city leading nowhere. Does people's desire to be photographed in front of the façade, as a way of asserting their identity, show an unconscious sense that the ruin is all there is? Perhaps as a façade, architecture is a face, a mask, a personification. This baroque façade is both an allegory in itself (a personification), and has allegorical designs upon it. It uses writing, having Latin, Greek and Chinese — no Portuguese — inscriptions on it. São Paulo is called locally, 'Da San Ba Pai Fong' (São Paulo memorial tablet), for its similarity to a Chinese memorial tablet: as if this writing in stone is both a manuscript which has been lifted through ninety degrees, and a monument; a work for memory and potentially both inviting and minatory; a gateway, which in Chinese thought, leads to transformation. 'Da San Ba Pai Fong' evokes the two-dimensional feature of the

43. Night overview of São Paulo

façade: the name comes after the fire that destroyed the church, so that the memorial is to death, and the memorial stone is a tombstone. Writing and erasure take place together, the signifier remains but the signified is under erasure. If São Paulo is approached as a text, the relationship of writing to death becomes a topic for speculation.

São Paulo may be analysed from the top of its five levels to the bottom.

The uppermost level comprises a dove surrounded by sun and a moon and four stars, and the pediment is surmounted by four obelisks and a cross. The cross is invisible from the ground below: if there is no place from which the whole façade can be seen, this belongs to the Gothic aesthetic, which stresses the part and not the whole (only God sees the whole).

The level below shows Christ under a scallop-shell canopy with, to the right and left of him, the emblems of his passion. To the left, the crown of thorns, a whip, the hammer, and pincers, and the reed on which the sponge was placed for him to drink from on the cross. To the right, are the nails, a ladder and a reed. On either side of these panels appear angels, one with the cross, the other with the whipping post. Panels to left and right of these contain respectively, the rope and a sheaf of wheat, the latter indicative in this land of rice, of the bread which forms the host. At the edges of this pediment,

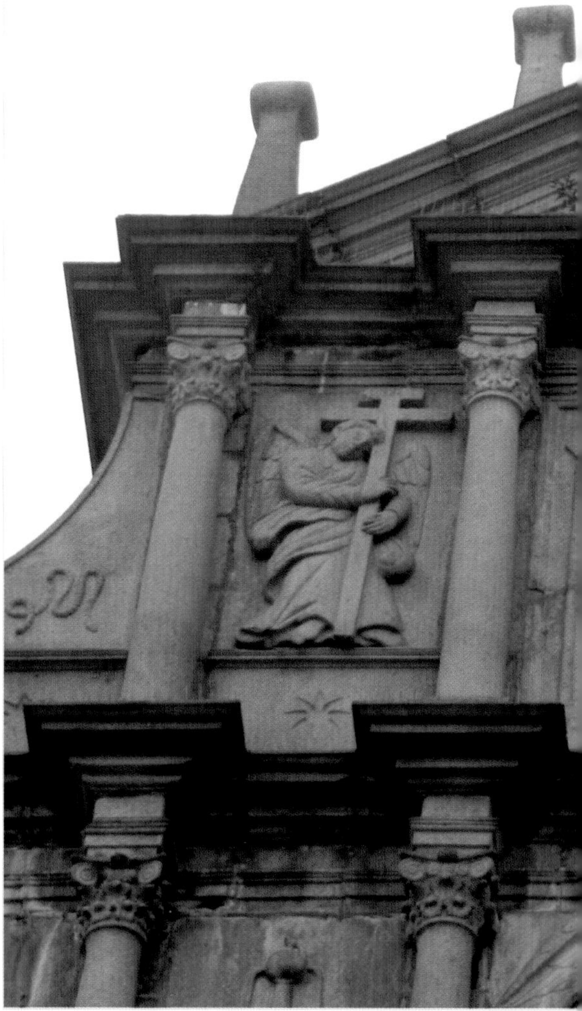

44. Upper two storeys

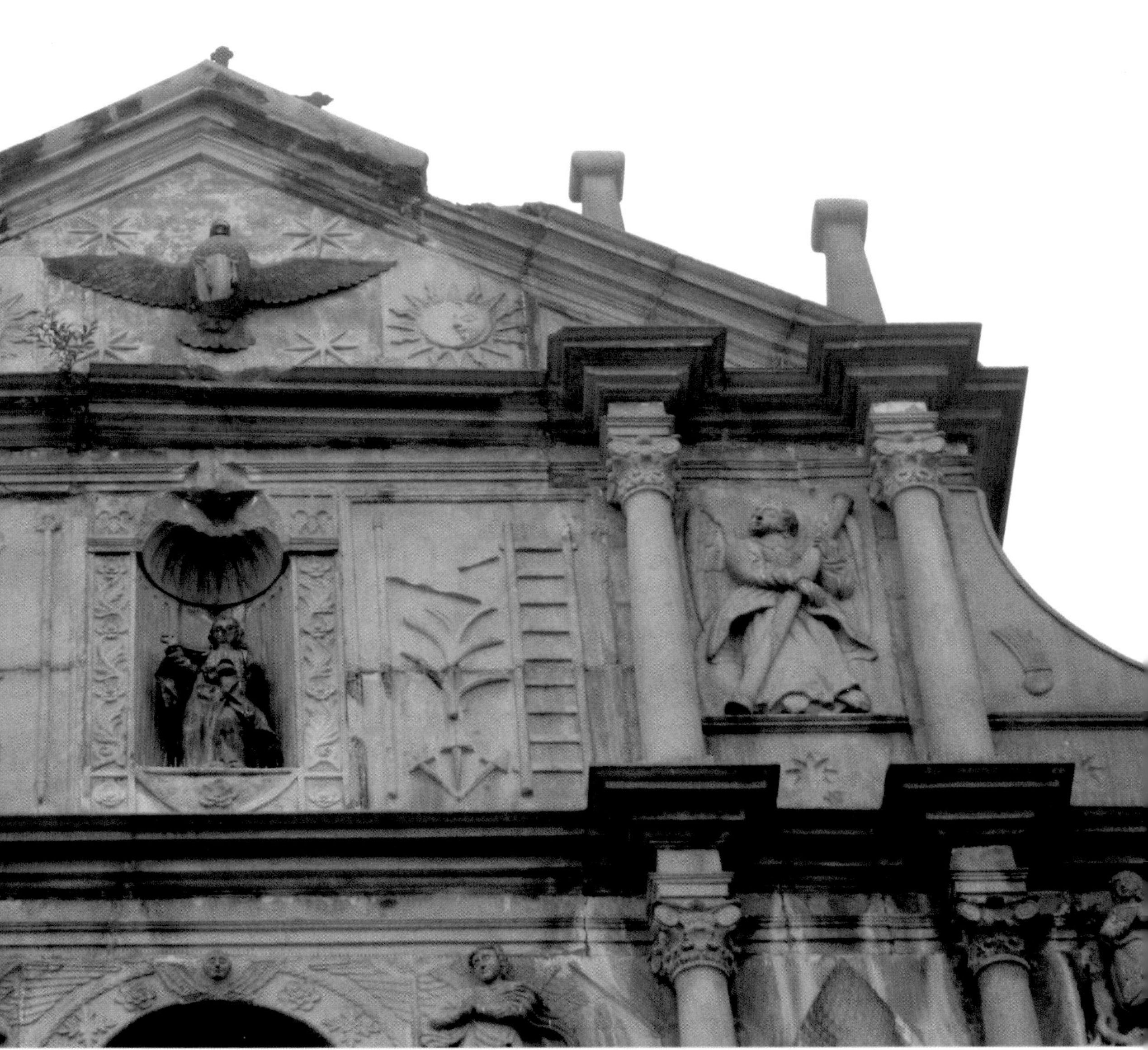

beyond the obelisks, are Chinese lions. The columns are surmounted by Corinthian capitals: this part of the façade represents the Church Triumphant.

The level below that is larger, and is given to a bronze Virgin Mary in the centre, framed by an arch.

To the right and left of her appear six angels, two praying, two making music, two swinging incense-burners, and then, between the classical pilasters, the fountain of life (left) and the tree of life (right).

In the panels going outward from these, there is, on the right side of the façade, a seven-headed dragon, surmounted by the Virgin. Chinese characters incised into the rock adjacent to her read: 'Holy Mother [larger characters] stepping on the head of the dragon [smaller characters]'. Dragons in Chinese represent the Emperor and power, while the Western dragon is demonic; the syncretism of the image does not take away from the potential implicit threat: Christianity destroys the power of the Chinese. Below the scroll forming the top of the pediment, there is a skeleton lying, pierced with arrows. Chinese characters annotate this as, 'Remember death; do no sin'. On the opposite side, there is a galleon, with the Virgin (as the star of the sea) above it, a reminder of Portuguese power. Beyond that, the devil, whose appearance is also Chinese, appears supine, with a woman's body. He is also shot through with two arrows, and the

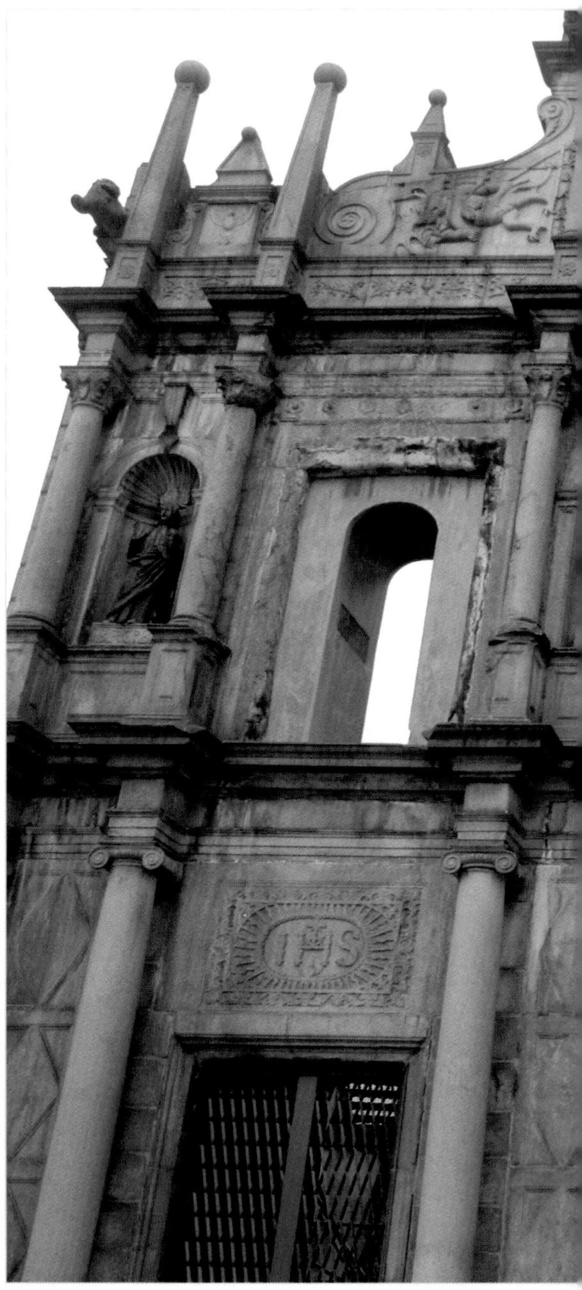

45. The first, second and third levels

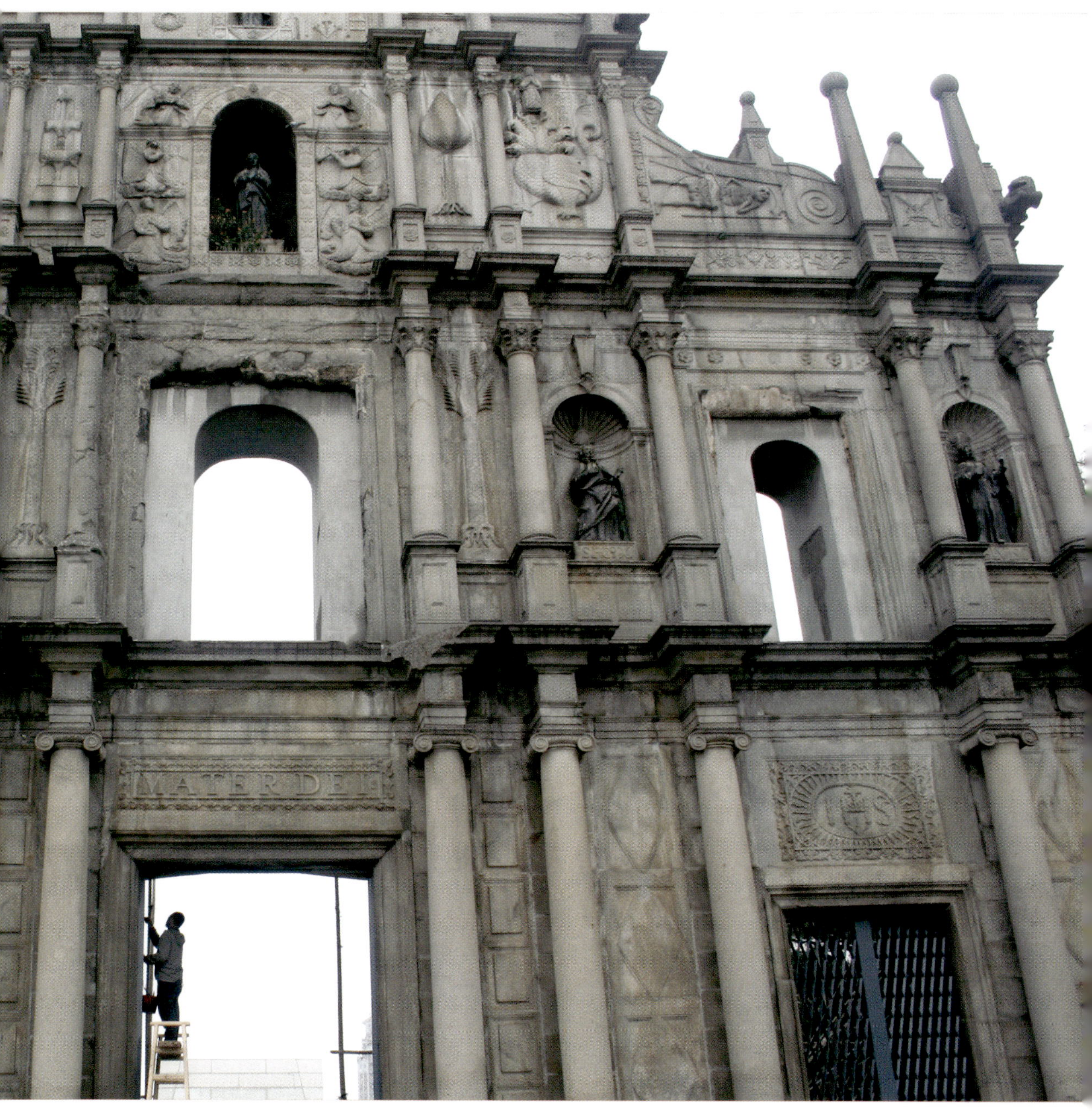

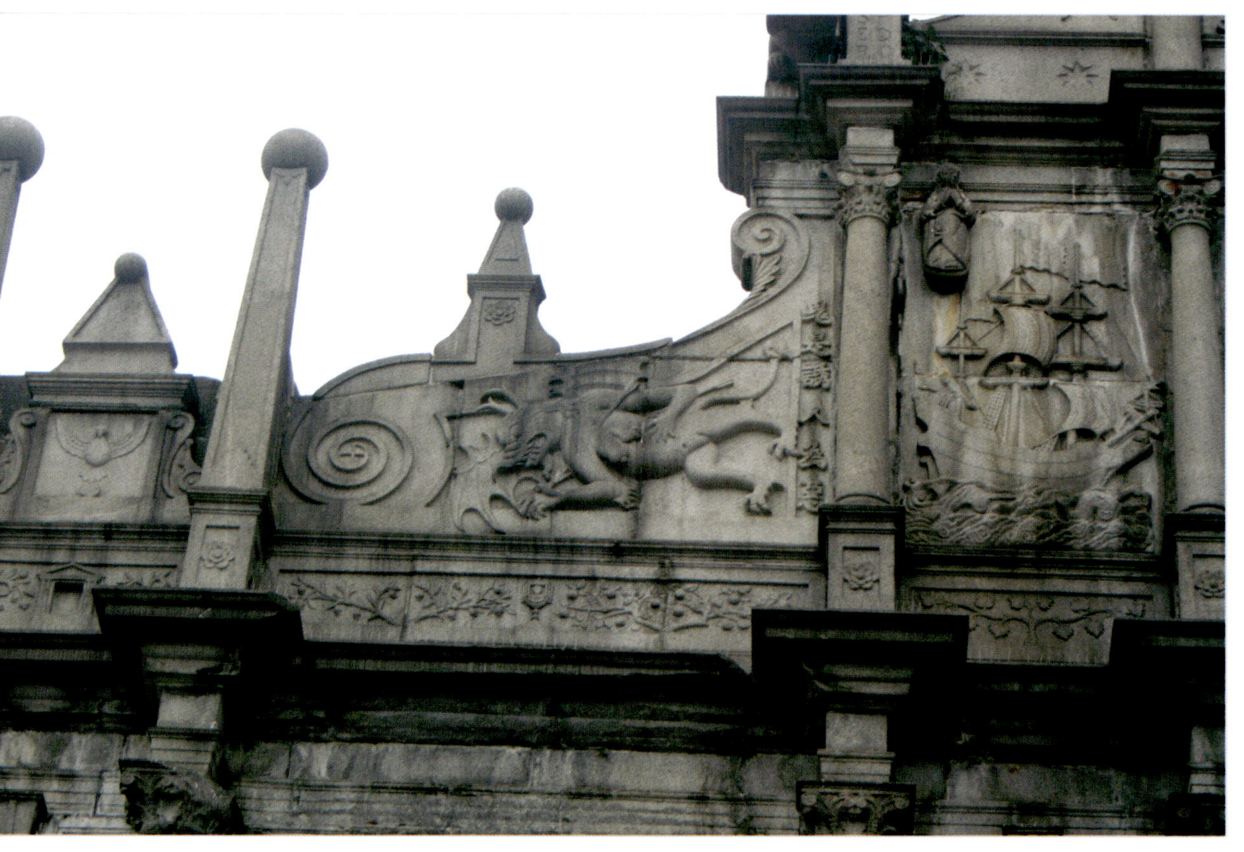

46. *Devil*

accompanying Chinese characters translate as 'The devil seduces, man turns to malice'.

These two representations, the devil and the skeleton, are medieval in character; skeletons began appearing as widespread images in Europe after the pestilence of 1348.[4] The skeleton (as a *memento mori*, like the skull of chapter 3) fits with the new European charnel houses which were contained within the city: this skeleton speaks of the urban

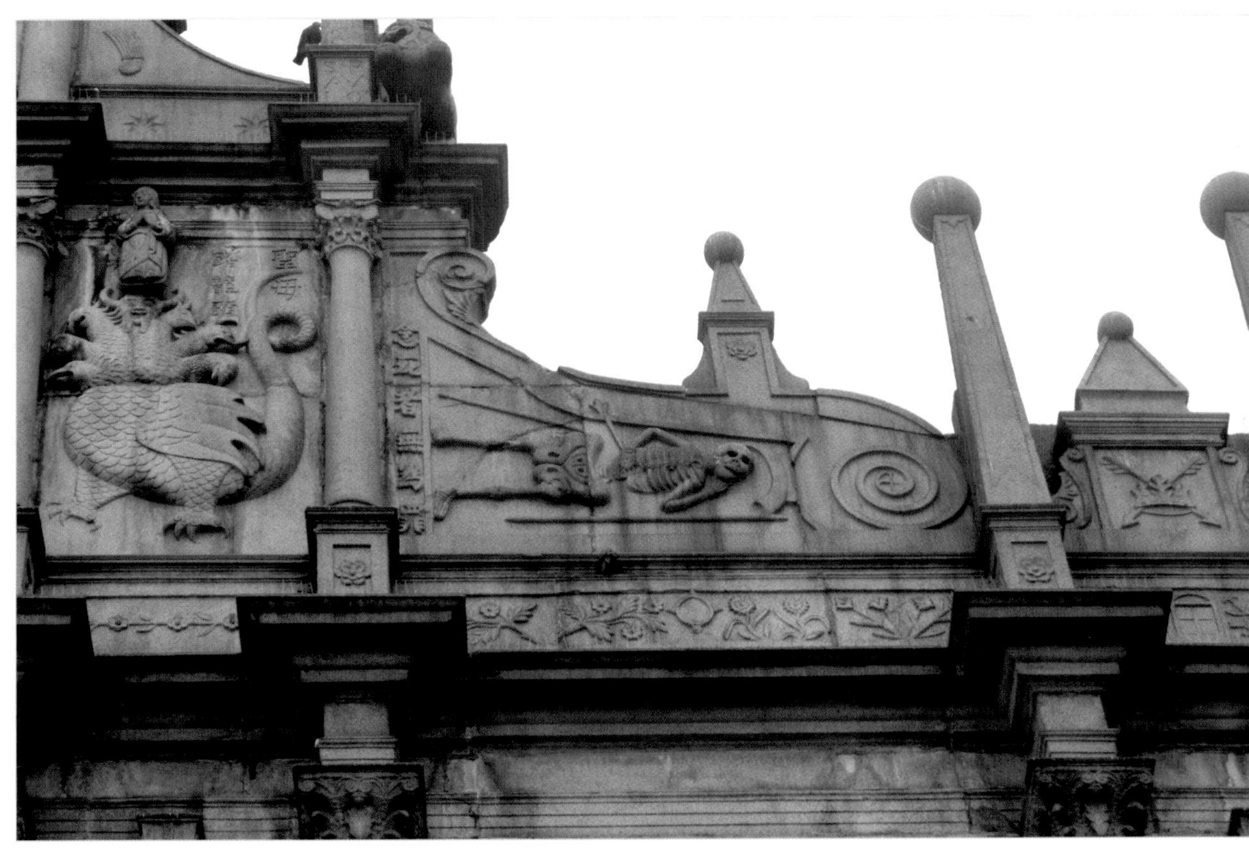

47. *Skeleton*

culture of Macao as a new city, but still a culture
built on death; as Derrida puts it in *Aporias*,

> there is no culture without a cult of
> ancestors, a ritualization of mourning
> and sacrifice, institutional places and
> modes of burial, even if they are only
> for the ashes of incineration [...]. The
> very concept of culture may seem to be
> synonymous with the culture of death.[5]

If the devil is a woman, that plays to a misogyny within Christianity which is memorialised here: the woman is either virginal or demonic. Allegorically and positionally, the devil, or the woman, and the skeleton answer to each other, as part of the visual culture of the late medieval which now recirculates high up in this commanding baroque, overlooking the city from its hilltop eminence. Beyond these figures, there are obelisks which frame a dove below a pyramid (left), and to right, a crown pierced by two crossed arrows. Under them, in a panel which surmounts the horizontal parapets, there are poppies (seeds of opium) and lychees, a Chinese fruit praised by Su Shi (1037–1101).[6] On this point, Roberto Gonzáles Echevarría is interesting, since he discusses how in Latin America, under Spain,

> studies have shown that it was in baroque churches that natives were able to include, in the cornucopia of figures, their own mythological beings, as well as elements of American nature, such as fruit that were exotic to the Europeans.[7]

Echevarría therefore finds in the colonial baroque the opportunity for syncretism, Christianity including a non-European, non-colonial force, which inscribes, or creates, a new nationhood through the inclusion of these figures and fruits. Perhaps the same may be true here. Colonial syncretism aims to produce a new imaginary nation through these visual images.

In the second level up appear saints, allegorical pillars of the church militant, like the ten framing pilasters of the level of the cornice, in which they are set in niches. They are, from left to right, St Francis Borgia, St Ignatius Loyola — canonised in 1622, so meriting the letter S beneath him; St Francis Xavier, of whom the same is true, and St Louigi Gonzaga (1568–1591), with a B for Blessed below him, as also for St Francis Borgia. It is unusual to find such figures of the early modern as the primary saints in such a façade. Their presence indicates missionary urgency and the possibility of martyrdom either in Chinese or Japan. Also on this level, there appear palm trees, emblems of the Orient, folded into this colonial discourse, like the lychees, and also like the Japanese chrysanthemums, which may be seen in the bases of the pilasters on the second level down, a reminder that this work owed much to Japanese artists who had been brought to Macao by Jesuits working in Nagasaki.

The last level is the ground floor, which is pierced by three doorways, with IHS written above the left and right ones. The *OED* brings out the instability of signification within allegory when it points out that 'the Romanized form of the abbreviation would be IES, but from the entire or partial retention of the Greek form in Latin manuscripts as IHC or IHS, and subsequent forgetfulness of its origin, it has often been looked upon as a Latin abbreviation or contraction, and explained by some as standing for *Iesus Hominum Salvator*, Jesus Saviour of men, by others as I*n Hoc Signo* (*vinces*), in this sign (thou shalt conquer), or I*n Hac Salus*, in this (cross) is salvation'. The sign either indicates the doorway, as Christ, or points to colonial imperialism (thou shalt conquer), or references the cross which is implied in image after image within the façade. Above the centre appear the words MATER DEI, 'mother of God', giving the central space to the woman who replaces the A-Ma goddess.

São Paulo: Interior

Going through this façade into the empty space beyond, now restored as much as possible by the contemporary architect Manuel Vicente, it will be seen that a Chinese temple, Templo de Na Tcha ('wild child'), built in 1888 as a shelter after an attack of the pestilence and extended in 1901 by a second gable-ended roof added behind the first, nudges into the space once occupied by the 1692

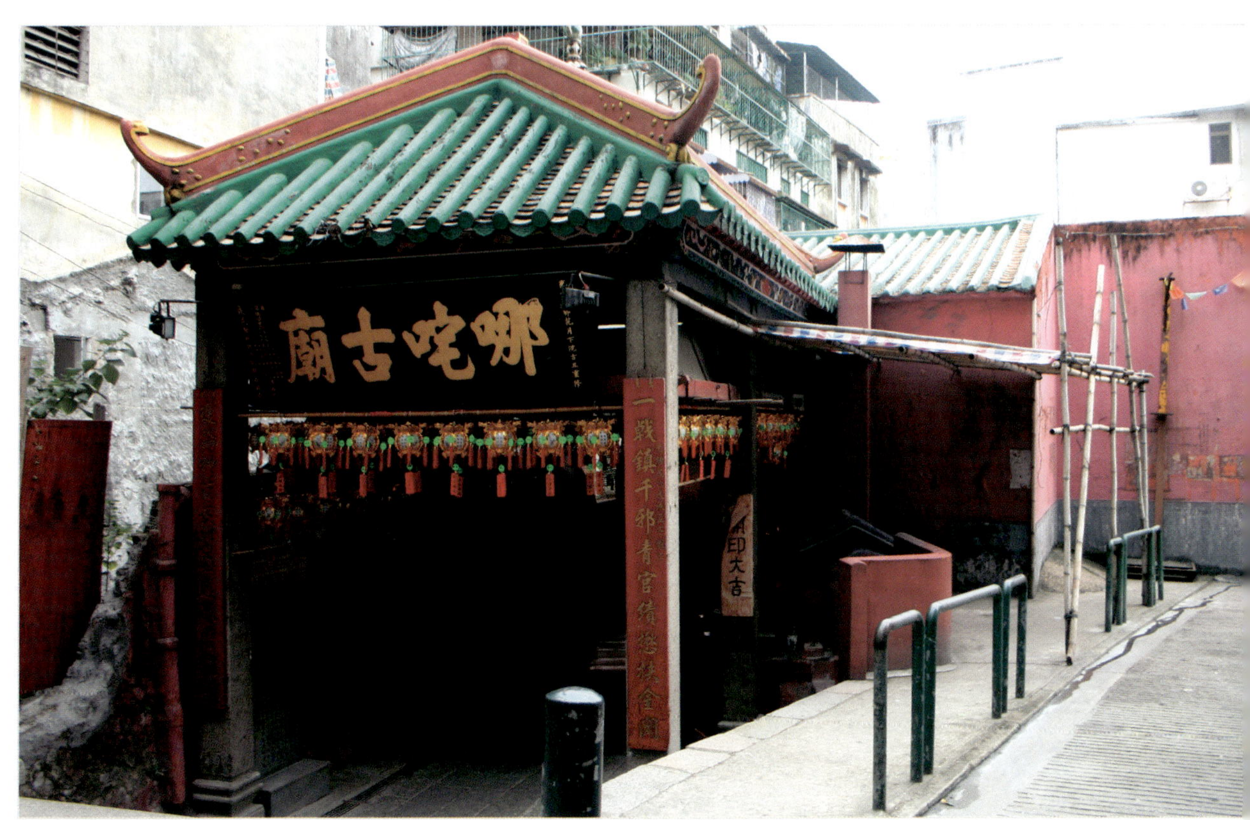

*48. Older temple of
Na Tcha*

chapel of St Francis Xavier. This temple has no courtyard, it pushes both into the road in front of it, and into the church-space. This temple can be seen to the right in photograph 66, together with its incense burner of 1898. Instead of showing it here, the photograph shows the nearby older temple of Na Tcha, which asserts itself cheekily between two streets leading to São Paulo.[8]

Na Tcha is the revolutionary but innocent Daoist child-god who does not know fear, and has to be put to death but is reincarnated. His presence in Macao is subversive, in the same way as his temples insert themselves into other spaces, including Christian spaces. This older temple for Na Tcha, at the junction of Calçada das Verdades and Travessa de Dom Quixote, is folded into the corner where the street divides into two: the lower street actually passes directly through the temple. The way the temple opens up into the tiny space is reminiscent of the extension of the Sir Robert Ho Tung Library. The folding of the temple resembles the art of origami: it is like a folded fan, the scallop-like shells resembling open fans.

In contrast to São Paulo, this temple has barely any façade. The sacred and the profane co-exist in the same space. However, once 'inside' the temple, there is the illusion of space created because of two doors, the one on the left continuing down into the sunlight and the street, and the one on the right opening into an interior, which is sandwiched

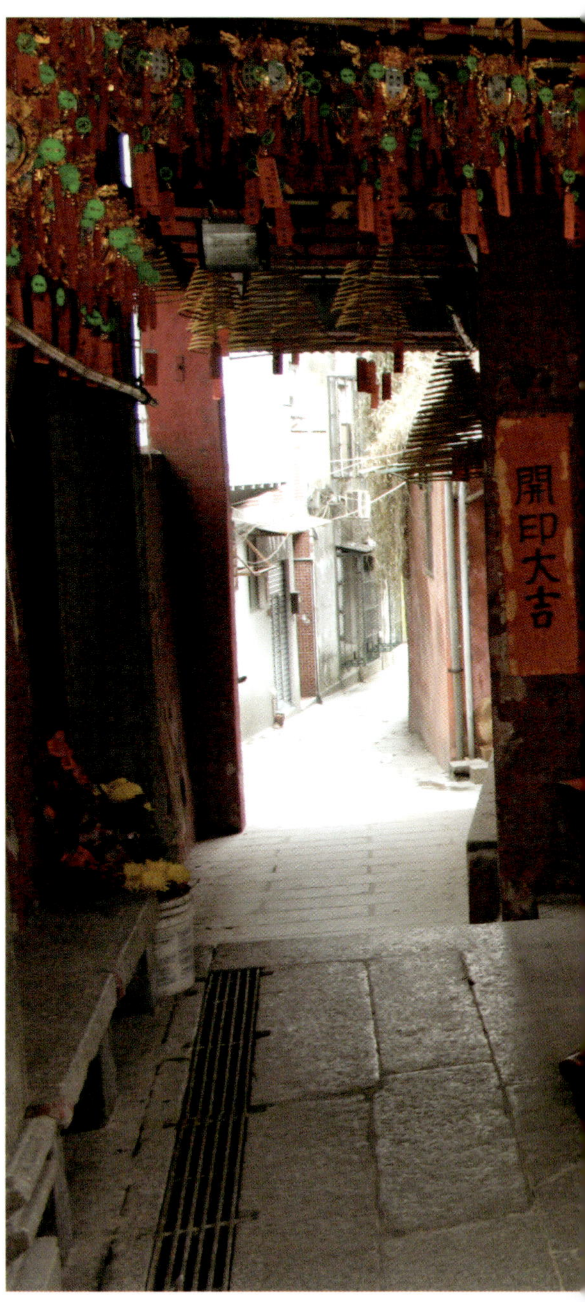

49. Folding of the older temple of Na Tcha

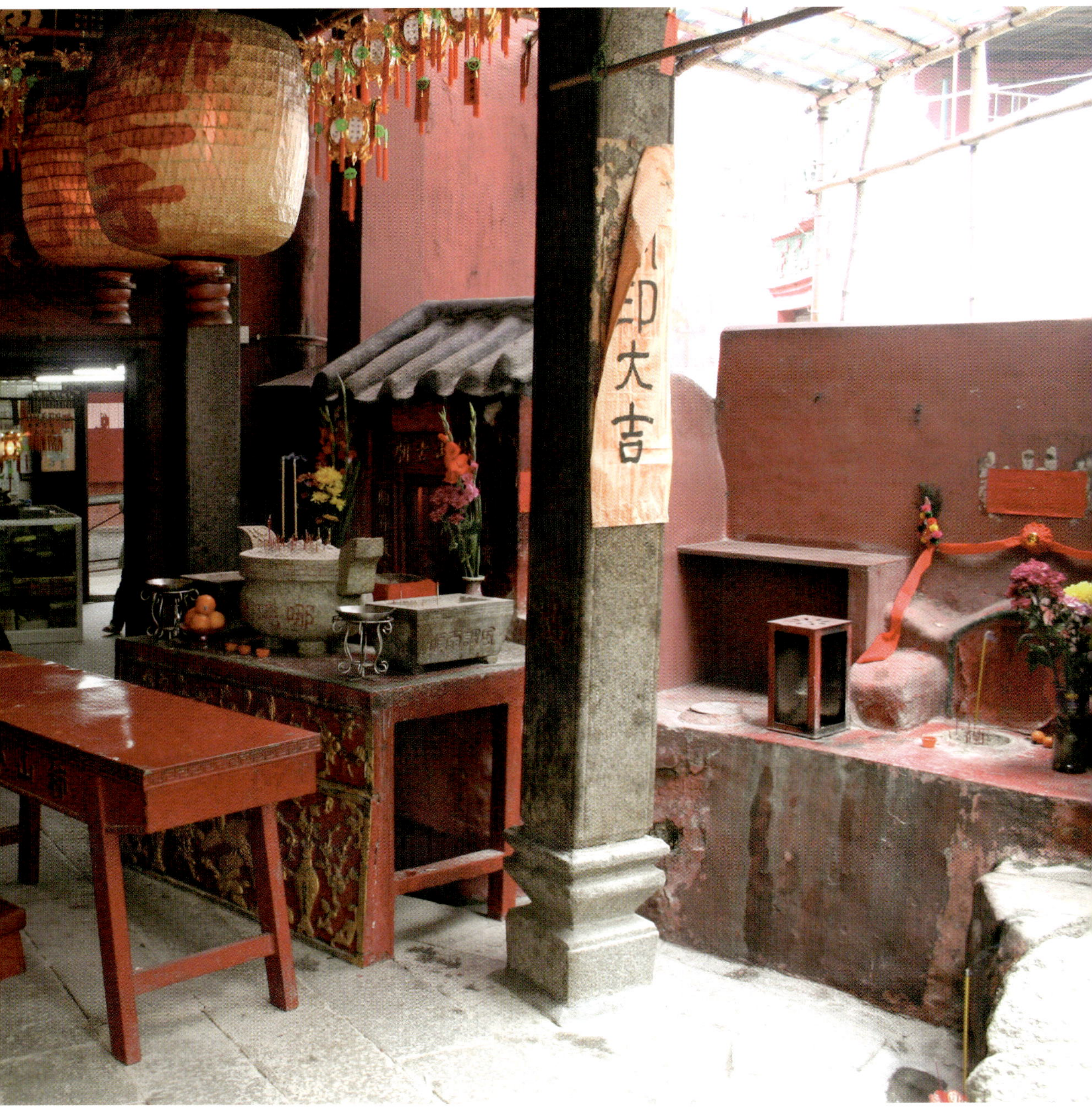

between the streets. While this building is clearly not baroque, Lacan sees 'the illusion of space' as an achievement of baroque architecture. While the architecture encompasses emptiness and death, the playfulness of the baroque that Lacan celebrates turns emptiness into space.[9]

Returning to São Paulo, beyond the chapels is the space of the chancel; here visitors may now descend into what was once the crypt. This once housed the body of Father Alessandro Valignano (1539–1606), the Italian Jesuit who worked in Macao and Japan, and made São Paulo College, adjacent to the church, the centre for the mission to China and Japan. Now, it is an ossuary, a library of bones. One skull that can be identified is that of the first bishop of Macao, the Jesuit Dom Belchior Carneiro (1516–1583), who was buried in São Paulo with a cross, and exhumed in 1835 after the burning of the church. His skull (shown in the photograph below) is flanked by an hourglass and a warning bell, and is now in the museum of Santa Casa da Misericórdia, founded by him as a hospital in 1569.

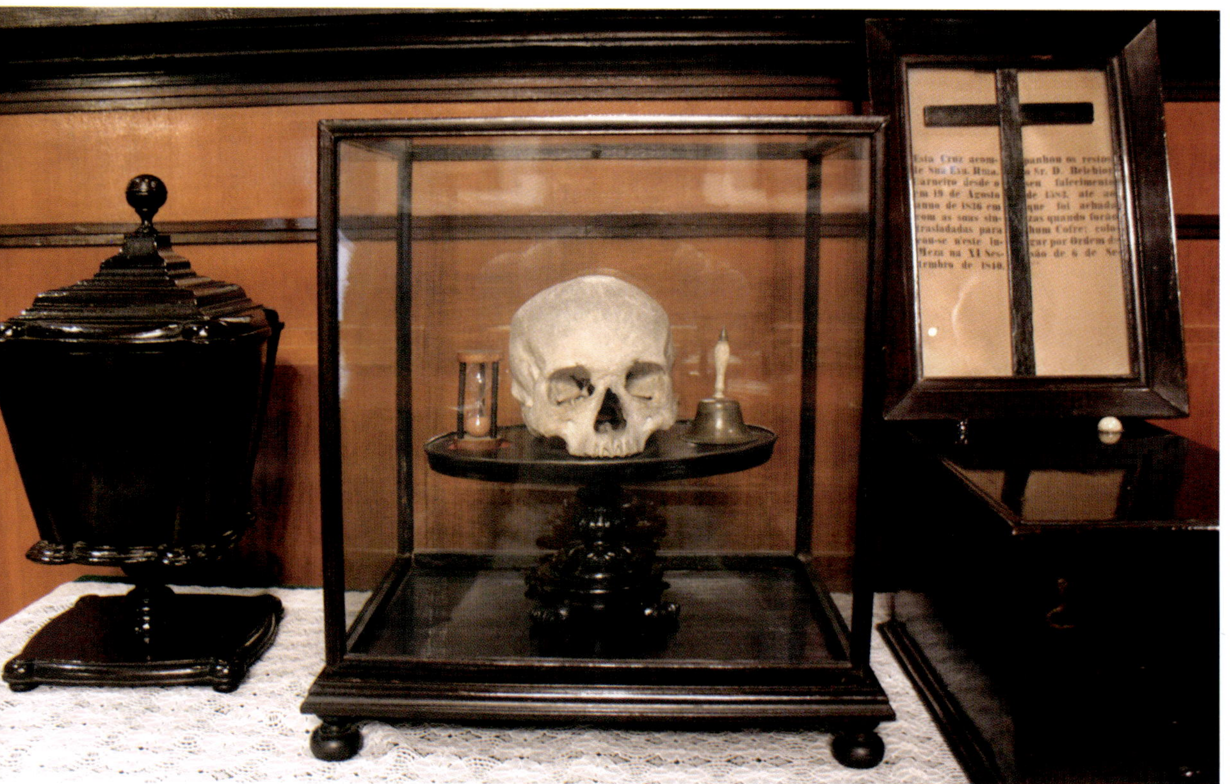

50. Skull, cross and urn at Santa Casa da Misericórdia

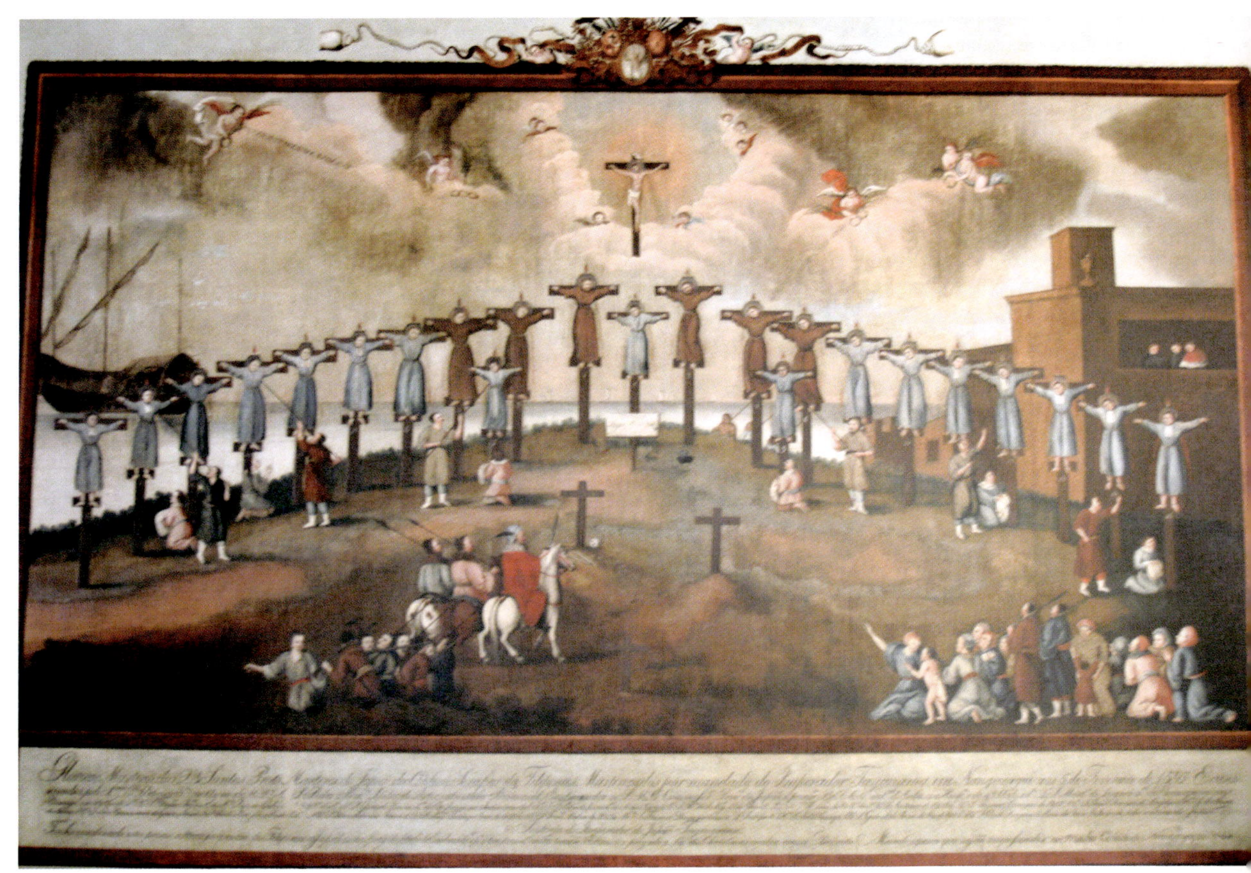

51. *Painting:* The Martyrs
of Japan

To the left of the ossuary but still in the crypt, there is a little gallery which houses colonial baroque art (one painting there, of St Michael, is discussed in the next chapter), including renditions of the life of St Francis of Assisi, and, most intended to effect an emotional response, the copy of a painting called *The Martyrs of Japan* (1640) by an artist whose name partially erased, lost, is Mateus van ... The photograph is of the original, now in the Bishop's Palace.

Here twenty-three Christians are shown as being crucified. In addition to these Franciscans, three Jesuits also were killed, but as this is a Franciscan painting, the Jesuits are not shown, though the Jesuit college — which must have been similar to the college of São Paulo in Macao — appears to the right of the painting. Nineteen names are included in the inscription at the base of the painting. The work is an example of figural representation because above the martyred Christians, there appears the crucifixion of Christ in a vision, to prefigure these sufferings. Further, the martyrdom of 5 February 1597, which this represents, prefigures yet another martyrdom of sixty-one lay members of an embassy from Macao to Japan who had come to try to secure withdrawal of a ban on trade which Japan had passed in 1639. This, then, is also represented in the picture. The economic crisis overlays the religious crisis.

The 1597 martyrdom depicted here had commenced with an incident in which a Spanish galleon from the Philippines, the *San Felipe*, had been wrecked off the coast of Japan and its cargo of silver had been appropriated by Toyotomi Hideyoshi (1536–1598), virtual ruler of all Japan, who took the incident as proof of the political menace caused by Christianity in Japan. He had six Franciscans, seventeen Japanese followers, three Jesuit lay brothers, included by mistake, crucified in Japanese fashion at Nagasaki.[10] The incident showed up the rivalry between the Jesuits (who

were largely for an independent Portugal) and the Spanish Philippine missionaries: the Jesuits accused the Franciscans of exciting Hideyoshi's anger by boasting of the power of the Spanish. As Charles Boxer (1904–2000) writes, the Jesuits 'were never tired of emphasising the contrast between peaceful, commercial Macao, which was a reassuringly open city (before 1622), with heavily fortified Manila, which was regarded as a menace by all the Asiatic races around the China Sea' (Boxer, *The Christian Century in Japan*, 238). The picture shows the crucifixions taking place on the coast with one ship lying off shore and several white sails being seen on the horizon as if to indicate that sea trade cannot be stopped by any one country. The artwork is interesting for its representation of Japanese officers on horseback who have come to enjoy the killings and whose posture resembles the antagonistic Jews in countless Renaissance paintings, while other Japanese resemble the Romans who carried out Christ's crucifixion. The painting is within a frame surmounted by a cartouche with, in another frame below that, a lengthy inscription. This attempts to stabilise the meaning of the picture so that the painting draws attention to itself as representation, not as realism. It encourages a divine *furor*, by showing Franciscans who are in a literal way undergoing the experience of Francis when he received the stigmata (which appears in an eighteenth-century painting to the right of this one). Baroque art here remains the art of ecstasy, the art of encouraging ecstasy.

The museum is past the ossuary where so many skulls are gathered. These answer to the representation of the skeleton on the façade of São Paulo, and supplement Derrida's sense of 'the culture of death' by showing how the baroque subject meditates consciously on death as perhaps colonialism does too. The English baroque writer of the seventeenth century, Sir Thomas Browne (1605–1682), was fascinated by the anonymity of newly discovered bones, saying 'What song the sirens sang, or what name Achilles assumed when he hid himself among women, though puzzling questions, are not beyond all conjecture' — but he turned away from these riddles (a marker of baroque culture) to ask about bones recently unearthed, 'who were the proprietaries of these bones, or what bodies these ashes made up, were a question above antiquarism' and concludes that 'to subsist in bones, and be but pyramidally extant, is a fallacy in duration'.[11]

Lacan discusses *The Ambassadors* (1534), Holbein's painting, in his *Four Fundamental Concepts of Psychoanalysis*. He says that the ambassadors 'are frozen, stiffened in their showy adornments. Between them is a series of objects that represent in the painting of the period the symbols of *vanitas*' [emptiness]. Lacan also refers to a 'strange, oblique, object in the foreground in front of these two figures'. It is an anamorphosis, a large skull that is so distorted in perspective that when the viewer sees the picture face on, it can only be recognised when the viewer looks back from the side. Lacan writes:

Holbein makes visible for us here something that is simply the subject as annihilated — annihilated in the form that is, strictly speaking, the imaged embodiment of [...] castration. [...] We shall then see emerging on the basis of vision, not the phallic symbol, the anamorphic ghost, but the gaze as such, in its pulsatile, dazzling and spread out function, as it is in this picture. This picture is simply what any picture is, a trap for the gaze [*regard*].[12]

Lacan's complex argument draws attention to an ambiguity within the painting. While the objects in the picture which assist exploration, and which Lacan calls the 'symbols of *vanitas*', are of the Renaissance (which 'explores universes'), the empty skull is baroque. (Lacan — or perhaps Holbein — comes close to deconstructing the difference between the Renaissance and the baroque, since the skull is also *vanitas*.) The argument can go further by reference to Christine Buci-Glucksman, saying, '*On pourrait définir l'oeil baroque comme un regard anamorphique*' (You can define the baroque eye as an anamorphic gaze).[13] Baroque culture creates the eye that looks awry, or, putting the point another way, a baroque image is that which looks awry, strangely, and uncannily, at the viewer. Lacan's prose identifies the strange, stain-like skull with what he calls the 'gaze' (*le regard*). The 'gaze' is not mine, looking at a picture, but something, which is nothing, looking at me. It is as if the skull, as represented, points to and contains within it something which cannot be symbolised within language, which Lacan calls 'the real'. He has already said that

> in our relation to things, insofar as this relation is constituted by the way of vision, and ordered in the figures of representation, something slips, passes, is transmitted, from stage to stage, and is always to some degree eluded in it — that is what we call the gaze.
>
> (*Four Fundamental Concepts*, 73)

The baroque image holds something in it which is beyond symbolisation, for which Lacan uses the terms 'the gaze' and 'the real' and even more obscurely 'the *objet petit a*'. In *The Ambassadors*, the skull indicates something that eludes the spectator, or the subject who thinks of himself as complete and autonomous. The skull, which can only be seen by looking awry, indicates that which will annihilate the subject. Lacan calls this negation 'castration'. It includes the loss of bisexuality and its replacement by a single subject identity, based on sexual difference. Insofar as the baroque is the art which brings this out, it stresses brokenness and lack of symmetry, even pain, through distortion of bodies, so that Lacan provocatively thinks of baroque architecture as an 'actualization of pain' (*The Ethics of Psychoanalysis*, 60).

Lacan always leads into speculation. Since he sees architecture as giving the 'illusion of space', it has to work to sustain that illusion of space, as something present, as opposed to invoking 'emptiness'. Speculatively, it could be said that the façade of São Paulo has to do too much work in (a) standing erect after the rest of the building has collapsed; (b) symbolising Christianity; and (c) symbolising Macao. (In Hong Kong, they have more mercy on buildings: in 2006, they pulled down Hong Kong's 'identity': the Star Ferry and its clock tower.)

The photograph (looking through an archway in the city walls which reveals its age in the stonework and which glimpses the newer Na Tcha temple on the left) looks at old cobblestones. It shows the poverty of the rear of the façade (its stonework as old as the city walls) and how it must be propped up from behind. Lacan suggests that the stonework is 'petrified pain' (*The Ethics of Psychoanalysis*, 60). There is a 'scar' of the roof on its back, like the trace of a whip-lash. While the façade shows the illusion of space, the skull shows the 'creation of emptiness' (140) because the bone contains nothing. ('Holbein' suggests 'hollow bone'.) The point holds both for the skulls which date from the time of the baroque, and to the anamorphosis in Holbein's painting.

*52. Gate with a view of the
back of the façade*

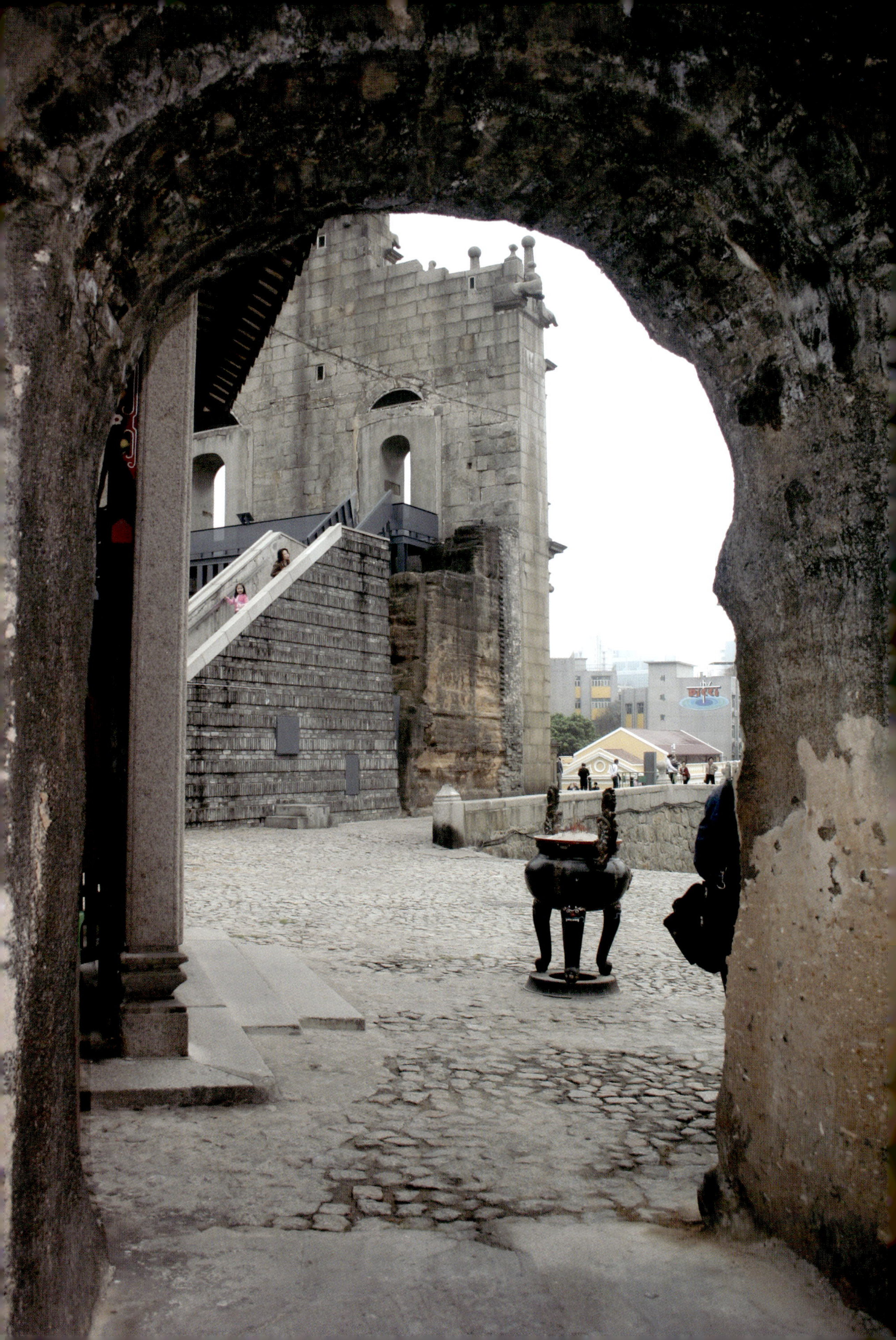

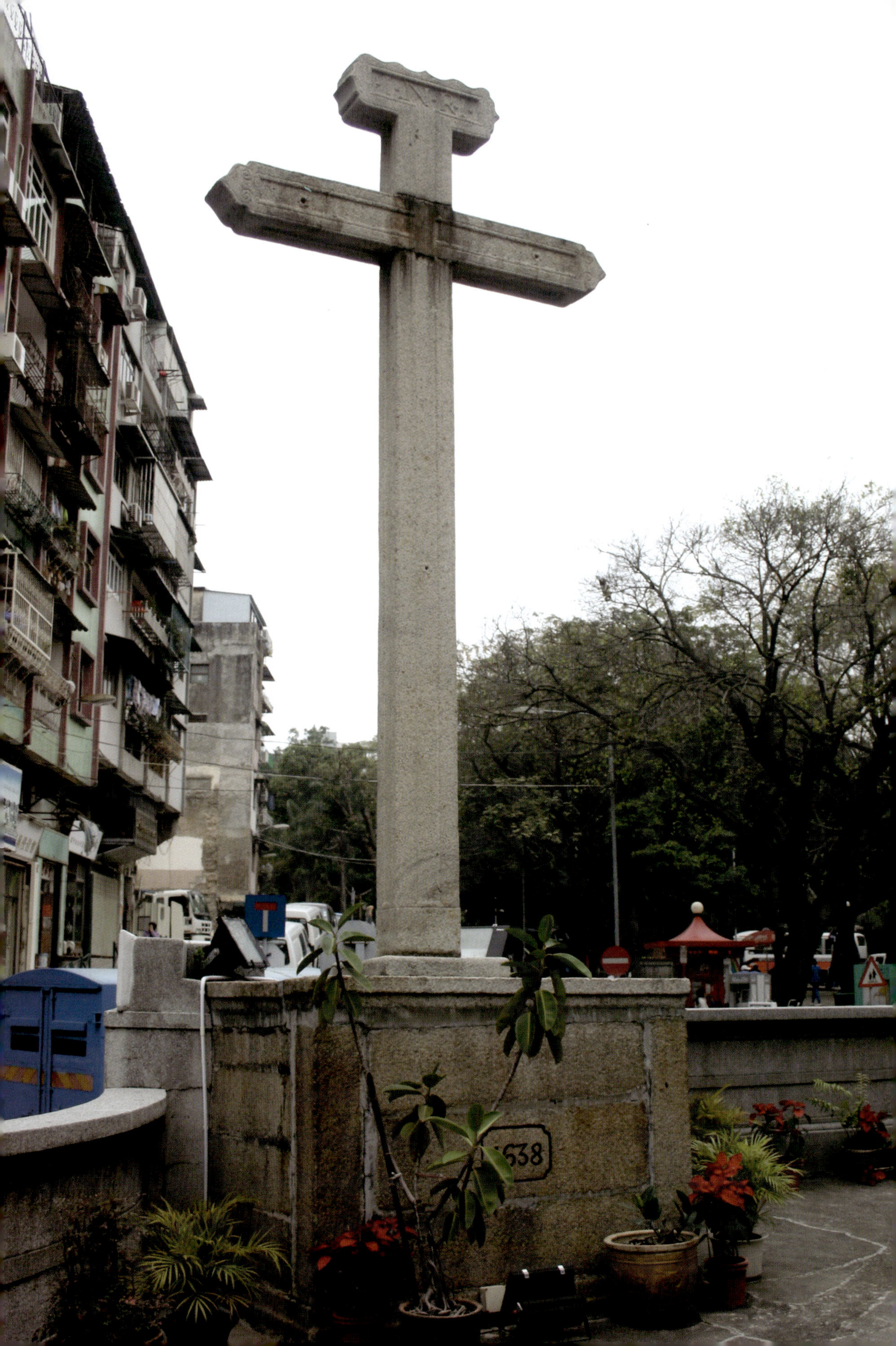

Chapter 6

Neo-Classicism

Portuguese colonisation has left traces everywhere in Macao, some of them Christian emblems, signs, which Chinese influences have made to resignify. A first example is the present classical church of Santo António, which has a Virgin and child in its entablature. It stands opposite the Camões Garden, which can be seen in the photograph, and replaces a church which was constructed in 1638, in place of another of 1560. It was burnt in 1809, rebuilt and burnt again in 1874 and repaired thereafter. The photograph shows in its entrance courtyard a cross of 1638, which once bore a crucified Christ. The empty cross means something in Christian theology, but it also suggests the loss of meaning over the centuries, leaving the object stranded, lacking a clear referent. In that way it connects with the melancholy that the cross inspires.

Portugal developed its seaborne empire in the fifteenth century, ahead of other European powers. To resume a history begun in chapter 2, it took Cochin, on the Malabar coast of India in 1503, Goa in 1510, Malacca in 1511, and reached China by 1513, under the command of Jorge Álvares. By 1517, Portuguese vessels had arrived in Canton (Guangzhou). By 1542, they had reached Japan, and their ships (carracks) facilitated trade between Japan and China — Chinese silks to Japan, silver bullion from Japan. The Portuguese acted as middle-men between two countries not officially trading with each other. From 1555 onwards, exchange of cargoes took place at Macao. Thanks to the influence of the Jesuits in this trade, Nagasaki became virtually a Jesuit city.

Up till 1555, the Portuguese had used two islands in the Pearl River estuary, Sanchoão (Sanzhao, near Macao) and Lampacau (part of Lianwan). The former island was where St Francis Xavier died in 1552, on the brink of going into China, his unrealised wish. His body was exhumed and buried in Goa in 1554. The person in charge of the exchange of cargoes at Macao became the effective governor of a new colony in 1557.[1] Not till 1575 did the Spanish arrive from the Philippines, going to Amoy in China, and so threatening Portuguese hegemony.

Macao, 'City of the Name of God in China', became a diocese in 1576, and was first called a city in 1586 (when, like Portugal, it was, technically at least, under Spain's control).[2] Between its founding and 1640, it built twelve churches, including Santo António, Santo Agostinho and São Domingos (discussed in chapter 4), São Paulo (chapters 4 and 5), and São Lourenço and São Lázaro, both discussed later. As the entrance to China, it attracted Jesuit missionaries, such as Matteo Ricci (1552–1610), mathematician and astronomer, born

53. St Anthony's Church, cross

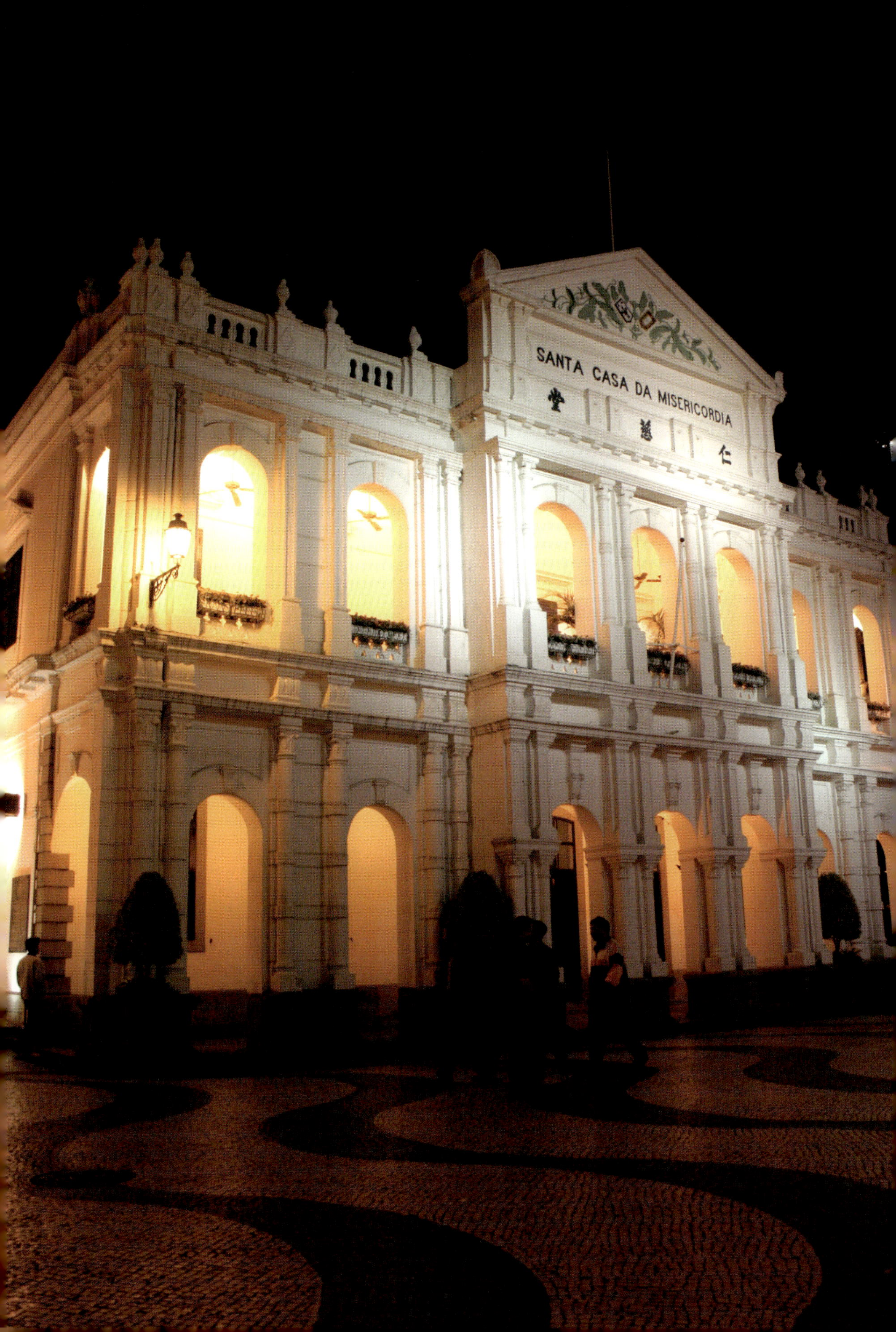

SANTA CASA DA MISERICORDIA
堂 慈 仁

in Italy the same year as St Francis Xavier died, and trained as a Jesuit by Alessandro Valignano (1539–1606). Ricci went from Lisbon to Goa in 1578, and then proceeded to Macao in 1582, with the determination of entering China. He went on to Zhaoqing, near Guangzhou in 1583, and to Nanjing by 1594, reaching Beijing in 1600. Macao's primary importance, which had made it a colony, declined around 1640, through several coincidences: the ending of the Ming dynasty; Malacca being taken by the Dutch in 1641, which limited the influence of Macao; and at the same time, the Portuguese's expulsion from Japan.[3]

Macao was officially part of Xiangshan county in China, and subject to Chinese authorities. According to Jonathan Spence, by the time of Ricci's arrival in 1582, its population was one thousand, five hundred of whom were Portuguese; others were Indian or Chinese women, children, with three to four hundred resident Chinese families who were interpreters, shopkeepers and artisans.[4]

Macao had colonial civic architecture, some memorialised in the museum of the old hospital, Santa Casa da Misericórdia in Senado Square (Holy House of Mercy). The Casa was last rebuilt in 1905, set up first by the Bishop Dom Belchior Carneiro, whose skull was seen in the museum in São Paulo (see photograph 50). The Casa da Misericórdia stands at right angles to the Leal Senado, first so

54. Santa Casa da Misericórdia

called in 1642. This, originally a Chinese council for meetings between Portuguese and Chinese, was set up in 1583, and created as the present building in 1783 (renovated after 1874, and several times in the twentieth century). Finally, in this colonial narrative, Macao occupied Taipa in 1851, and Coloane in 1864.

Matteo Ricci comments on how Macao came into being from the previous trade on the islands, and alludes to the A-Ma temple, which supplied Macao with its European name:

> This kind of trafficking went on for several years until the fears of the Chinese gradually vanished, and they granted the visiting merchants a trading post on the point of a nearby island. There was an idol erected there called Ama. It may be seen today and the place is called Macao, on the Bay of Ama. It is more of a protruding rock than a peninsula, but it soon became inhabited not only by the Portuguese, but by a motley gathering from the neighbouring shores, eager to barter for all sorts of merchandise ... the prospects of quick fortunes were an enticement to the Chinese merchants to take up residence on the island, and in the course of a few years the trading

post began to assume the appearance of a city. Numerous houses were built when the Portuguese and the Chinese began to intermarry ... the King of Portugal granted charters to the new city, and with Pontifical authority, had a Bishop appointed there to facilitate the administration of the sacraments and to lend the proper ecclesiastical dignity to divine services.[5]

Ricci perhaps refers to Macao as an island because at that stage the isthmus of the peninsula was covered by water at high tides.[6] Following on from what Ricci writes, and his allusion to Macao's bishop, reference should be made to Macao's cathedral. It was constructed in 1576 as a wooden building, and replaced in 1622. In the nineteenth century, another cathedral followed (designed by José Tomás d'Aquino), consecrated in 1850 and effectively destroyed in an 1874 typhoon. It was not rebuilt in concrete until 1937, and it was refurbished in 1993 (by L.T. Piñero Nagy). It is neo-classical, with two towers added to the sides of its central granite façade, looking back, not forwards, in terms of design.

Photograph 55 is of a tiny square to the left of the Cathedral, a newly opened space (by the architect Francisco Pinheiro) including a new fountain, and a nearby cross. The fountain, with religious motifs, picks out sea-horses which are also found worked into the tiles of the pavement, and it has baroque monsters suggestive of Bernini's fountains in the Piazza Navona in Rome, on a much reduced scale, and like that fountain, this more modern one equally suggests a global aspiration in the baroque (there is a globe and a cross surmounting the fountain). The twisted column and the suggestions of shells on which the monsters rest imply one aspect of the baroque — its heterogeneity — while the more ordered sea-horses imply the baroque's directed and controlling nature.

The end of the 1840s also saw the completion of Government House, which was originally built as a residence for the Viscount de Cercal, and bought by the colonial government in 1884 as an example of Portuguese domestic architecture.

Spence comments that when Ricci arrived at Macao, he found that Valignano, whose mission in Macao — where he was to die — was principally meant for the Japanese, had already there with him four Japanese Christian converts from noble families to whom he was teaching Latin, Portuguese and Spanish. The idea was to take them back to Europe, to raise funds for further missions in the East. Led by their principal Mancio Ito, these first Japanese ambassadors to Europe arrived in Lisbon in 1584 and returned to Japan in 1590. Spence also draws attention to the danger of the trade with Japan, when in the same year a ship went down off the coast of Formosa (Taiwan), and 200,000 ducats'

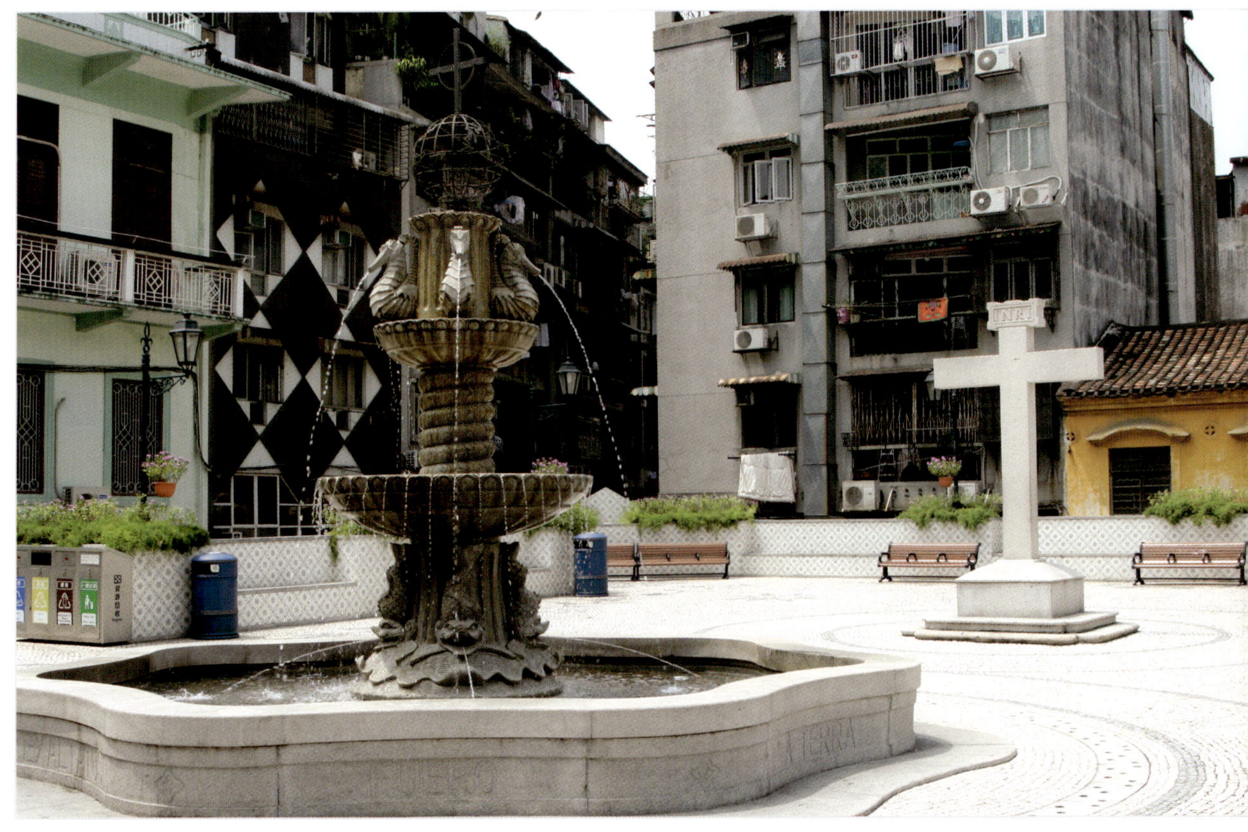

55. *Fountain outside the Cathedral*

worth of goods were lost (Spence, *The Memory Palace of Matteo Ricci*, 177–8). It was that which supplied the wealth of Macao and of the Jesuits, who had shares in the trade.

The cross of St Anthony may be compared with another, that of St Lazarus, to be seen on the right of the courtyard of the church (photograph 56).

St Lazarus' Church memorialises another hospital which was set up in 1569, and a temporary church which was replaced by another in 1633. It was set up outside the colonial city by Bishop Belchior Carneiro, intended, as the name Lazarus suggests (because it recalls the Biblical Lazarus (Luke 16), who was both a beggar and by association a leper), to treat lepers. These were normally held in hospitals outside the city. (How lepers were treated before the early modern period is the theme of the beginning of Foucault's *Madness and Civilization*.) The present church recalls the earlier situation. The hospital had the name 'Our Lady of Hope' (Nossa Senhora da Esperança). Its present-day courtyard has a cross of 1637, which also bore the crucified Christ.

The present neo-classical church is less heavy in appearance than St Anthony's, its façade pleasantly picked out in green and white. It looks asymmetrical because of the bell tower that is joined onto its façade at the right. In its pediment it has a simple motif which includes a cross (for faith) and an anchor (for hope). The church was rebuilt in 1885, and enlarged in 1967.

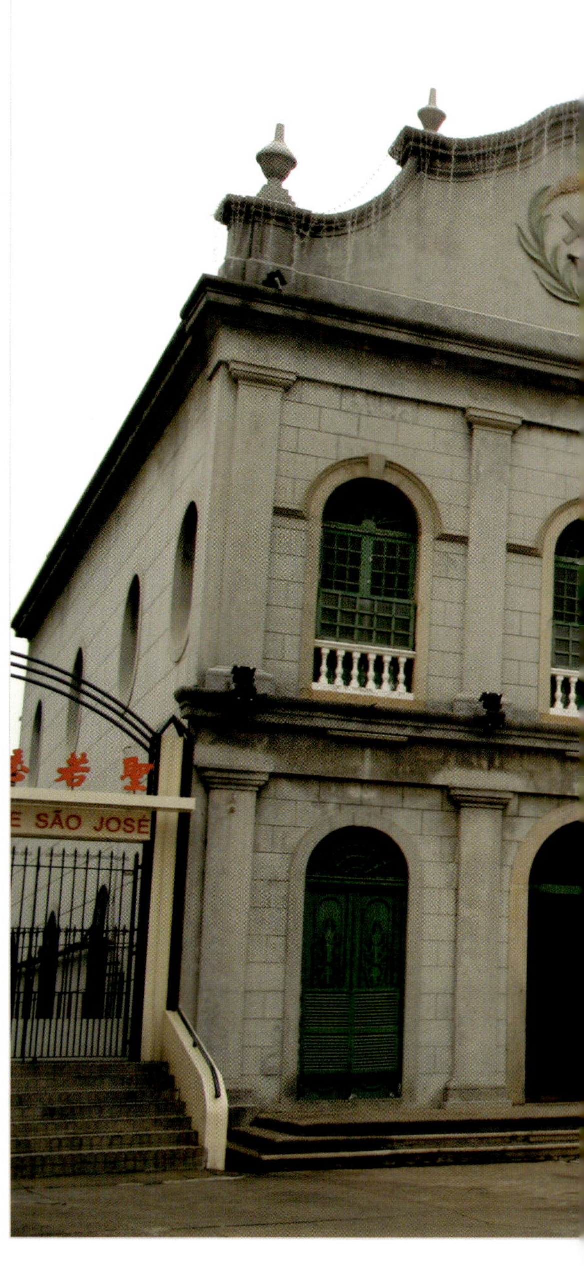

*56. St Lazarus' Church,
with cross*

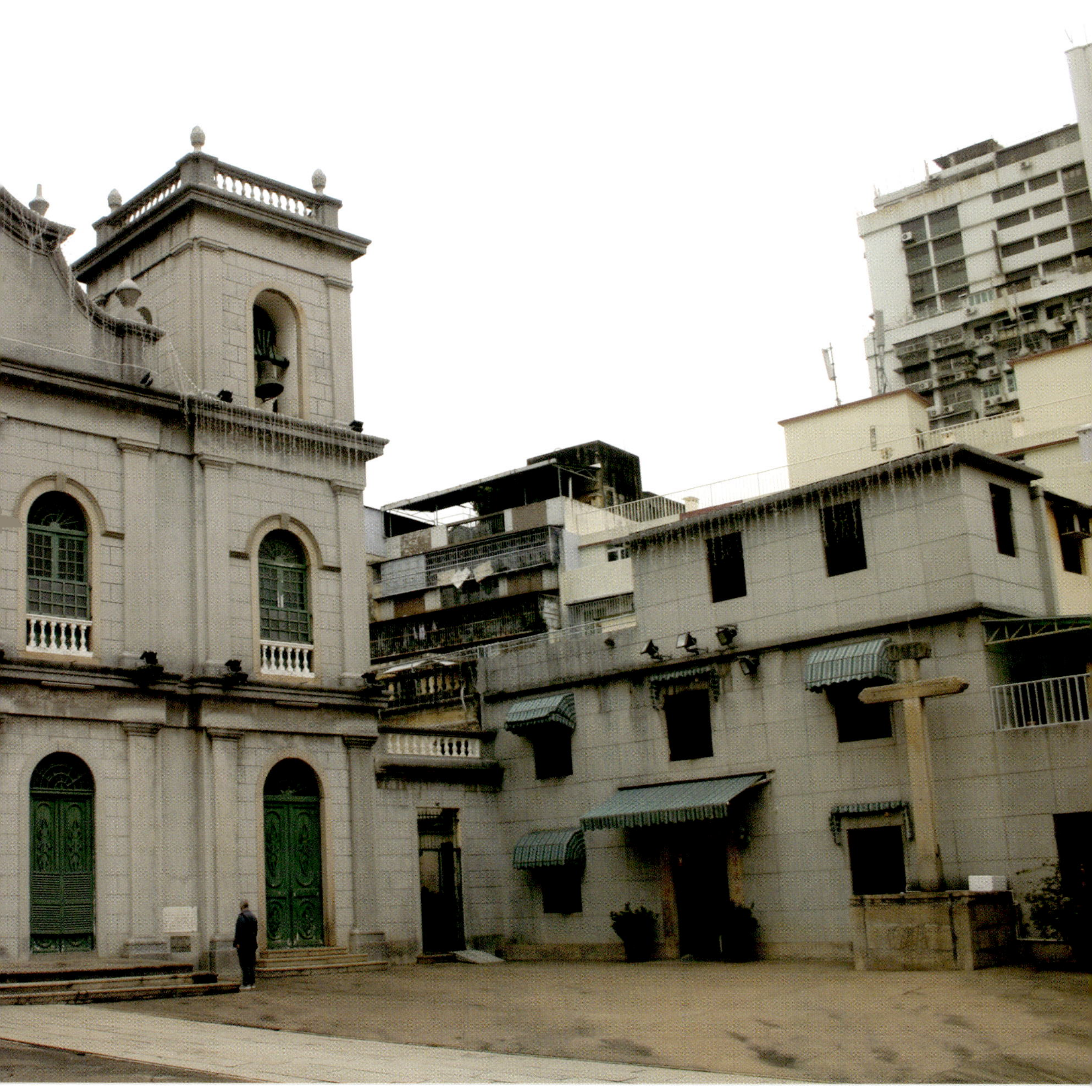

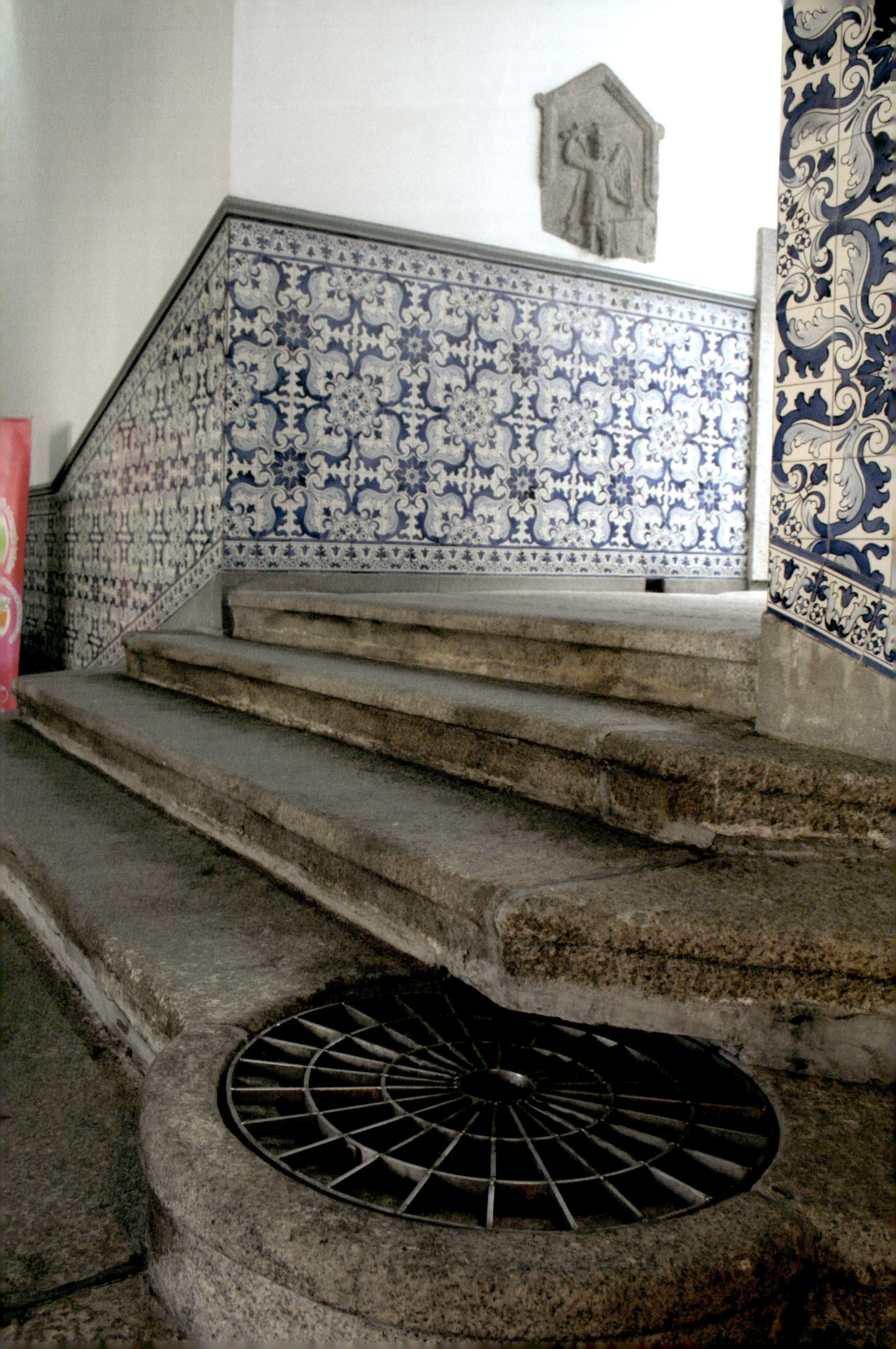

Besides these traces, there can be seen emblematic figures which have been left over from somewhere and included in the atrium of the Leal Senado, which is a neo-classical building, having a central main façade surmounted by a pediment and flanked by granite Doric columns. The photograph picks out the blue and white ceramic tiles, the broad stairs that go up towards the garden at the back of the building, the well which indicates the prime importance of this building for early colonisers, and, on the left wall of the staircase, a bearded angel in a Gothic frame, who has an uplifted sword in his right hand, and scales in his left. He wears a cloak, and is girt with a belt, and has distinctive leggings, which are perhaps Japanese or Chinese, and the clothes may possibly suggest Oriental motifs. This is a tiny fragment, much of whose significance has been lost, but which may be compared with the Archangel Michael who appears in a marvellous oil painting in St Paul's crypt.

The significance of this angel of the Apocalypse (photograph 58) is that the painting used to hang in the church when that belonged to St Paul's College, whose ruins are to the right of St Paul's. Two things must be considered: the College, and the painting of the angel. The College began life in 1579, and emerged in 1594 out of a previous church, Madre de Deus, which had been founded in 1565 by the Jesuits Francisco Peres and Manuel Teixeira. It had had its wooden roof replaced by a tiled one as early

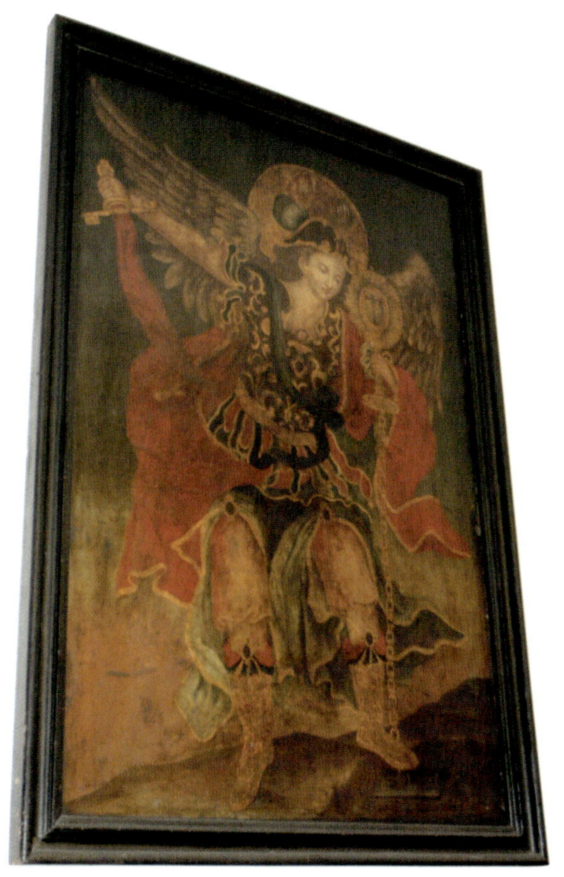

58. The Archangel Michael

57. Angel of Judgement and well

as 1571, as a gift from a captain of the Japan trade, António de Vilhena. The College seems to have been the place which held the first library, however small, of western books in China: at the height of its existence, some five thousand of them. In times of danger from the Dutch in 1603, it was where people left their valuables for safe-keeping. The College remained until it was closed in 1762, after the suppression of the Jesuits in Portugal in 1759; along with St Paul's, it was burned in 1835.

The painting is inscribed as 'Sino-Portuguese, Nanban influence seventeenth century'. Nanban is Chinese and Japanese for 'southern barbarian', and refers to the trade between China and Japan, which was carried on via the Portuguese. It has been attributed to a Japanese pupil of the Jesuit Giovanni Nicolo, whom Ricci called 'the first master under whom both the Japanese and Chinese learned to paint in European style, to the great benefit of both national churches' (*Journals*, 180). The painting, then, is the work of a Japanese trained by the Jesuits in Nagasaki and Macao. The speculation is that it hung over St Michael's altar in one of the chapels in St Paul's.

This angel has an air of movement (whereas the stone angel in the Senado appears static, his cloak hanging firmly behind him), appears feminine in his features and in the folds and waves of his robes, though he is a soldier; he seems Japanese, down to the general look of his armour. The angel of the Senado, however, is certainly masculine. In Revelation 20.1, St Michael comes down out of heaven 'having the key of the bottomless pit and a great chain in his hand'. In photograph 58, his right hand bears a sword which is flowing red fire, and the key is associated with it. In his left, he bears a crucifix which shines with a burning light, part of a monstrance holding the Eucharist. Hanging from it is a golden chain with a weight attached to its end: this he will use to bind the devil and keep him in the abyss, glimpsed to the bottom right of the picture, weighed down so that he should not rise again for the duration of the Millenium. In his helmet which has plumes above it, he has a crucifix, while above his breastplate is the head of an angel, as if he is presented again in a *mise en abîme*. His clothes are spangled with twelve stars, suggesting Revelation 12:1.

These two angels of the Senado and of St Paul's College both imply authoritative judgement taking place in the new colony, judgement which holds both for the here-and-now, and for the future; they also imply the apocalyptic (which is associated with the baroque), the unveiling of the end of the world. Both angels are decisive, neither has features in any state of shock, both convey a single message.[7] The inscription for the picture of St Michael says that the Eucharist is a guarantee of the power of missionary work, so that the apocalyptic episode is specifically an allegory for the work of the Jesuits. The picture shows an emblematic fire and keys, and an emblematic gold chain to bind evil, which depends from the sign of Christ on the cross. Everything in the picture is theatrical display, intended to preserve this single richness of meaning. The angel is a messenger with an allegorical message, which the painting conveys as univocally as it can.

Missionary activity in the baroque can be associated with the apocalyptic itself. For example, baroque representations in Latin America of St Francis (1181–1226), founder of the Franciscan order of friars, represent him as flying, and identify him with the angel of the Apocalypse (i.e. St Michael): in this way, putting together missionary journeys with the dangers and fears of the Apocalypse.[8] Apocalyptic thought has been discussed by Derrida in an essay called 'On a Newly Arisen Apocalyptic Tone in Philosophy' which draws attention to the Apocalypse in at least three ways: first, as an unveiling which removes everything hidden; second, as a series of messages, each of which demands interpretation so that there can be no finality even in the Apocalypse; and third, as an invitation to the other to 'Come'. Each of these ways suggests how the Apocalypse opens things up. The psychoanalytic critic Julia Kristeva discusses what she calls 'abjection', by which she means the processes by which an individual tries to secure his individual selfhood. The Apocalypse for Kristeva means the collapse of such anxious self-protection, which is maintained, she argues, in language, by binary codes (e.g., day/night, man/woman, nature/culture) which structure thought and which prevent thinking about what lies between and is repressed, veiled, by these oppositional codifying elements.[9] In contrast to this opening up, this apocalyptic sense which undoes repression, missionary activity, while it does indeed open up other countries, does so at the price of closing down a relationship with the 'other' (because missionary work is colonising). There is no possible evocation of the other to 'Come' within missionary and colonial activity, but this ambiguity is not recognised in the militarism of the painting.[10]

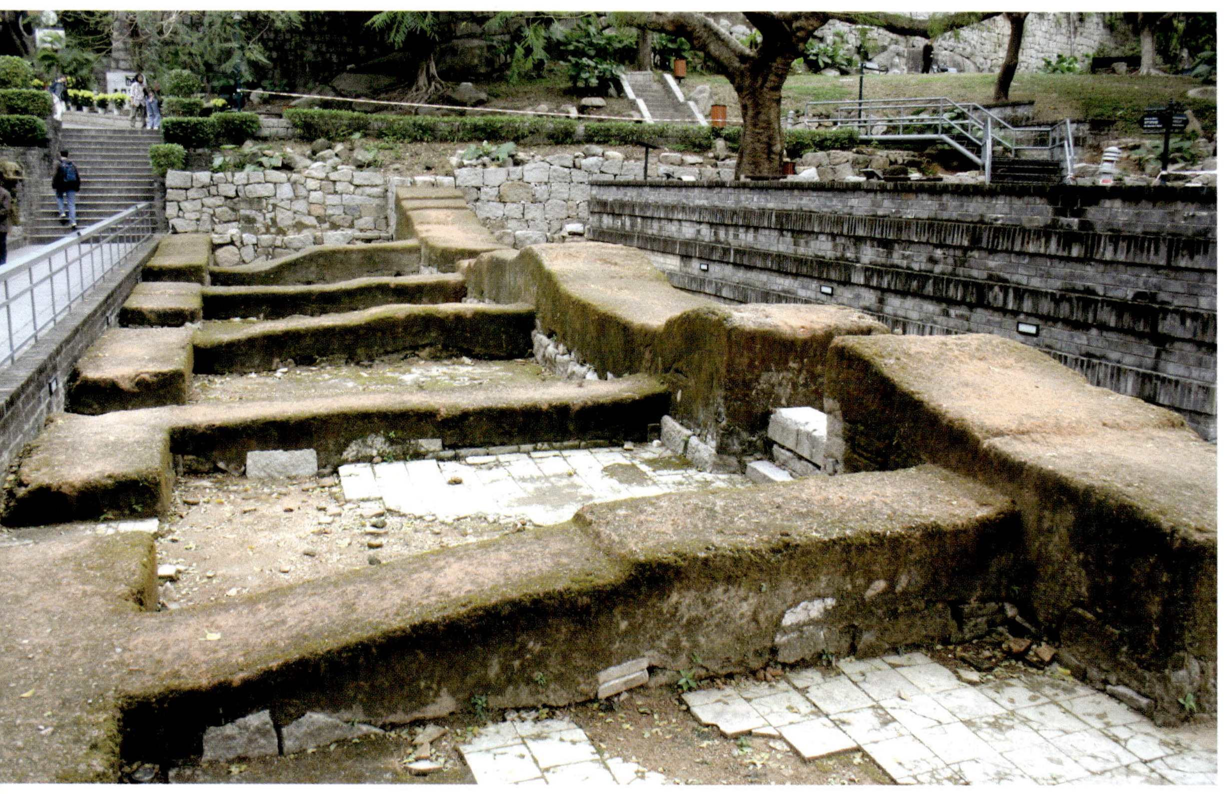

59. St Paul's College

St Paul's and St Paul's College are part of what is old in baroque Macao. This photograph shows the ruins of the College, with a south corridor on the far left (now built up and modern), and rooms to the centre of the picture: going back from the front, the watchman's tower (perhaps), the atrium, cubicles, and behind these, dilapidated portions of the college wall, which extends further to the right.

St Lawrence's Church, in the southwest of Macao, is also on an old hill site, close to the harbour. It was from early on associated with typhoon warnings, and was called 'Fong Son Tong' — 'wishing for favourable weather with timely wind and rain'. It dates from a wooden church built here between 1558 and 1560, and was rebuilt in 1618 (in clay) and stone (1803). In 1844, the same year that the rebuilding of the Cathedral began, it was redesigned by José Tomás d'Aquino, and its interior was renovated in 1954 by Father Costa Vaz; it still retains a wooden ceiling.

The photograph shows a church on a hill, fitting the image of colonial Macao, and also like Saõ José (photograph 19). It is a wealthy, middle-class area; the church is approached by ornamental staircases, which though asymmetrical, because the retaining walls to right and left of the central gate do not match, run parallel to the road. The two sets of

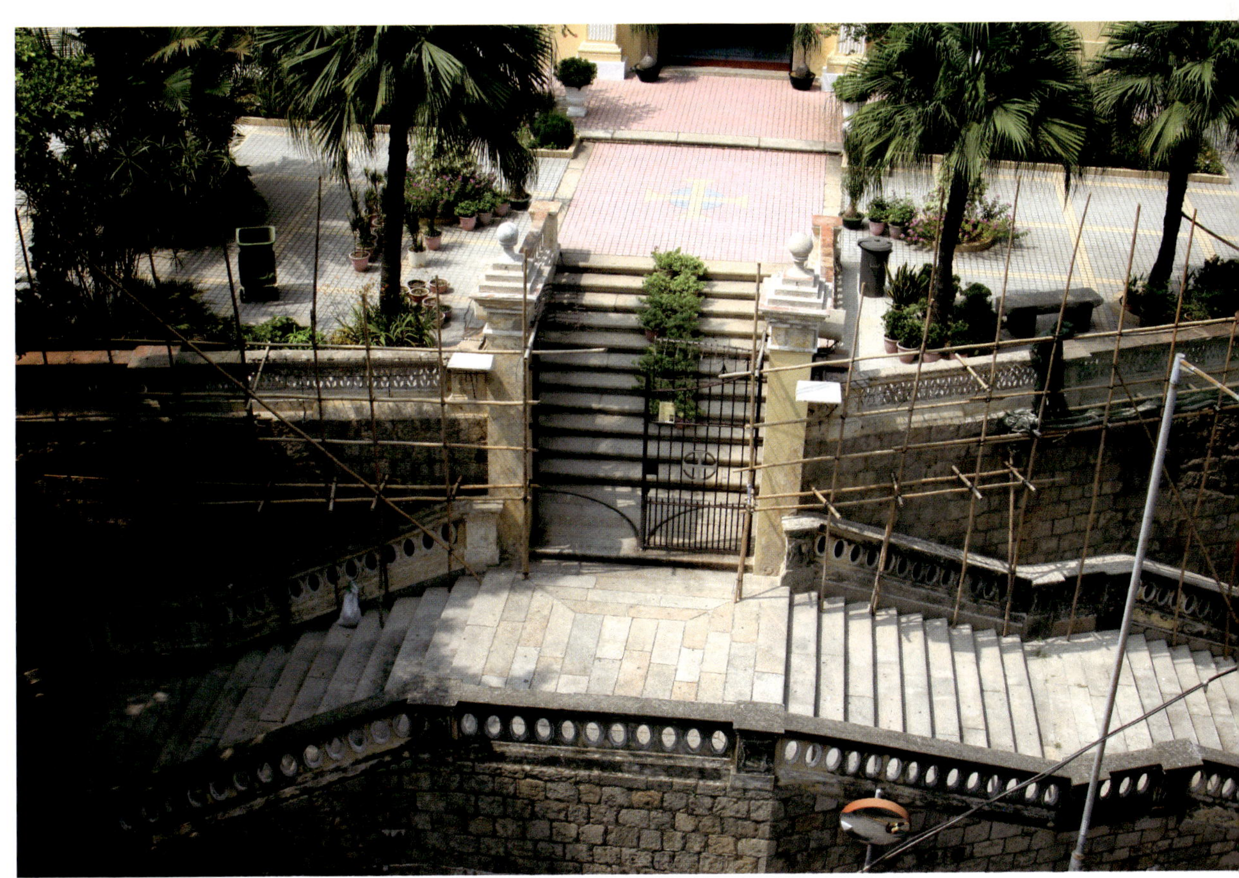

60. St Lawrence's Church

stairs meet at the top, giving a sensation, seen from above, of a rolling wave which rises then falls. The visitor at the top then goes through an entry-gate, to ascend further stairs to arrive at the platform where the church is built. The space in the street in front was portrayed by George Chinnery, who lived in a street to the left of the front of St Lawrence's which bears his name (though the house is gone). In 1841, before the building of the present edifice, he made a pen-and-ink sketch of the outside of the old church, and an oil of the same scene. In neither case is the church seen. The pencil sketch shows three Chinese, two playing a game and one watching, and with pigs nearby. Two Chinese, one holding an umbrella, are going up the steps. Another, with a child, comes into sight along the road, driving a cow. The words 'Sketches in Macao G[eorge]. C[hinnery]' are set into the wall of the stairs of the church. In the oil painting, in the foreground, next to the staircase, two men are playing, and another is watching. Behind them, under the platform on which the church is situated, is a gang of workmen, three working on the ground, two on the platform, winching up a bucket of water from a well to another platform, which is primitive and wooden; it is rough industrial labour.[11]

The façade comprises a central entrance with Doric fluted pilasters and ornamental triglyphs above, flanked by a bell tower and a clock tower. The central entrance appears neo-classical, with its neat pediment above the first floor, but the baroque is hinted at with the additional, curved pediment above a more triangular regular pediment. Inside the upper pediment appear a cartouche and an 'M' (compare the M to be seen in the Guia Chapel, photograph 73). Other baroque elements appear in the decorations in the upper parts of the towers, with characteristic curves and folds. There is an equal falsity about the lintels above the first-floor window of the central bay. But these details noted, it remains the case that the façade carries the baroque within its neo-classicism, not the other way round, which again means that it is not truly baroque since it is under constraint as the baroque could not allow itself to be. A baroque design appears above the faces of the clock, but that looks Victorian, and acts as a marker of bourgeois culture in itself. The emptiness of the panels between the tower and the pilasters on either side tells a story of absence. The neo-classical looks more restrained, more Eurocentric, than the baroque, and so points to more repression. Inside is a flattened wooden ceiling, shaped to allow the light to come in through circular windows in the side walls. There are no aisles, unlike the other churches, Santo Agostinho and São Domingos. The outside central bay is narrow, so the altar is pushed back into a position of restricted visibility, contrasting with the flamboyance and theatricality of São José, which is just around the corner, behind this church.

61. St Lawrence's Church

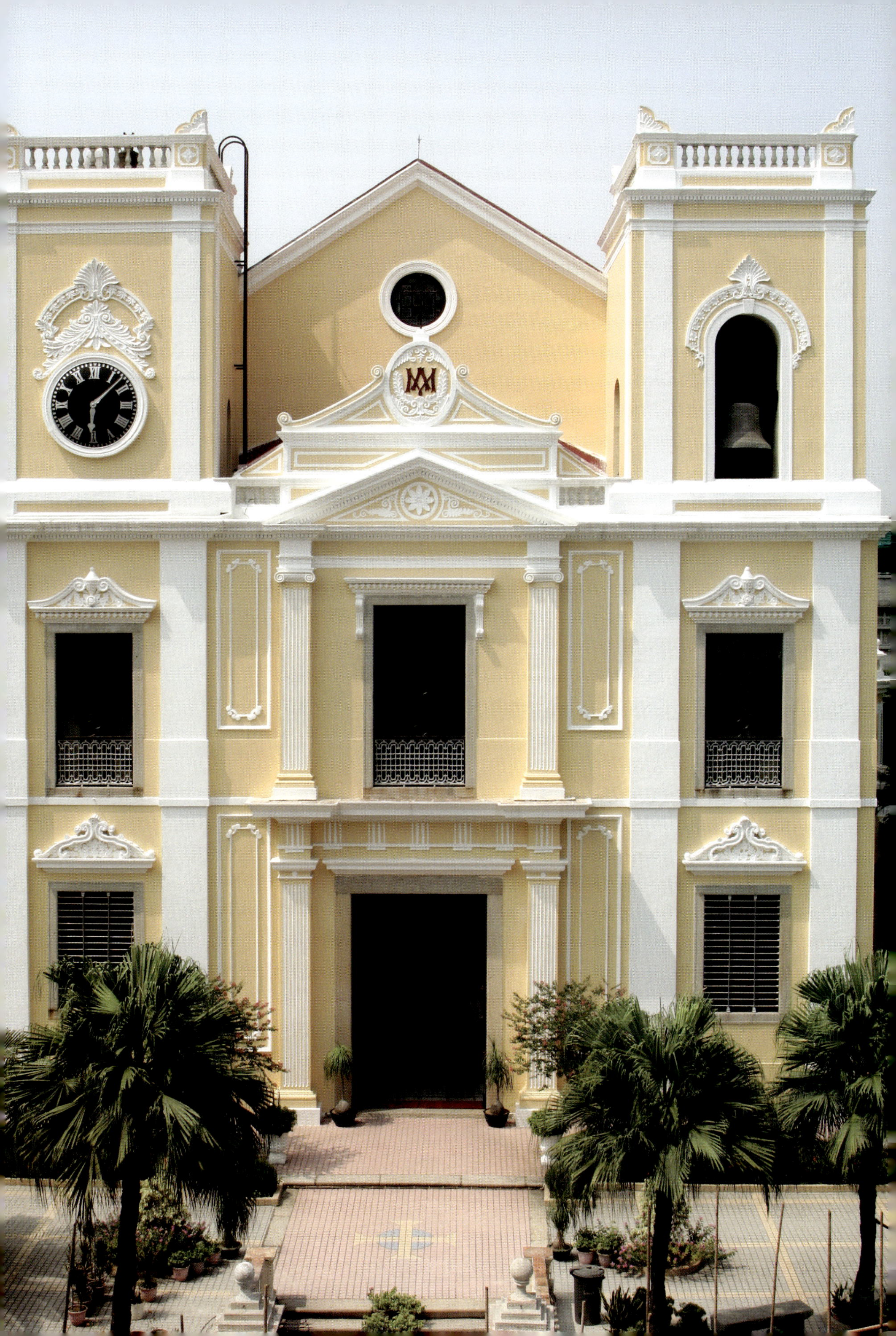

Chapter 2 showed the square in Taipa village (photograph 12). Looking away from the square to the water, four colonial houses can be seen, each in green and white, but with red sloping roofs which deny a roof-terrace. The view they had in the 1920s has been altered by the aggressive new developments on reclaimed land beyond it.

The museum devoted to the home and interior of a colonial civil servant is of 1921. It is of a classical, south European style (which also looks American, because of its 'wrap-around' verandah, on a platform or low balcony, going round two sides of the house). The two photographs show the two sides of the verandah (the word is colonial: Portuguese, imported into India, and so, in the eighteenth century, back into Europe).

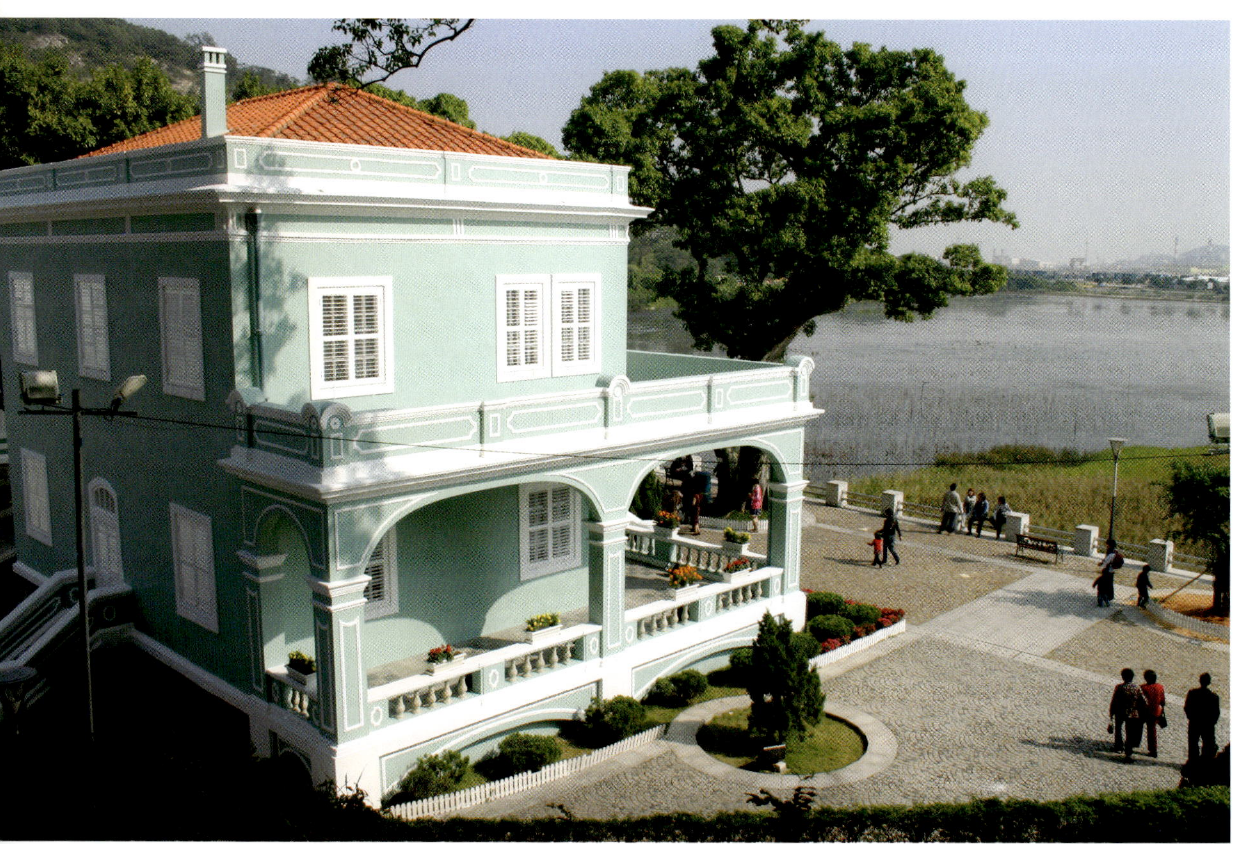

62. View of colonial house

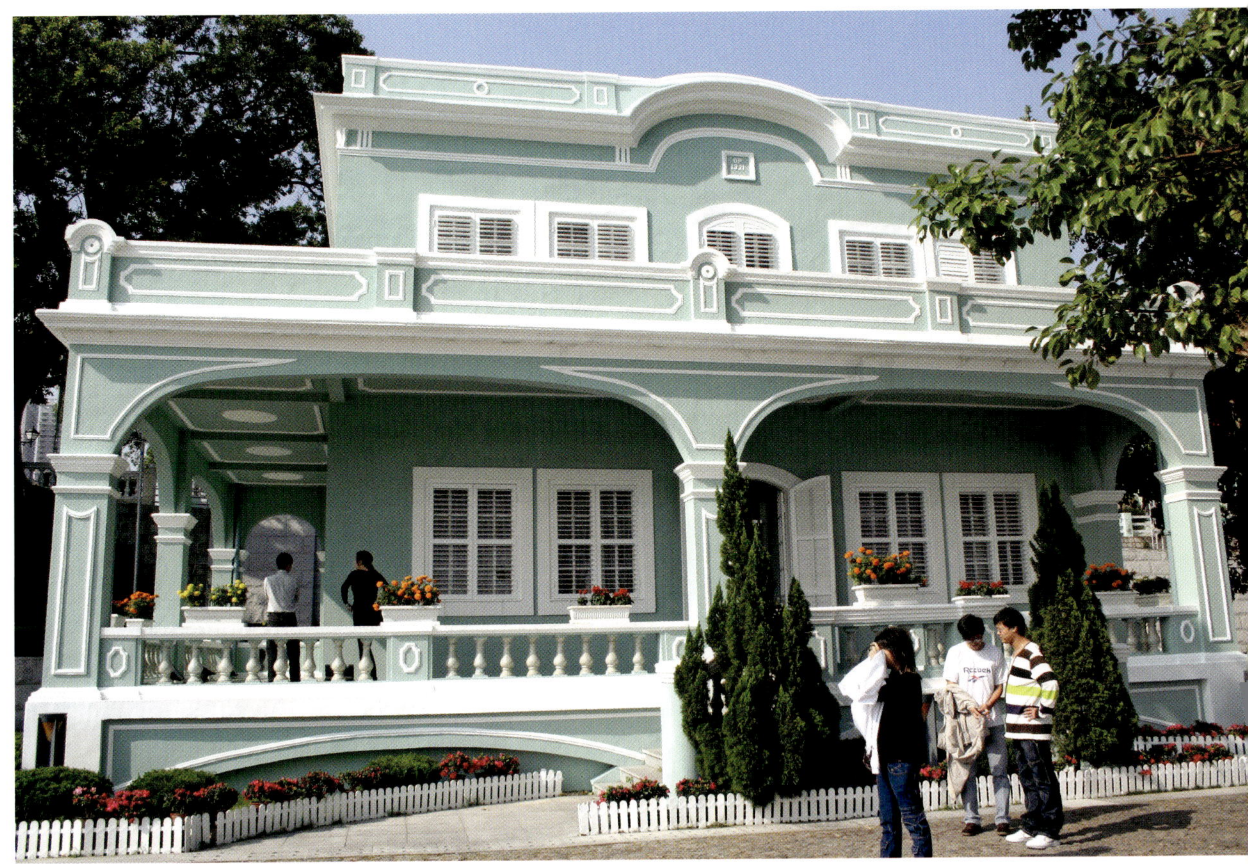

63. Front view of colonial house

If the verandah had been on three sides, it would have had some symmetry, but as it is, however pleasant the exterior, it brings out a poverty within colonial architecture: the arches of the verandah are unrelated to the house and its windows, and the front door of the house is placed behind one of the arches, because of the decentring caused by this lack of verandah. The house and its façade, amusingly, do not relate, and the house is too small for the verandah.

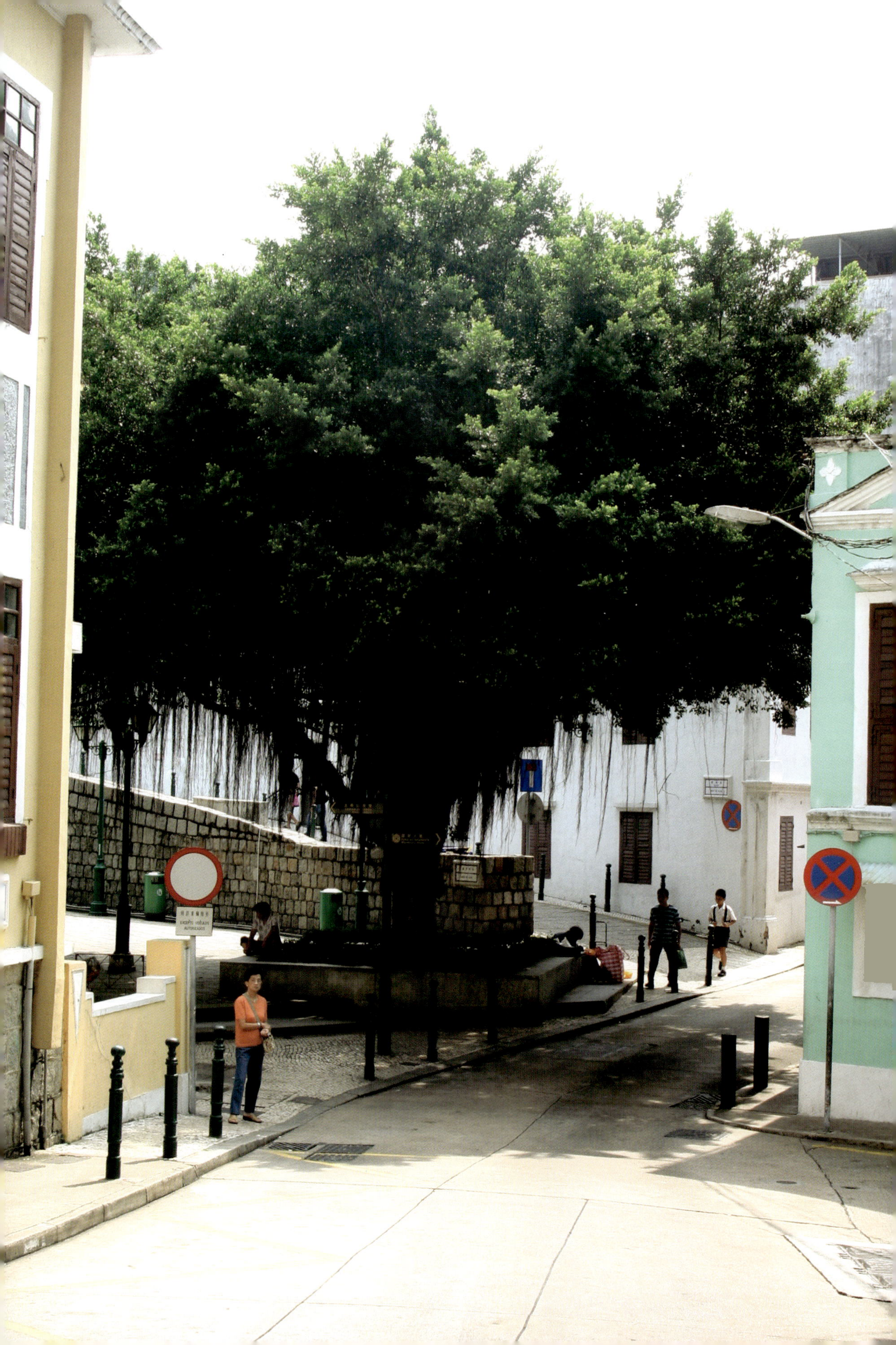

For one of the most attractive colonial sites, there is the Mediterranean-looking Lilau Square, near St Lawrence's church, which was one of the first Portuguese residential areas, with a regular water-supply (its present well — the second noted in this chapter, and there are many others in Macao — was constructed in 1994, to replace a much earlier one). 'Lilau' means 'well of old women [grandmothers]'.

The photograph gives a glimpse of the square; the well is hidden. Buildings in the square are of the beginning of the twentieth century. Johnny To's Hong Kong gangster film, *The Exiled* (2006), set in Macao in 1998, just before the transfer of sovereignty, uses Lilau Square as a site where two groups of gangsters who grew up together, are waiting to confront each other: the film uses much lower high-rise buildings (six floors only) for hoodlums shooting each other from the top of the building to the bottom; these buildings can be found in Macao still, but no longer in Hong Kong.

The next chapter looks at the defences that colonial architecture built.

62. Lilau Square

Chapter 7

Walling the City

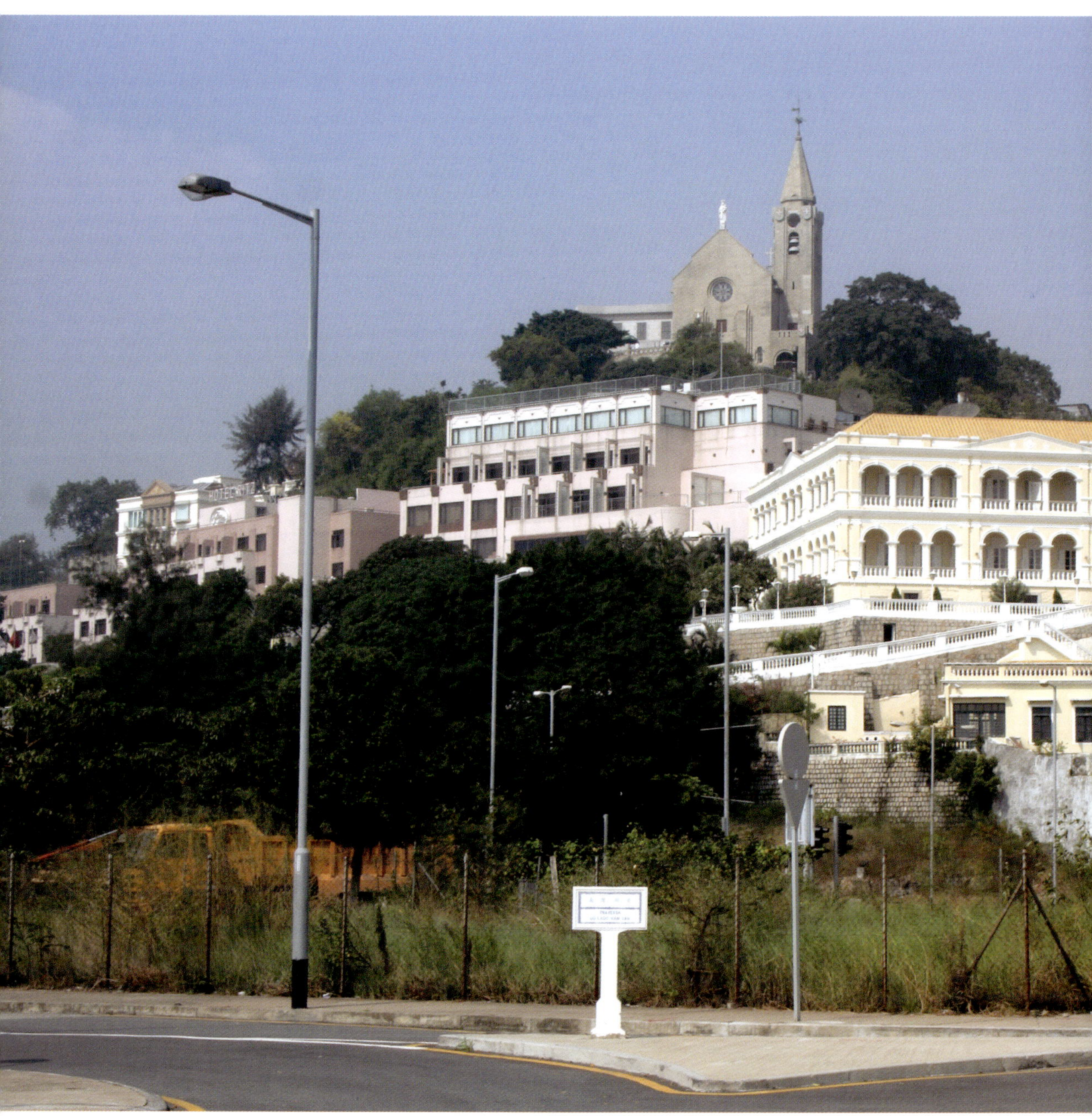

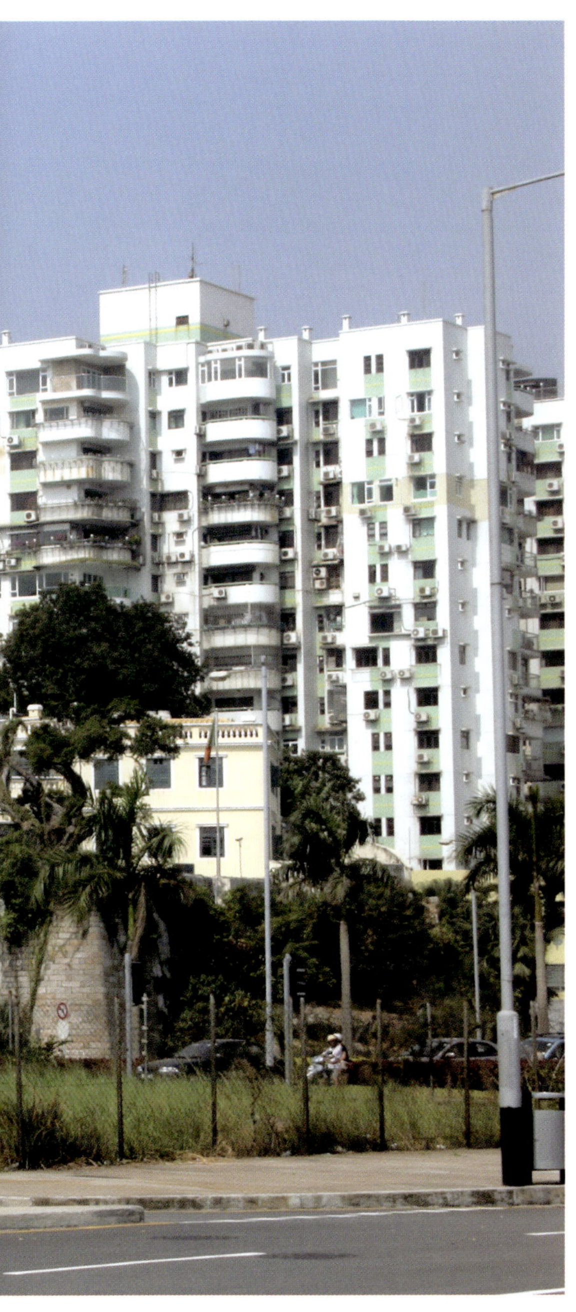

65. Walls along the Praya Grande

Beginning from the A-Ma temple, the Portuguese built forts along the Praya Grande, the Inner Harbour, and on the hills of Macao. The photograph shows walls and a bastion, and looks up beyond the old Bela Vista hotel towards the Penha Hill, site of a fort, and to the Penha Church. The walls are now integrated into Macao's nineteenth- and twentieth-century architecture. Exploration of them starts behind the ruins of St Paul's College, with the hill, fifty-seven metres above sea level, which supports the Mount Fortress (Nossa Senhora do Monte: now housing the Museum of Macao). Early settlers in Macao lived around this hill, and in the space between it and the southwest part of Macao.

Mount Fortress (see photograph 106) was built in 1617 by Jesuits (Father Jeronimo Rho and Francisco Lopes Carrasco) using the existing city walls as a partial foundation: walls to the north ran from there down to the Inner Harbour as a defence against the north. Walls began to be built to enframe the city from 1569 onwards, made of 'chunambo', or 'taipa' (Portuguese): earth, straw and lime and shells with wooden strips placed between them for cohesion. Jorge Graça says that chunambo gets stronger with time, and would not crack under fire from cannon-balls, but would absorb them. After the Dutch invasion of 1622, walls and defences became more serious. The Jesuits' fortress was taken over by

119

the governor, Dom Francisco de Mascarenhas, in 1623. He improved it, making it a fortress, to serve as a residence for governors (until the 1740s) and soldiers (the latter until 1965).

Viewed from above, it appears trapezoidal. Each of the four corners has a bastion, and in plan and appearance it looks like a European castle, one intended, with its huge cistern, to withstand siege for two years, and with cannon focused on the west, south and east. It was not so much against China but against the Dutch, at war with Portugal (then under Spanish rule): the Dutch tried taking Macao in 1604, 1607, 1622 and 1627. The Dutch seaborne empire had begun growing after 1581, when the States of Holland formally renounced allegiance to Philip II of Spain (who had annexed Portugal in 1580), and compelled Spain to a peace in 1648, with the Treaty of Münster. This was eight years after Portugal had gained its separate status again. By then, according to Charles Boxer, 'the Dutch were indisputably the greatest trading nation in the word, with commercial outposts and fortified "factories" scattered from Archangel to Recife and from New Amsterdam to Nagasaki'.[1] (In Japan, the Dutch were the only European traders allowed after 1639, ending the 'Christian century' when Portugal had been the favoured partner).

The photograph shows a fragment of the city wall near the Na Tcha temple, with an entrance.

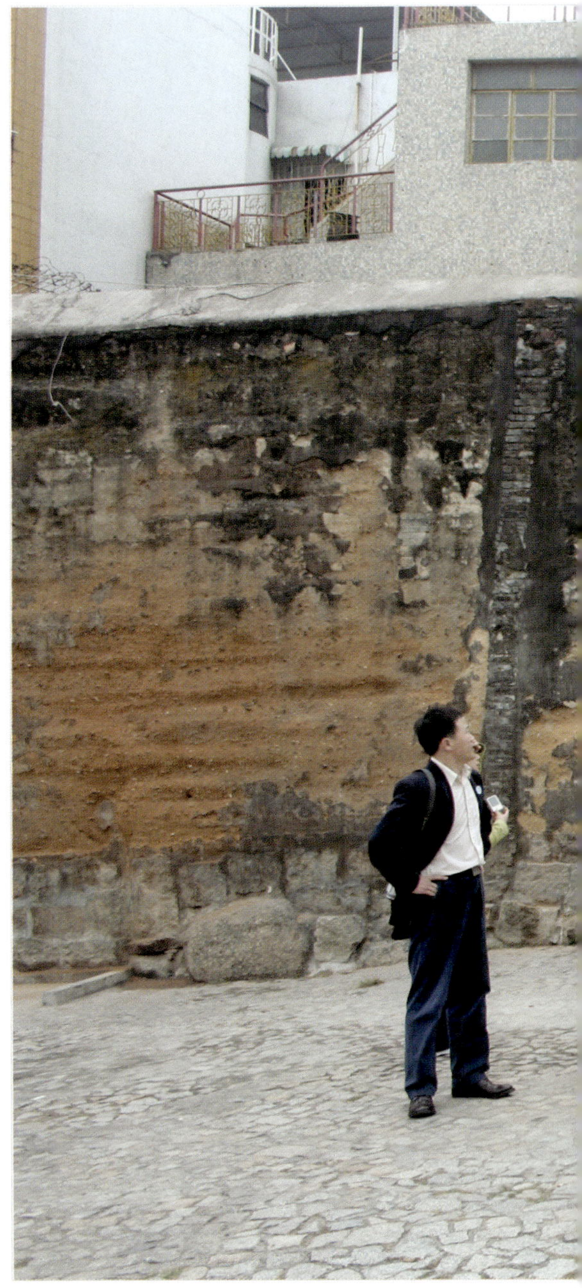

66. City walls

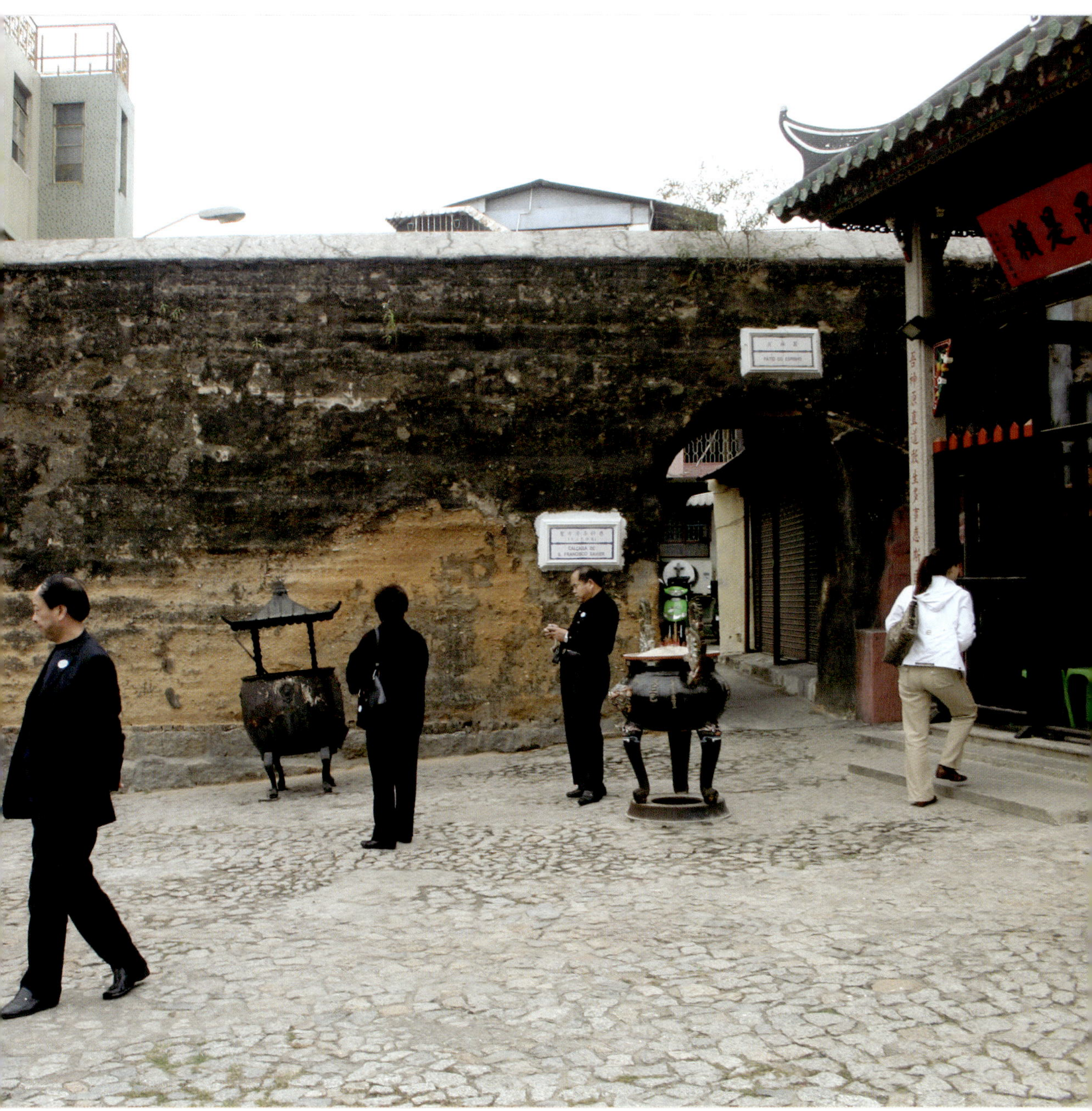

We look through a rough opening, in reverse
direction to photograph 52, towards apartments
which are technically outside the walls, in the
'suburbs' (what was called, historically, the 'Chinese
bazaar'), with a glimpse of a motorbike, with a cross
on a house incongruously behind it. Two religions
confront each other from either side of the wall,
just as the Na Tcha temple has, between it and
the wall, a further shrine to a minor god. There
are Chinese urns, one for burning paper-money,
the other a tripod for planting lighted joss-sticks,
with lions' legs (a lion's head, in colour, appears on
the urn itself). They have pushed their way into
the open space, creating something heterotopic in
this area.[2] The two greens, the three cameras just
visible, the hipped roof versus the flat roofs, the
blue writing against the red inscriptions, and the
sense of apartments behind the walls looking down
on events inside the walls are reminders of how
spaces change their looks by chance. The tourists in
black from the mainland, dispersed in the square in
front of the temple, looking at different direction,
contribute to the heterotopic atmosphere where no
protection seems needed.

Jorge Graça discusses some fourteen fortresses built
in the seventeenth century, some demolished. The
Barra fort, designed for cannon fire, and situated
near the A-Ma temple — on the southern tip of
Macao, on the shoreline at the entrance to the Inner
Harbour — resisted Dutch attack in 1622, though
it was not completed until 1629. It was to include a

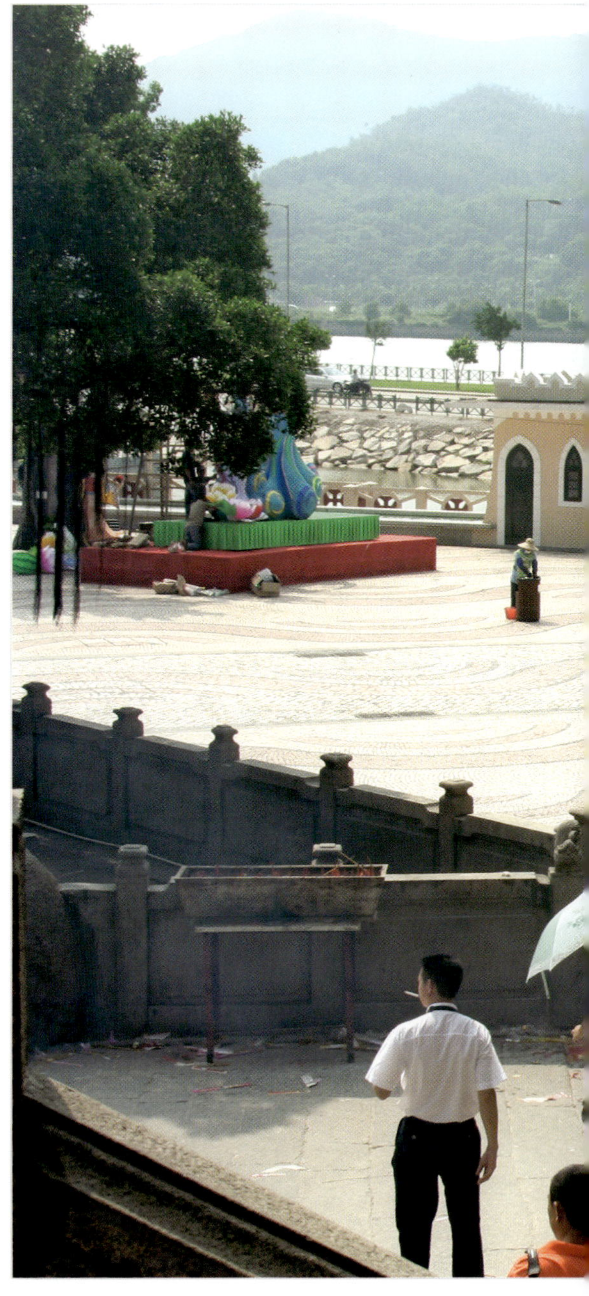

*67. View from temple:
towards the mainland*

122

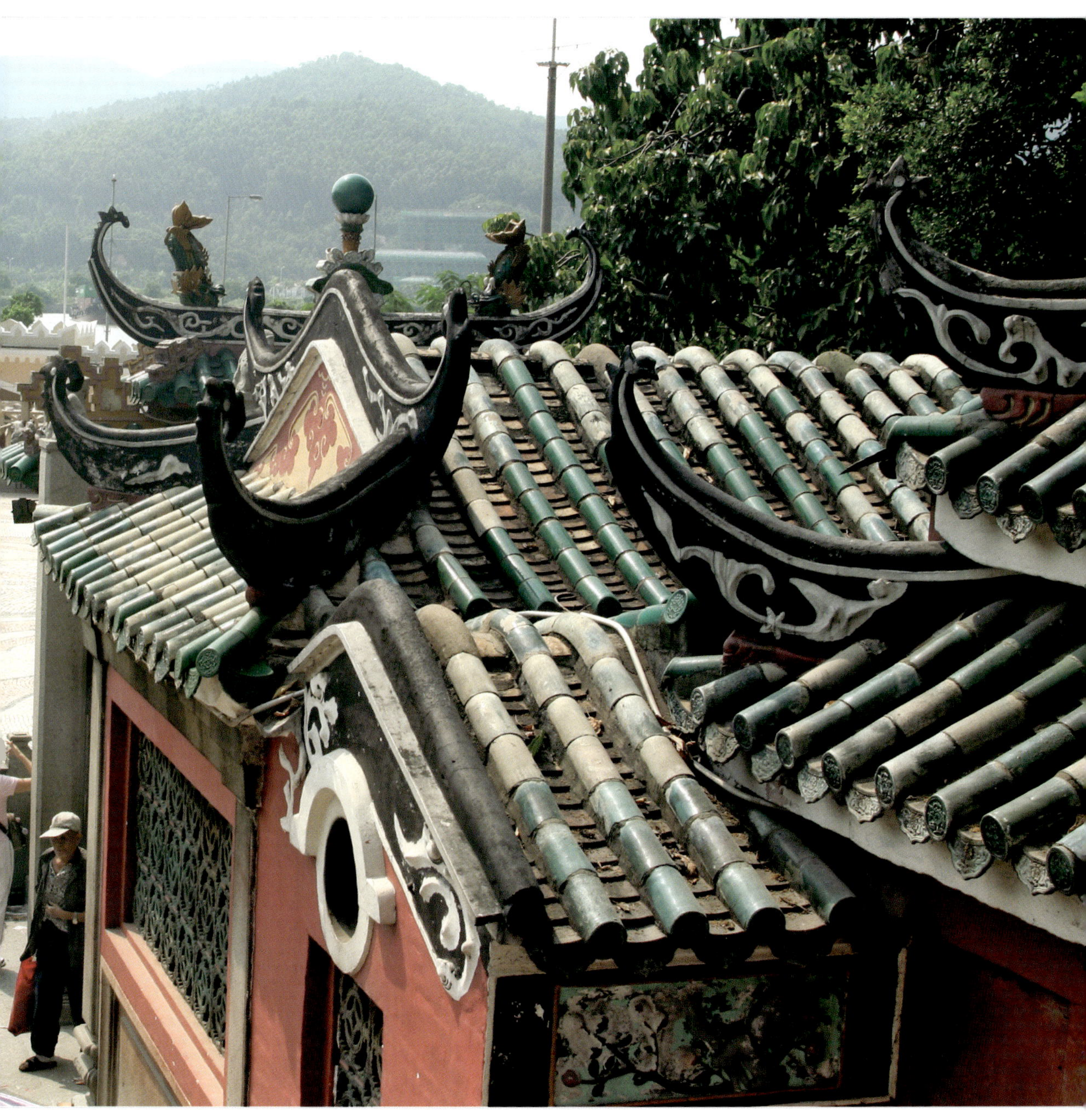

chapel to St James (São Tiago, built in 1740). The São Francisco Fort, on the Estrada São Francisco, now inland (it was on the coastline when built, in an alignment with the Barra Fort), was built against the Dutch in 1629, and had a convent with it; it was rebuilt in 1864, as a protection against Chinese. Another fort, Mong-Ha, appears in chapter 11.

Perhaps the most significant fort is Guia (Nossa Senhora da Guia), built before 1622, but extended in 1637, and intended, according to Graça, to defend Macao from piracy.[3] The most interesting part of this fort, on the highest point in Macao (ninety-four metres above sea level), is the Guia Chapel, which is seventeenth-century and stands next to a Victorian lighthouse of 1865, and renovated after being damaged (like much else in Macao) in September 1874 after a typhoon. An elegant curve in the line of the lighthouse is a belated reminder of the baroque, and it contrasts with the much more rectangular outline of the Chapel, which has, on its other side, a campanile with a bell, to tell the hours and to give warning.

The Guia Chapel is dedicated to Our Lady of the Snow (feast of August 5), and is a neglected gem. The visitor walks underneath a balcony (for the choir) into the tiny chapel, whose thick walls are a reminder that this chapel was to be defended. There is a barrel-vault ceiling, with an arch to support it, and the visitor looks towards a statue of Mary and Christ in a miniature baldacchino. There is a side-chapel to the left. The walls have been whitewashed, but they and the ceiling contain frescoes, most in a bad state of repair.

Photograph 68 shows the arch, halfway into the building, and behind it the vault-shaped roof. The visitor looks back to the balcony and the west end, and to a little Gothic-like trefoil design in the rear window. Below the gallery, in the floor, is a tombstone, which bears the date 1720, because it reads: AQVI JAS AE / STA PORTA / OS CRIS˜ POR / VENTVRA POIS NAO˜ ME / RECE SEVCORPO / TAO˜ HONROZ /A SEPVLTURA / 1687 / 1720 ANNO [Here lies at this gate the remains of Christopher (or Christóvão), by venture, for his body does not deserve such an honourable sepulchre].

The eye is arrested by the sinuous lines of branches growing upwards past the topmost support for the columns, following the curve of the arch on either side, and which nearly meet in the middle, before the tendrils turn away again. The plants, whose stems are reddish-brown, seem to grow out of a Chinese rocaille formation, as the motifs of flowers which are also red and brown, and which are put over other plants whose leaves are green, seem Chinese (see p. 1). The rocaille formation, which is in dark green, is just underneath the line of the capital on both sides, so that it seems, wittily, as if the plants come from roots in rocks

68. Guia Chapel — roof

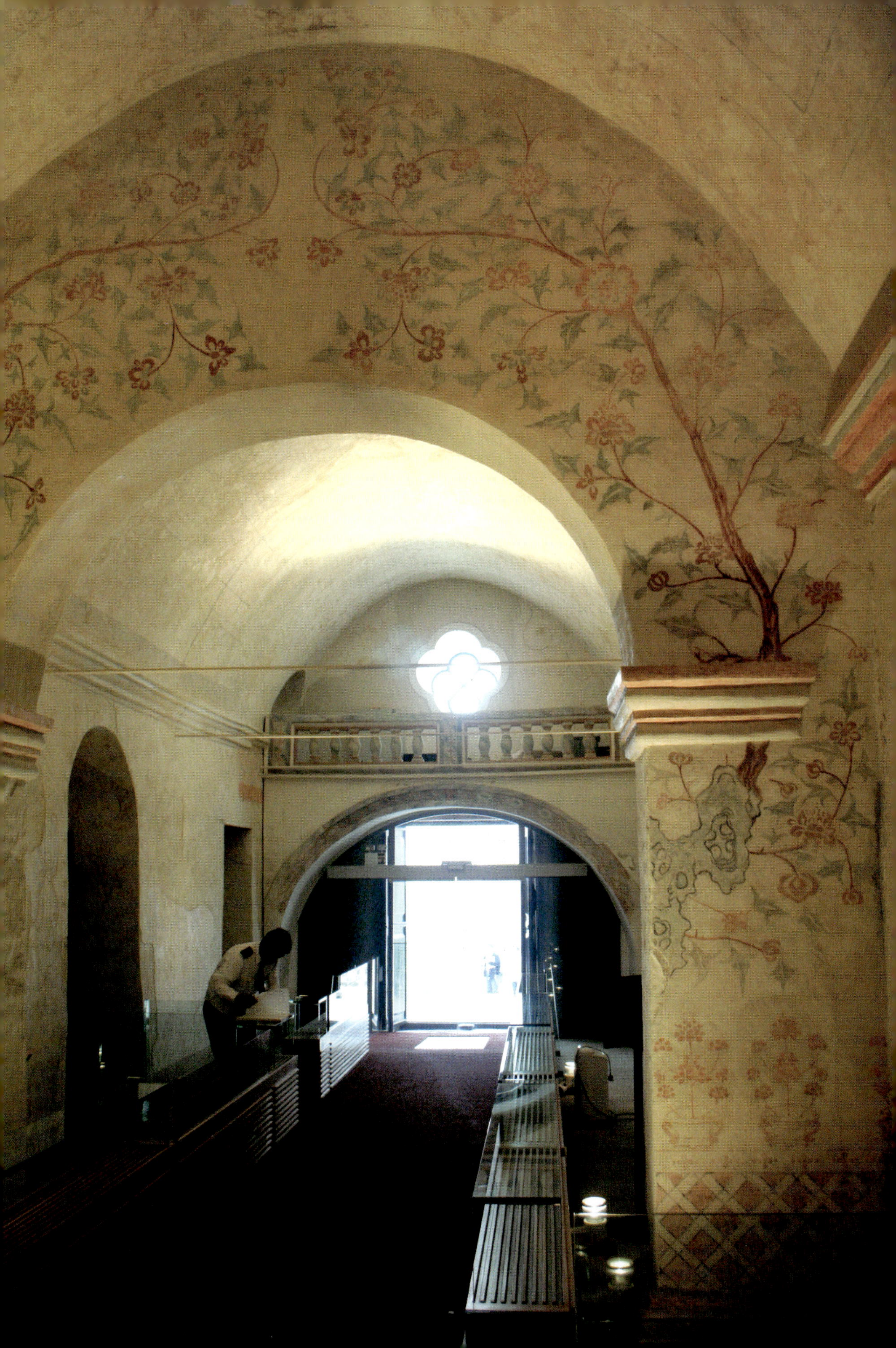

which then force their way above ground, above the line of the supports for the column, which then becomes the ground level. Two large flowers from these branches seem in symmetry with each other, echoing the window at the back. This Chinese-like decoration has replaced any Christian symbolism, or representation of saints, and it seems more rococo than baroque in its playfulness and lightness. Below the rocaille formation are two sets of flowers in shallow urns which are again Chinese in character and which may be borne by handles. Three shoots rise out of each of these urns, the central one of which divides again into a cup-like formation, which continues the central stem up to the topmost flower. The urns are shown in a western perspective, as if we are looking down on them slightly. This sense of enclosed space, which is realistic, as if the artist was trying for a still-life representation (except that the flowers are not seen in any perspective), is added to by the point that the urns seem to have serrated edges, as if the decoration continued into the fine detail of the base of the urn and the underlip, as if making these urns like cartouches. And below these urns is a line of six flowers seen from above, their petals wide open, and below that a cross-hatching pattern intersecting into the base of the arch. The plants in the two urns are artificially placed, while the plants that grow above are more natural, growing up out of the rock towards the sky. Art and nature come together in this overall design.

Some frescoes in the side-chapel show something other than this playfulness. One is badly worn, medieval-looking, and set in the southern wall of the chapel. It is high up, under the barrel-vaulted ceiling, which has panels of flowers, central cups of flowers which are also crowns, surrounded by ten other flowers seen in burst-out form, lilies and in each corner, a lily-like flower. They are in poor

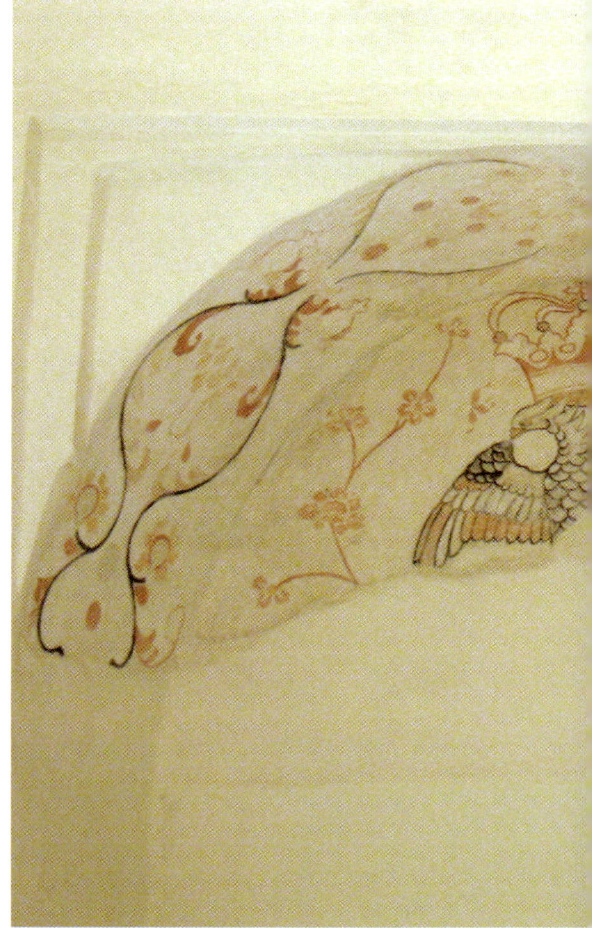

decorative order, the execution is crude (each lily looks different), and the relative absence of specific religious imagery seems important. Everything here of the fresco-work and the figure of Mary, seems Gothic in inspiration — late Gothic art in the seventeenth century — though the surrounds, the flowers, and the abundance and proliferation of flowers seem also baroque.

In the first fresco shown here (photograph 69), there is a picture of John the Baptist as a child, which is over the door. John cradles a tiny lamb in his left hand (had this Chinese artist ever seen a sheep?) and carries a flag in his right hand. He is surrounded by the blue heavens, but he stands upon the rounded earth, as if taking possession of it. Perhaps John is there to celebrate victory over the

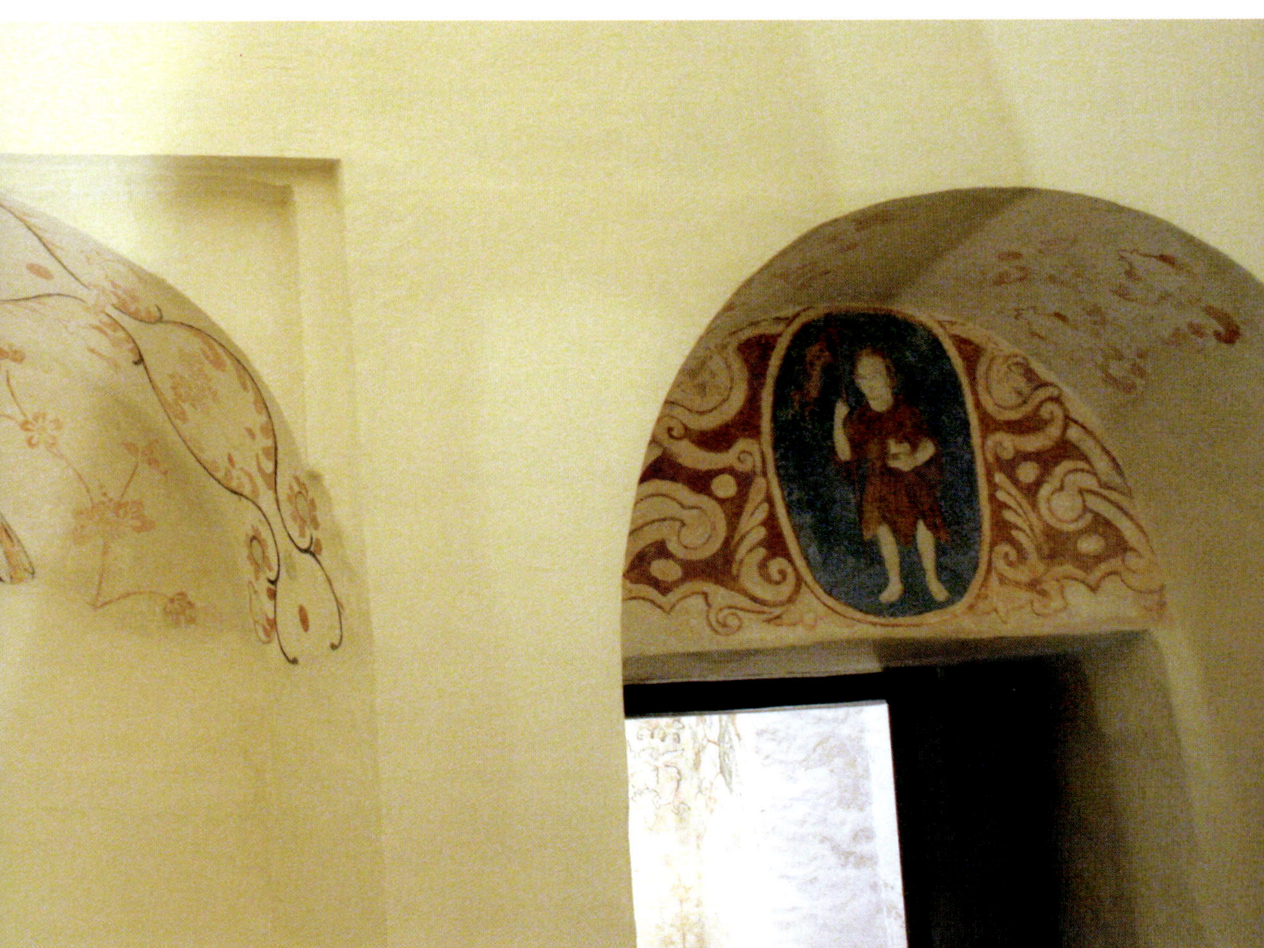

69. John the Baptist and wall

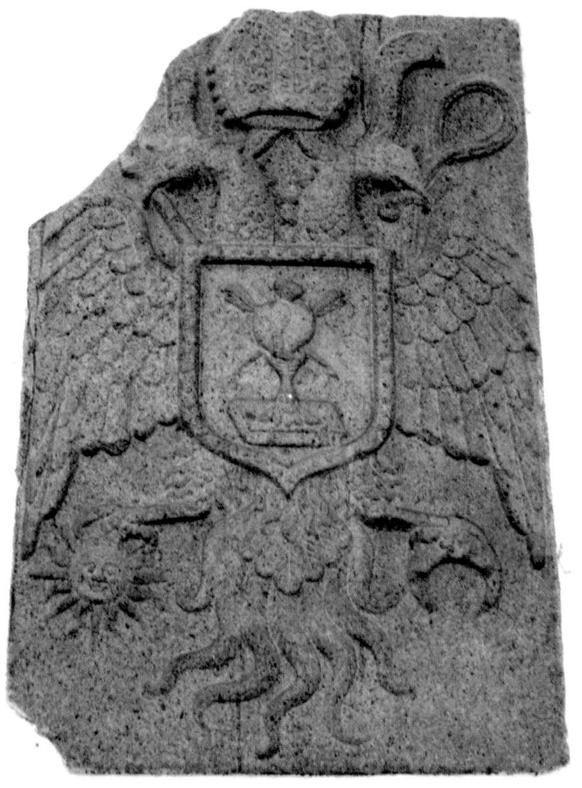

70. Eagles in stone

wings outspread. Perhaps the double-headedness joins spiritual and secular powers into one, into a single crown symbolising total power; perhaps too it suggests the dominance of this bird as it flies east and west simultaneously. Nothing about the painting of the two halves of this bird is quite symmetrical, nor are the flowers which are behind it, nor is the more intricate design of flowers which are set into the underside of the arch under which the eagle is seen, with a crown which is pushed awkwardly right up into the space between the wall and the ceiling. The fresco compares with a stone fragment seen in the Leal Senado.

In this badly weathered stonework, the eagles, which seem to rise out of fire like phoenixes, use their talons to hold the sun and the moon, both given faces. Perhaps they suggest universal imperial power, East-West; or masculine and feminine power combined.

Dutch on St John's day, 24 June 1622. He is inset into a golden frame which is surrounded by a design which attempts to fill the semi-circular space, with a winged, almost bat-like formation, but the two halves of the cartouche fail to match.

Inside this side-chapel appears the fragment of a fresco, with a crown supported by the heads of a double-headed eagle, seen in profile, the

In the chapel, power appears fragmented; the fresco is damaged, and the next design that appears, on another wall, is of gold flowers with a red background, and apparently unrelated to the lion leaping above.

Here, in the inward turn of the arch appears the fresco of a reddish tree, installed in an urn with S-shaped handles. The tree grows upwards and branches into three. The stems divide and form ovaloid structures, each containing a flower, so that there are three flowers, no doubt associated with the Trinity, seen going up to and disappearing into the ceiling. On the side are flowers growing downwards. The central branch with its cup-like structure, (the cups repeating the container of the urn), is nearly duplicated below in another dwarf arch, or niche, for a statue on the left-hand side of the wall which is otherwise nearly empty. The exception is that there is no urn in the lower arch. The floral design is repeated at several points in the vaulting on the underside of the arches; for example it can be seen in photograph 69. In the lower arch, the petals of the three layers of flowers are sharply different; they form a corona in the lowest, and blossom in the middle. The topmost flower is different again, and could represent the tongues of fire associated with the Holy Spirit on the day of Pentecost (Acts 2). Fire and flower are one. But beyond these flowers is the sharp and sinuous outline of the shoots of the plant, which form such sensuous, even erotic curves, and the general suggestiveness of the design makes for what resembles curving elephant trunks underneath the second row of spreading-out shoots. Next to the flowers in the upper part of the arch is a Chinese lion, already mentioned. His mouth is open, he is in three-quarters profile, with eyes looking down towards where the altar should be. His front paws are raised, as if aggressively, and as if standing on its rear legs, but those legs are invisible because the rest of the wall has no decoration, nor is it clear, given the fragmentary state of everything, to what extent the other parts of the chapel were

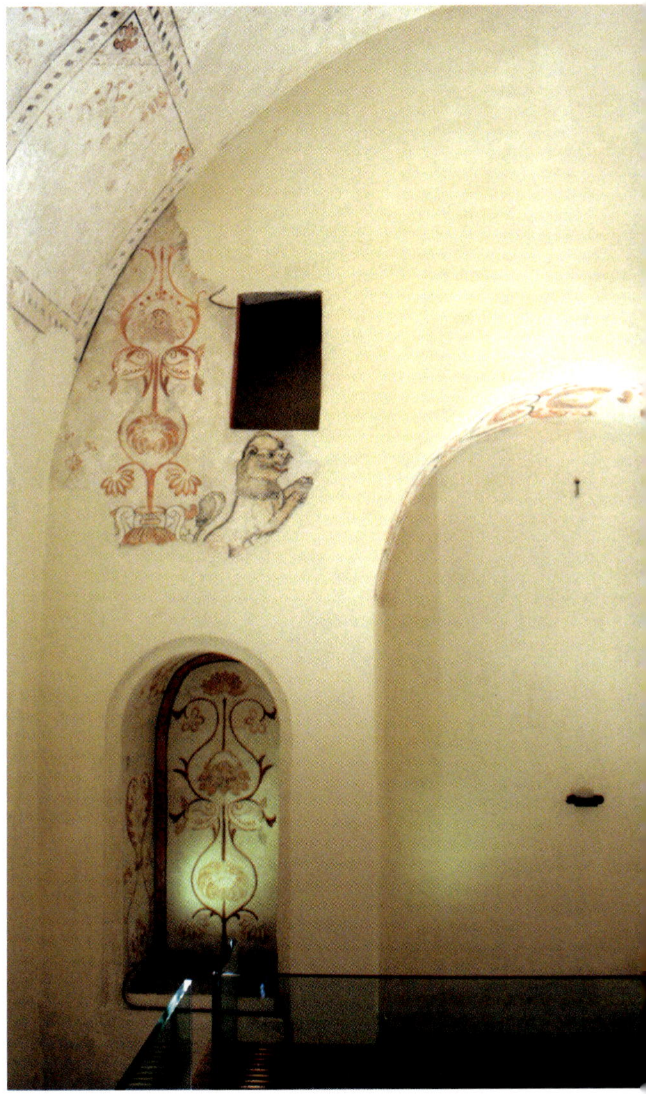

71. Lion and floral design

decorated. The lion's tail curves and curls and appears like another flower, or as if its S-shape corresponded to the handle of the urn. However much it is ready to spring, a certain fineness and delicacy in its shape suggest something feminine in the chapel's decoration.

Back in the chapel's main part, a complex design in the wall can be picked out: lions supporting two classical pillars which rise up and act as the frames for a cartouche, which contains five angels — four surrounding an angel's head with wings, with a banderole above him. On the other side of each pillar there is a further cartouche, and there is no symmetry in the way these cartouches frame the pillars.

The Chinese lions, with human faces, look in different directions, as if they were about to pull in reverse directions, as if the whole effect was about to come apart. These lions are different from the one in the Lady Chapel, because here they are in service, supporting the pillars which, however, are only sketched in. The feet of the topmost angels to the right and left are concealed in the imaginary space of the sky which is concealed by the framing of the cartouche. To read the episode here is almost impossible partly because of its state of repair, partly because of the execution, partly because the subject and the themes seem so anachronistic. But that is its point, and it makes the picture part of colonial baroque culture. It seems that the art of this chapel

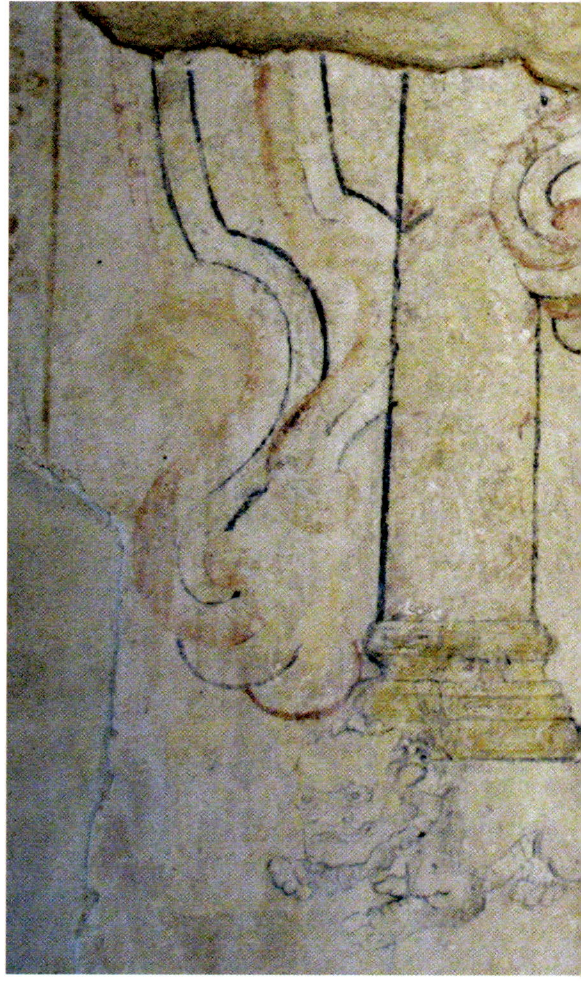

has come from colonial subjects who have painted the chapel with only fragments of knowledge. If this art which is of the baroque period is Gothic, that brings out a point about the anonymous painters who worked on these walls and ceilings; this is not classical art, of which there is plenty in Macao, because the classical contains what Ruskin would

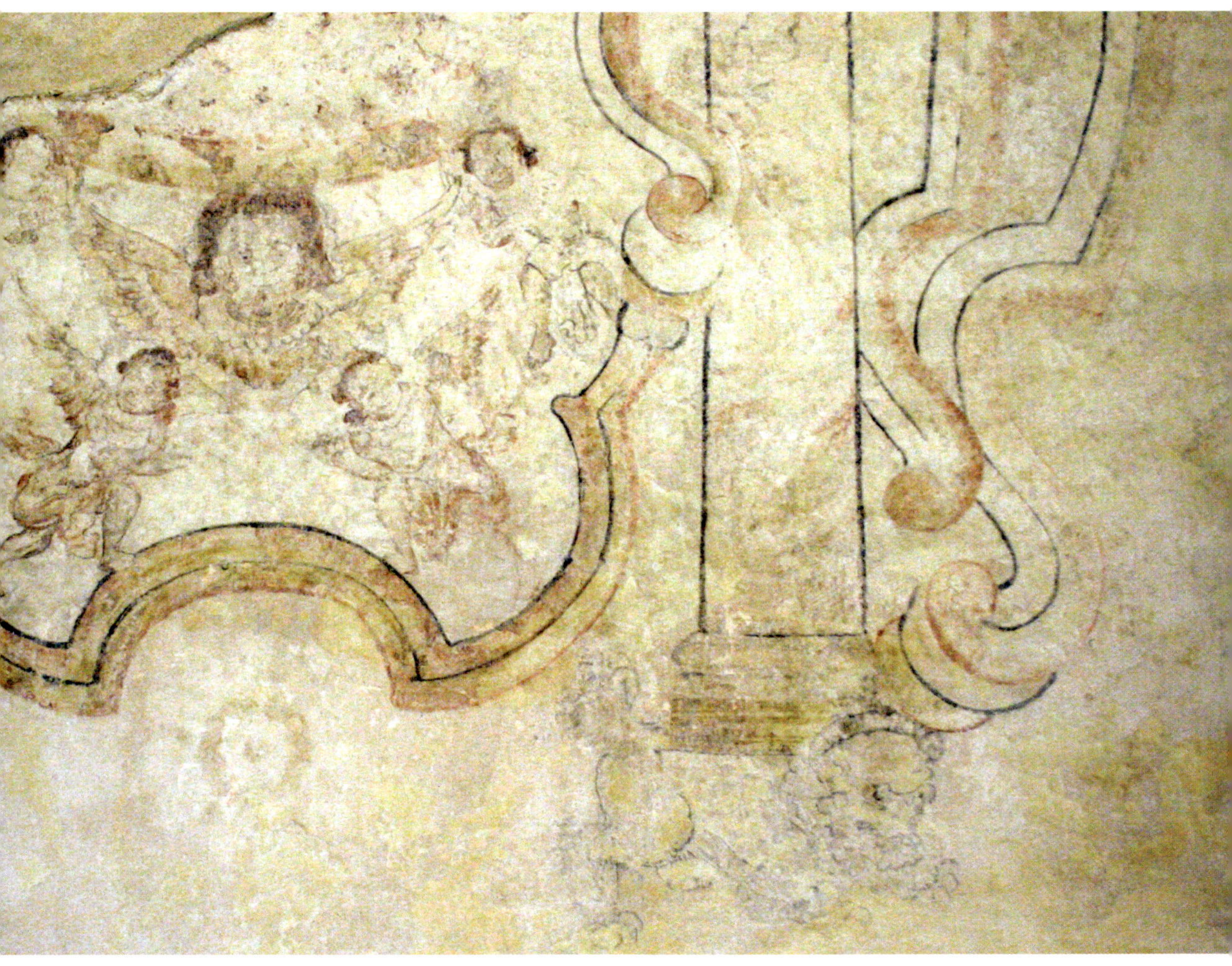

72. *Angels in cartouche*

call the 'demand for perfection' which is 'always a sign of a misunderstanding of the ends of art'. In contrast, Gothic art allows for failure, which can only come from individual creativity; 'no great man ever stops working till he has reached his point of failure' and 'imperfection is some sort essential to all that we know of life'.[4]

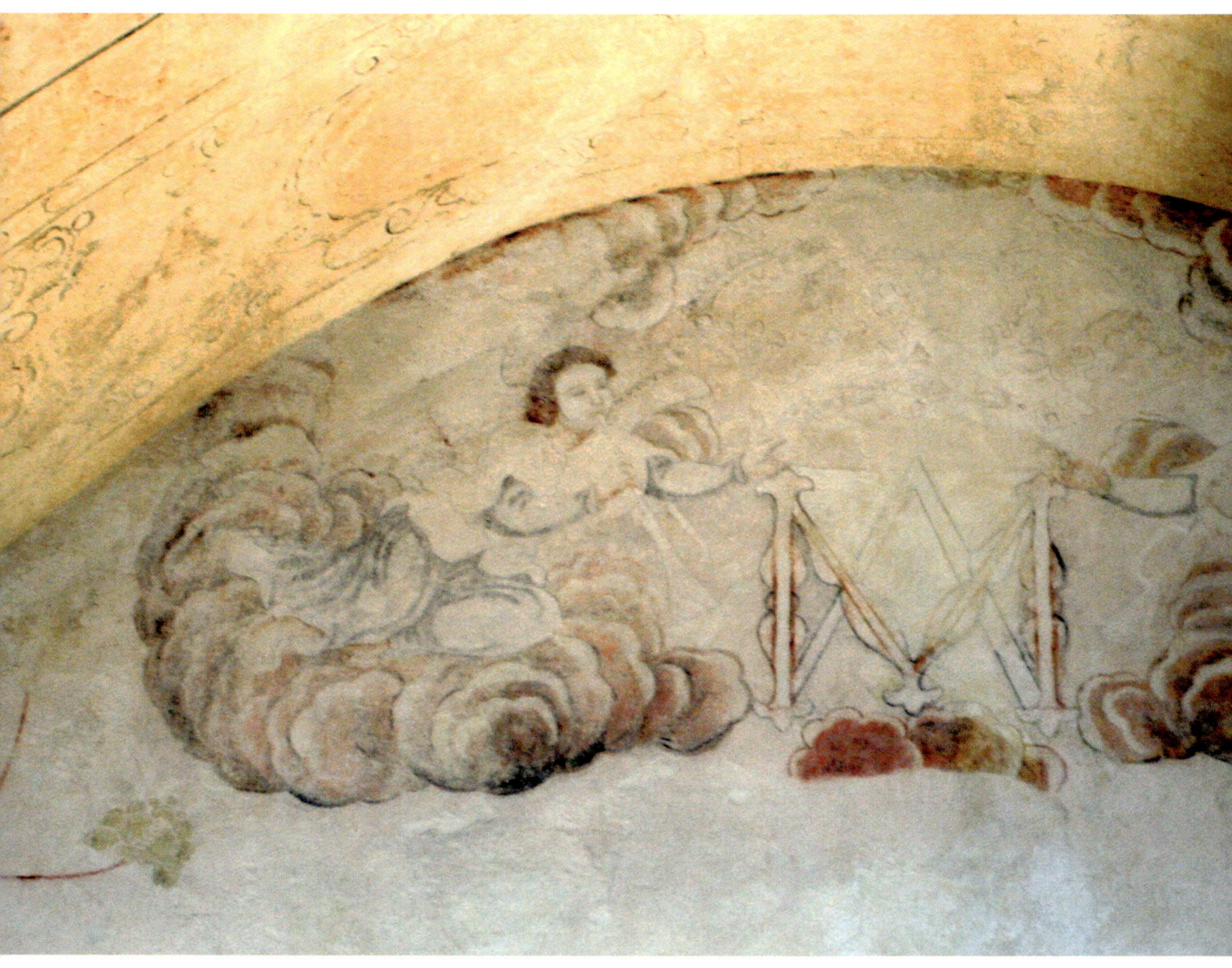

73. *Angels flying and playing*

The central cartouche in this fresco could well be on the ceiling, as indeed there are such *trompe l'oeil* effects in the vaulting of the main chapel.

Trompe l'oeil is at the heart of baroque, and two examples of it may be picked out in the upper part of the barrel vaulting. The first, illustrated here,

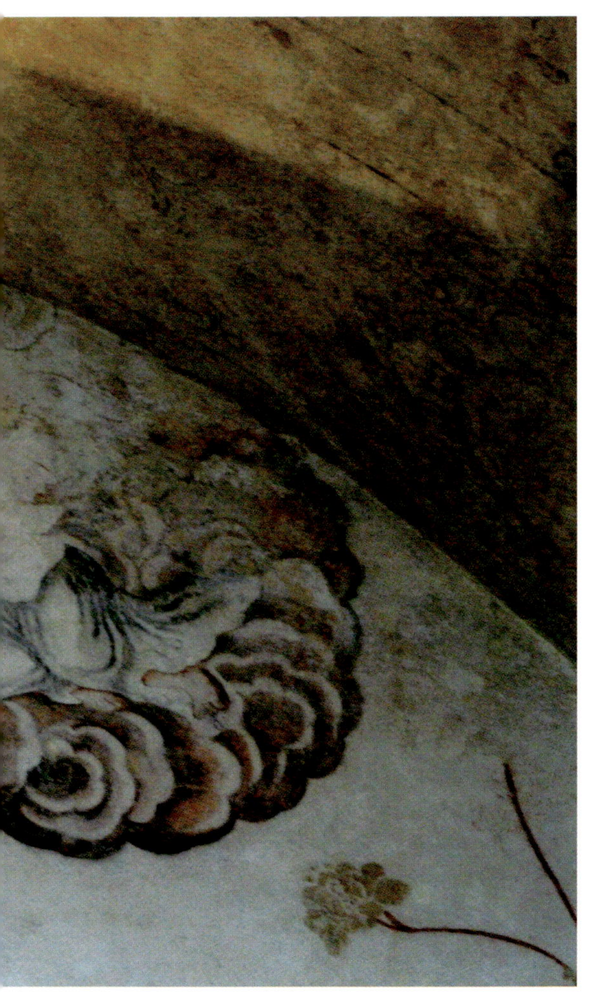

shows the playfulness of the two angels on clouds in the upper part of the central arch, resting on cloud-like flowers, and holding between them a highly decorated letter M (which is also an Alpha, and also a V for 'Virgine'), one with the left hand and one with the right, their other free hands holding pipes which they are playing. They are seen on arrival

into the chapel. They appeal to the illusionistic, they seem real, resting on clouds above the viewer, and yet their playfulness appears in the writing that they carry between them, which draws attention to another layer of reality, that of signs. Above, in what is technically the nave of the chapel, appear cartouches, one of which contains the sun and the moon, the moon having a face. (They recall the sun and the moon on the façade of St Paul's.) The effect of the ceiling, if it existed anywhere else, would be of intricate baroque folds, which would have been brought out by elaborate plaster work and mouldings and breding; but here, the fold has almost been pencilled in, ruled by lines which do not disguise the point that this ceiling is the work of a draftsman who works two-dimensionally, and makes no effort towards a three-dimensional effect. The result is baroque and not baroque, baroque which exists as if only on a sketchpad, the more playful because of that. The ceiling has not been reproduced because the artwork is too faded, as it almost was, for photographs 72 and 73.

This Guia Fortress remained a military area until 1976. The Moorish Barracks, on Barra Hill, located in 'Quartel dos Mouros' near the Inner Harbour at the opposite end of the town evokes new barracks (like those for São Francisco near the town centre) which were opened in 1874, when the Italian architect Cassuso designed a building in Moorish style to accommodate some two hundred Muslim Indian policemen from Goa, in a building up of the police force, after Macao had made itself an overseas province of Portugal (1844), and independent of China (1849, the incident involved the assassination of the Governor Ferreira do Amaral: it is memorialised in the border-arch between Macau and mainland China). The building became the offices for customs police in 1905. Built into a hillside, and so playing with different levels, and high above the street level at the front, it is enframed on three sides by verandas with Moorish-style pointed arches.

While the motivations of the colonial government, which had to strengthen the police force in the nineteenth century using non-Chinese and non-Portuguese policemen, is interesting, it is unfortunate that the buildings call Indian Muslims 'Moorish', and that a fake exoticism was required to accommodate the new forces of law. The building is not baroque, but neo-classical, with Moorish additions, but its back has been greatly changed with new buildings, and the designs here are not neo-classical, but much more elaborate and playful, with another attractive spiral staircase.

The visitor who walks away from the barracks towards St Lawrence's church and the centre of Macao reaches Lilau Square via the Mandarin's House, which suggests a different architecture, theme of the next chapter.

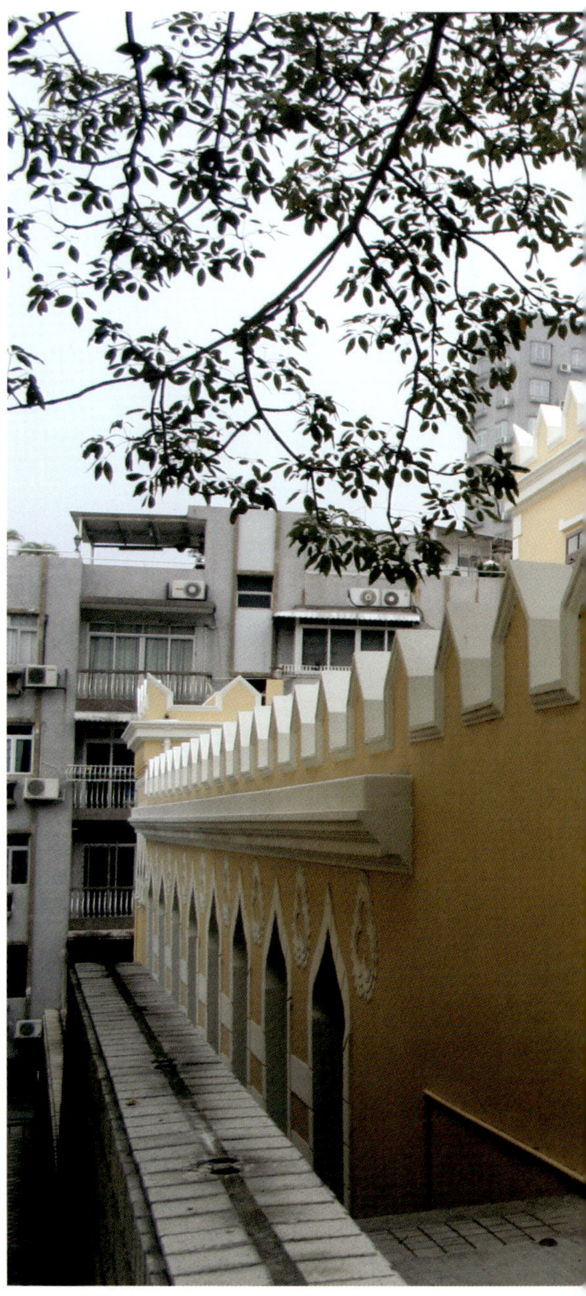

74. Moorish Barracks

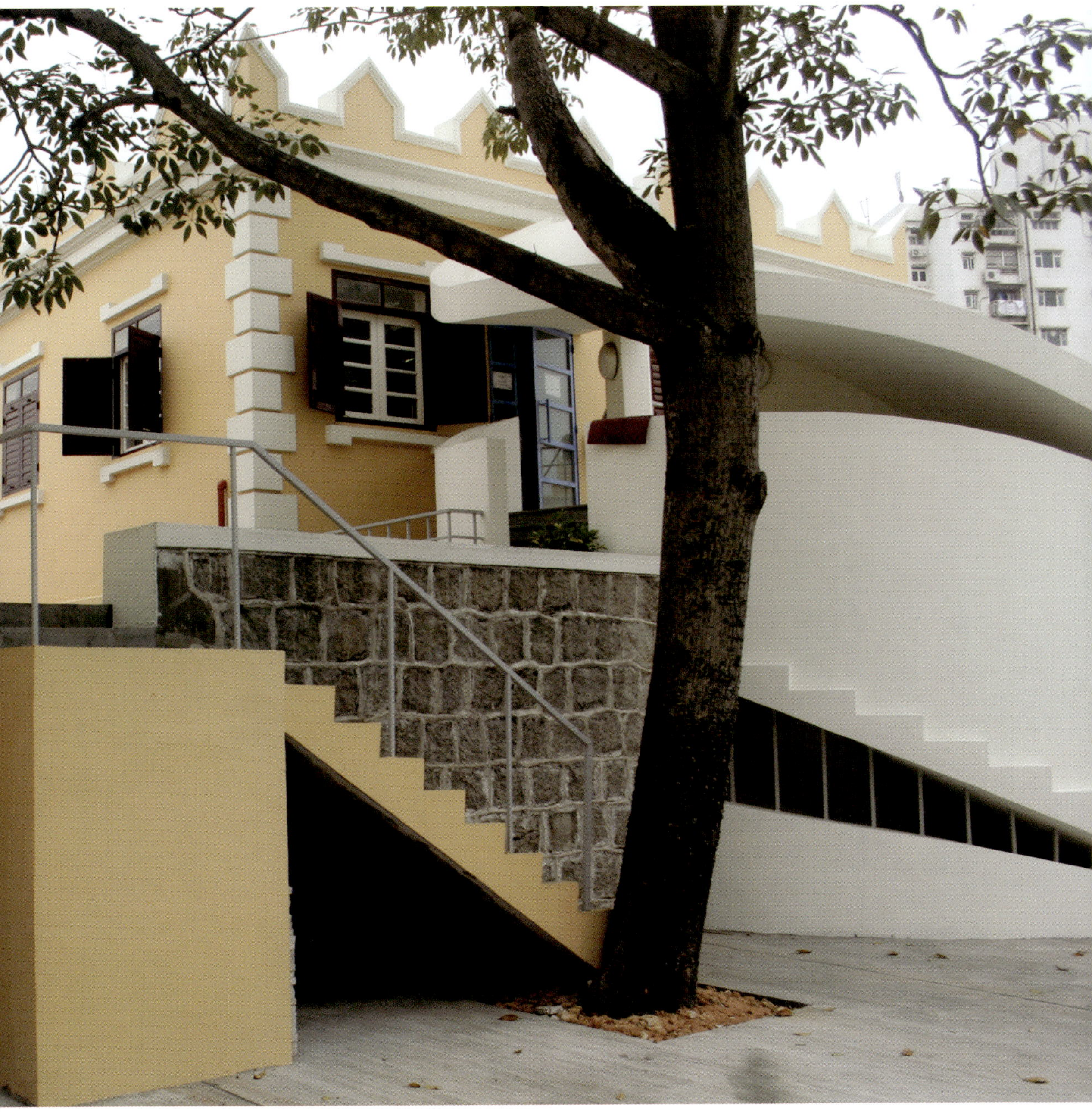

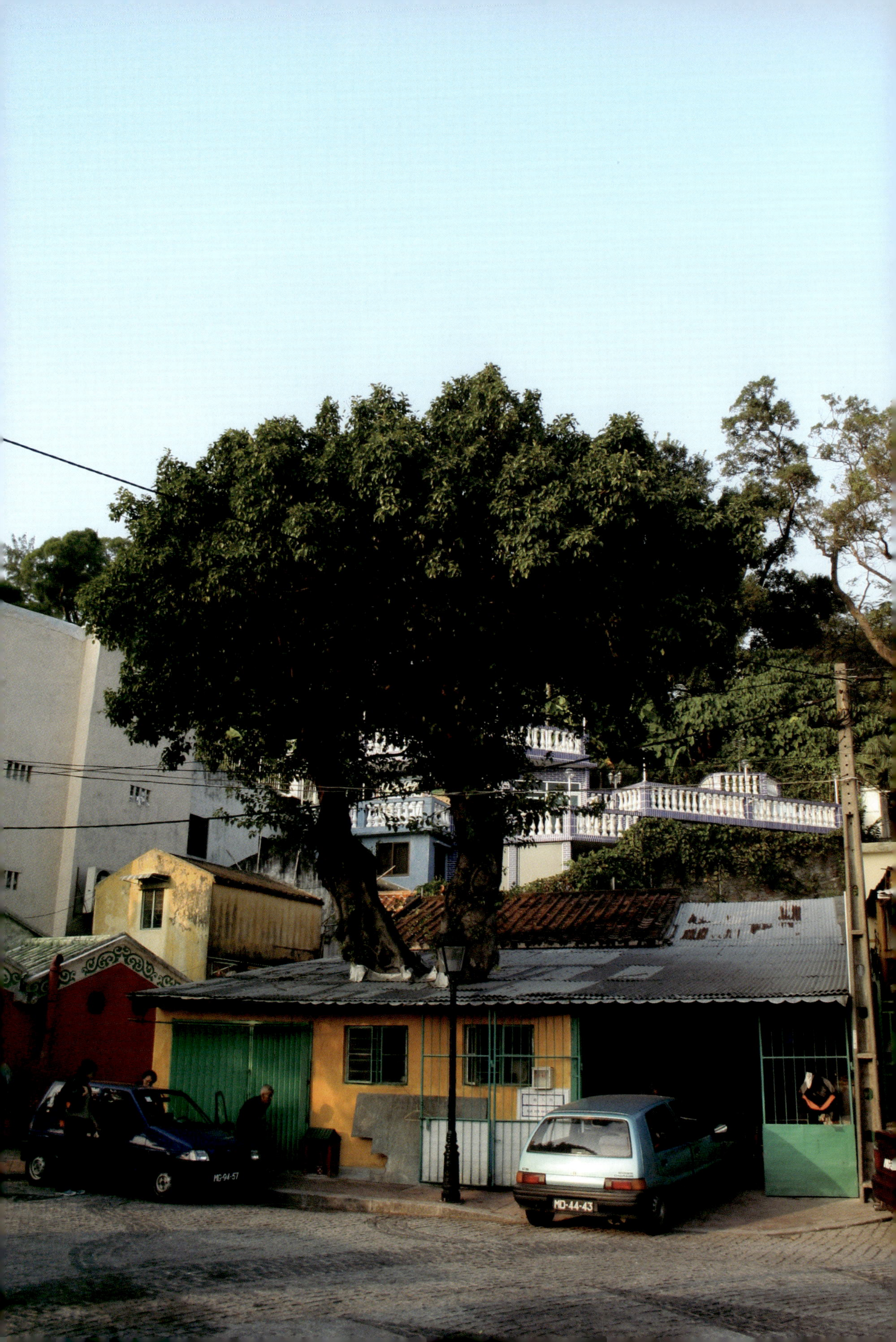

Chapter 8
Macao's Chinese Architecture

Nature and culture stand in nice relation to each other in Macao. These two photographs of Coloane bring out their integration. In photograph 75, corrugated iron has been cut to keep the trees in place and growing upward: the shacks which are so roofed have been built in front of a Chinese house. In photograph 76, the Daoist temple, which looks towards the sea and towards seafarers to whom it offers protection, has been integrated with landscaped rock, which rises higher than the roof. The baroque also integrates nature and culture, and our examples will discuss this through Chinese architecture.

This chapter considers buildings and spaces, all Chinese in design, which are the opposite of the official, civic and defensive buildings that represent the public face of Portuguese colonialism. They often show a certain repression of the baroque, preferring the neo-classical. They either criticise, silently, the colonial idea, or by their existence they form alternatives to it, or they indicate its limitations. Among many possible examples, only those which are part of the 'heritage' of Macao are discussed: a garden, a Mandarin's House and the A-Ma, the most famous temple of all. They are looked at as examples which help us to read the baroque because in many ways they are baroque themselves.

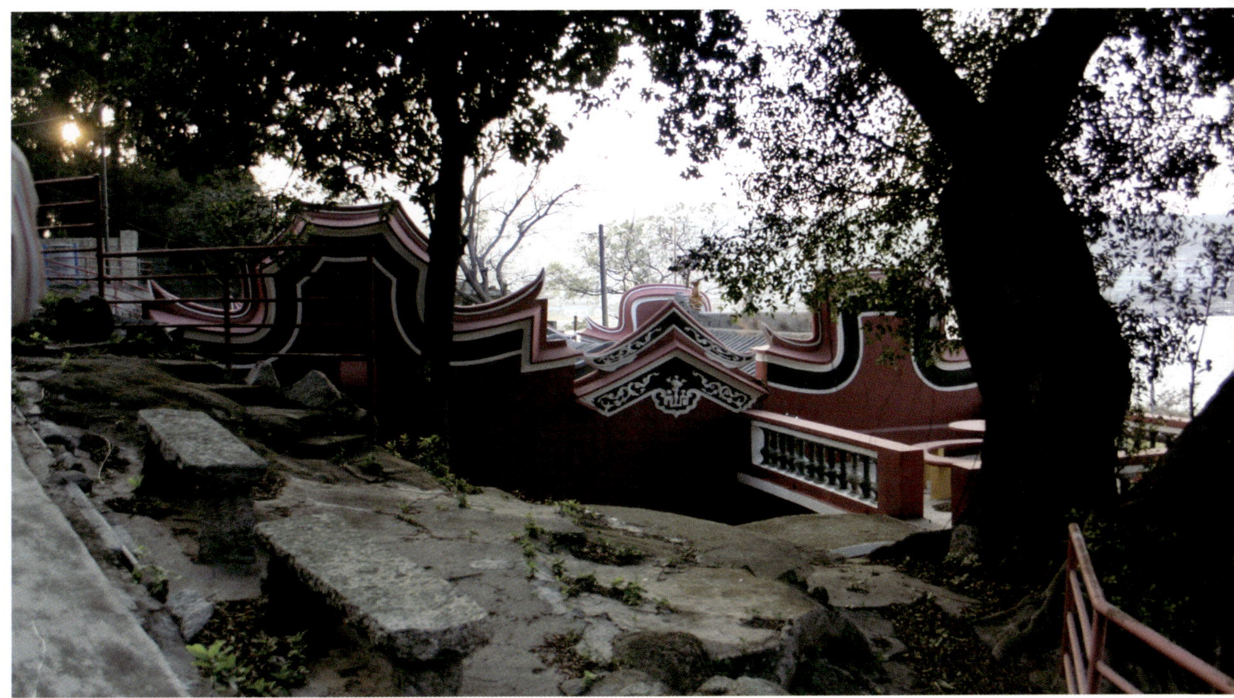

◀ 75. *Trees and houses, Coloane*

▲ 76. *Tam Kung temple and rock*

Lou Lim Ioc Chinese Garden

A first example of an 'other' space is the Chinese garden, Lou Lim Ioc, which is inside the busy city, surrounded by high-rise flats as may be seen in the photograph. Hong Kong has no Chinese garden; whoever would wish to visit a Chinese garden must come here, short of going to a mainland site, such as Suzhou, another UNESCO heritage site since 1997.

The visitor enters through a moongate into a series of spaces which are made up by bamboo; by miniature sculpted rocks in the form of arches, reminiscent of Chinese mountains in Chinese art; by the presence of water; by paths which divert the visitor as much as possible, taking him eventually over the bridge which itself branches and folds nine times, as if resisting the spirits; and by statues, such as the one of Kun Iam below (see p. 154). The only straight line in the garden is in the western-style house (where Dr Sun Yat Sen stayed in 1912), which may be seen to the back of the photograph here. It contrasts with the usual Chinese halls in Chinese gardens in its straightness of design. The length of the verandah is reproduced in photograph 78.

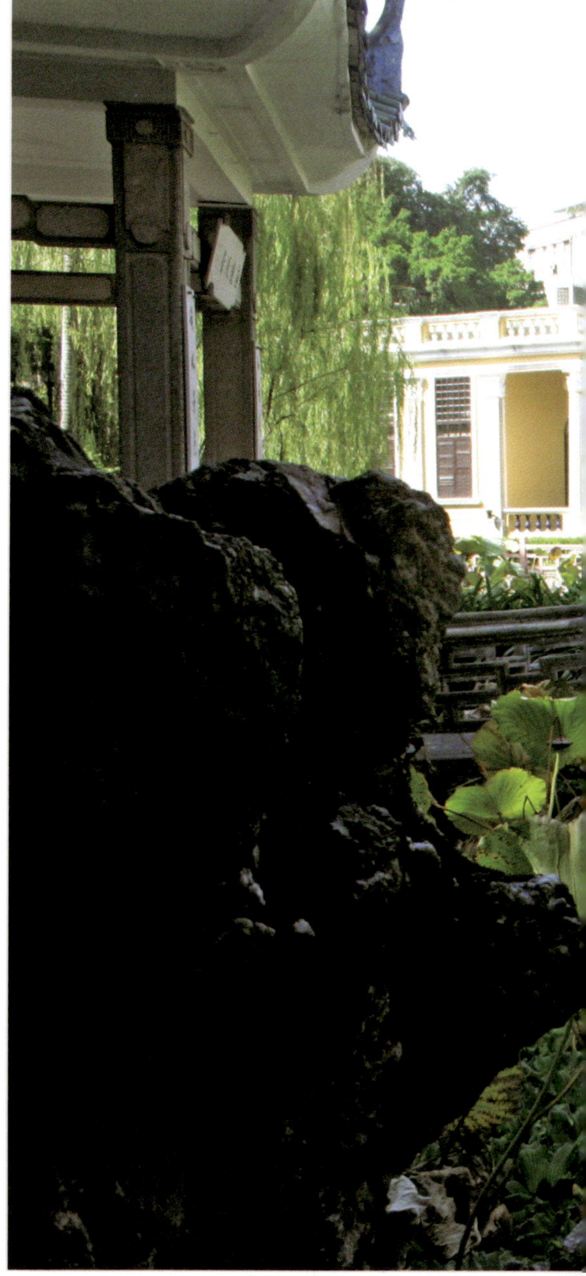

*77. Lou Lim Ioc Garden: view
from a false hill*

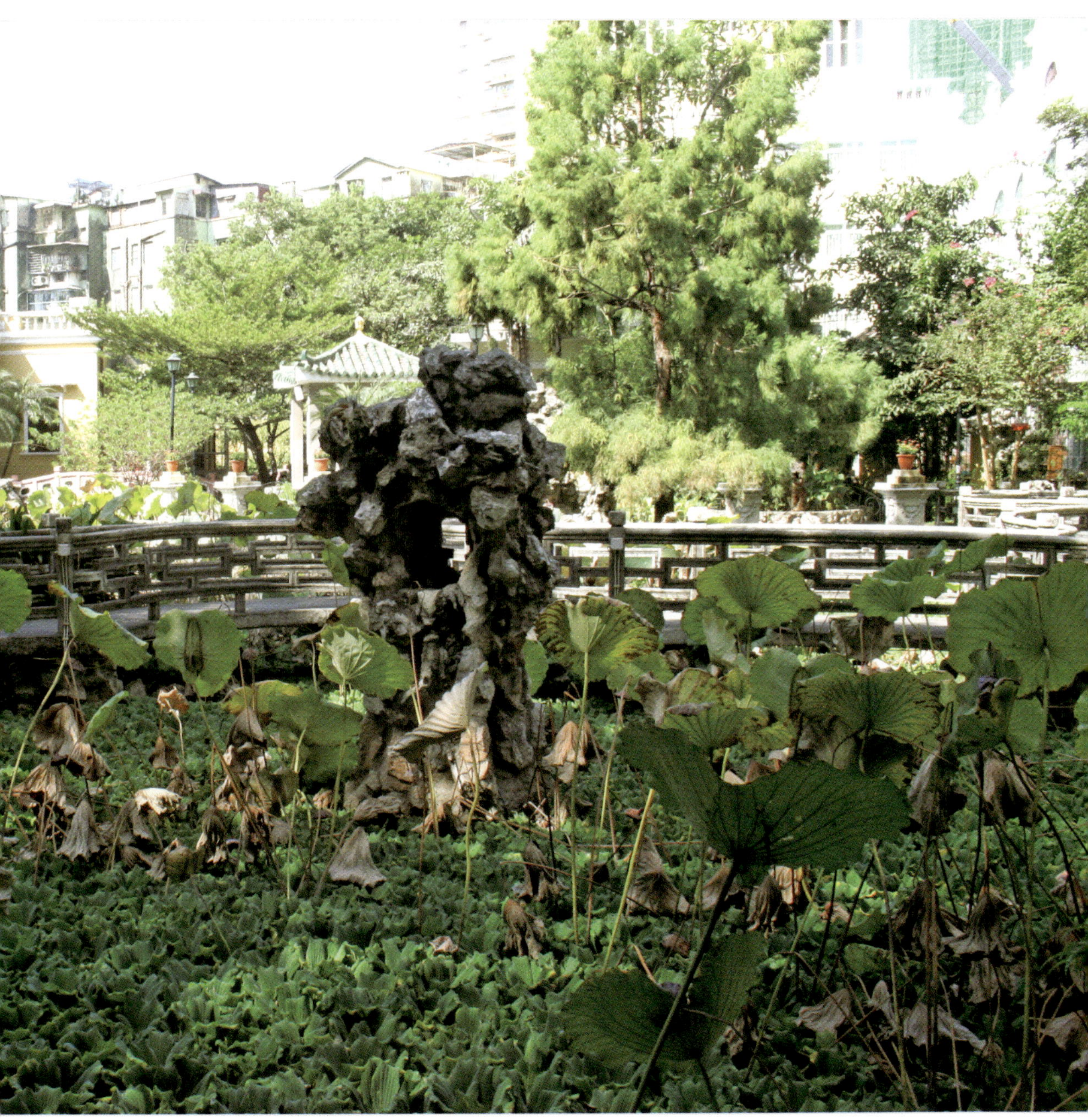

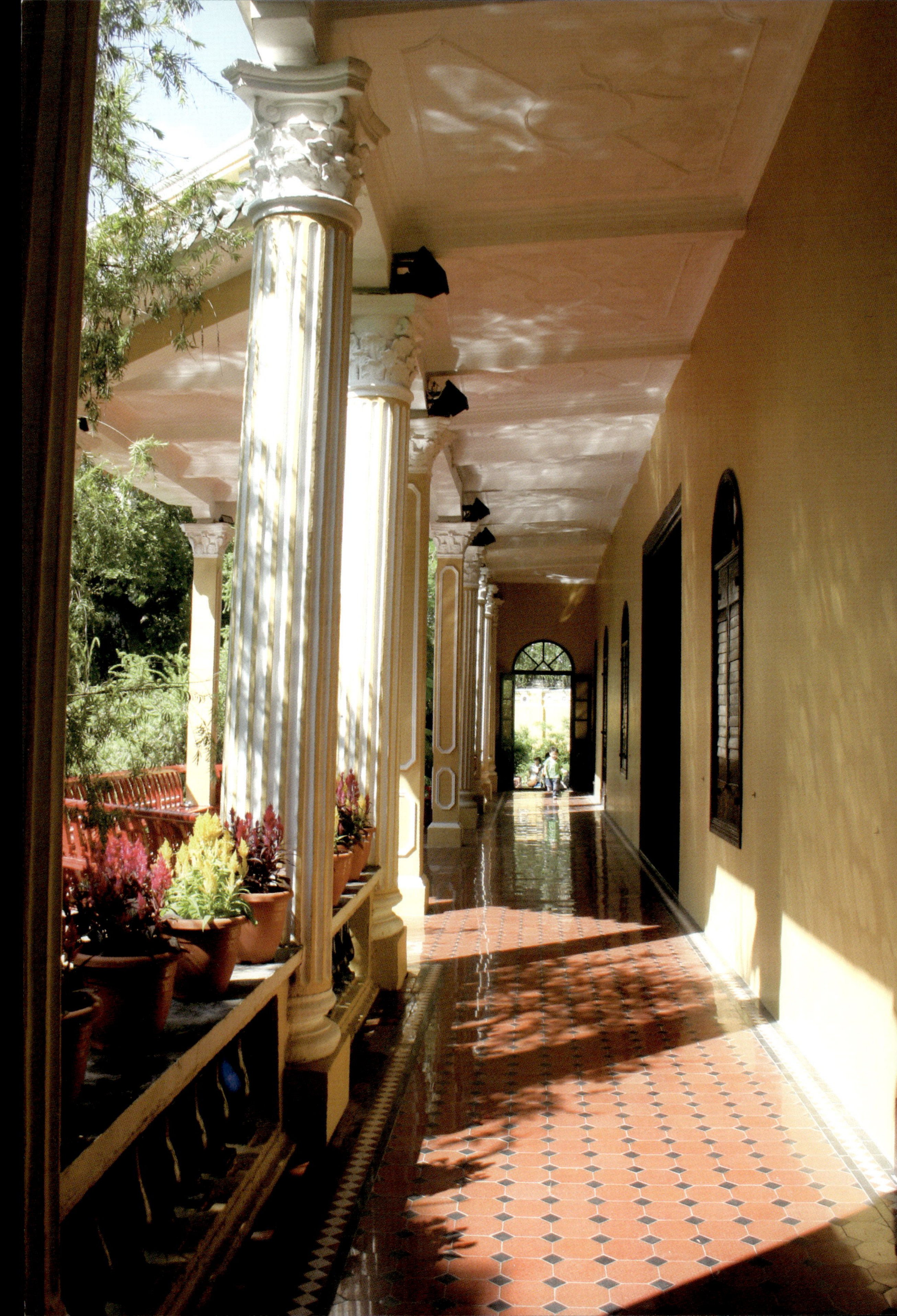

The western-style house ('Spring Grass Hall'), a good resting-place (and a museum of art), however fine, speaks of the neo-classical, of which Blake wrote: 'Improvement makes strait roads, but the crooked roads without Improvement are roads of Genius'.[1] The Chinese garden reproduces such unimproved roads. Everything depends on the visitor being able to look back at where he or she has been, and to consider it from a different prospect, and to see the various features of the garden — the pavilions, open structures themselves, the resting-places, the

different vegetation-formations, all of them in three dimensions (paths, hills and ponds). Walking around all of them is only possible by walking round the garden, not round individual features. The different prospects mean that the sense of being 'inside' or 'outside' is disturbed, just as much as it is for Derrida (see chapter 2) and for the baroque; each feature is contained in a tight structure and yet it is an open area, inside and outside at the same moment. In the photograph of the bridge, the pavilion which is its entrance is also within the garden.

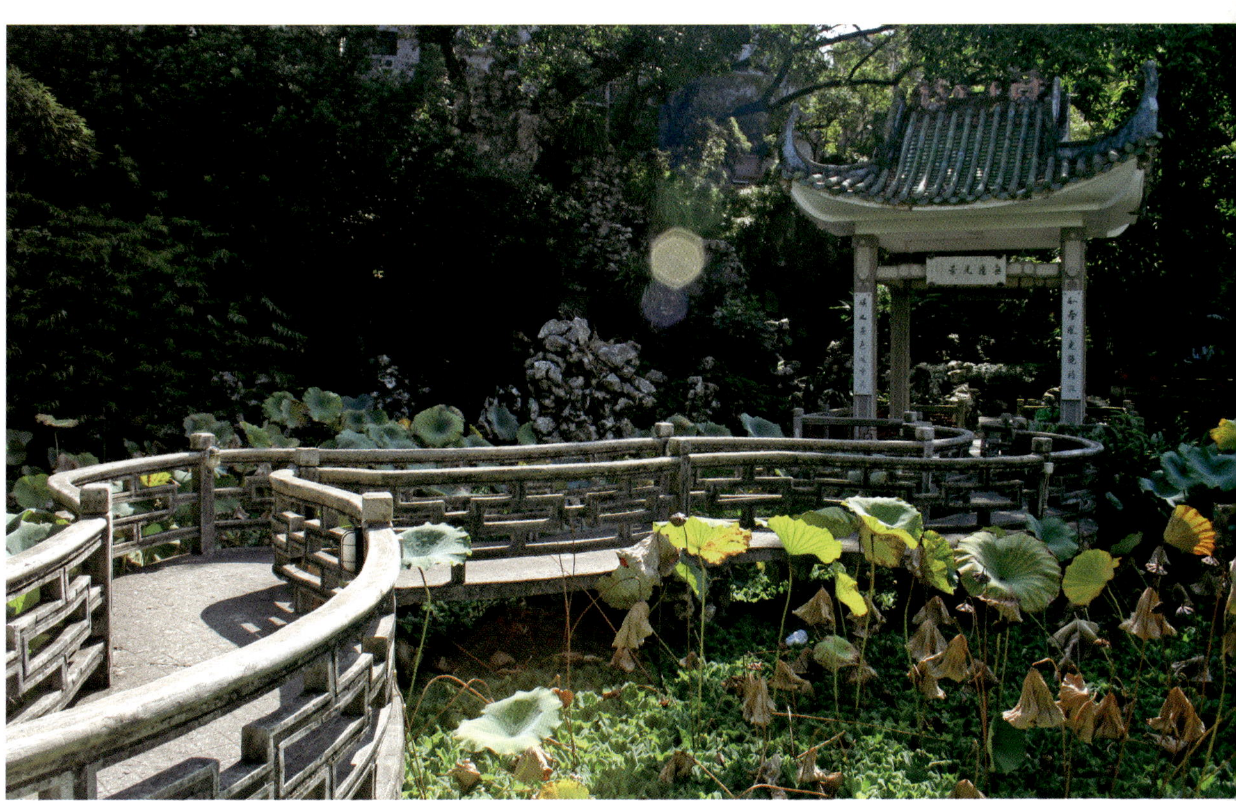

◄ *78. Verandah of the western house
in the Lou Lim Ioc Garden*

▲ *76. Lou Lim Ioc Garden: nine-turn
bridge and pavilion*

The individual paths which turn, and the sense of the ability to be always faced with several directions at once, which is associated with the Chinese garden, suggests the linking that Borges makes in his short story 'The Garden of Forking Paths' between the book and the Chinese garden. The imaginary book, which is called *The Garden of Forking Paths*, is a library in itself, because it allows for all events to take place simultaneously, in different spaces and in different times. The point is the significance of the library as baroque. Chinese gardens have their influence throughout Macao, such as in the graceful turn of the staircase in the side-garden of the Sir Robert Ho Tung Library and the bends of the garden path.

In this garden, the Chinese influence is generalised. Borges draws his inspiration from the library discussed in chapter 2, and the baroque, and from the labyrinth, and the Chinese garden comprises and sums up all these. It is a library, always designed for the scholar, and permitting the person inside it to go down several paths, as a good library does, and to see different problems from different aspects. 'The Garden of Forking Paths' even allows for the idea of the book which exists in an endless loop, so that the person reading it would never be able to complete it. As the Sinologist Dr Albert says to the Chinese Dr Yu Tsun who has come to kill him, while explaining to Yu the riddle that he has been trying to work out:

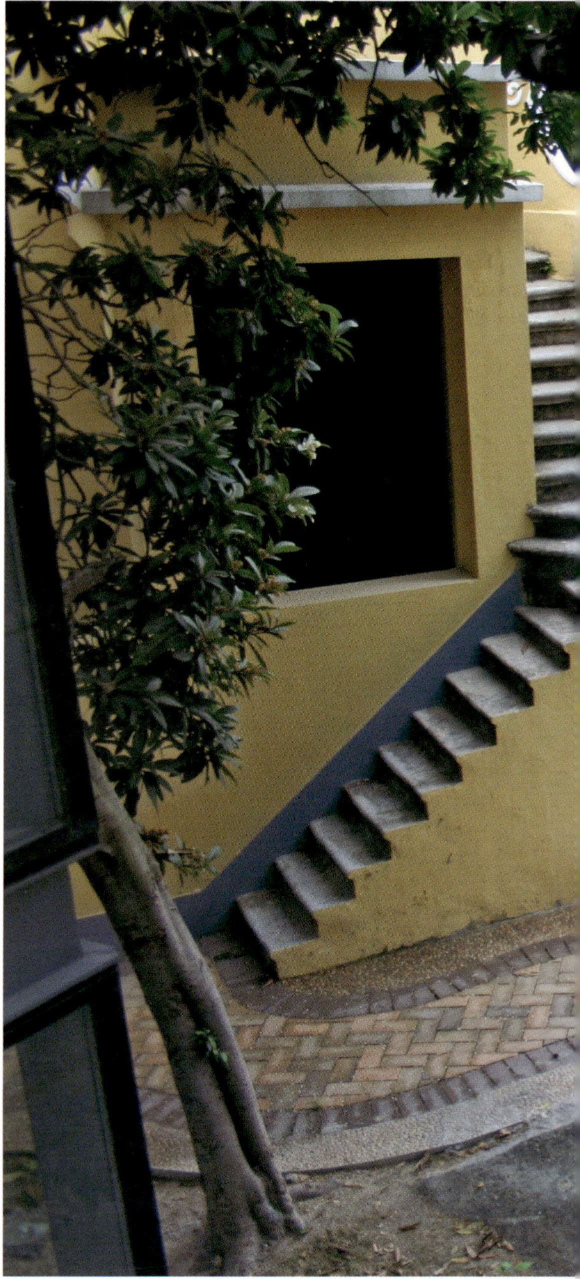

80. Garden in Ho Tung Library

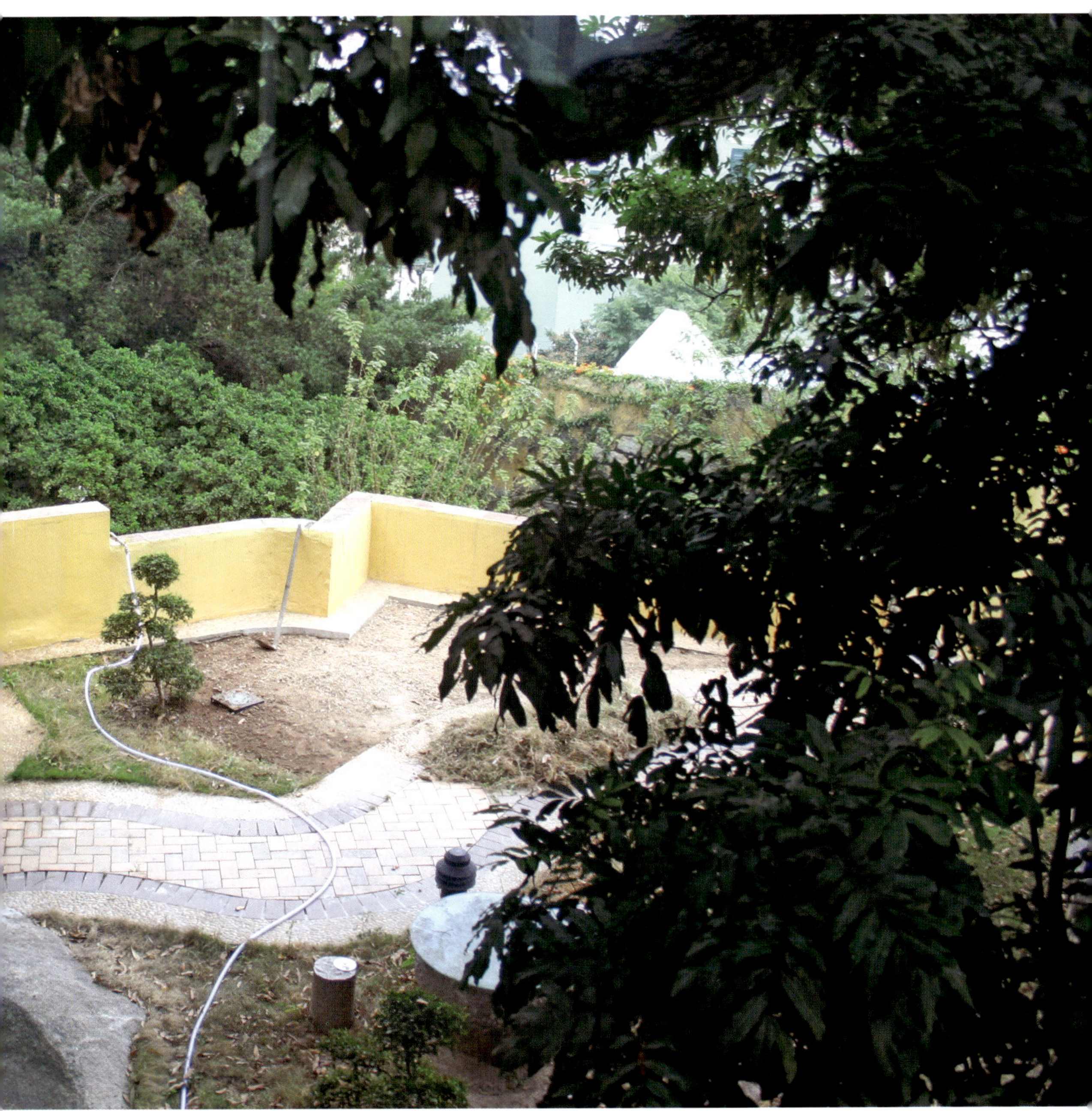

Ts'ui Pen [the scholar he is studying] must at one point have remarked, 'I shall retire to write a book', and at another point, 'I shall retire to construct a labyrinth'. Everyone pictured two projects; it occurred to no one that book and labyrinth were one and the same. The Pavilion of Limpid Solitude was erected in the centre of a garden that was, perhaps, most intricately laid out; that fact might well have suggested a physical labyrinth. Ts'ui Pen died; no-one in all the wide lands that had been his could find the labyrinth. The novel's confusion — confusedness, I mean, of course — suggested to me that it was that labyrinth.[2]

The point that relates to the baroque here is that in making these identifications, one thing is never seen as single; it pluralises and gathers many meanings. The labyrinth is the exact term to describe what is happening within baroque thinking, as is also the library and the Chinese garden. It is not surprising that Borges should have taken his inspiration for the Chinese garden from Cao Xueqin's Chinese novel *Hunglou Meng* (*The Story of the Stone*, or *The Dream of the Red Mansions*), which appeared in 1792, because the novel seems to be analogous to the rococo in its delicacy of style, and also because *Hunglou Meng* exemplifies a garden of 'forking paths' — in both the garden described in the novel and its narrative. In chapter 17 of *Hunglou Meng* the buildings and scenery in the garden (Prospect Garden) must have a name inscribed, to be written, to make the garden complete. There are empty spaces which have to be filled up by Chinese names for the particular part of the garden. Culture (inscription) comes in to make nature (the garden) fully 'natural': in the garden, culture supplements nature, making these two inseparable. In photograph 79, which gives a prospect of the pavilion at the end of the bridge, the Chinese inscriptions over the pavilion that also gives a prospect read, at the top: 'Boundless Scenery', or, 'Boundless Time'. In the same way, the inscription on the left column could be translated 'The Scenery that Entertains People Could be Found Here'. Similar inscriptions can be found on the other side of the pavilion; for example, one inscription (not visible here) reads 'Green Water Brown Hills Twisting Bridge Bending Willow'. These inscriptions name many times over, but there is no single name: there is the sense that naming could go on for ever; there could not be completeness. They are supplementary, they do not define the meaning of that particular part of the garden, but rather, they add to it. They are like allegory, if that is understood as meaning 'speaking other'. Other meanings proliferate, and the subject (or scholar, or father) who has the authority of naming loses mastery because of the disseminating plurality of the names. Rather than limit the meaning of the garden, they add to the play of difference. In Derrida, writing disrupts the sense of language as having certain limitable meaning within it — what Derrida calls 'presence'. Its possibilities appear as it departs from a known and established meaning. The Chinese garden is the place where textuality is glimpsed, the endless play of difference. On that basis, the Lou Lim Ioc Garden suggests a Chinese baroque.

Lou Kau Mansion and the Mandarin's House

The Lou Kau mansion, hard by the Senado Square, in the Travessa da Sé, going up to the Cathedral via the square discussed in chapter 6, is situated in what was once a business area — and before the Opium War (1839–1842) the site of a silk factory — but which later in the nineteenth century became a residential district. It was built around 1889. It belonged to the Chinese bourgeois Lou Kau, who commissioned the Lou Lim Ioc Garden. It shares features with the other Mandarin's House, which is currently under renovation: examples are the 'flower bird' design under the roof. In both Mandarin's Houses and in the A-Ma temple, this motif runs from front to back along the sides of the building.

The Lou Kau mansion, a grey brick building, looks from the front as if it has two storeys, with two slightly protruding wings and a central section, which has a door, and a protective screen behind it,

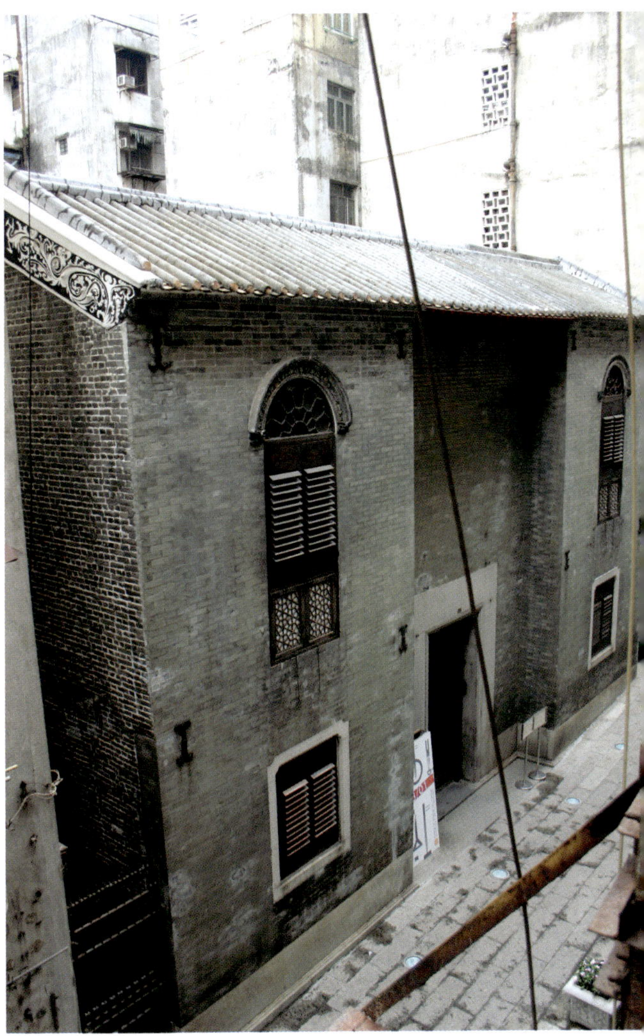

81. Exterior of Lou Kau mansion

and, unlike the side wings, no window above it. The windows to the right and left look classical, western. Because the central panel is set back, the roof eaves overhang the front door and give it protection from the wet.

Nothing on the outside of the house prepares visitors for the inside. Although the inside looks regular, logical, even symmetrical, it is a maze of rooms and empty shafts, or wells, from roof to ground floor, and of windows from rooms looking out into rooms, of windows from rooms looking out into space, and of rooms seen across spaces with intervening gaps and wells. When standing on the first-floor level the courtyards appear as abysses because the eye cannot see any floor below. When standing on the ground-floor level of the courtyards, it is like standing on the floor of a well with the eye being led to look up. Stained glass windows catch the light and allow the eye to pass beyond and also baffle vision. It is the technique of the Chinese garden, carried into domestic architecture, where space is folded into space, and where people look across space to another discrete space, and it is impossible to tell outside from inside. This is deconstructive architecture — where space is so enfolded within space, there is the possibility of thinking of heterotopias; though this is bourgeois space, there is a criticism of bourgeois predictability and uniformity.

To try to describe the interior: beyond the entrance the house has a courtyard which is open to the sky, and rooms are behind it, which culminate at the back in an ancestral hall which looks theatrical, like a stage because of the surrounding Chinese frame resembling a proscenium arch. The theatricality is even further suggested by the presence of doors like wing-doors just to the audience side of the arch. But any suggestion that this theatrical space can be understood singly is demolished when the eyes look up and see that above the proscenium arch is a gallery where the shutters open out so that people can look out at the audience from the upstairs space. The eye's vision is baffled because the audience become spectators and spectators audience. As in all good theatre the distinction between actor and spectator cannot be sustained.[3] The ceremonious space below for the parents to receive visitors is a discrete area, but there is another life above it in the galleried space above, which is at the highest place in the building.

As in baroque art, above the earthly scene, and in an uninterrupted continuum with it, is the space for the gods looking down (see photograph 51: Painting: *The Martyrs of Japan*). In Foucault's discussion of that most baroque picture, *Las Meninas* (1656) by Velasquez (1599–1660), attention is drawn to the way the king and queen, who are being painted by the artist who stands prominently in the middle

82. Theatrical space

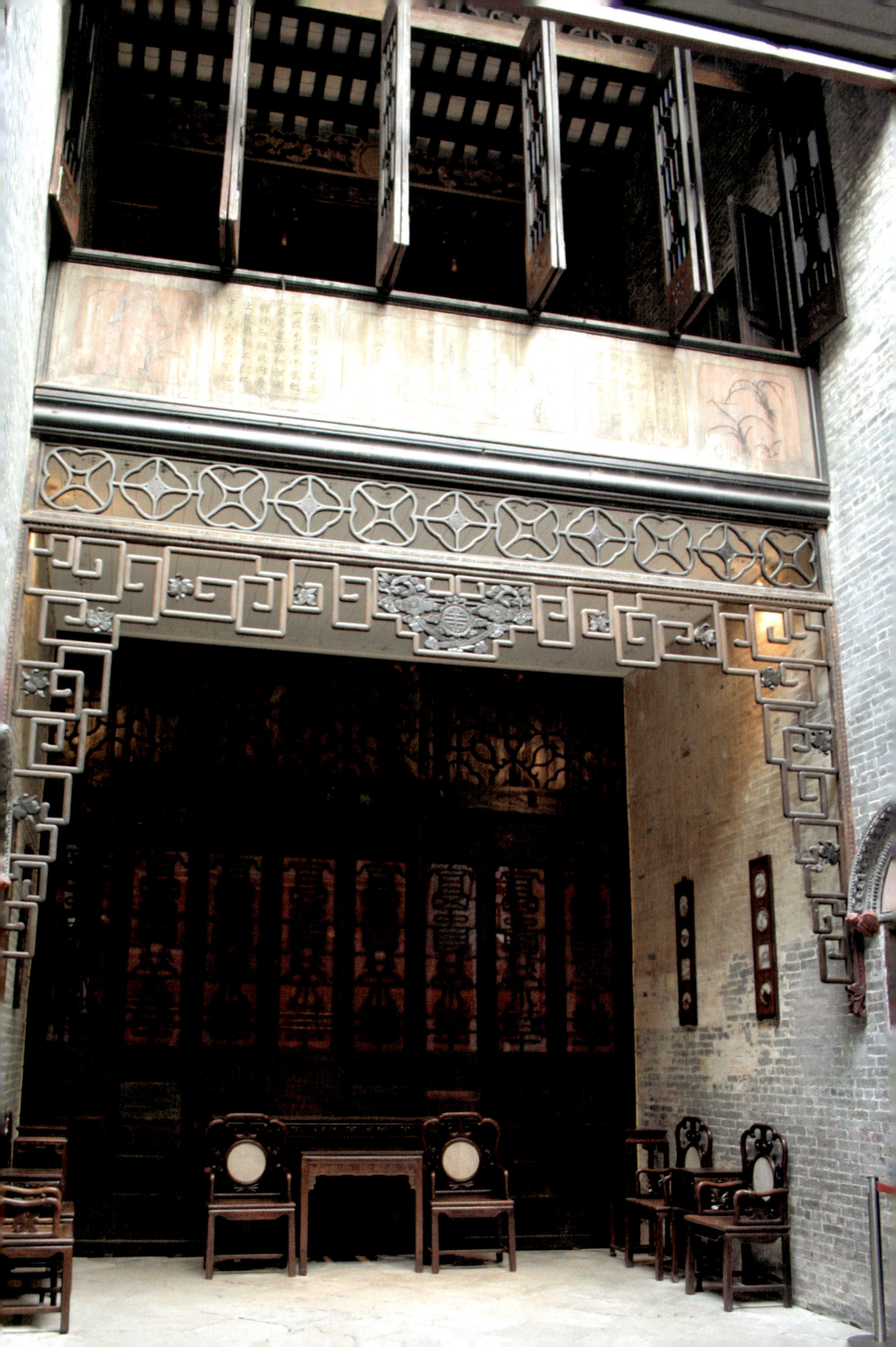

of the picture, are reflected in the mirror which directly faces the viewer. Their position is outside the picture, for they are to be imagined as placed where the spectator is positioned to see it. And though they are outside the picture, they are also inside it, within the mirror. As Foucault puts it, 'the entire picture [meaning the King and Queen, who are in the imaginary picture that Velasquez is painting] is looking out as a scene [note the theatrical reference] for which it is itself a scene'.[4] Visibility, meaning the conditions for vision, is what is painted. The phenomenologist Maurice Merleau-Ponty (1908–1961) who precedes Foucault, says, 'painting celebrates no other enigma but that of visibility'.[5] Visibility is that which enables something to make itself seen. Visibility looks at me, and I look because I am looked at. In Velasquez's painting, however, Foucault's reading disagrees with Merleau-Ponty, because he puts no emphasis on what it is that is looking, only on the people who are objects of display. So that the picture shows what Foucault calls 'the gaze which has organised it, and the gaze for which it is displayed'(15), i.e. the King and Queen, but does not show the invisible subject who creates the picture.

Power is theatrical in the baroque; it is on display, as it is in this ancestral hall, but it knows its display is illusion because real power is elsewhere, invisible.[6] Baroque plays with illusion because it does not tell you where the power lies. As with Velasquez's painting, the owners of the house occupy a double place. They have the privilege of possession, so occupying the space that looks towards the 'stage' and also being in these throne-like chairs on the stage that looks down the length of the building. And, as in all good theatre, behind these thrones is the suggestion of illusion, of screens, and light behind screens, which correspond to the baroque sense of 'life as a dream'. And authority is de-centred, and relativised by the sense of space above the throne-room.

One difference between what Foucault describes in his essay on Velasquez, and how power is on display in the Mandarin's House is this: in the European baroque, the mirror is prominent; for example, in *Las Meninas*, the King and Queen are seen in the mirror. There are no mirrors at all in the Mandarin's House, at least as it is displayed today. In Foucault's argument, the mirror supplements vision, but 'it is in vain that we say what we see; what we see never resides in what we say' (9). This is because power is always invisible. Yet the space of the house teases the eye by making it see across abysses, across different spaces. To recall Lacan, it gives 'the illusion of space'. It tells you that what you see is not all there is; as Foucault writes about the picture, 'perhaps it is hiding as much as and even more than it reveals' (15). So Foucault writes that 'it may be that, in this picture, as in all the representations of which it is, as it were, the manifest essence, the profound invisibility of what one sees is inseparable from the invisibility of the person seeing — despite all mirrors, reflections, imitations, and portraits' (16). I cannot see myself, even (or especially) if I look in a mirror; that is the lesson of *Las Meninas*. The subject must remain unknown to himself. I cannot see what there is to be seen; that is the lesson of the Mandarin's House, and it can therefore afford to dispense with mirrors, which therefore perhaps play a lesser role in Chinese culture. Except, of course, that the rooms that are looked at are mirrors of the room that the spectator is standing in. What I see is illusion. Lacan shows a fundamental invisibility at work in art when discussing *The Ambassadors* (*The Four Fundamental Concepts of Psychoanalysis*). Two years later, Foucault, in 1966, took this other baroque work of art, *Las Meninas*, and argued a similar point as Lacan. The argument also applies to this Chinese work of art, which therefore can be claimed as 'baroque'. The same point holds with the Chinese garden: it is a real space in the city, but it is a space which celebrates itself as illusion.

To resume discussion of the geography of the house: on either side of this central area, there are rooms in the side bays. Doors in the central courtyard, with classical surmountings, suggest that it is an exterior space. The windows have stained glass and interesting ironwork, which recall their equivalents in the seminary at São José.

In São José, the photograph looks out through ironwork and blue glasswork into a garden with

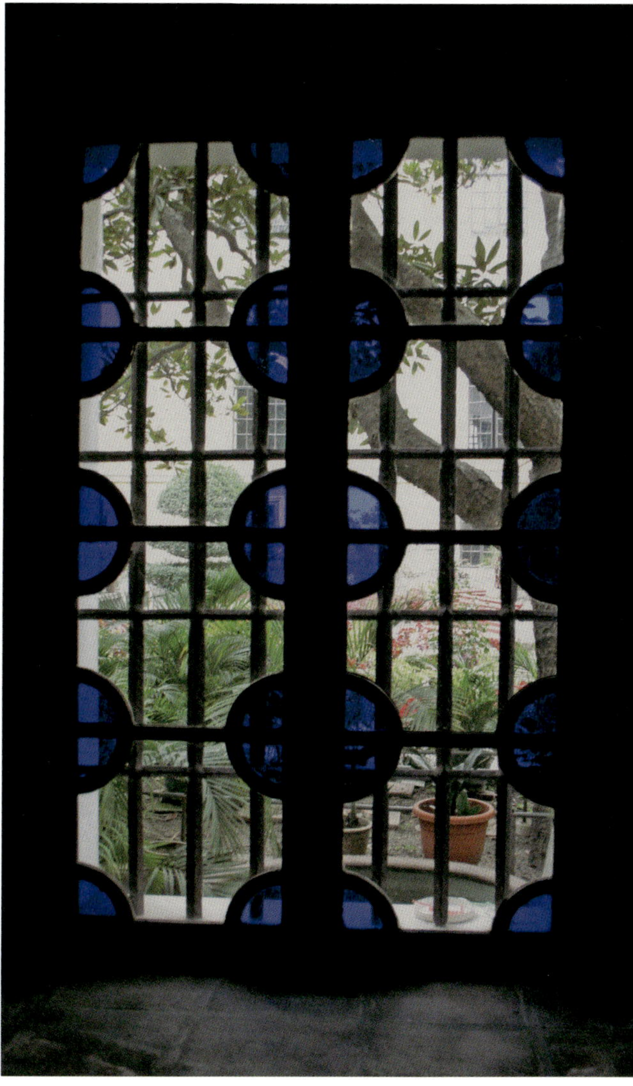

83. Garden and stained glass together

149

a well at the centre. Here the eye passes through, but in the Lou Kau mansion, it does not: the eye sometimes stays with the windows, which then become decoration in themselves, and sometimes the eye passes through layers of space, different 'sheets' of space.[7]

In this secular, 'Chinese baroque', the viewer's eye does not pass through the glasswork to the sky, but into 'sheets of space', which are also folds of space, just as the windows, when opened, are folded back. Ultimately, vision leads through window after window to find, eventually, the street at the back: even there, there is a window to look back at the eye looking. No one can be in a picture without being a picture to someone else. 'And if I am anything in the picture', says Lacan, 'it is always in the form of [...] the stain, the spot'.[8] One meaning of 'stain' has been given (see above, p. 95) in considering the anamorphosis in Holbein's painting which baffles vision. But while 'spot' means 'stain', it is also a pun, meaning a 'spotlight', that which gives a pool of light. In the theatrical space of the house, open spaces act as spotlights, giving light and illumination. The effect is of darkness and light together. The effect of being in the house is to be both occluded and to be brought out, as if in a baroque picture. The house gives both closings and openings.

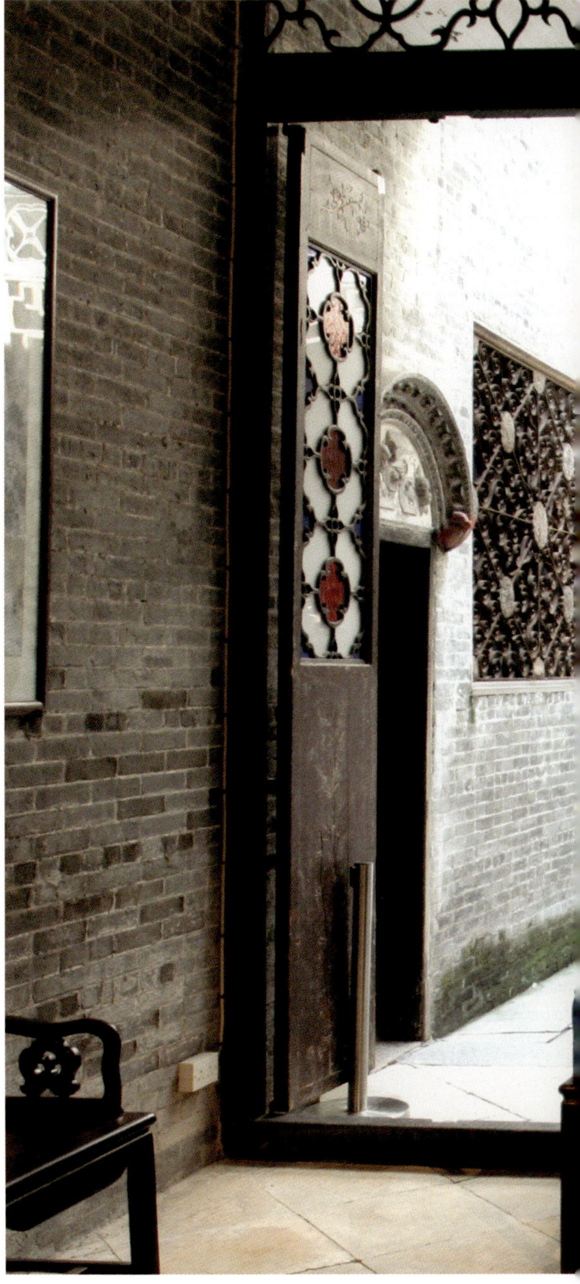

84. Stained glass

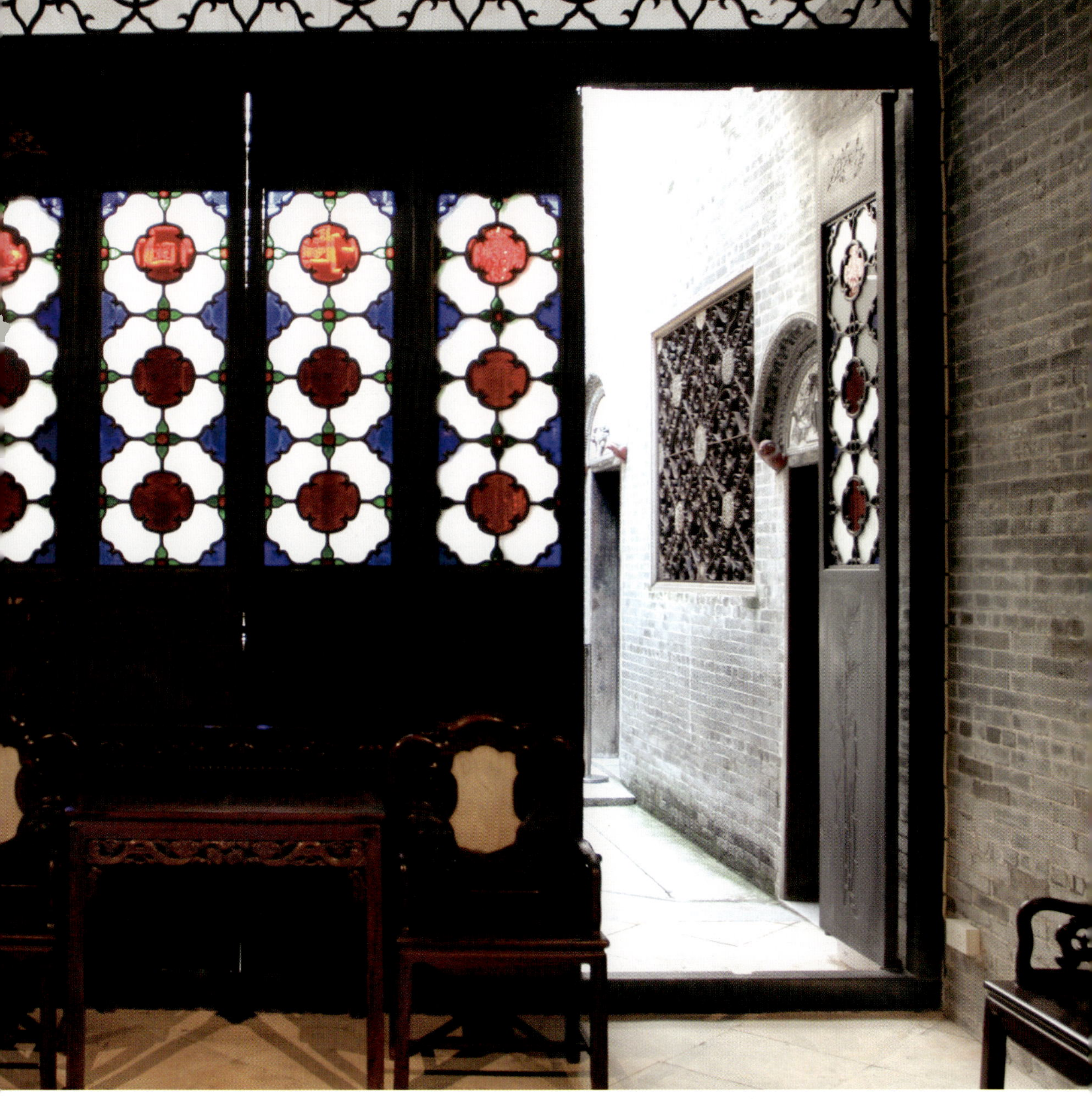

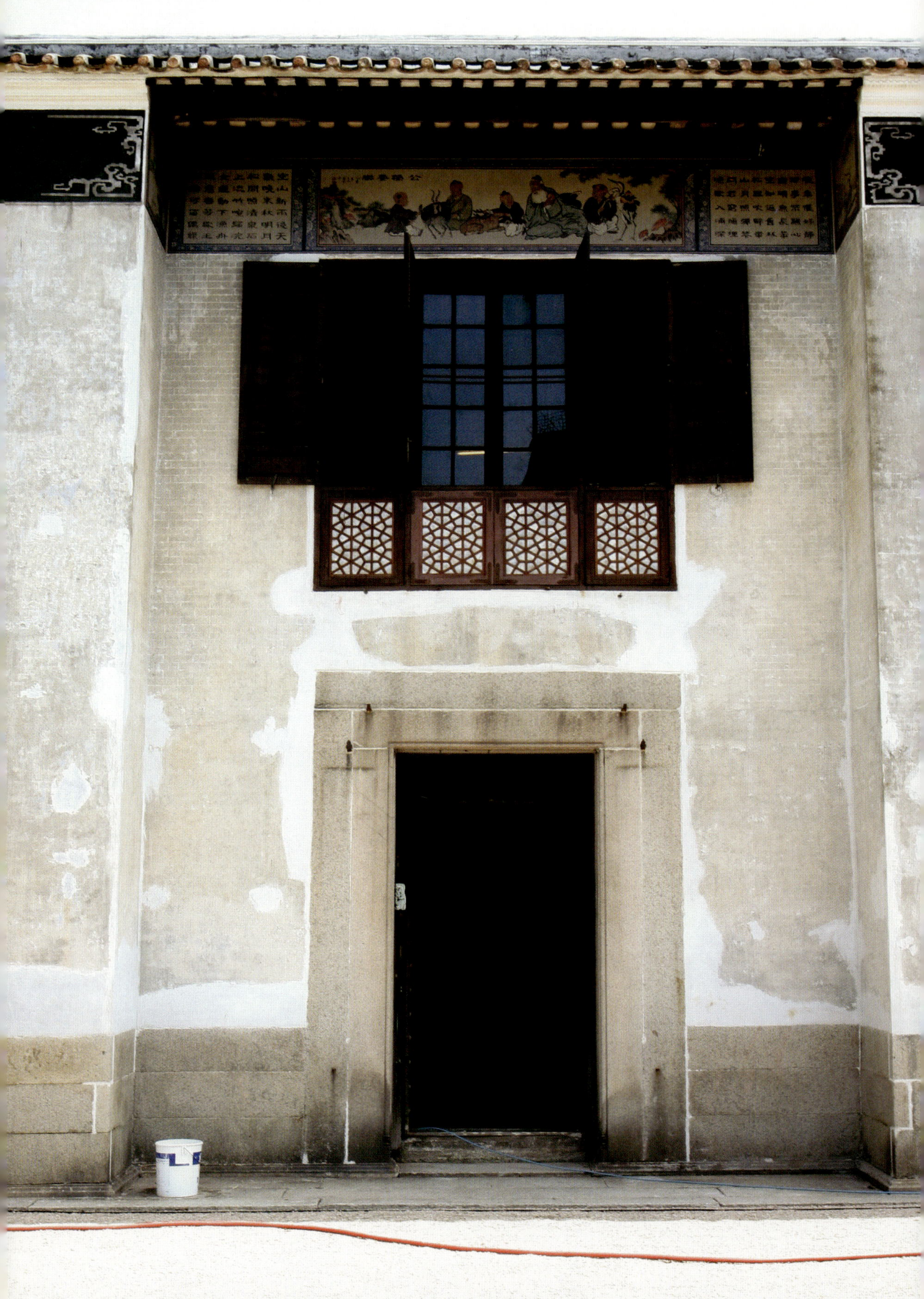

Photograph 85 shows three levels in the Mandarin's House, the door, windows and pictures which are on three sides in a recess underneath the roof. The frontal picture shows a grandfather and four children playing, with animals like a lamb, a deer and a crane, surrounded by trees and rockery, perhaps in a garden. The top window is like a *jalousie* window (French: means both jealousy and a window with blinds and shutters, from which one can see without being seen.)[9] To right and left of the picture appear poems celebrating old age and nature.

In the Lou Kau mansion, the side courtyard wall has at its summit writing extolling the virtues of study in order to become an official. In the middle, there is a raised picture showing birds soaring to the heavens and a lion on top of a hill surrounded by trees and flowers, which are not in proportion. This symbolises the rewards of scholarship. And beyond that level, surmounting a protective grid above the courtyard, a wall design has two parts: a central roundel of mountains and water, with fishermen in boats, the whole picked out by being surrounded by bright shapes, of fruits, such as starfruit, bananas, pineapples, oranges, cucumbers, and of animals such as chickens, birds, fishes, and, above and below the roundel, faces. The one above is of a red bat,

the marker of well-being. (These red bats are just visible as corbels on the doors in photograph 82, except that their faces are those of lions.) In the design, the animal below is yellow, and may also be a bat. Bats are also found in the labyrinthine structure of the design enclosing or being enclosed by the objects which have been collected as if in a Chinese cabinet, like a case of curiosities. It is rococo, playful, and near to kitsch — but a lack of blandness in it just keeps it from that. Certainly, it is the aestheticising of the life of the official, to place these *jeux d'esprit* (jokes, or games of wit) at the top of the house, where they cannot be expected to be seen in any detail. The eye goes up and up till it is lost trying to see the heavens; the cornucopia (a horn of plenty) or sense of abundance in the design suggests that there is no need for jealousy.

85. Mandarin's House

A-Ma Temple

The last example is the A-Ma temple. Chapter 6 referred to Matteo Ricci on the 'idol erected [...] called Ama. It may be seen today and the place is called Macao, on the Bay of Ama'. The A-Ma temple is at the base of Penha Hill, in the south-west part of Macao, right on the sea front, land now reclaimed. Older than colonial 'Macao' and giving its name to it, it associates with other Ming (1368–1644) temples: those of Kun Iam, a goddess of the sea (her huge, modern statue is near Macao's Cultural Centre, on reclaimed land, and her temple is to the southeast of Mong-Ha Hill), and Lin Fung ('hill of lotus'). Lin Fung temple, to the northwest of Mong-Ha Hill, includes a statue to Governor Lin Zexu, who attempted to repress the opium trade that Britain was practising on the Chinese. (The place where he adulterated opium with chalk in 1839, an incident which proved to be the beginning of the outbreak of the Opium War in 1840, is in Humen, in the Pearl River estuary).

In the A-Ma temple, Ricci's 'idol' is A-Ma, once a fishergirl, now a goddess of the sea. The photograph shows an entrance on the left which leads up towards three separate temples, climbing up the hillside. On the right a circular, full-moon-shaped window looks into the main courtyard, behind which is the main hall. Four characters are seen above the window: they are a demand for unity. Above that appears a vision of a rocky landscape,

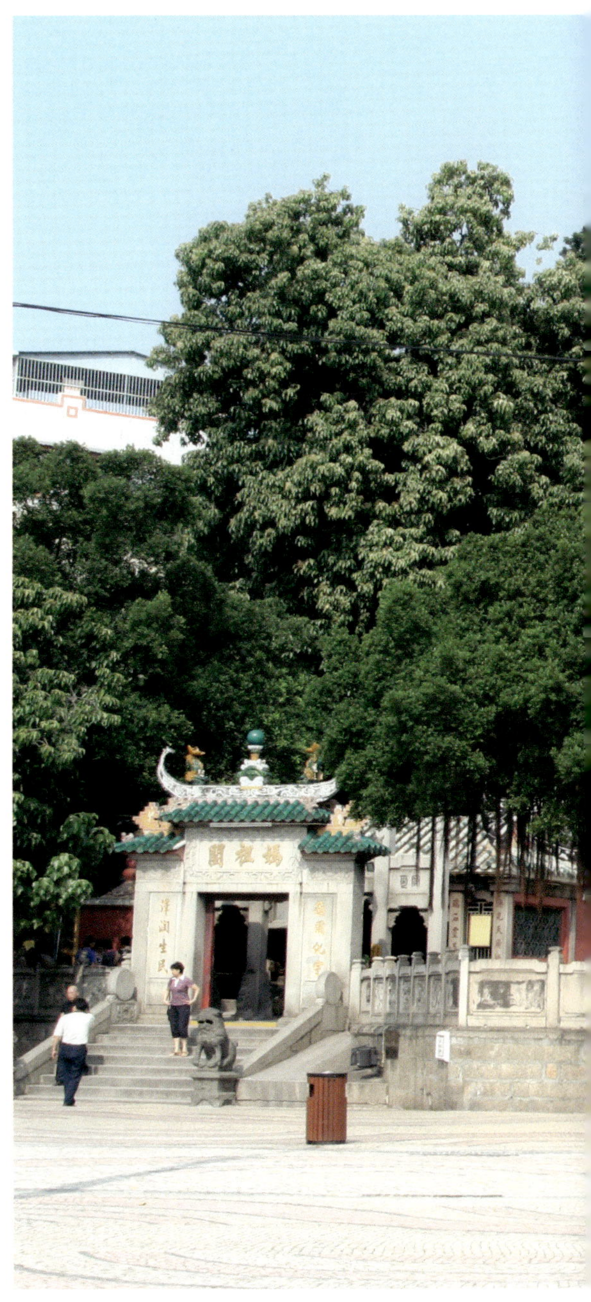

86. *A-Ma temple*

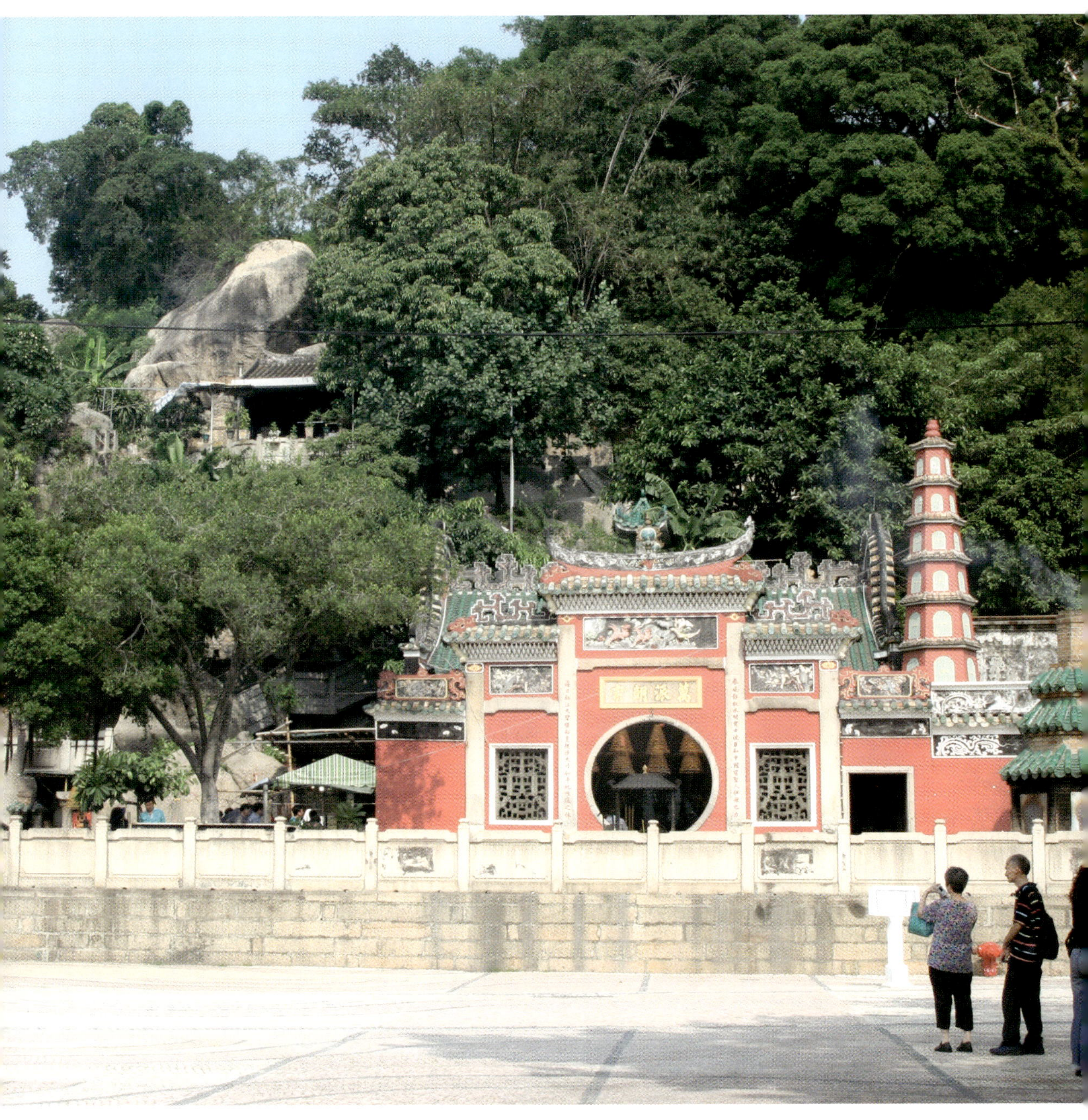

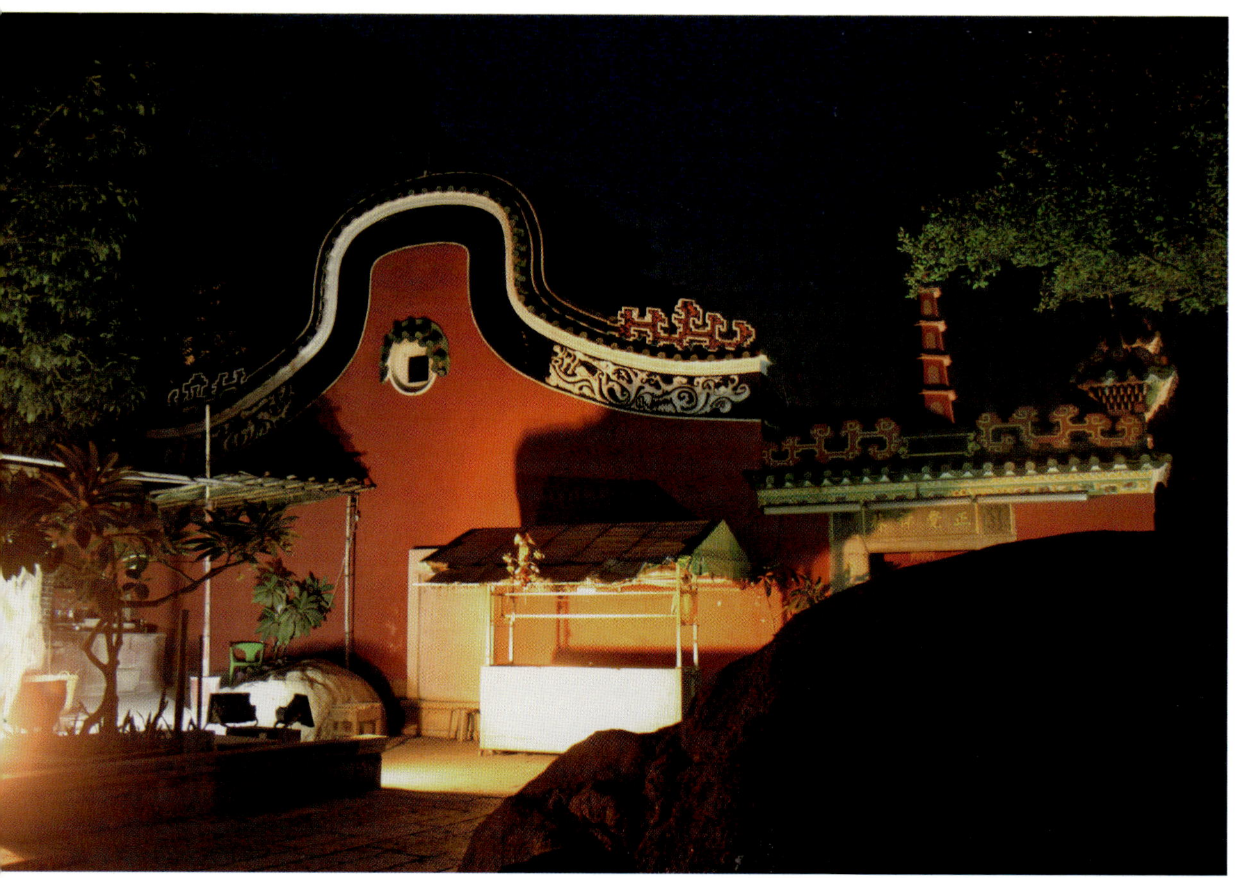

87. Exterior of main hall

with two twin-tailed mythical lions and three birds. The two characters for 'lion' allows for the pun which implies 'everything that happens [what is signified in two lions] happens according to your wish'; the appearance of these lions is therefore playful, punning. Above this appears a traditional Chinese roof, surmounted by the outline of a ship design, and in the middle, topmost of all, appears a design where a pearl, or gem, or globe, is held aloft, the architectural design implying fire.

In photograph 87, we look at the left-hand wall and roof of the main hall, so that the pagoda, also visible in photograph 86, is seen behind the hall. The main hall of the temple, behind both the façade and the courtyard that it gives onto, is of one storey, and its roof is a single rise and descent (compare the double roof in photograph 33, of the Sam Kai Vui Kun temple, which may just be glimpsed half way down the street on the right). The roof, in both cases, reverses the western idea, which pitches the roof at the centre as one looks at the building; here the roof's summit is as if it has been turned ninety degrees, so that only from the side is the rise and fall visible: but this gives to the architect the opportunity of creating a curve for the gable, whose sinuosity seems baroque-like, however anachronistic the term may seem. And yet this gable also has the function of limiting what would happen in the case of fire. The elaborate wave-like roof-top of A-Ma temple evokes a sense of femininity, perhaps echoing the goddess worshipped in the temple, as a contrast to the masculine hero worshipped in Sam Kai Vui Kun temple (see chapter 4) under a twin A-shaped roof-top.

The denial of a single sharp apex softens and replaces rigid symmetry with the line of beauty, which is decorated in four bands, one of them being the green Chinese tiles, which are also seen making up the lintel above the roundel in the wall, and which is decorated in a style that suggests popular art. There are intricate and abstract patterns, in a full-bellied shape formation (the technical term is 'flower bird belly'), now black on white, now white on black, and with designs above in ceramics. The design here replicates that of the Mandarin's House (photograph 85) and of the temple in Coloane (photograph 76). Beneath, under the awning, appears an inscribed stele set against the wall.

The next chapter opens with a discussion of what use European colonisation made of this temple.

Chapter 9

Colonialism and Modernity

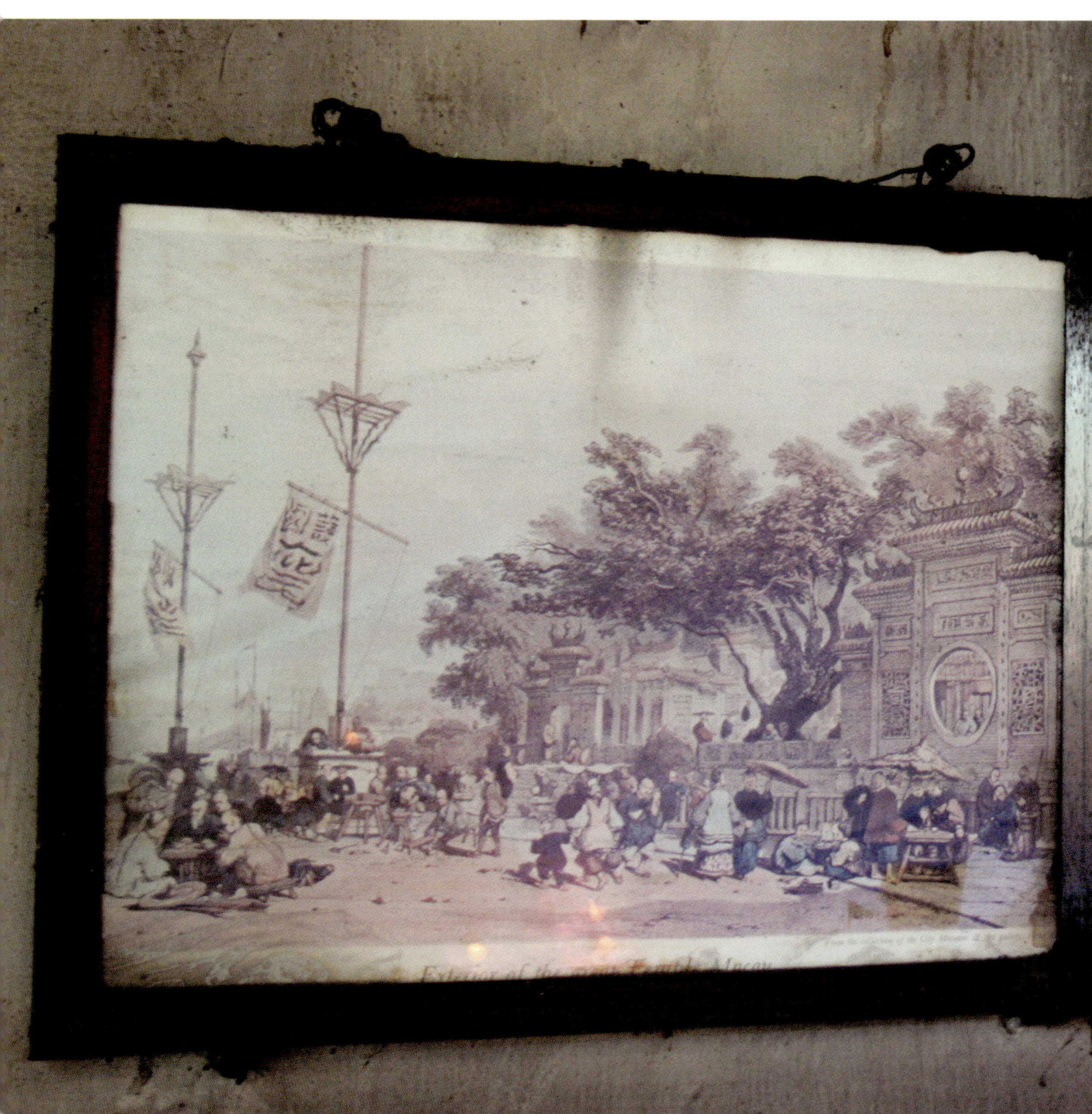

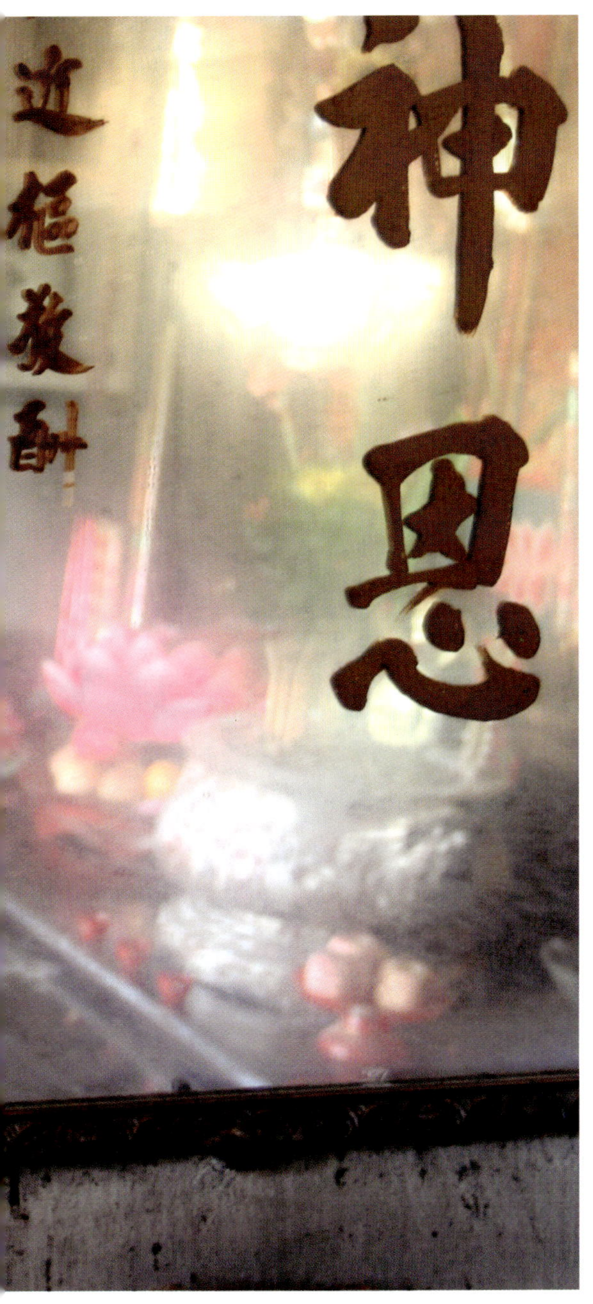

88. Interior of A-Ma temple

The A-Ma temple was repeatedly painted by Western artists, for example by George Chinnery (1774–1852) and Auguste Borget (1808–1877).[1] A copy of a faded Borget representation appears adjacent to the mirror in the photograph, which shows the interior of the highest of the shrines which are set into the hillside. Chinnery, London-born and trained at the Royal Academy, painted scenes from four different colonial situations: the English in Ireland, where he lived from 1795 to 1802; the English in Calcutta, where he lived from 1802 until 1825; and Macao where he went after leaving India, and where he was to die in 1852. The fourth is the British in Hong Kong, which Chinnery visited and painted in 1846. Chinnery also visited Guangzhou, eighty miles up the Pearl River, where foreign merchant-houses existed in the 'concession' yielded by the Qing rulers to the British in 1760.

Guangzhou, Amoy (Xiamen) and Macao had been opened as ports to westerners in 1685, but this had come under restriction. France established a factory in Guangzhou in 1728, Sweden in 1731, America in 1784. By 1759, trade was restricted to Guangzhou, with thirteen merchants (the Co-*hong*) licensed to deal with foreign trade; they built a site for factories (*hongs* — first citation in the *OED* gives 1726) outside the city walls. Guangzhou became part of London's visual culture through the 'dioramas' (i.e. panoramic views of cities) which were on public

159

display; a panorama of Guangzhou was shown by Robert Burford in his Panorama building off London's Leicester Square in 1838.[2] The street where the thirteen *hongs* existed remains in present-day Guangzhou: Shishanhang Lu.

Western paintings of Macao require discussion of 'modernity', whose art form, the critic Linda Nochlin argues, is the fragment; this introduces the idea of the ruin.[3] Modernity was defined by the French poet Charles Baudelaire (1821–1867) in his essay, 'The Painter of Modern Life' (1859), as 'the transient, the fleeting, the contingent'. It suggests particularly the conditions of new urban culture, especially in Paris.[4] Chinnery's art is less interested in the 'fleeting moment'. While colonialism associates with modernity, colonial art, it seems, tries not to be modern. While colonialism depends on transport, movement is restricted in Chinnery's Macao to junks and sampans; even his portraits of traders, such as William Jardine or James Matheson, are static figures, with no ships seen in landscapes or seascapes behind them. His portraits of Tanka boatwomen make them figures of the shore.[5] The nearest he approaches 'the fleeting moment' is in a representation of the Praya Grande, where high winds are suggested by the flag blowing and by the fishermen's reactions to the waves. As if emphasising fleeting change, the sun shines on the convent on Penha Hill in the background.

The photograph shows one way of thinking about modern Macao. It shows a street near the Inner Harbour. At first sight it seems unexceptional, with modern high-rise flats and shops, but the middle block has cut in two an older arcade of shops and lower-rise houses, leaving the arch on the left completely suspended, while the building on the left itself has been already cut into by another building of different height. The busy street does not notice the change.

In the nineteenth century, Baudelaire felt himself a victim of the effects of the rebuilding of Paris, which he describes in 'Le cygne' (The Swan) (1859). One verse runs:

> Paris change! mais rien dans ma mélancholie
> N'a bougé! palais neufs, échafaudages, blocs,
> Vieux faubourgs, tout pour moi devient allégorie,
> Et mes chers souvenirs sont plus lourds que des
> rocs.

> [Paris changes! But nothing in my melancholy
> has changed. New palaces, scaffoldings, blocks,
> old neighbourhoods, everything for me becomes
> allegory,
> and my dear memories are heavier than rocks.][6]

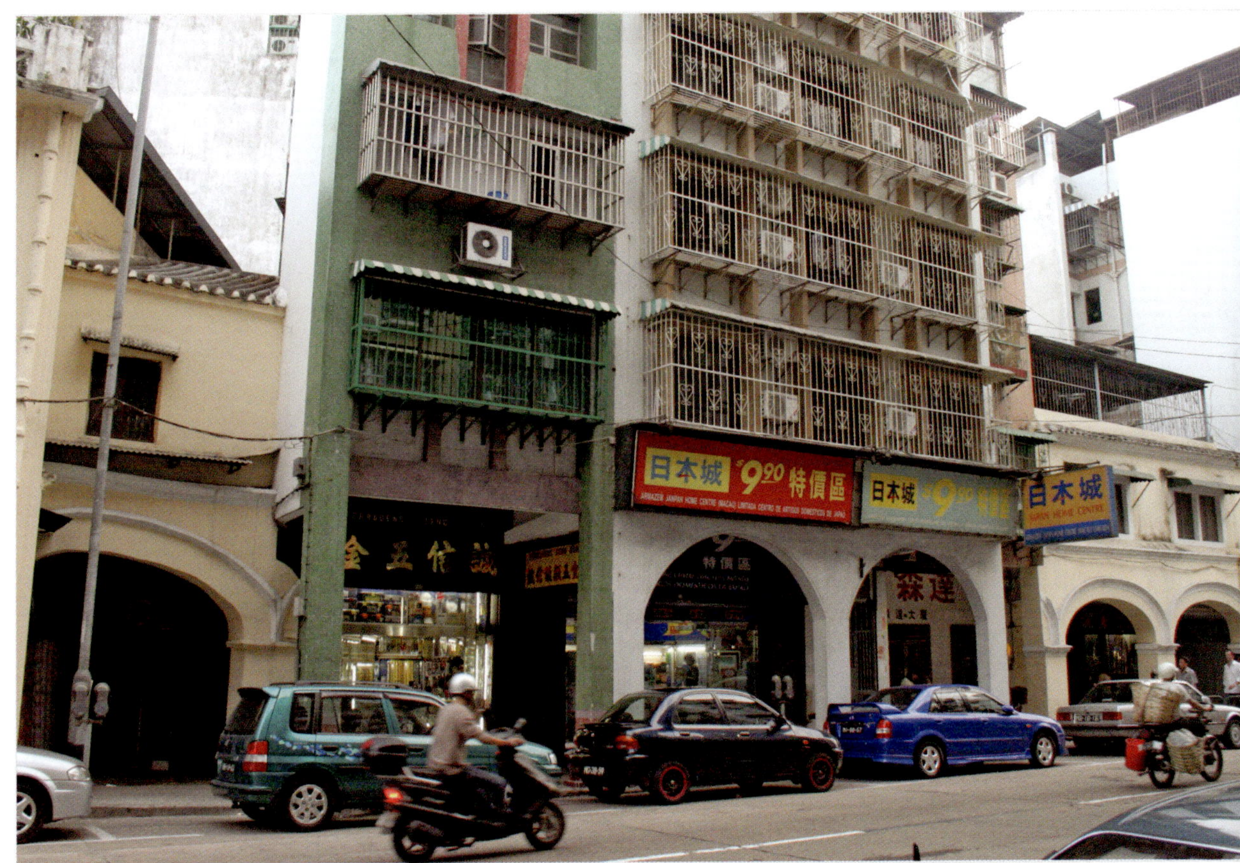

89. Inner Harbour road

Everything in the restructuring of Paris turns the city into something unreal, having no more reality than allegory. In allegory, one thing substitutes for another in an interchangeability which can go on forever, like the 'new palaces, scaffoldings, blocks, / old neighbourhoods' of the poem. Nothing seems real in its own right.

These photographs of a street scene (Pátio da Lenha) illustrate tradition, modernity and decay. They are taken from two angles to bring out contrasts: the age of the street as indicated by the cobbles and signs of a drain in photograph 91, which looks down towards the shrine, towards the Portuguese/Indian word 'INDIGO' which is matched by the colour of the motorbike. The shrine appears to the right in photograph 90, at the back in photograph 91, in close-up in photograph 92. Photograph 90 draws attention to the Chinese house, whose ornamentation beneath the gable suggests that it was not poor. It has red paint at ground-floor level, because of the shrine (on the left) to Shi Kang Tong ('The Brave Stone') of Tai Shan (the holy mountain in Shandong Province), and another shrine to the local land god on the right (photograph 92). Local and 'foreign' spirits are juxtaposed. Besides the two central shrines, there are four on the right, one on the left. The diamond shape above the central shrines has the character meaning 'prosperity', or 'good fortune'. It is repeated in the papers stuck to the wall, and on the front of the pot which contains the joss-sticks.

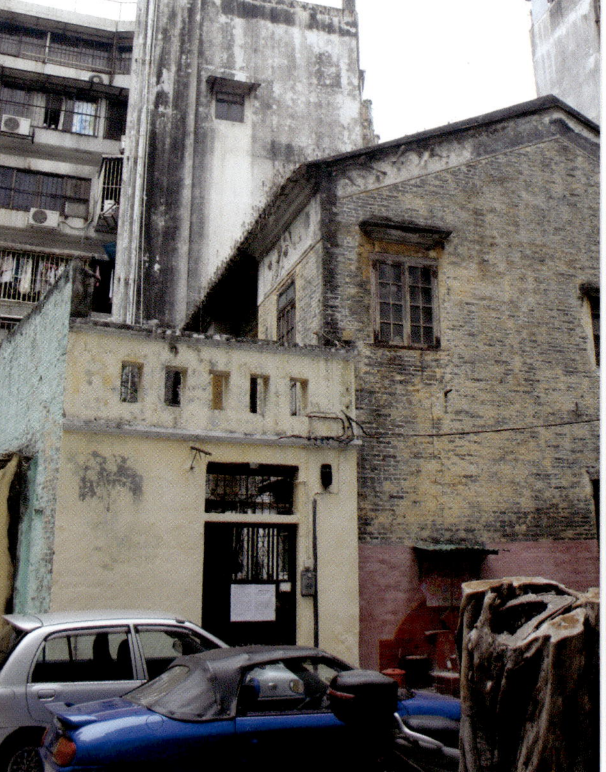

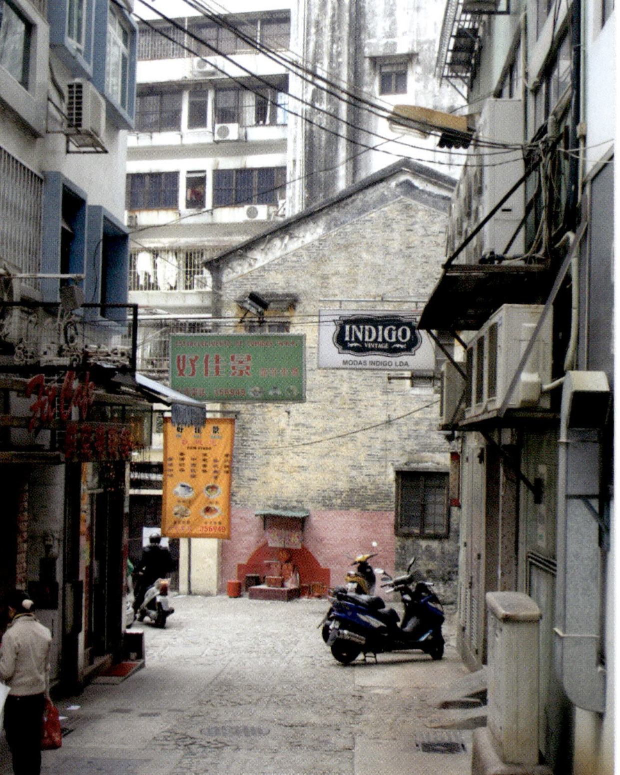

▲ 90, 91. Street scene　　　　　　　　　　　　　　　*92. Shrine ▶*

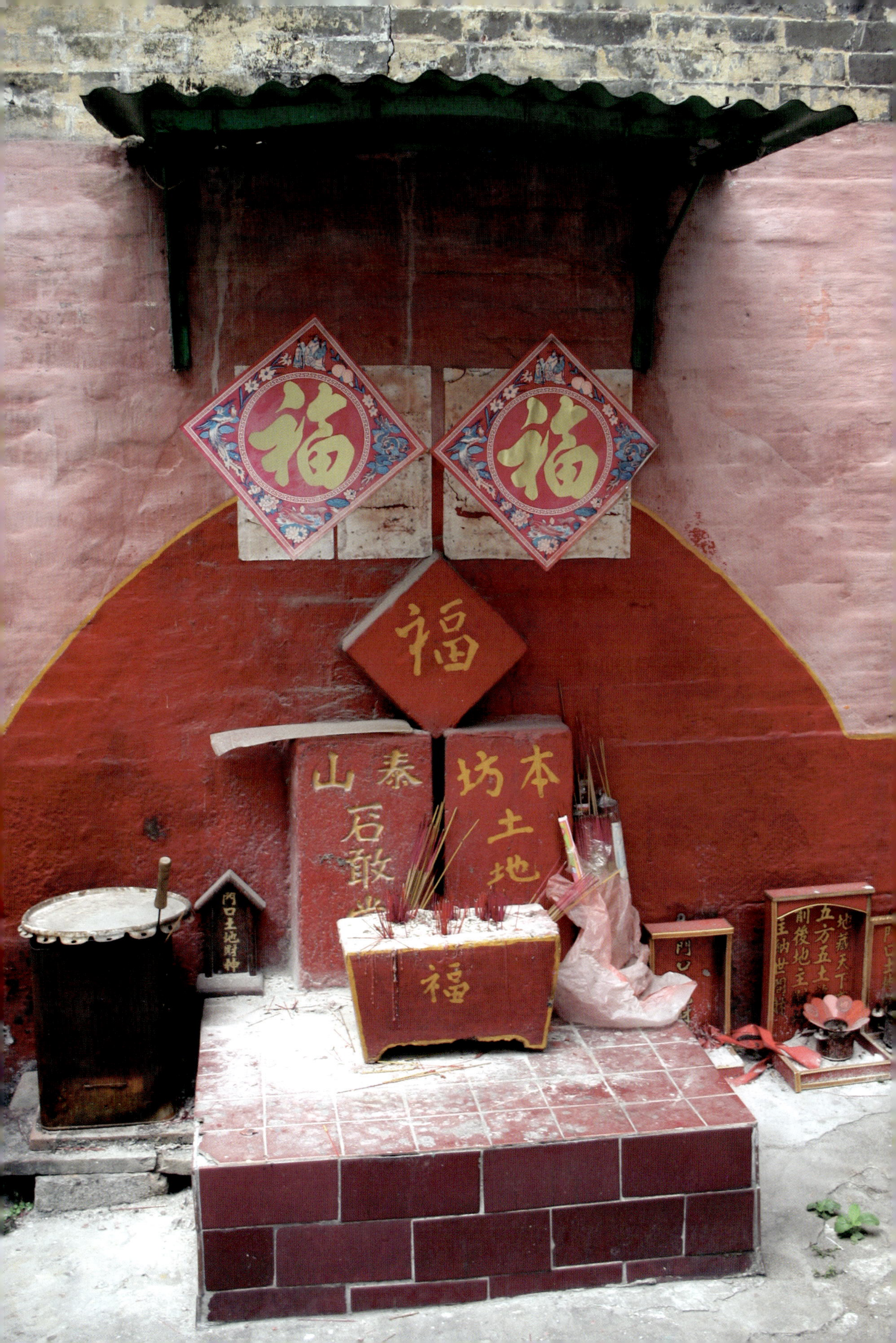
福
福
福
泰山石敢當
本坊土地
門口土地財神
福
地藏天下
五方五土
前後地主
門口

There are also, to the left, two closed containers for burning paper money. One was designed for this purpose, the other has been recycled from being used as a container. Since it is not 'proper' to put these unused joss-sticks next to the shrine, it seems that no boundary is recognised between the sacred and the profane. This miniature temple has been added to a pre-existent wall; the green shelter completes it in an improvised manner, being also pre-used material that has been included here like bricolage.

But these elements of tradition have met with signs of modernity. The Chinese house has had pushed up against it another building, due to be demolished. Older high-rise buildings appear behind, and in the front of the picture there is the stump of a tree: another ruin. But everything speaks of discontinuity and change, even the motorbike and the cars, two parked, one passing, like everything else in photograph 90. Photograph 91 shows how the 'memories' in the tree and the shrine and in the Chinese house have been enframed by high-rise forms of the modern.

The photographs show that when everything in the city is under change, it is no longer the place of permanent structures but of memories which may persist, haunt and weigh the person down, though the form of the city has changed. Old buildings which have been bulldozed have gone but they stick in the memory ('memories are heavier than rocks'), and new buildings do not have the same reality.

Benjamin follows Baudelaire in making the 'modern' city the place of melancholy and of allegory, and so, like the baroque. Buildings may be thought of as allegorical. Their ruin relates to melancholia, and produces memories, 'souvenirs' in Baudelaire's poem. These heavy 'souvenirs' compare not only with the 'souvenirs' which are the little cakes made and sold in souvenir shops (see photograph 6), but with the plentiful light 'souvenirs' which flatten memory that are offered in hi-tech photography; the plurality of photographic images guarantees that the individual picture can never be looked at. To consider the baroque is to engage with memory, and with the memory of ruins.

Baudelaire saw the paintings of Borget, who had sketched Guangzhou, Macao and Hong Kong in 1838, and reviewed his art when writing about the Parisian Salon of 1845:

> Eternal views of India and China. Doubtless it is all very well done, but they are too much like travel-essays or accounts of manners and customs. There are people, however, who sigh for what they have never seen — such as the boulevard de Temple, or the galeries de Bois! M. Borget's pictures make us sigh for that China where the very breeze, according to M. Heine, takes on a comical sound as it slips past the little hanging bells, and where

nature and man cannot look at each other without laughing.[7]

The metropolitan critic comments on underdevelopment and on colonial nostalgia, and discusses the Borget painting visible next to the mirror in the A-Ma temple (photograph 88). The temple is mirrored by Borget's art, but the colonial mirroring is patronising; but here, it has been absorbed into the everyday life of the temple, the profane alongside the sacred. Baudelaire's sense is that China has been rendered comic, miniature, insufficiently differentiated from the non-human. Any metropolitan, Parisian taste that likes these pictures responds to what has never been seen. Baudelaire argues against the art which paints the colonial scene.

In contrast to the sense of the temple as rural, in a site of under-development, is the temple in an urban situation, adjacent to a market.

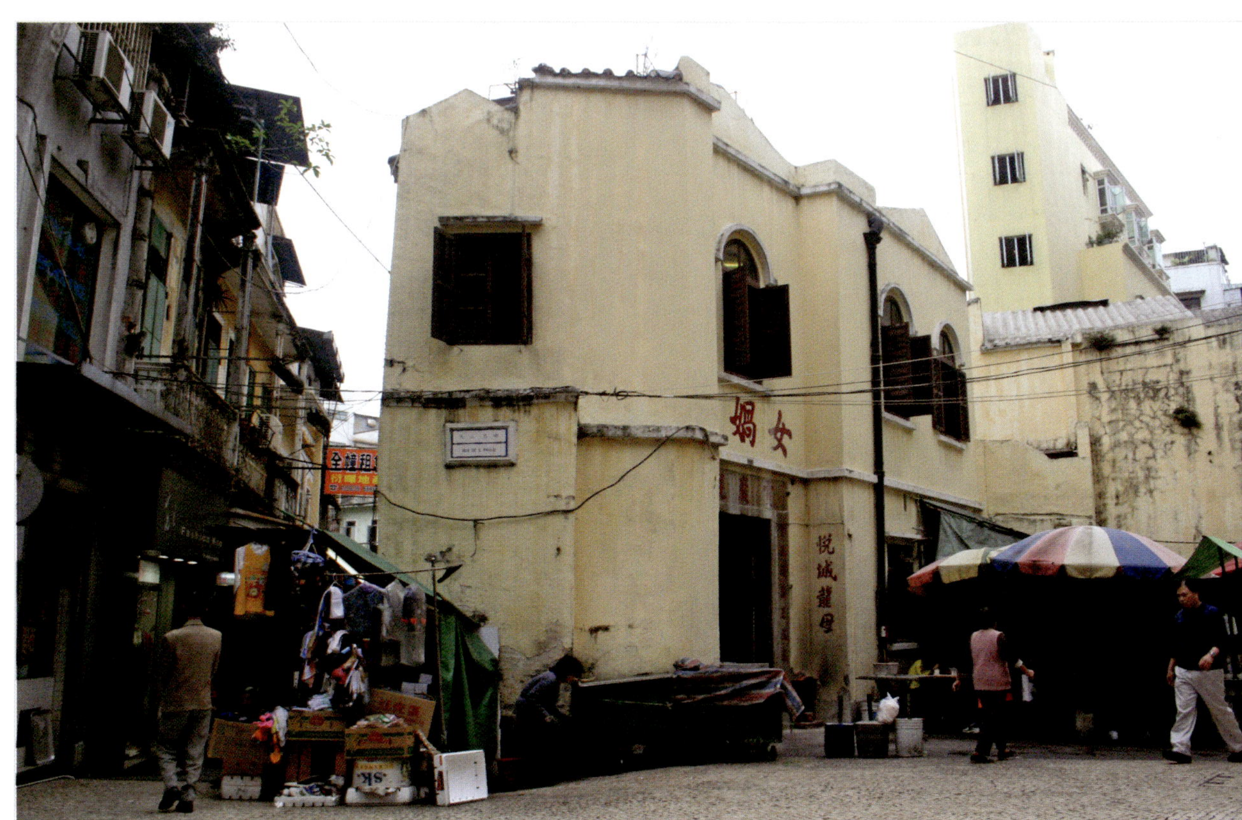

93. Temple of the Snake Goddess

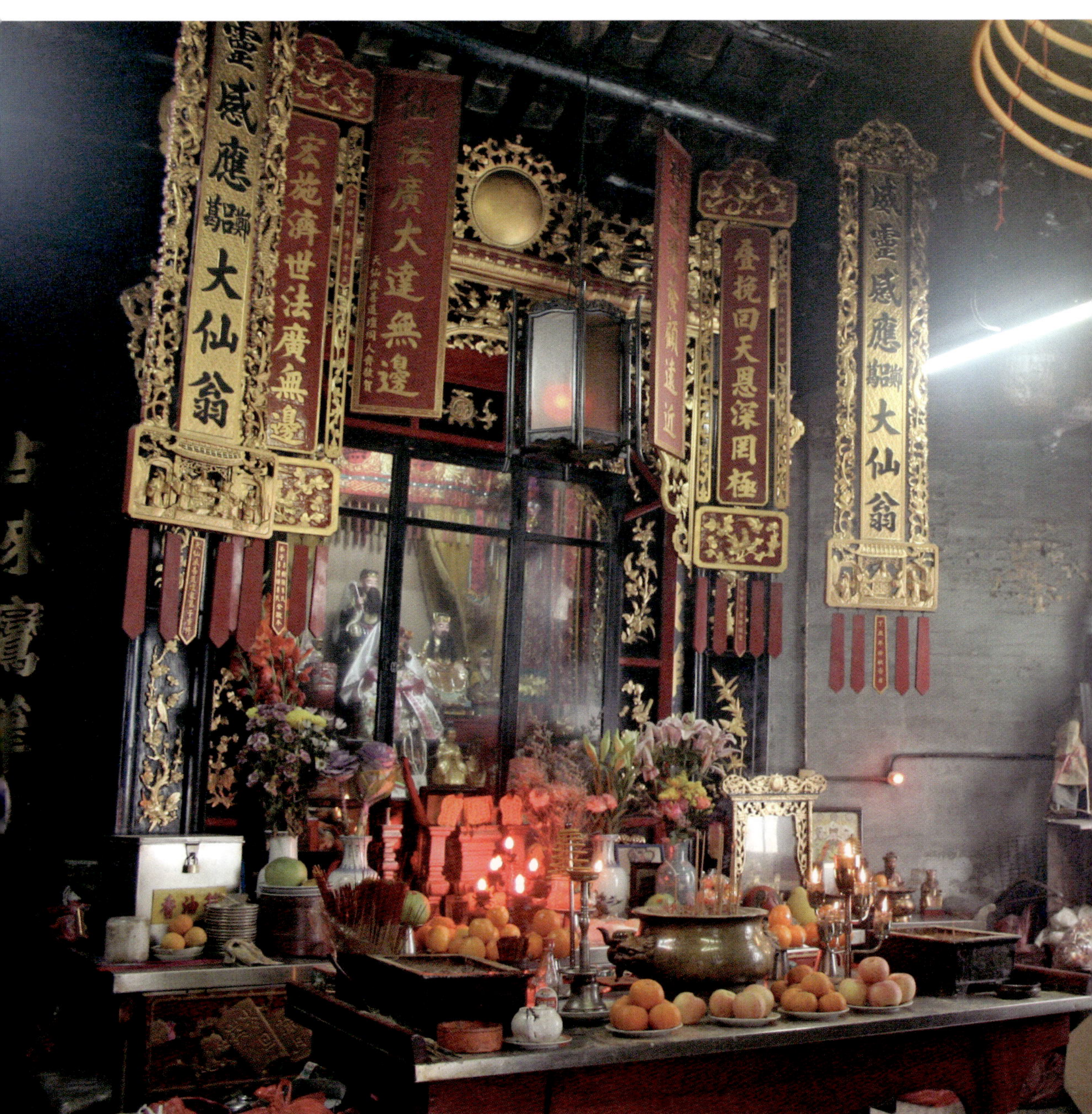

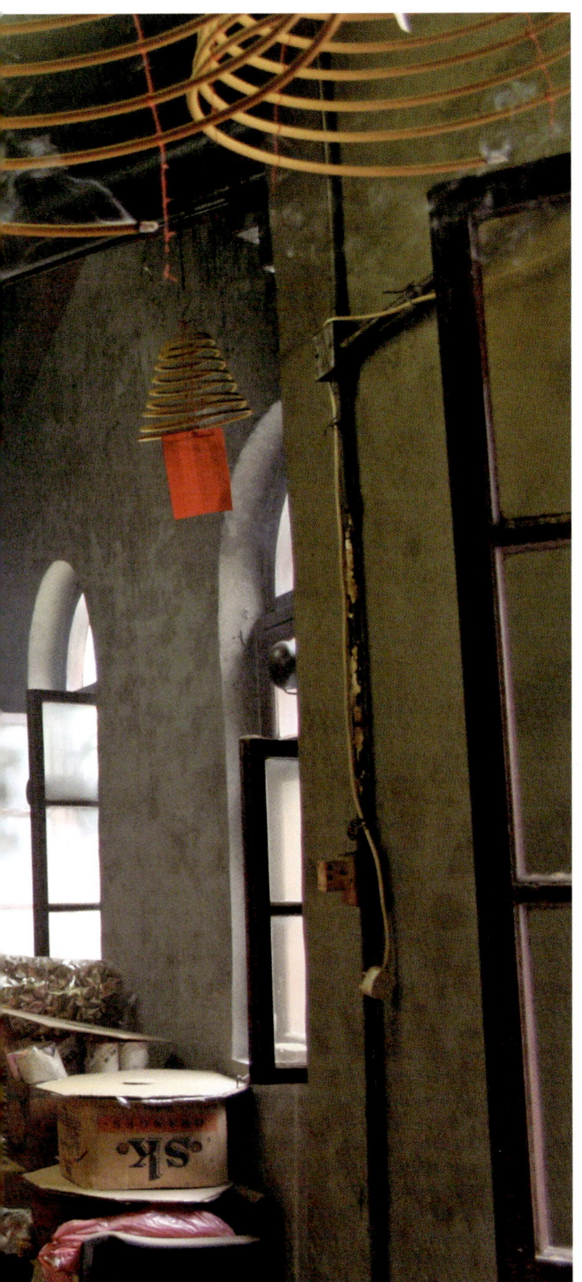

94. The interior of Temple of the Snake Goddess

The temple of the Snake Goddess, on the Rua de São Paulo, with the words 'Daoist Temple of the Holy Rock' written on the lintel so that it houses two divinities, is distinctive, being enshrined in the fold formed by two streets meeting and creating so narrow a space that the shrine must be placed upstairs. No two walls are symmetrical here, while the urban setting makes it appropriate for the shrine to have windows; the temple is simply an ordinary house. A temple associated with prostitutes, which adds to its urban character, it was originally situated in the market place, but that temple burned down in 1914.

Borget's pictures of the A-Ma temple, seen on an angle and idealised in its extensiveness and completedness, is a background to between forty and fifty people, all diminished in size. Some are walking, some seated at tables: there seems little attempt at individuation. Save for their size, these are the figures of the opening chorus of an Italian opera where everything is on display. The sense of urgency in the movement of the people (even the wind seems strong, in the way it blows the flags) infantilises them, but nothing in the picture justifies this urgency. Another picture, in an incompletely rendered setting, shows two Chinese seated, discussing business over a basket of fish, with three others watching on, one in profile on steps above, one leaning over in a bent position, one older man watching, also in profile. The annotation refers to Chinese faces that Borget says 'beamed with joy'. It is as if self-consciousness is denied them; they are miniaturised by their qualities.[8]

This is also partly true of Chinnery. Macao is made English — even its Portuguese aspect is diminished. He has a will to diminish the size of the Chinese figure, as in a pen-and-ink sketch of São Domingos church with street vendors, where he has written in shorthand 'figures correct right size'.[9] This picture exists in a tiled reproduction, part of a mural below the Cathedral Square of photograph 55.

The reproduction shows how the image changes its signification. Chinnery sketched São Domingos, which was then new, having been substantially rebuilt in 1828, with Chinese who are thereby reduced by the picture, in the sense that it does not take their 'otherness' seriously. Now the reproduction of Chinnery becomes a diminishing of his work. The church that he depicts is just round the corner from the mural, and there is a nice touch of parody in turning Chinnery into so many tiles.

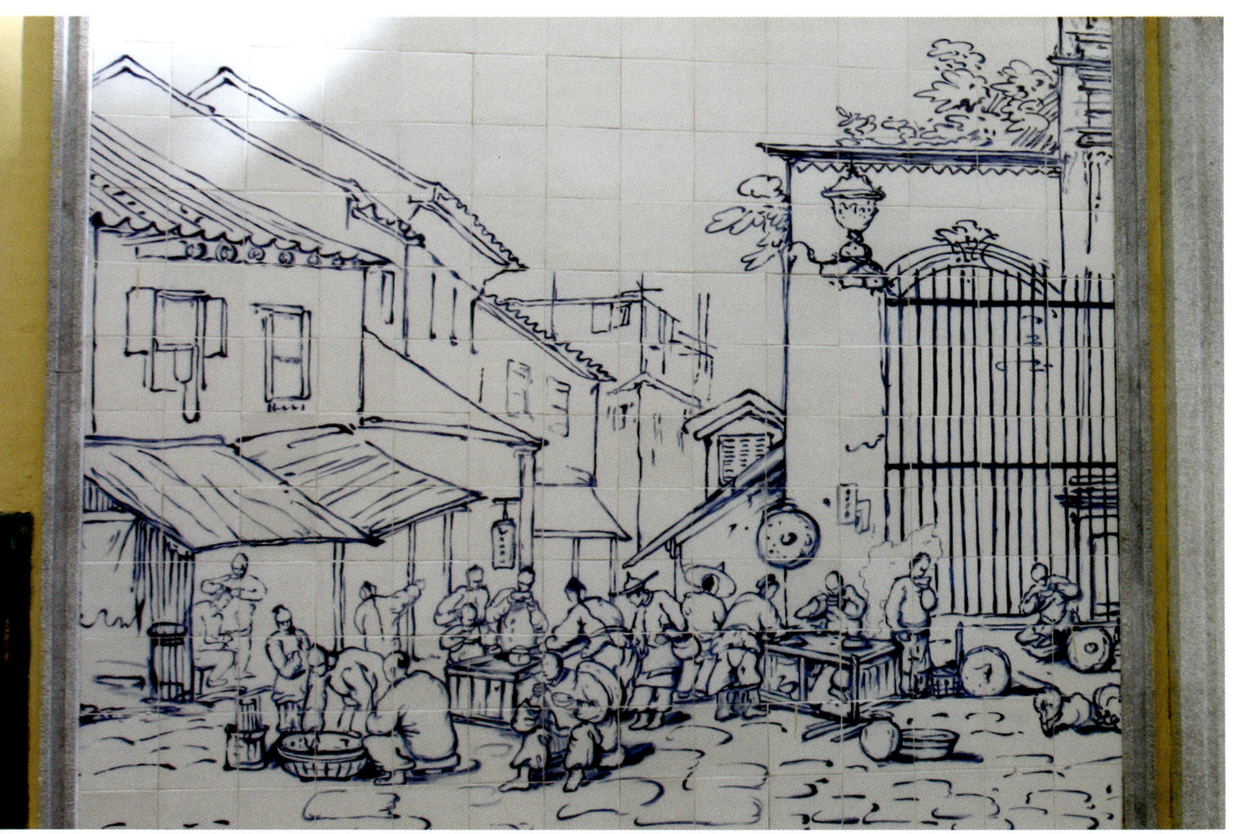

95. Reproduction of Chinnery

Chinnery's shorthand note indicates that he thinks he has a privileged vision of the Chinese. There is no turning away from that European assurance. Yet the façade of São Domingos is no more substantial than the people; an emptiness in it makes it tendentially a ruin. Perhaps because Chinnery lived in the colonial context, rather than simply visiting Macao like Borget, there is some resistance to interpreting the colonial other. Chinnery's sketches, more fragmentary in character, as if refusing the temptation to unify insights to render a complete scene, seem more interested in 'the transient, the fleeting, the contingent'. Though there is something of caricature in his sketches of street-traders, vendors, workers and boat people, they are part of an observational art interested in feet and hands, and in other neglected aspects of life: non-domestic dogs, pigs, cattle. The sketches' fragmentariness suggests that they have no will to complete or totalise; they are loose ends excluded from a narrative of colonial progress, they cannot be framed.

Chinnery painted Macao when a more intense, non-Portuguese colonialism had begun. William Hunter (1812–1981), an American writer on Guangzhou, a member of the American company Russell and Co., says Macao was, from 1762 until the taking of Hong Kong, the 'summer resort of the residents of Canton [Guangzhou]', who were compelled to leave that city every six months. In 1848, its population was 6,000 Portuguese and 55,000 Chinese.[10]

An early display of Chinnery outside Macao was at the Boston Athenaeum in 1827.[11] America had been active in the China trade since the 'Empress of China' had sailed in 1785. The Philadelphia merchant Benjamin Chew Wilcocks, American consul in Guangzhou from 1813–1822 and importer of Turkish opium into China, retired in 1827, taking a self-portrait of Chinnery with him while Chinnery's portrait of him followed a year later. Another merchant, Nathan Dunn, opened a Chinese museum in Philadelphia in 1838. Harriett Low (1809–1877)'s journals describe coming to Macao (1829–1833) as the niece of a Salem shipping executive, William Henry Low, who wanted her to care for his invalid wife (her illness might be called the psychopathology of colonial life).[12] Chinnery painted her, and the Lows. Her journal, which comments 'Oh hard is the lot of spinsters in Macao' (224), describes continually meeting the same people and dancing quadrilles, and while needing to marry, also needing to keep her distance from men. It discusses her reading, fiction and history, the library she visits, how newspapers come in, the lateness of news, the visit from an Italian opera group performing Rossini, whose life she reads about in the library, meeting Dr Bennett, a phrenologist who discusses Spurzheim, who had died in America (232). She notes that it was exceptional for a ship to arrive from Calcutta in seventeen days (142), and that 'Canton' to Macao took two days.

As Unitarian, she regards the Portuguese Catholic population of Macao with distaste. But Americans seem to have been independent of Portuguese restrictions on who lived in Macao; she says, after the family had ignored a request to go, that 'the government of Macao is only nominally Portuguese' (86). The Chinese population are distanced, the 'most singular' and 'most united' of any people (33), but otherwise not seen except as objects, as when she sees them as slaves, the women with feet bound as 'mere toys, for the idle pleasure of their masters, crippled and tortured merely to please them' (177). She says she 'came home and talked to Uncle about the Chinese, their cruelty, their recklessness of life, their belief concerning a future state, etc. It is almost impossible to know what they do believe, there is such a variety of sects ...' (220). She refers to a Chinese *hong* merchant's saying 'that if he should live again as a man, he would be a Chinaman, but if a woman, he would be an Englishwoman' (221). She notes that the Empress of China has died and that there are to be a hundred days of mourning throughout China, and 'the men are not allowed to shave for that space of time, so we shall have some beautiful-looking servants' (217). She sketches with Chinnery, while noticing Macao's weather, and typhoons, each of which drowns seafarers (106, 137–8). She thinks, like him, in terms of the picturesque, which becomes a technique for not seeing other lives:

How I wished for Mr Chinnery's talent for painting, that I might sketch for you [her sister, to whom she writes] the beautiful scene before me, the large and handsome church, milk-white, with a splendid flight of stone steps, and surrounded by trees and shrubbery. Just beyond, the fort, stretching into the bay. Beyond this again, you can see the roads [channels for shipping], and the little boats skimming over the surface. In the distance, two islands of high ground can be discerned, and the beautiful ship heading towards her much desired home. A little farther in, is a little European boat flying along under her full sail, and any quantity of Chinese boats are in sight. Now can you not imagine that we have a pleasant view from our terrace?

(61–2)

The church's whiteness suggests an envy of Macao's Mariolatry and of the cult of virginity, and shows how the secular Puritan sees cleanliness as beauty. The language is of nostalgia: 'desired home'.

The photograph of Our Lady of Carmel Church in Taipa is neither pure white nor is it of one that Harriett Low could have seen, since it was not built till 1885, but that it has no inscription on its frieze

96. Our Lady of Carmel Church

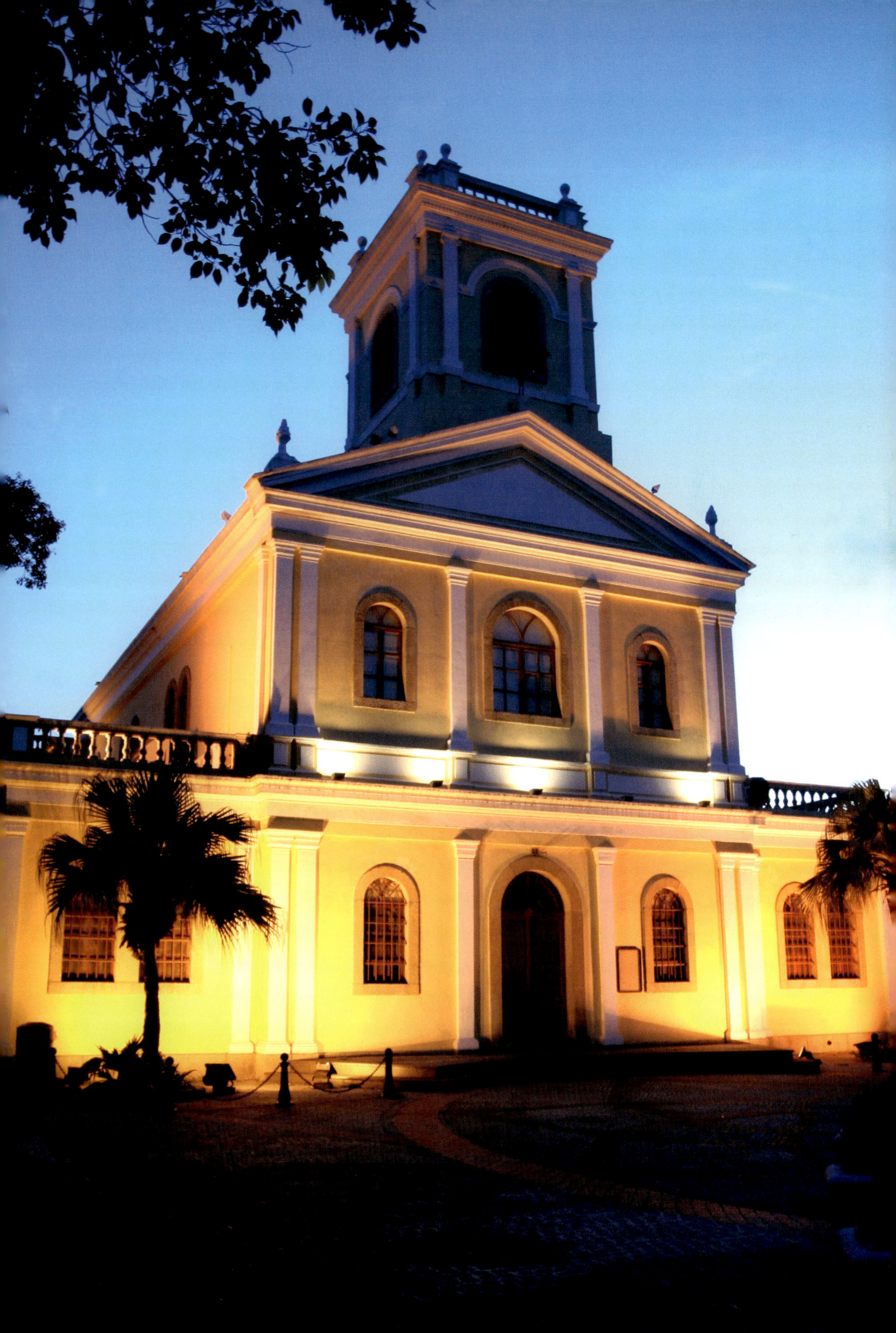

(it does not actually say it is a church) brings out the point that nothing in Low's description is specific: colonialism cannot quite inscribe itself fully onto its buildings.

Harriett Low's perception depends on a sense of aura, moving out towards the distance, not seeing. Once, she refers to a steamboat, the *Forbes*, 'loaded with that precious drug, opium' (65). That is as close as she gets to what the East India Company was doing with the China trade, though she notes occasional trouble with the Chinese, who are antagonistic to the East India Company (95–6).

After 1830, Chinnery sent portraits from Macao to London's Royal Academy for engravings to be made from them. The first, for 1830, were of Robert Morrison (to be discussed in chapter 10) and *Portrait of a Hong Merchant* ('Houqua'). He is framed next to a classical pillar, a Chinese cup next to him on a table and a Chinese lantern hanging behind him; his Chinese clothes make him eighteenth century, not modern.[13] Later came: *Thomas Colledge, Esq., Member of the Royal College of Surgeons, London, and Surgeon to the British Factory in China, attending at his private Opthalmic Infirmary in Macao.*[14] In 1846, he sent *Self-Portrait of the Artist at his Easel.*[15]

Dr Colledge in his surgery is surrounded by four Chinese. One on the far left crouches, blindfolded, passive, as if excluded by the red curtain that hangs over the classical pillar. A classical urn appears behind him. A woman, seated, has had her eyesight restored through Colledge's work, and her son, with a pigtail hanging down his back, bisecting his white jacket, kneels in gratitude holding up a letter of thanks on red paper to the doctor who dominates. An older Chinese servant is to the right. A painting within the painting, behind Colledge and his servant, is of the hospital where the viewer is supposed to be: it is a *mise en abîme*. The hat of the Chinese boy on the floor to the left, with an umbrella with a vermilion tip to it, laid down, as it were, before his entry into European space, contrasts with the white scroll on the floor to the right. The blind man has one hand resting on his knee; there is no pointing to his blindness, as if he lacks self-awareness, while the woman whose sight has been restored is equally passive; her hands are not seen. What dominates are Colledge's hands, the right hand extended over the woman, on her head, having just lifted her glasses up to her forehead. He looks as if he is blessing her, while his left hand is held out in a position that individuates the index finger, as if he is teaching, Christ-like. He has turned his body round to talk to his servant; his left hand engages him, but will move back to the woman's face. The son, whose hands are complemented by his bare feet, presents the red book with his right hand towards Colledge's left, while his left hand touches his mother. The servant has both hands on the table, in a position of readiness contrasting with the blind man.[16]

Chinnery's *Self-Portrait*, also framed by red drapery, shows, on the wall behind, facing the viewer, a framed view of the Praya Grande, while on the easel, which is at an angle parallel with the red drapery, appears an Indian landscape, of an overgrown Indian tomb, or mosque, with figures in the foreground. It looks dilapidated, broken down. In the self-portrait, the artist's appearance in black jacket and white trousers is distinctive, and recalls other portrayals, including China traders.[17] It aligns Chinnery with these speculative merchants, and with the professionalism of Dr Colledge in his surgery, with which the self-portrait may be compared, since both pictures conceptualise vision. Colledge gives vision, under the authority of the artist, who shows in his *Self-Portrait* that vision is what he also gives. As the Chinese woman in Dr Colledge's surgery had glasses, supplements to vision, so here glasses appear too, and the painter's eyes are not concealed by them, since, being put on his nose, they leave the eyes free to look at the viewer. Derrida, writing about vision and the blind, compares spectacles, as detachable from the body, to the fetish.[18] Chinnery holds a brush in his right hand, while his right leg, by being crooked over the other, lets him support his palette and a supplementary three brushes in his left hand, which has smudges of vermilion and whites on it. As regards the landscapes shown in the picture, the chronological order in which the paintings were done is reversed, for Macao represents completed work, and India incomplete; hence India is a vision,

a dream, not a reality, or an absence, since it is not finished. Perhaps the studio is imagined to be not in Macao; certainly the absence of personal detail in the studio diminishes particularity in the portrayal of places.

The use of vermilion (the brightest red colour) is a signature for Chinnery, for whom it seemed to operate as a mannerism in portraiture. Conner cites Chinnery writing to Maria Browne (1786–1828), an amateur painter in Calcutta: 'There is something about Vermilion very curious — Vermilion is vermilion'.[19] Vermilion is present in the curtain, the artist's lips and the palette, but not in the painted landscape of India, as though the artist knows that he must apply it somewhere to give the landscape definition, as a work by Chinnery; it has not yet become historical, or personal; it has not quite achieved presence. Something seems lacking, as it so often does in colonial art. The picture either shows something coming into being, which will be identifiable with the artist, or the work of memory, India as something remembered. But if so, memory may be of nothing that has existed: the picture, unlike a photograph, does not say that this has been, that the scene represented can be thought of objectively; rather, it is part of colonial nostalgia. And that nothing supplements memory is apparent from the point that nothing within the painting of India can be accounted for by what stands behind Chinnery and to his left: a table with a bottle and mixing bowls and a sketch pad, and an unopened portfolio of work. There is no alterity, since no actual sketch of India is shown, as if nothing can give the vision to the artist. So Chinnery's self-portrait frames Macao as a place and a commodity, given status by its position in the artist's studio, while it brings into being a timeless India, unaffected by colonialism, but still broken down. Chinnery identifies himself by his self-presentation as a bourgeois portraitist (who paints in the pursuit of money), and he represents himself as a landscape painter (who paints for the pursuit of art). This portrait painter does not paint people, save as objects within an imagined landscape: but equally the landscape painter does not paint places. Perhaps vermilion implies what Lacan, in *The Four Fundamental Concepts of Psychoanalysis*, calls the appearance in the picture of the stain, the spot (see chapters 5 and 8). Chinnery is looking at himself, but the stain, always 'present' in the picture, puts opacity over against the viewer, including Chinnery looking at himself, making full vision of the self impossible.[20] The subject paints himself within a mirror, and paints himself being looked at by a mirror. Portraiture becomes an art which shows the impossibility of completeness; the vermilion which would complete everything is also a way of reducing what can be seen, bringing in the stain.

Derrida discusses the self-portrait, saying that in it 'the figure, the face ... sees its visibility being eaten away; it loses its integrity without disintegrating'. So 'the pictures of ruins [are] ... the figures of a portrait, indeed, of a self-portrait'. He concludes by discussing ruins, saying: the 'naked face cannot look itself in the face'; it needs the supplement, it is incomplete, a fragment.[21] The artist of the colonies cannot be separated from what he has objectified: he is caught up in the same absence. If the baroque is the culture of the ruin, ruins are historical, like here in Chinnery's painting, associated with colonialism, part of the void it creates, needing, therefore, the supplement. The colonial spaces in Chinnery's self-portrait are differently rendered. India becomes a pastoral ruin, but Macao, shown with the Praya Grande, has been urbanised, as the framed picture of the hospital in 'Dr Colledge in his Surgery' attempts to give the city depth.

Fragmentation is everywhere in Macao, as with this bisection of a classical building in Taipa village street (Rua do Regedor). The western building, which is one of a series, many of them broken up into halves and overgrown with weeds, is split by a different Chinese one-storeyed house design (note the roof). Derrida calls the ruin:

> not a negative thing. First, it is obviously not a thing. One could write ... a short treatise on the love of ruins. What else is there to love, anyway?

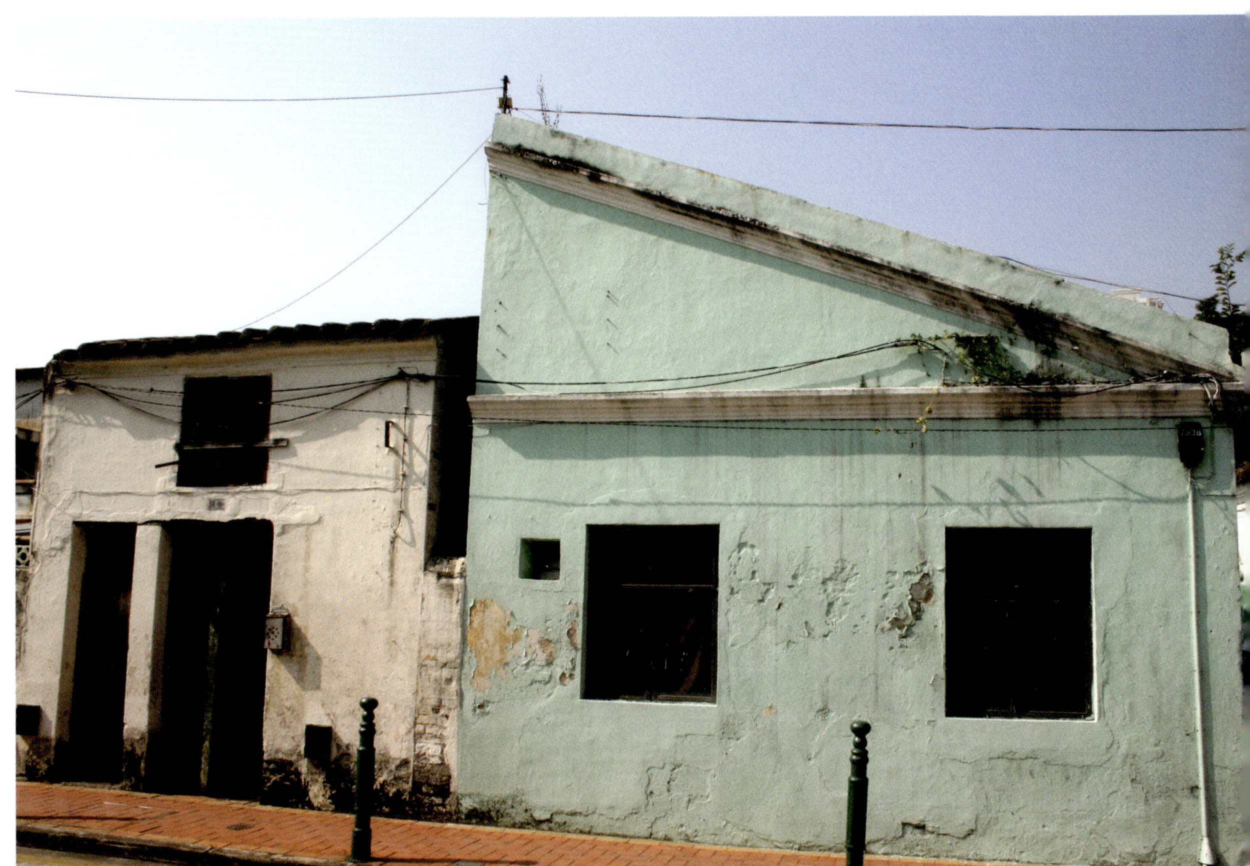

97. Taipa ruins

One cannot love a monument, a work
of architecture, an institution as such
except in an experience itself precarious
in its fragility: it has not always been
there, it will not always be there, it is
finite. And for this very reason one
loves it as mortal, through its birth
and its death, through one's own birth

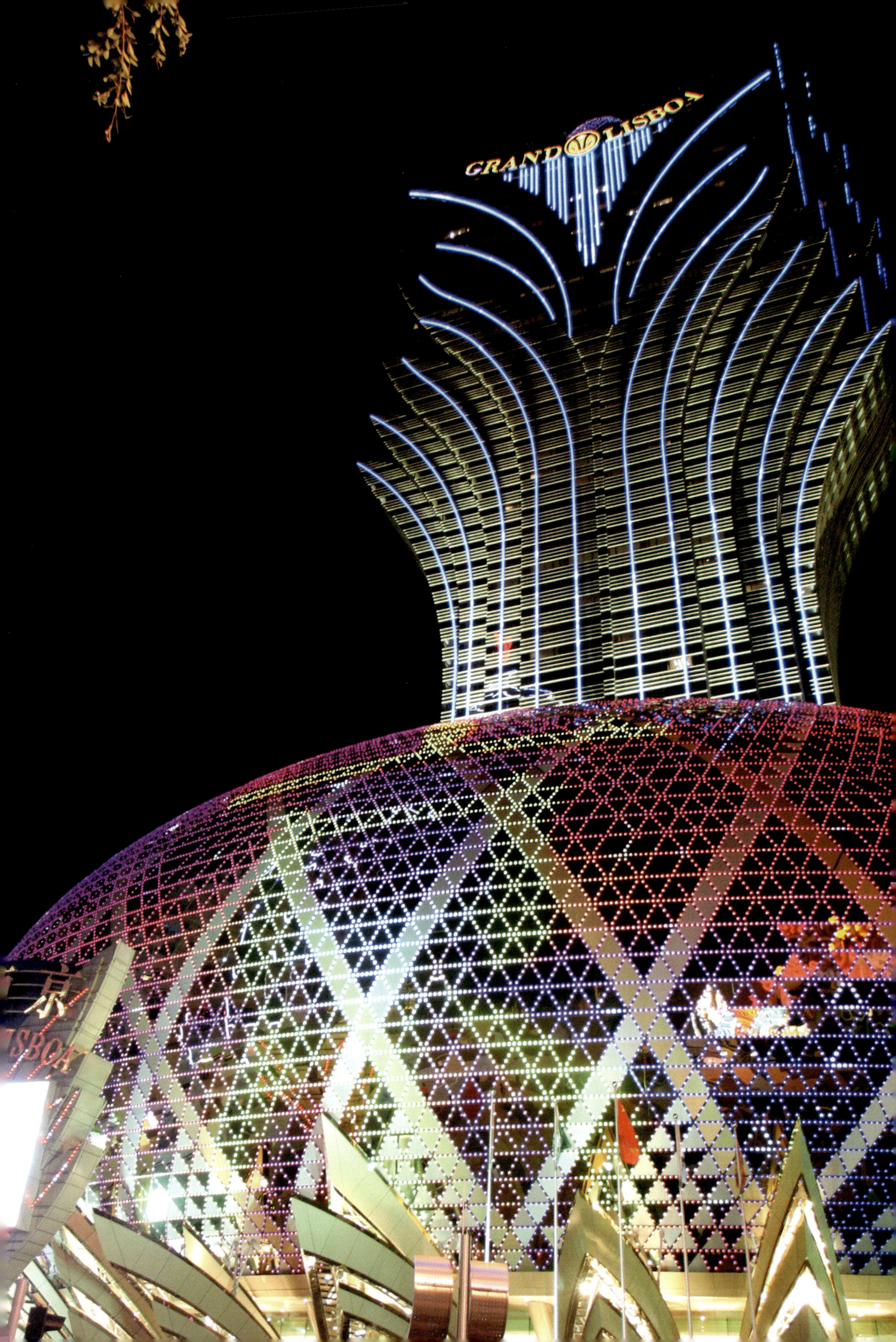

GRAND LISBOA

and death, through the ghost or the silhouette of its ruin, one's own ruin — which it already is, therefore, or already prefigures. How can one love otherwise than in this finitude?[22]

Alongside these ruins in Macao, Chinnery's Macao is fragmented in another sense. Buildings are already ruined, like the façade of the church of St Paul's or in his picture *Old Houses, Macao* (1835).[23] Here, a discontinuous line of houses runs at an angle from left to right on old brick platforms, with three indistinctly rendered Chinese figures in blue, two with straw hats, completing the pastoralism of the scene. Macao, before it is developed, is already ruined. In *View of the Praya Grande from a Doorway on Penha Hill* (oil on canvas, 1834), the door's surroundings are overgrown, and it seems to serve no function; on the crest of a hill, it frames a distant view of the Praya Grande, far off, even faded, light, almost white against the dark browns and yellows of the forepart of the picture.[24] The colours are echoed in two Chinese figures in the painting, one distantly seen looking away from the viewer through the door, and one older, with an open basket, displaying goods for sale, seated in the corner made by the doorway and the wall. Both pictures place the ruin outside time and modernity.

Beyond the work where Chinnery incorporates deliberate ruins, there is the sense of non-completeness, that the work holds within it the existence of another ruin, which enables memories which are unintentional, because they are unconsciously remembered. These enable reading, and imply that these landscapes of Macao may be taken allegorically. Chinnery's art becomes an archive bearing witness to memories he cannot know. Painting the ruin brings into awareness the 'void' in the city's 'unwritten biography'. Chinnery may be excluded from the life, and the history, of the Chinese in Macao, but his work shows up that gap.

What of Macao's present modernity? The photograph shows the Grand Lisboa (DLN Architects) going up from a base resembling a lotus, the city's flower, a motif also used by its precursor over the road, Casino Lisboa, which can be seen on the right. The forty-four storeys above resemble fireworks or water ejaculating as a fountain. Both casinos, the first built in 1972, are the works of Stanley Ho, whose career began in Macao, but the second is the oversized son to the father, who, by being naming after Portugal's capital city, makes them both the sons of Portuguese rule, and commentaries and mockeries of that rule. The lotus of the Casino Lisboa can be seen brightly illuminated in photograph 99.

98. The Grand Lisboa

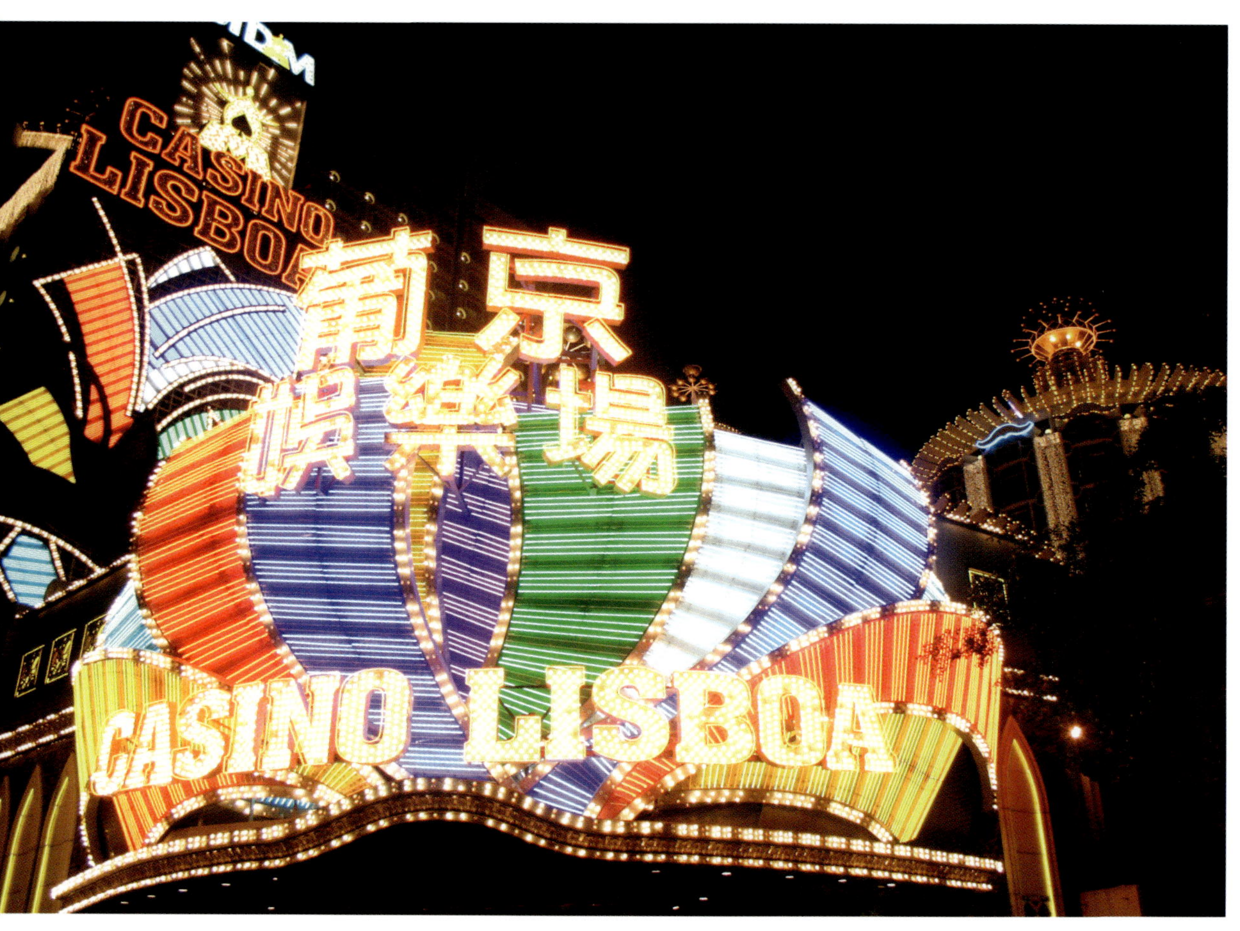

99. Casino Lisboa

The new building, and the kaleidoscope of colours, seems Macao at its most self-confident. When Derrida writes about the ruin as at the heart of deconstruction, his comments may sound overly consolatory, reconciliatory. But Benjamin, too, indicates that the best way of reading an architecture so confident may be to see it as bearing the signs of its own ruin within it. He discusses new buildings and calls them ruins, saying that 'Balzac [1799–1850, French novelist] was the first to speak of the ruins of the bourgeoisie'. For, thinking of the rapid developments of nineteenth-century capitalism,

> the developments of the forces of production had turned the wish-symbols of the previous century into rubble, even before the monuments which represented them had crumbled…

One city-structure giving place to another conveys the idea of each moment dreaming the next. No urban development can stay still, rather,

> with the upheaval of the market economy, we begin to recognise the monuments of the bourgeoisie as ruins even before they have crumbled.[25]

Ruins are not romantic signs of decay, but show that any structure is marked by incompleteness. The new building has the signs of its death upon it, indications that it must be a dream of how it can be upgraded. A new building becomes a dream of the next building; it becomes obsolescent; it has the sign of death upon it. There cannot be a complete building, or city, any more than there can be a complete thought, hence 'allegories are in the realm of thoughts what ruins are in the realm of things'.[26] This passage was quoted before on p. 58 with reference to baroque images. It suggests that allegory, meaning describing one thing in terms of another (compare p. 144), shows that thought never understands itself, never knows its own meaning. Similarly, 'things' seem to be self consistent and complete, but are split, fragmented, self-divided. Understanding the baroque as both allegorical and the art of the ruin helps us to see the Grand Lisboa as in ruins.

Camões and the Casa Garden

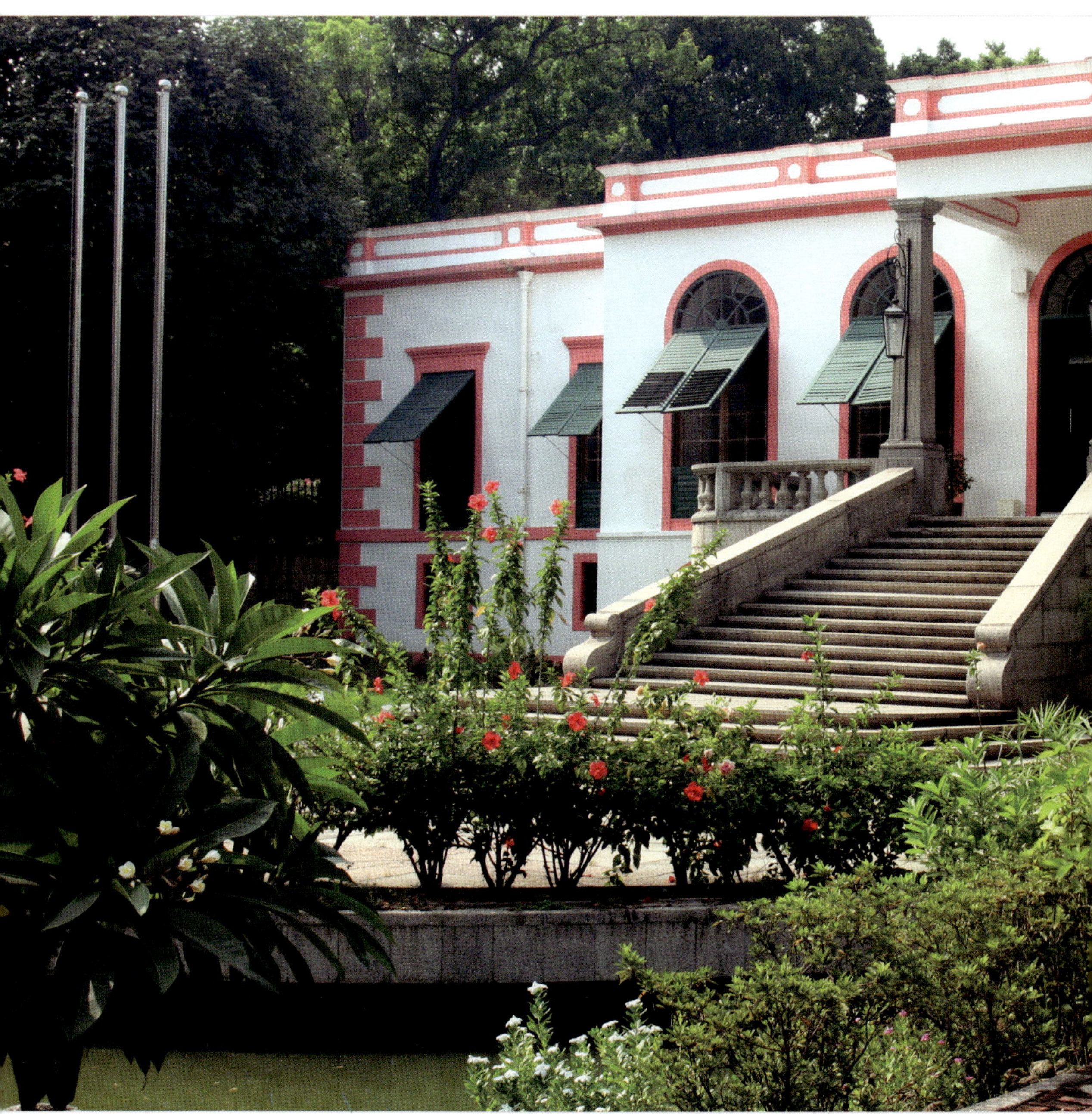

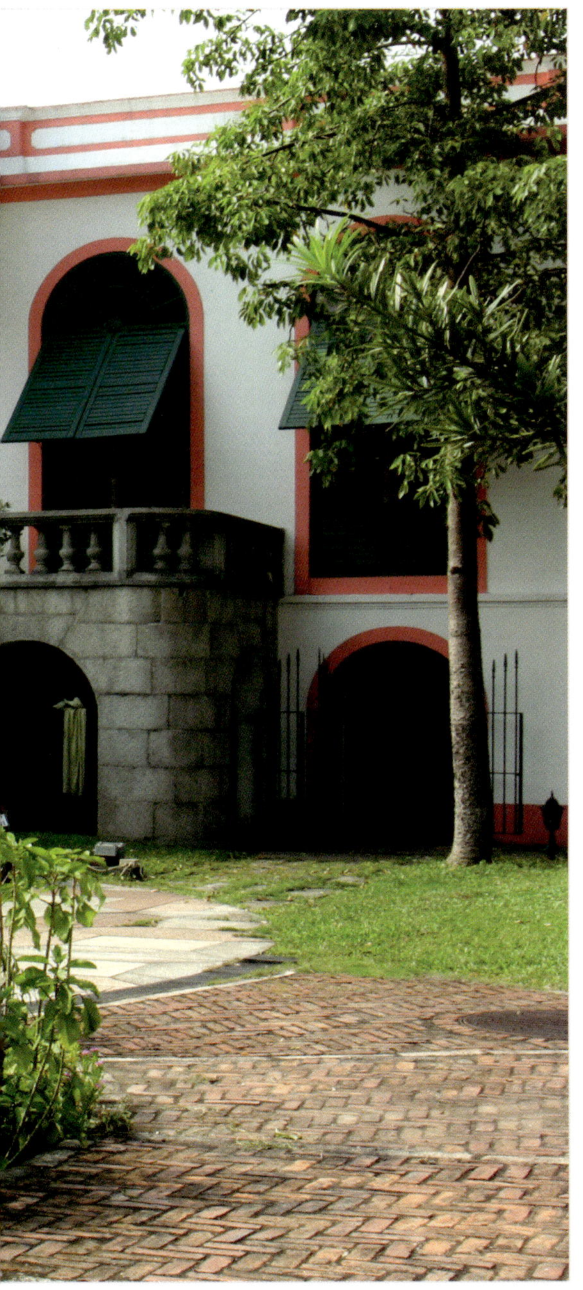

100. Casa Garden

This chapter looks at four sites associated with Portuguese and later colonialisms. Three may be visited together: the Casa Garden, the Protestant cemetery and the Camões Garden; the fourth is on Coloane.

The Casa Garden is part of a villa, built perhaps in 1770, and later belonging to a surgeon and insurer, Manuel Pereira, a leading name in Macao (another Pereria, a merchant, has his portrait hung in the Casa da Misericórdia). It was leased out to William Fitzhugh in the 1780s, and so to the British East India Company, and then to James Drummond. Here Lord Macartney stayed in 1794 after his embassy to Beijing. In 1885, it was taken over by the Portuguese government.

The visitor goes from a low platform on five wide steps, up another staircase which narrows up towards the front door, which is now — after a renovation which changed a sloping roof for a flat one — on the first-floor level of the building. (The ground floor is for the servants and for storage.) The house, with its pond in front, is neo-classical in style, with two bays on either side of the front door, and two wings on either side of that.

Part of its garden, to the right as the visitor approaches, was taken over as the Protestant cemetery, and in 1821, a small Protestant chapel was built there, named for Robert Morrison (1782–1834), translator for the East India Company who is buried in the cemetery, like Chinnery, who painted him and two Chinese assistants working behind him on his Dictionary, and on his Bible, and prayer-book. Morrison appears in academic robes, holding the charter for the Anglo-Chinese College.[1] He stands as an example of the necessity for double-thinking within colonialism: aware of opium-dealing, he justified his activities for the Company for which he worked, on the assumption that he was enabling the bringing of Christianity to China, as the Protestant answer to Ricci.

Chinnery's interest in ruins means that, unconsciously, he painted what the baroque represents. One Chinnery pencil sketch is of the tombs, where the low graves are for the three children of Thomas and Caroline Colledge who died in infancy.[2] A tall column to the right, surmounted by an urn and framed by trees, memorialises John Crockett (1786–1837), who captained an opium storeship, the *Jane*. The urn above contrasts with the one below, dedicated to another infant, at the foot of this grave.

The photograph, which shows a corner of the cemetery and illustrates colonial melancholy, indicates what Chinnery worked from. The column is an allegory, in that it suggests the man as a column of society. It compares with the heroine's first sight of the odious priest, Mr Brocklehurst, in *Jane Eyre* (1847), Charlotte Brontë's novel written ten years after Crockett's death: 'A black pillar! — such, at least, appeared to me at first sight, the straight, narrow, sable-clad shape standing erect on the rug: the grim face at the top was like a carved mask, placed above the shaft by way of capital'.[3] In this photograph, the funerary urn placed above the column becomes a head: rather than being a portrait, this face has been depersonalised into an allegory of death and of ruin. In literature, the device of personification allegory turns a quality (e.g. Love) into a person (Venus). In this allegory the reverse has happened. The person is represented by the dead emblematic object, the tallest thing in the cemetery. He is the opposite of what is meant by 'personification allegory'. Instead, it is more baroque, since the pillar and the capital imply the breakdown of meaning, or rather, they turn meaning into loss and death.

The urn and the one below are like the baroque examples found in São José, and the one in Chinnery's picture of Dr Colledge in his surgery. They imply in the case of Crockett that the masculinity which dominates in the service of colonialism is melancholic, because it is associated with death. It is also associated with the desire to create memories which enforce the idea of the melancholy of colonial service. The idea is recorded in the epitaph inscribed to the man:

101. Tomb of Captain Crockett

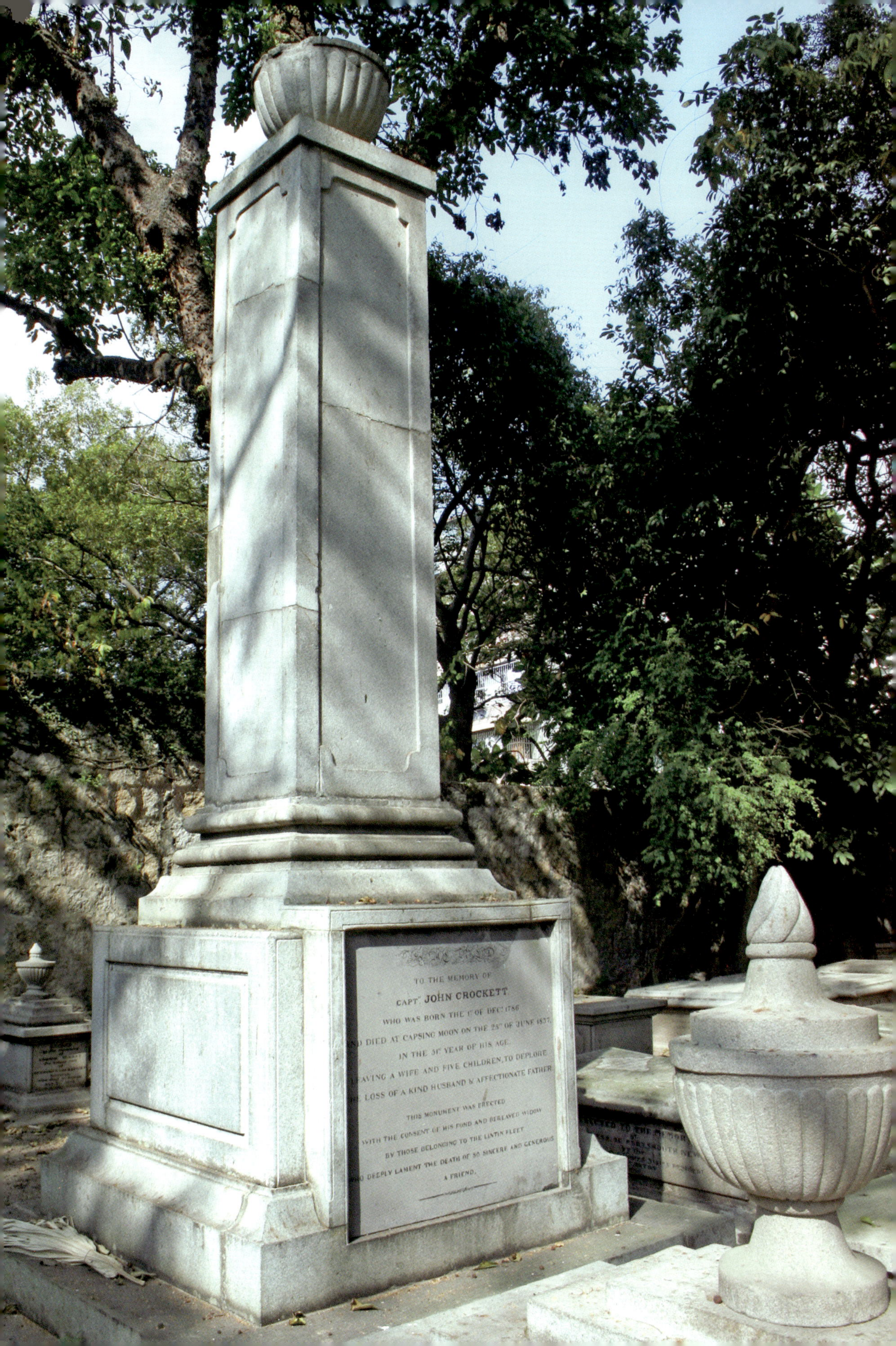

TO THE MEMORY OF
CAPT. JOHN CROCKETT
WHO WAS BORN THE 1ST OF DECR 1786
AND DIED AT CAPSING MOON ON THE 25TH OF JUNE 1837,
IN THE 51ST YEAR OF HIS AGE.
LEAVING A WIFE AND FIVE CHILDREN, TO DEPLORE
THE LOSS OF A KIND HUSBAND & AFFECTIONATE FATHER
THIS MONUMENT WAS ERECTED
WITH THE CONSENT OF HIS FOND AND BEREAVED WIDOW
BY THOSE BELONGING TO THE LINTIN FLEET
WHO DEEPLY LAMENT THE DEATH OF SO SINCERE AND GENEROUS
A FRIEND.

To the Memory of Capt. John Crockett who was born the 1st of Dec 1786 who died at Capsing Moon on the 25th of June 1837 in the 51st year of his age, leaving a wife and five children to deplore the loss of a kind husband and affectionate father. This monument was erected with the consent of his fond and bereaved widow, by those belonging to the Lintin fleet who deeply lament the death of so sincere and generous a friend.

That the narrative of the tombstone obliterates everything to do with Crockett's activities except the reference to the Lintin fleet which was commandeered by Jardine and Matheson in 1835, is indicative as is his death in Hong Kong waters. All that is given is his bourgeois status as a family man and the sense of the loyalty he commanded. A tiny and selective life is created, trying to fix his identity in generic terms, on the basis of his death and becoming allegory.[4]

The Protestant cemetery is an attractive space, whose raised tombs became the theme of nineteenth-century art.[5] The photograph, taken from the Casa Garden, looks down into the upper section of the cemetery, while to the left, behind the trees, in the cemetery's lower section, can be seen Crockett's pillar; the surrounding trees are taller than it is. This lower part of the cemetery also contains, not seen here, a well, a kind of life in death.

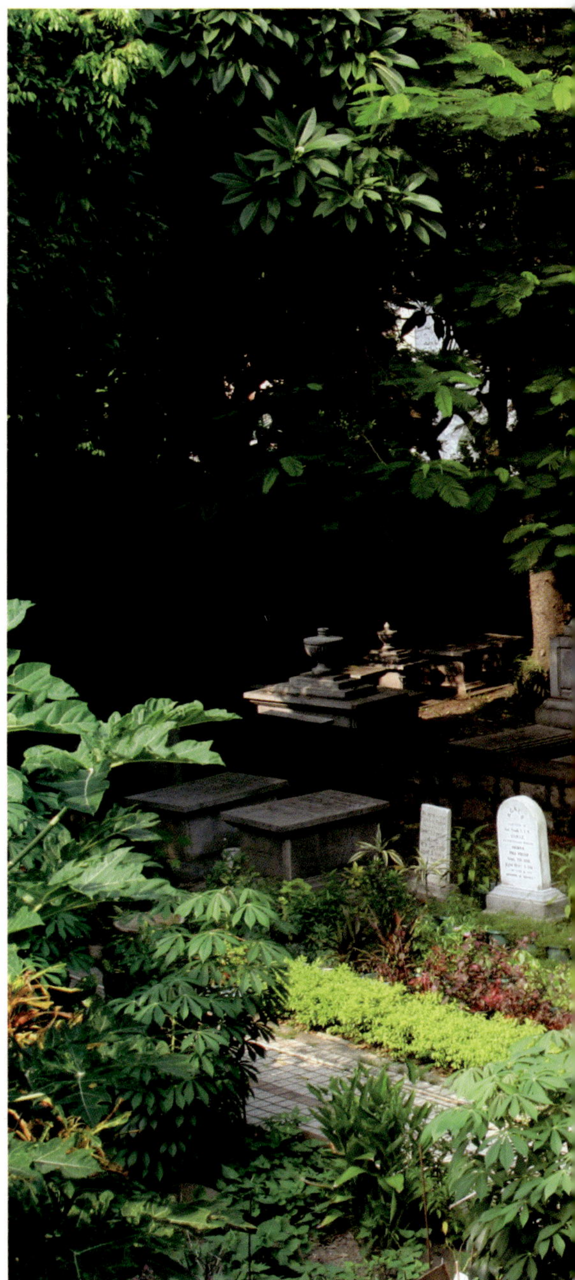

102. Cemetery

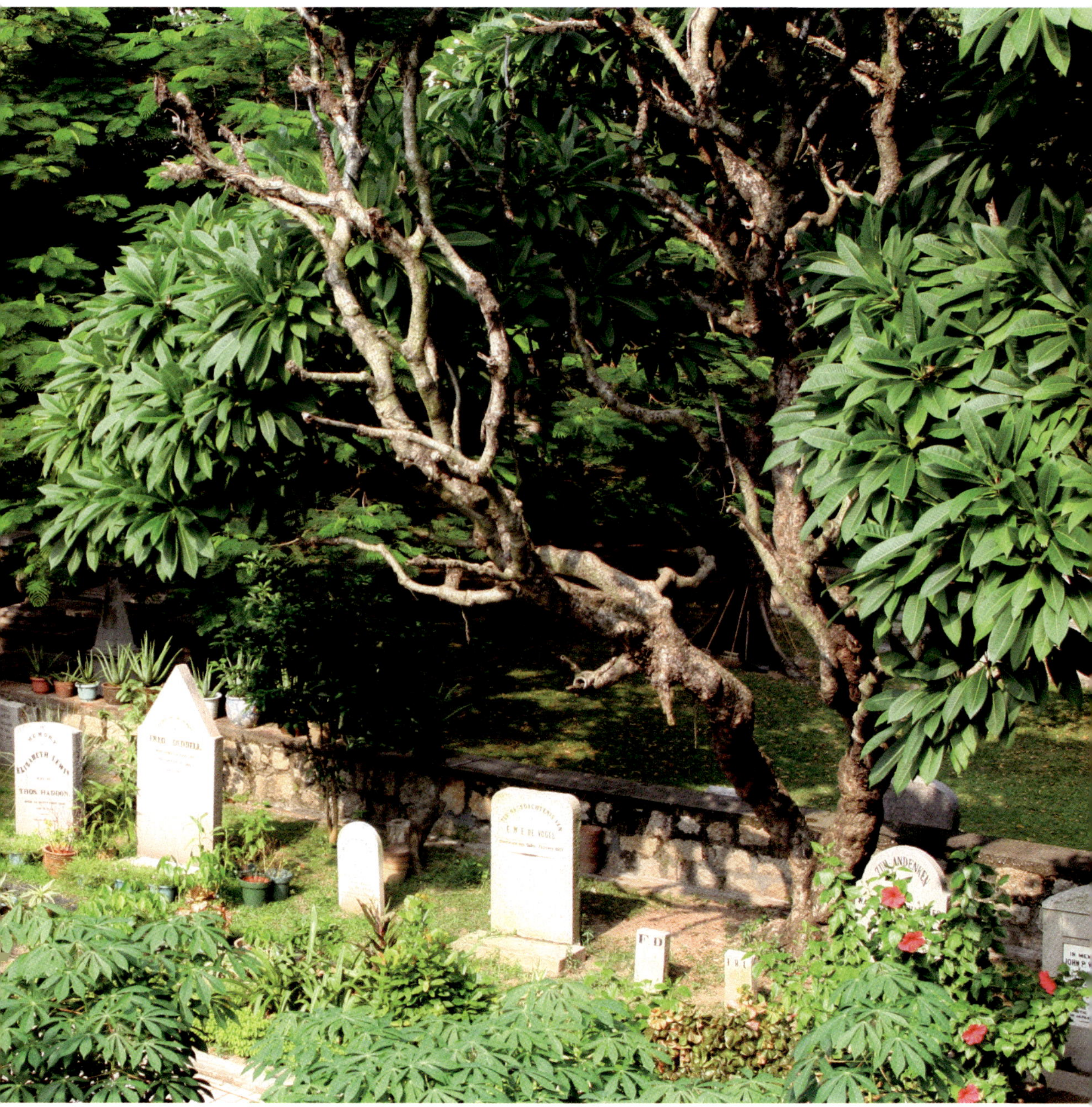

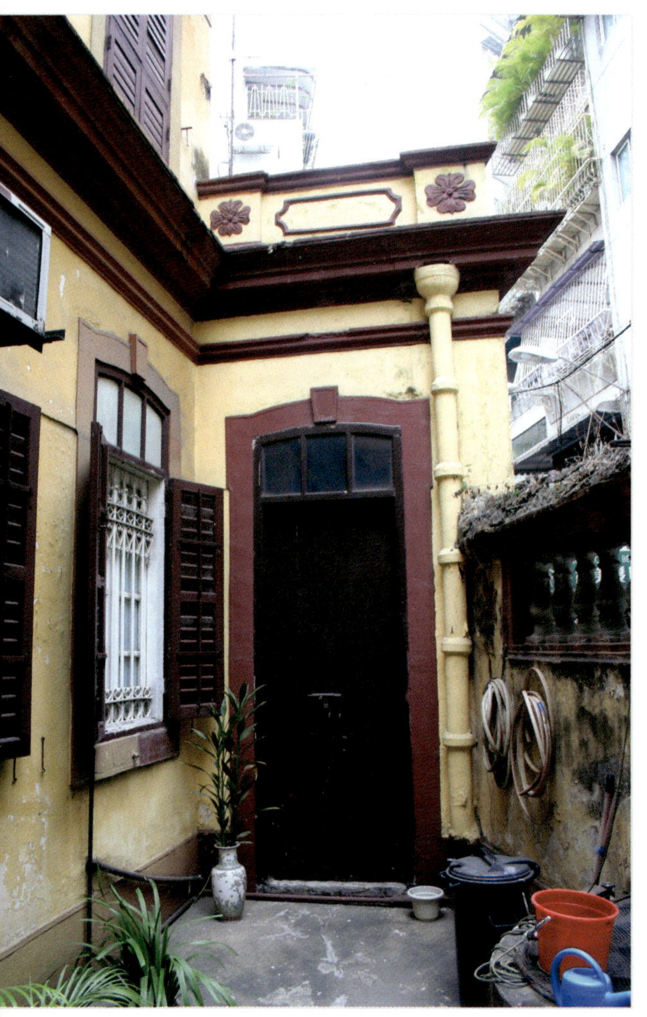

103. Well in courtyard

Macao, as noted earlier, has many wells, from this to one in the courtyard of the Ricci Institute, and another in the Ho Tung Library and two in the Mandarin's House. Another example may be noticed casually in the yard of one of the 1920s classical houses, in light brown and dark red, colours that are so much a feature of the city. This house and yard has a balcony, seen to the right of photograph 103, which gives onto the Travessa do Padre Soares.

The well, to the right-hand side, may be contrasted with the vase and plant that stands beside the door. There are five vessels for containing things here, and the sense of abundance is continued in the green plant life that hangs from the high balconies glimpsed at on the other side of the street outside. A bucket is on top. This is an in-between space, between the house and the road. The well in the Protestant cemetery is also not easily noticed, because of the graves.

The Camões Garden

Ruins, for the eighteenth century, were associated with the picturesque, which as a colonial practice keeps the painter and the scene at a distance.[6] Chinnery, an artist of the picturesque, like others, was drawn to the grotto in the Luís de Camões Garden adjacent to, and once part of, the Casa Garden, the garden already mentioned in chapter

104. Grotto

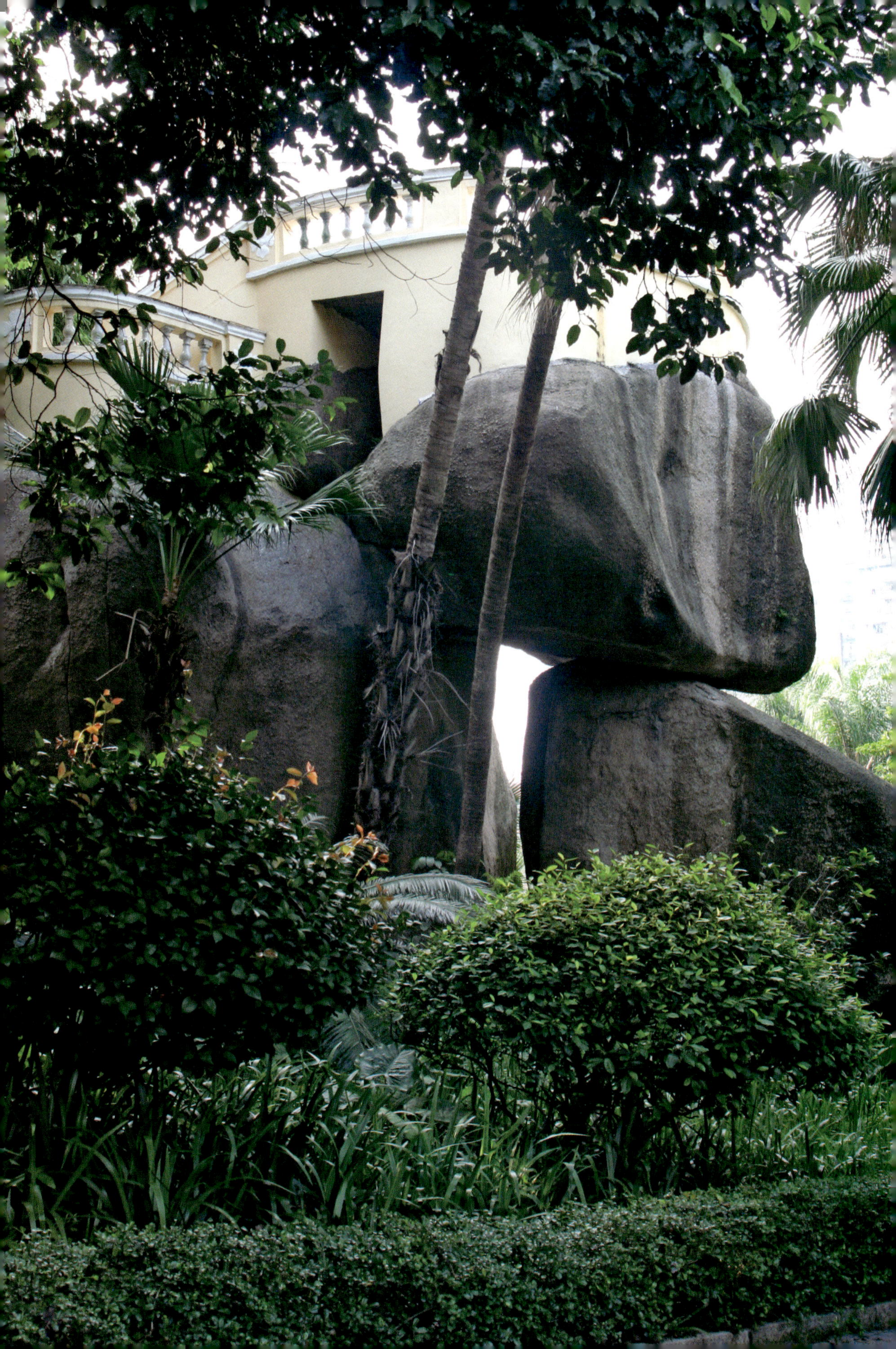

2 for the library in it.[7] This Camões Garden, now considered in more detail, has at least four significances. It recalls European colonisation and leisure. Second, today, it is popular with Macao people, who use it in many ways: for leisure, for carrying birds in cages, for playing Chinese chess. Third, it recalls the ruin, as baroque and as rococo, in the rock-formation in the middle of the garden. Fourth, it invokes Camões, author of *The Lusiads*, who has been turned into a gentleman of leisure, reflecting on the imperial enterprise. The grotto, also crucial to Chinese Gardens, is central to the Camões Garden. Funded by Lourenço Marques, who lived at the house as one of the Pereira dynasty, it was renovated in 1849 and a bust of Luís de Camões was erected at its mouth, emerging from the dark space between the rocks, on the assumption that the *Lusiads* had been written there. By identifying him with the grotto, itself a theme of Chinnery, placing his work on it, and centring it in the gardens, they make him a melancholic who writes with a sense of looking back from the eighteenth or nineteenth century. The bust, Camões' head and shoulders (there is no extant likeness that the sculptor could draw on, and no photograph is given here), shows him with a ruff which separates his head from his body, in a way that makes him truly proto-Cartesian. Camões is

made a poet laureate. In 1999, a new plaque was put up in both Portuguese and Chinese. The poet of empire becomes the great humanist poet, and *The Lusiads* embodies Portuguese universalism.[8]

In *The Lusiads*, Lusus is described in the poem as a follower, or son, of Bacchus (1.39, 7.77, 8.2–4). And Bacchus, who seems in the poem to be like the Devil himself in his opposition to the Portuguese conquests in the East, is jealous of the effect that they will have there (see canto 6, stanzas 30–34). It is as though the Orient was, for the coloniser, the very sphere of the Devil. *The Lusiads* was written at some time around 1559, but not published in Portugal till 1572, eight years before Portugal itself was annexed by Philip II of Spain, in the year of Camões' death, and went into what was called its 'Babylonian captivity'. Portugal remained Spanish until 1640, though it seems that Macao remained Portuguese. *The Lusiads* was composed after Camões had gone out in colonial service to Goa, and it was completed in Lisbon. An unreliable tradition says that Camões' poem was written in Macao. This could make it tendentially baroque. But is it baroque?

The Lusiads was intended as advice and warning for the King, Sebastião (ruled 1557–1578), advice that was to prove fruitless, as the King died without leaving an heir, and so gave the advantage to Spain. The Spanish annexation marked the beginning of the end of Portugal's sea-borne empire's triumph: Holland and the English moved in to complement Spanish colonialism and the Dutch invasions of Macao have been noted.

As classical epics do, the poem begins in the middle of things, with Vasco Da Gama on the way to Asia, arriving on the coast of East Africa (canto 1). In canto 2, Jupiter tells Venus of the victories that await the Portuguese in the East, and portrays the conquest that Vasco Da Gama will make by going in a straight west-east direction (whereas, in fact, some of Portugal's African territories were taken after their success in India). The King of Malindi (in present-day Kenya) asks Vasco Da Gama for details about his country, and the voyage. This introduces canto 3, which begins Da Gama's narrative of the history of Portugal, and on how it became a single nation in 1128 under Alfonso Henriques.

This narrative, which includes the taking of Ceuta (Morocco) under the auspices of Henry the Navigator in 1415 (4.49) — the event seen as initiating Portugal's seawards expansion — ends in canto 4, with the introduction of the character of Manuel I (ruled 1495–1521). His dream of the rivers

of India is given (4.69–75). Manuel commissions Da Gama to make the journey to India, and the canto concludes with the ships sailing from Restelo beach at the chapel of Belém (i.e. Bethlehem), at Lisbon, as happened in 1497. Belém is a significant monument, because the Manueline style of architecture developed on the basis of what Da Gama brought back from India. Its major examples were to include the Mosteiro [Monastery] dos Jerónimos, which was begun in 1502, as a memorial to Da Gama, who was to be buried there. Other distinguished examples of this style are the Mosteiro de Jesus in Setúbal (1490–1510) and the church and chapter-house of the Convent of Christ in Tomar in the district of Santarém. Here, the decoration of one window, which is otherwise Gothic, designed by Diogo de Arruda, gives the heart of Manueline architecture, which would have been known by Camões' time, if it was not already known in 1497.

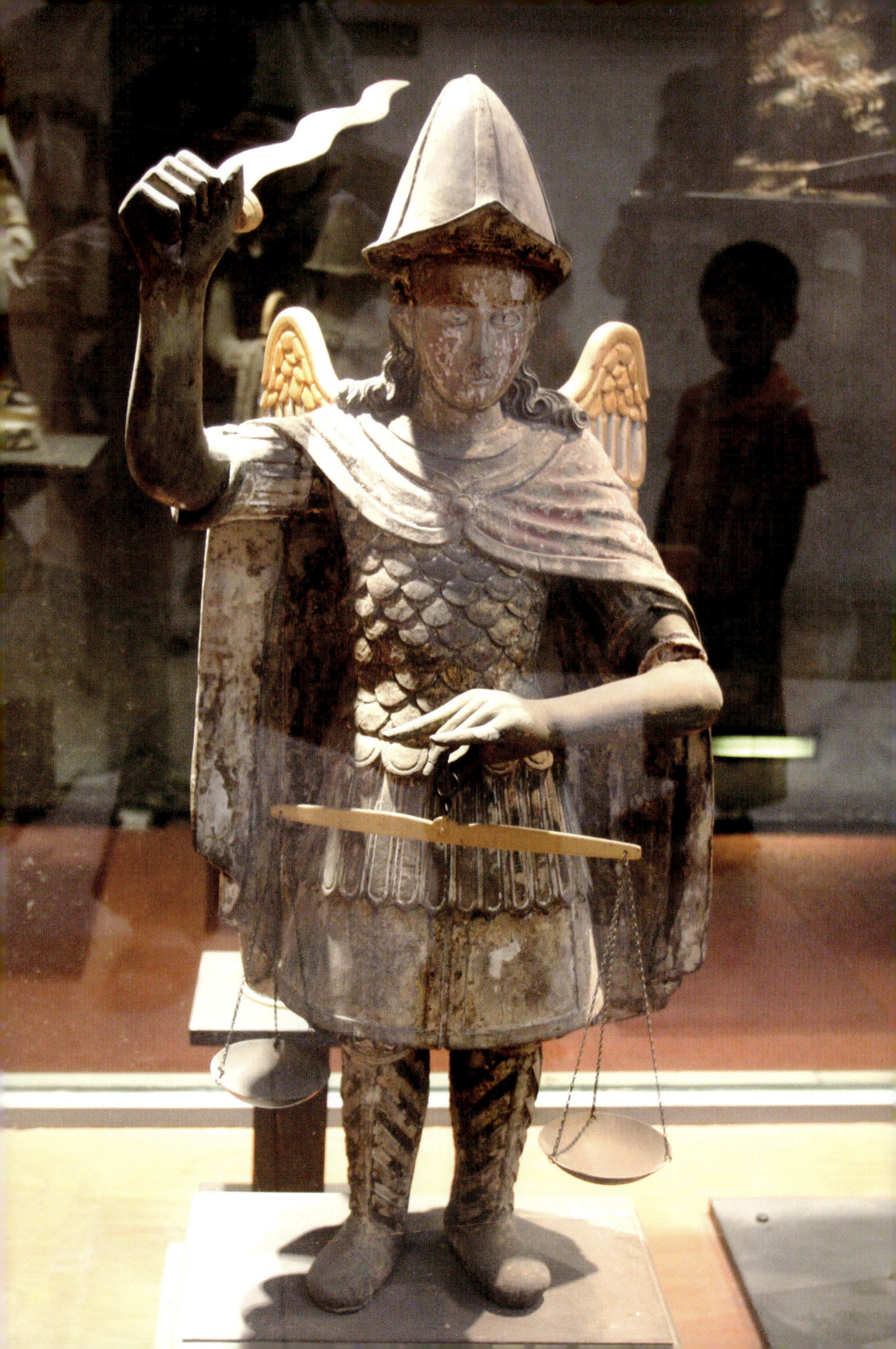

In Manueline architecture, exotic naturalism derived from colonial encounters and discoveries and maritime motifs appear. There are twisted rope formations and sculpted living forms. The rocaille already noted in Macao also suggests the dominance of the Manueline style, which helps to join together Gothic and baroque and makes the point that the baroque in Portugal, which was then re-imported into Macao, also derives from colonialism, from Portugal's experiences in Asia.

But the poem's triumphalism, as the seafarers are about to set sail at the end of canto 4, is suddenly broken by a solemn warning from an old man attacking the pursuit of fame and ambition. This makes the poem ambiguous. The speech is an energetic rebuke against the Portuguese sailing from Lisbon to India. It lasts for the final eleven stanzas of canto 4, as the old man damns, comprehensively, mankind, the Portuguese, and the first men to sail in ships. The warnings will be repeated in canto 5, with another figure, the Titan Adamastor.

Canto 5 narrates the journey, which began in 1497, going as far as Malindi, and includes the account of rounding the Cape of Good Hope, where in an extraordinary episode, Adamastor, who is an allegorical personification of the Cape, gives warnings of future deaths by shipwreck and drowning of those who dare to pass from the Atlantic into the Indian Ocean by going round the Cape (5.39–60). (The Cape of Good Hope had been rounded by the Portuguese Bartolomeu Dias (1450–1500) in 1488 and he called it the Cape of Storms. João II renamed it the Cape of Good Hope, because of the promise it opened up for reaching India, but Dias was, eventually, to be drowned there (5.44).) This warning from Adamastor comes exactly at the centre of the poem. Adamastor is a cloud, amorphous, a monstrous figure, the Cape itself, part of the elements and part of the landscape, and a figure in his own right. He comes and goes, but he has the power to ruin. One commentator speaks of him as though he was an 'optical illusion'.[9] This, by itself, makes this allegorical creature baroque; he is also a figure of nature, the personification of the waterspouts, and of the storms. Further, he does not quite disclose his name. 'Call me Adamastor', he says (5.51). And in doing so, he shows that the baroque is always concerned with what is riddling, or secret, or enigmatic, not quite disclosing itself.[10]

In canto 6, the King of Malindi sends the voyagers on their way across the Indian Ocean, and after a disaster which is orchestrated by Bacchus and prevented by Venus, the ships arrive at India. In canto 7, Da Gama talks to an official, the Catual of Calicut, who asks him about the scenes from Portuguese history depicted on the banners of the fleet. This produces another narrative, in canto 8, of the heroes of Portugal, up to the time of Henry the Navigator (1394–1460), third son of King

*105. Imperial Power: c17 wooden statue,
the Archangel Michael, St Paul's; compare
photographs 57 and 58*

João of Portugal (ruled 1385–1433), founder of the Avis dynasty. More details about him appear. With the advantage of the existence of a newly unified Portugal, which set the country apart from any other European state, Henry initiated the country's seaborne adventures, which included the slave-trade on the west coast of Africa. According to Camões' translator, William Atkinson, Henry 'sought communication with the mysterious Prester John, ruler of a Christian Ethiopia; he sought new channels of trade for his country; he sought to discover, perhaps to annex and colonise, new lands; he sought to extend the Christian faith at the expense of Mohammedanism; and the ultimate objective of all, he sought a sea-route to India and the East', and the East for him 'meant spices, the most sought-after commodity of the Middle Ages'.[11]

Canto 9 shows the Portuguese avoiding treachery from the Samorin of Calicut, and the mariners escaping and being taken to an Island of Love, which has been devised for them by Venus. Tethys (Thetis), the goddess of the sea, reveals herself to Da Gama, and canto 10 includes her prophecies of the extent of Portuguese domination. They will go as far as China and Japan. She includes a reference to Brazil, where the Portuguese arrived in 1500 (10.10–44, 50–73, 93–143). But the poem ends soberly, with warnings to the King, Sebastião, urging him to respect those who serve him overseas, just as the poem had begun by warning him (1.6–

18), as if with the sense of the imminent collapse of the Portuguese empire and the Avis dynasty.

The seventeenth century indeed saw the decline of this Portuguese empire, because of new colonialisms arising from the English East India Company (founded in 1600) and the Dutch East India Company (founded in 1602, after the Netherlands gained independence from Spain in 1581). Macao became a colony in the last days of Portugal's unquestioned success: Camões saw failure ahead, and even builds into the poem two references to being shipwrecked (7.78–82, 10.128), which are both symbolic and also perhaps autobiographical, and which pull the poem towards the centrality of Adamastor's curses. Both references appear in passages which are full of a sense of personal injustice being practised on him.

The Mount Fortress, its mock-Solomonic columns shown here curling in opposite directions, indicating baroque decoration of a seventeenth-century fortress, is a reminder of how the Portuguese seaborne empire could not survive Dutch attack. Some commentators think that Camões wrote the passages full of hope about Portuguese history (in cantos 3 and 4) before going to Goa, and that much else was written after his return. As one critic argues:

Before the *Lusiads* was published in 1572, then, the old Camões saw the

Oriental conquest … as mere vanity
and total ruin. The creative literature
of Portugal's sixteenth century opened
with laughter and pride in that
adventure. The so-called Renaissance
epic of the modern world, through
its dedication and finale directed
to the monarch, and through its
prognostication of gloom in the words
of the 'velho do Restelo' brings us to
the frontier of the Baroque age. This
strangest of epics … flies apart at three
junctures: beginning, middle and end,
all sections composed after the poet's
passage to India. These junctures undo
the very business of the epic.[12]

This argument sees something double in Portugal's
national text, making it both Renaissance and
baroque: Renaissance, as to its beginnings, describing
a hero (Vasco Da Gama) who has no self-doubts and
no inner quarrels with himself; baroque, because the
poem and the poet are full of self-doubt and inwardly
conflictual. This shows in the various attacks the
poem makes of the power of money to corrupt (see
the endings of cantos 5, 6, 7 and 8). Much of what
is said here has to do with the knowledge of how
corrupt imperial rule was in the East.

Camões' poem, finally, turns things towards illusion.
The poem comments on the island of love:

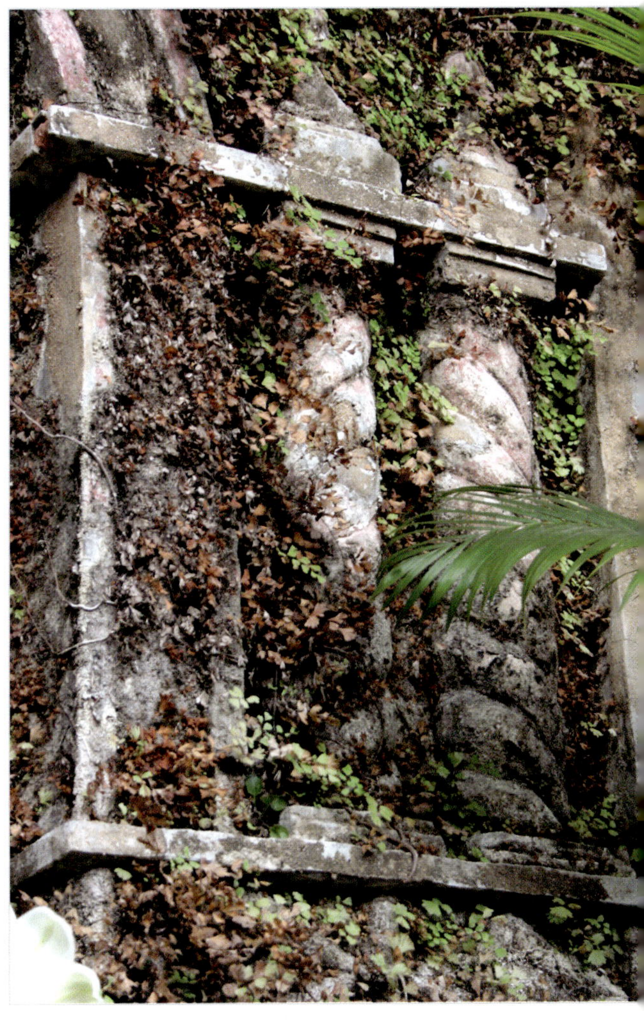

106. Mount Fortress (detail)

193

For the ocean nymphs in all their beauty,
Tethys, and the magic painted island,
Are nothing more than those delightful
Honours which make our lives sublime.
Those glorious moments of pre-eminence,
The triumphs, the forehead crowned
With palm and laurel — these are what is meant
And what this island's pleasures represent.

Those immortals whom men of antiquity,
In their love of great deeds, imagined
Living there on starry Olympus,
Soaring on fame's happy pinions
Through brave acts, or through
Mighty labours which were thought
Virtue's path, rocky and precipitous,
But ending in delight and happiness,

Were enjoying only those rewards
The world bestows for the superb,
Deathless achievements of heroes
Who, though human, became divine; ...

The poem adds that 'fame ... added strange titles,/
Such as gods, demi-gods, immortals, / Deities,
heroes, and the like' (9.89–91, 92, 1–4).[13] The
movement of the poem, then, is to see everything as
allegory. What had seemed material triumphs now
becomes only the consciousness of work well done.
Classical gods must disappear into mere moral
qualities, subject to the authority of Christianity.

What Benjamin calls 'the struggle against the pagan
gods, the triumph of Christianity, the torment of
the flesh' (*The Origin of German Tragic Drama* 220)
condemns the pagan world to illusion. Adamastor
himself, because of his unfulfilled love for Thetis,
is condemned to be a destructive figure. There is
a link between the melancholia of allegory, and
the sense that much has been lost when so many
energies can only be seen as allegorical. The poem
gives the success of empire, but threatens to remove
it as not substantial, illusionistic. In this way, the
baroque grows out of disillusion with empire.
That *The Lusiads* repeats the Virgilian epic (i.e.
The Aeneid) and its prophecies of the future glory
of Rome, with recommendations to bring peace,
already makes it a 'ruin', repeating a heroic past
(as Don Quixote tries to do). (And since Virgil had
been 'Christianised' as a prophet in the Middle
Ages, that 'ruin' embraces Christianity too.)

Piracy

In chapter 2, Coloane Library was discussed. It
is round the corner from the chapel of St Francis
Xavier, dating, like much else in Macao, from 1928
(see photograph 107). Another outstanding and
attractive example of miniaturisation in Macao is
the square outside the chapel of St Francis Xavier
in the village of Coloane, the furthest (now non-)
island of Macao. As a chapel is characteristically a

*107. Overview of square outside
São Francisco Xavier*

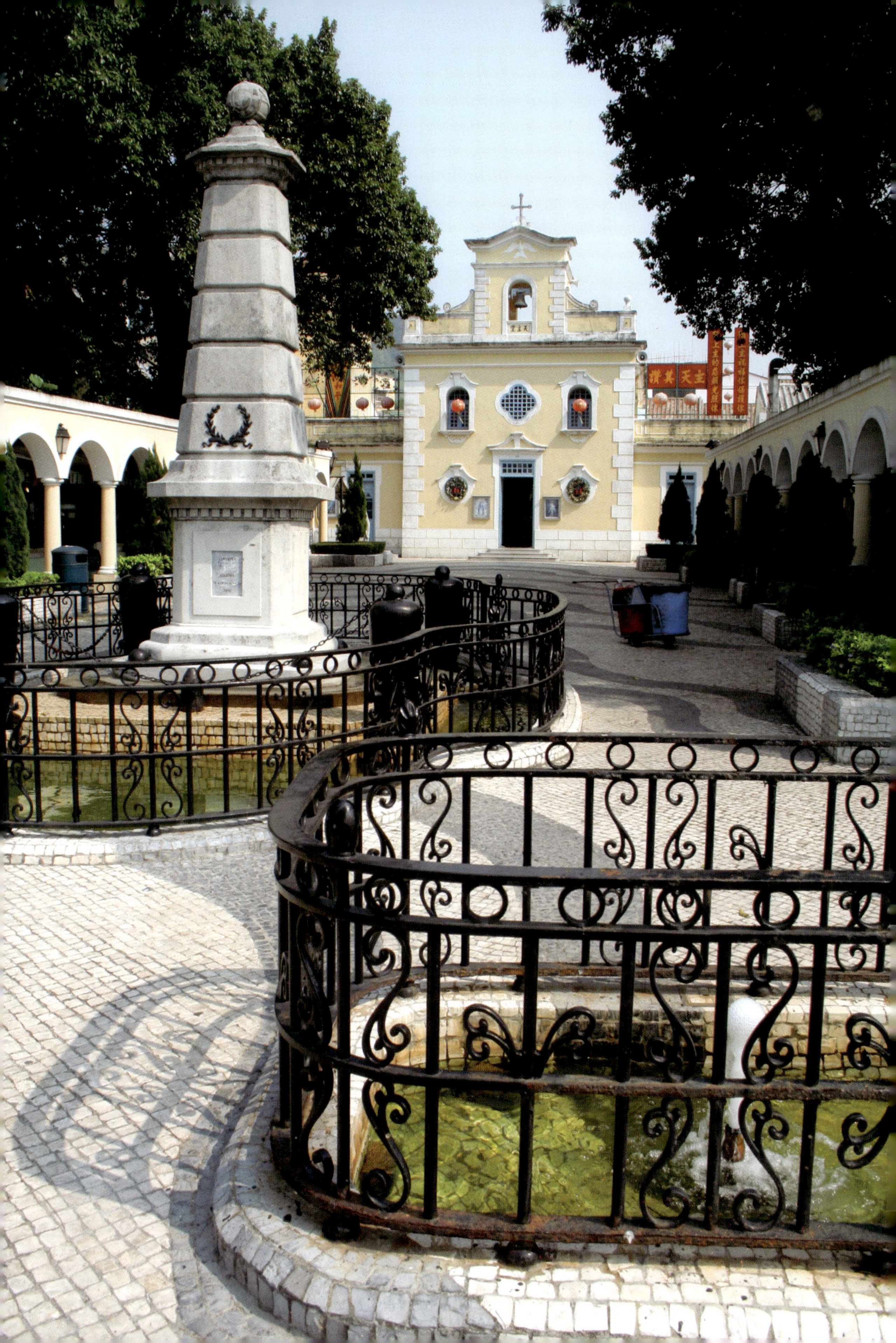

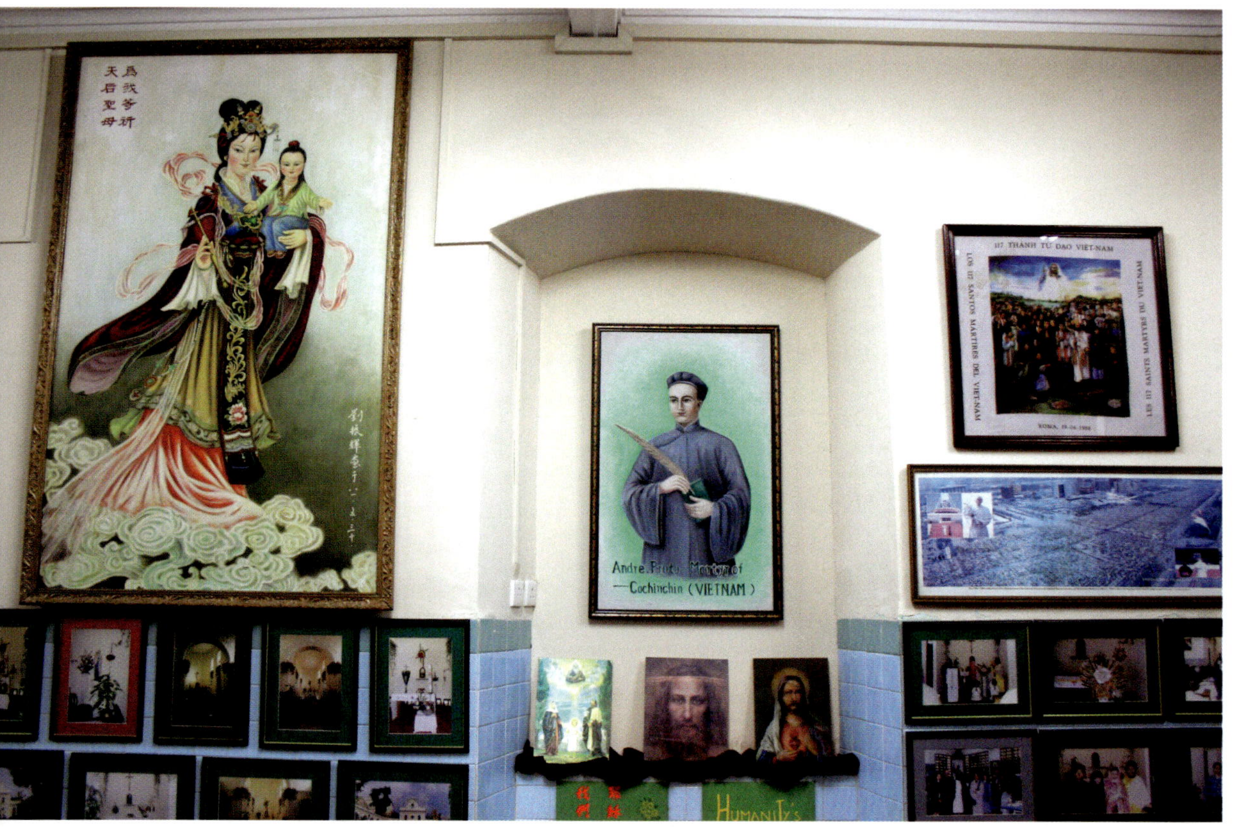

*108. Paintings in São
Francisco Xavier*

miniaturisation of a church, so the colonnades of the square (Jardim Eduardo Marques) outside the chapel repeat in miniature the colonnades in Senado Square and the black waves that make up the paving of its stones. Before noting a specific detail in this square, a detour should be made to the chapel, which originally housed a relic, the wrist bone of St Francis Xavier. It is an archive, with paintings which show the infant Christ with the Virgin Mary represented as a Chinese goddess (the Virgin Mary also looks Chinese in Baroque paintings visible in the Bishop's Palace).

Adjacent to this Chinese Madonna are other reminders of Christianity and colonialism, the pairing celebrated in *The Lusiads*; a photograph taken in Seoul celebrating 103 martyrs in Korea, another which recalls 117 martyrs in Vietnam who were canonised in 1988 in Rome. Between this and the Virgin Mary is a portrait of a Chinese missionary who has taken the name of André Pinto, martyred in Cochinchin: a reminder of the French in Vietnam, and the multiple ways in which colonialism has worked itself out, for this martyr is himself Chinese, though he had taken the name of an early Jesuit (André Pinto, 1538–1588) who came from Portugal to Macao.

In the square: the Jardim Eduardo Marques on Coloane has, as photograph 107 shows, fountains and a classical-style monument of 1910, standing in water, surrounded by cannon barrels and cannonballs and an artillery shell. Standing at the western approach to the square, the monument is dedicated to the memory of a fight between the people of Coloane with pirates, their leader named Wu, which is remembered every 13 July. It is a reminder of the power of piracy which is relevant to *The Lusiads* because the Portuguese seafarers themselves could easily be seen as pirates, as Bacchus accuses them of being, when they arrive

at Mozambique (1.78–79, see also 2.80, 8.53, 8.67, 8.74).[14] Piracy as part of the history of Macao begins with the coloniser and continues to the present, and the huge critical literature on it raises questions about the liminal nature of the pirate, and the relationship of this strange community, often homosexual in tendency, to communities on shore.[15] It asks questions about the relationship of their violence to sexuality and to state violence. In the case of the 1910 battle, where ships from offshore pelted pirates who had taken refuge on Coloane, it is ironic that one of the cruisers was called *Vasco Da Gama*.

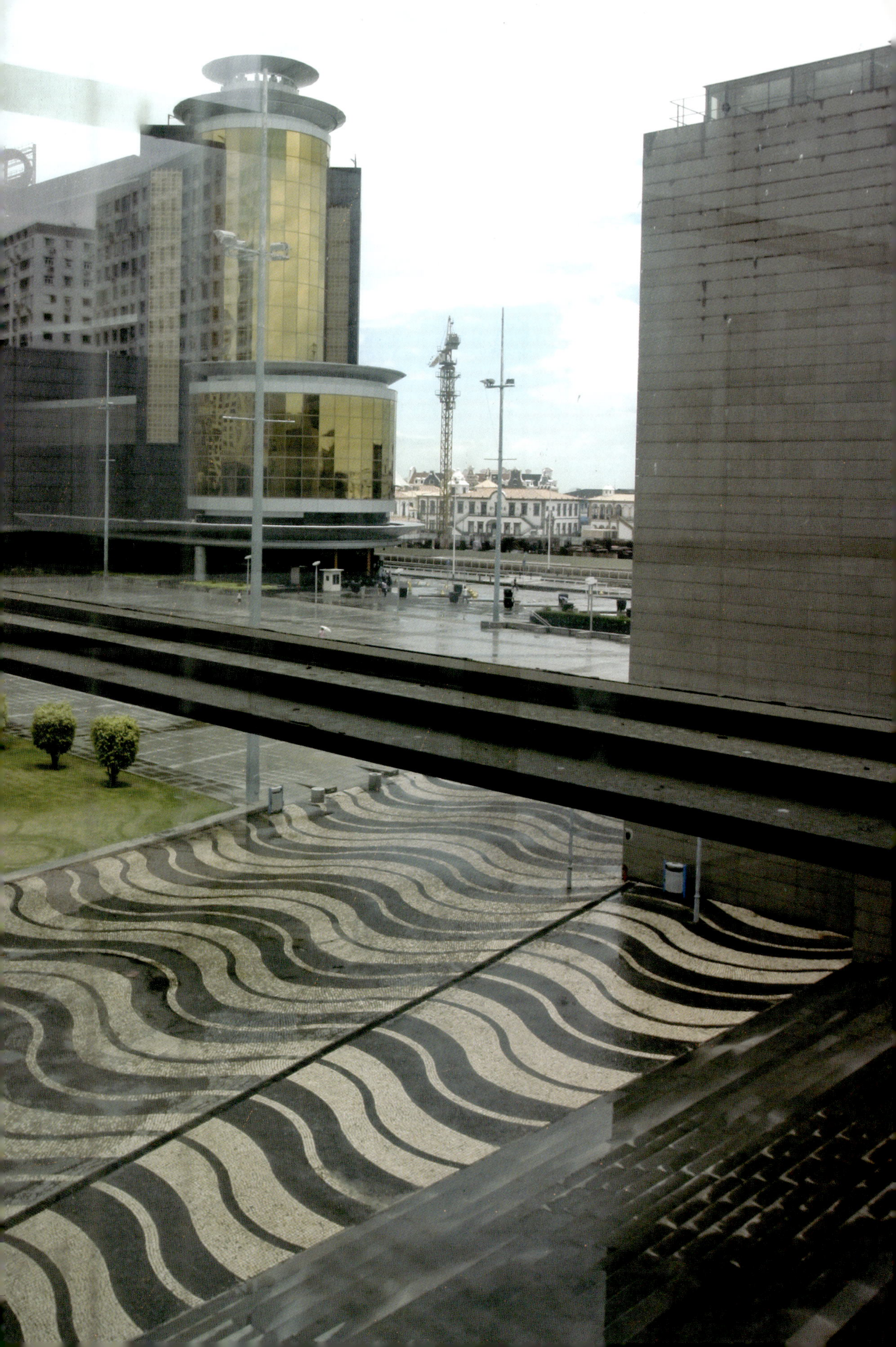

Chapter 11

Is Postmodern Macao's Architecture Baroque?

Like photograph 88, photograph 109 plays with illusions that are already there, looking out onto reclaimed land from inside Macao Cultural Centre (1999, architect Bruno Soares), with stairs mirrored in the glass, surveying illusionistic floor-levels, which though flat appear to be bevelled, across to the rounded towers of the Sands Casino, the lower one being seen here. These towers have been compared with UFOs, or with rockets, or more suggestively, with syringes, sucking money out of the gamblers. Beyond Sands is Fisherman's Wharf. Art and illusion are put against each other, except that art is also illusion. This reclaimed land is the part of Macao where visitors who come from the jet-foil which ferries gamblers and others from

Hong Kong will find themselves initially. And this seems to be inhabited so much by new casinos. It requires getting beyond this space, past the large international hotels, to get to the older, baroque Macao.

This chapter, and the next, suggests that there has been a desire to see modern Macao in Venetian terms. This certainly appears in the architectural work of the Lisbon-born (in 1962) Mário Duarte Duque for the Legislative Assembly and the Supreme Court (the Court of Final Appeal).[1] These are both situated on the Nam Van Lake, and jut out onto the water. The Legislative Assembly is the simpler building, basically rectangular, but this is

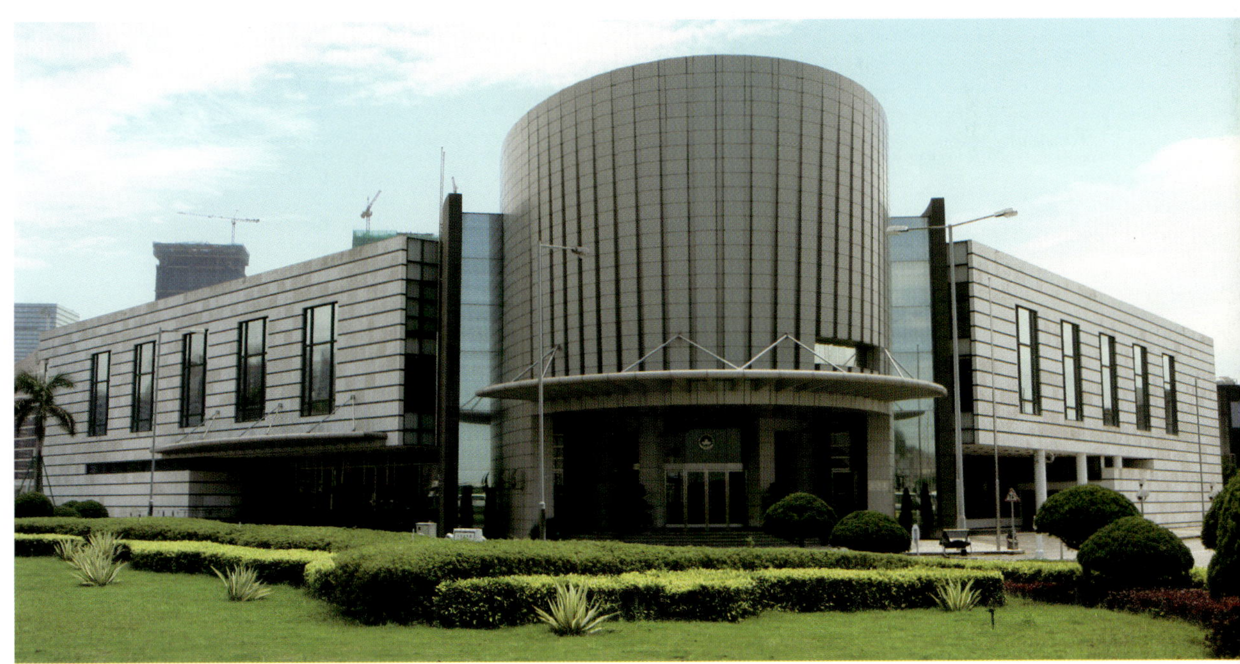

◄ *109. View of Sands from Museum of Fine Arts*

▲ *110. Legislative Assembly*

disguised by placing its main entrance onto a corner of the building, away from the waterfront.

The entrance comes out in a bevelled form which continues the sense of an ovaloid shape, which is how the floor-space of the atrium appears inside. The entrance has a massive overhanging canopy, looking from the side like an open mouth, and is so arranged that though it is perfectly symmetrical, it looks a little off-centred — an effect helped by the steps up to it which are not curved but cornered, and by its possessing only one window above, set to one side. The rounded corner above the entrance, massive, has no features at all, but looks like the blank wall shape that Herman Melville in *Moby-Dick* described the sperm whale as having for forehead. A blind wall, then. If the entrance may indeed be thought of as slightly off-centred in appearance, the symbolic intention may be to say to the person who approaches the building that however much they think they know, they are not quite equal to the proceedings of the legislators. The absence above the entrance of a flanking window to balance the other and the paucity of windows seem to deny transparency in government (the contrast with Norman Foster's glass-dominated Reichstag building in Berlin (1999 — the same year) is obvious). It seems to give nothing to the person approaching. The entrance faces onto empty grassland and away from casinos on the other side of the Nam Van Lake, as if blind to their existence. If it looks at anything, it is back to Penha Hill, and to the buildings climbing up to Penha Church from the line of old trees that marked the Praya Grande and the limits of land (see photograph 65).

Behind the Legislative Assembly stands the Court of Final Appeal (1999) — the Tribunais de Segunda e Última Instâncias: ultimate, appropriately, because this is as far as the land gets before the sea. Its position enforces the point that behind government stands the rule of law. It has been designed as virtually two buildings, linked at the upper storey. The one that looks out to sea has, predictably, a prow like a ship's. The one that looks to land, and towards the Macao tower, is more traditional.

The buildings are separated by a passageway wide enough to take a car, and the building to the left displays, as the visitor looks into it, a Dr Caligari-like Expressionistic exaggerated sense of perspective, where lines recede in grossly accentuated diagonals. (The shadow cast by the building to the right only intensifies the feeling of potential menace.) The left-side building, in fact, seems to be leaning on the other. (What does Justice lean on?) Throughout these two buildings which are in fact one, the rectangular box-shape which makes it, or them, functional, has been disguised, either by decorated diagonals, or by corners which have been inverted, or kinked, turned outside instead of in, the effect being to look playful and individualistic, in a form of shaping the building which is associated at its fullest with Daniel Libeskind's Jewish Museum at

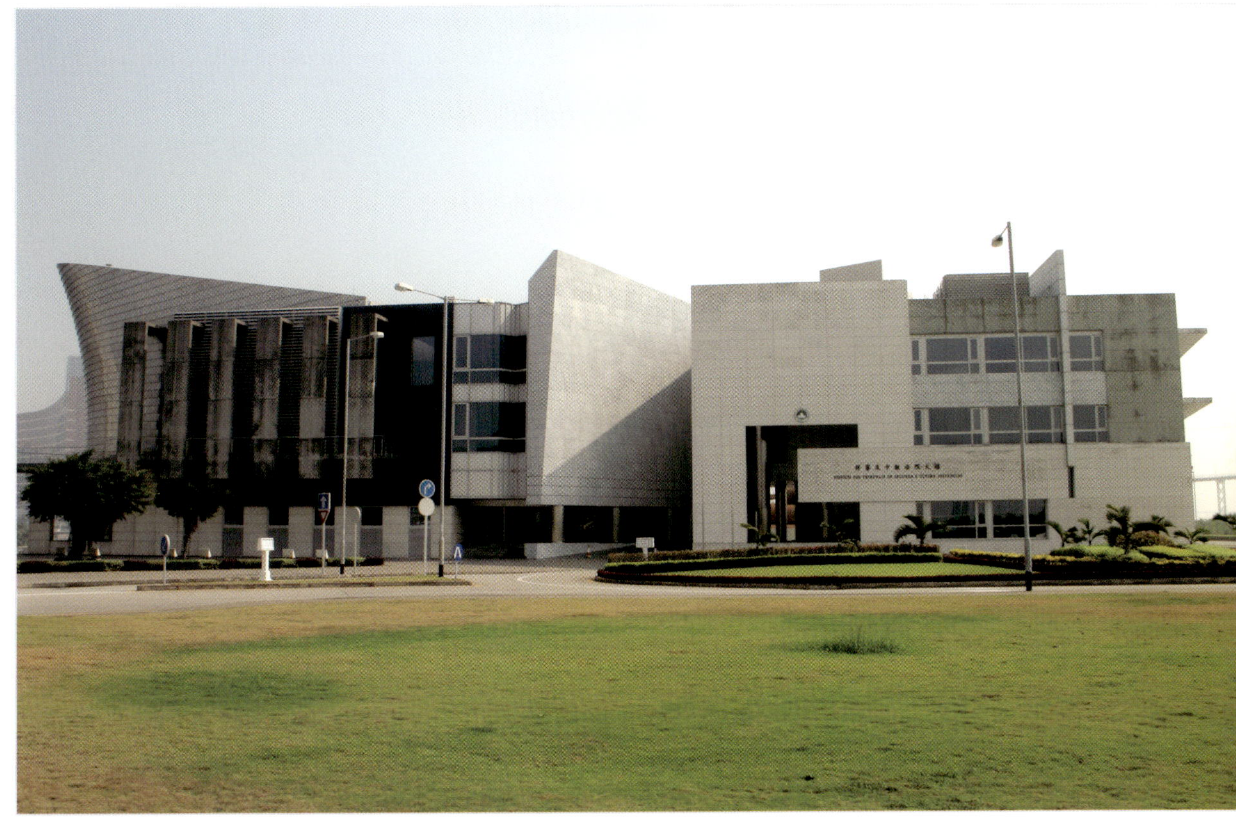

111. Court of Final Appeal

Berlin (2001). The building to the right shows its modernism with its horizontal lines, and its postmodernism with the horizontal tongue that intrudes onto the rectangular C-shape (it resembles the Chinese character 'dented'). The tongue looks attractive, but its value is no more than decorative, like everything else in this building, not integral to the function of the building, whose dents and kinks are meant to imply that the law is able to meet each individual case, and has no single uniformity within it.

Since it is hard to design monumental architecture, that which must embody state ideology, it is pleasant to turn to the Kindergarten Dom José da Costa Nunes (1997), also designed by Duque, and situated as the hill descends down the Rua da Fonte da Inveja, to the Estrada da Vitória. Duque was commissioned to add to an existing art deco–style school, and to incorporate the new development into a fast arterial road that was adjacent to the old school. The school is approached alongside it, down the hill, and the first thing that is seen is a sloping shape whose exaggerated diagonal emphasises the road's descent, and which looks like one half of a child's see-saw. This reaches down to the other building, with which it makes contact via a footbridge adjacent to the carriageway, which cuts through the kindergarten layout. Behind the façade the road is completely concealed.

For the buildings on the right there is the teaching block of five levels surmounted by a roof which comprises part of a broken rectangle (photograph 112). The right building, located more uphill, houses a single-storey indoor theatre hall (photograph 113). The external wall already described evokes a yellow paper-folded bird, also with features extended into the air, which are solely decorative.

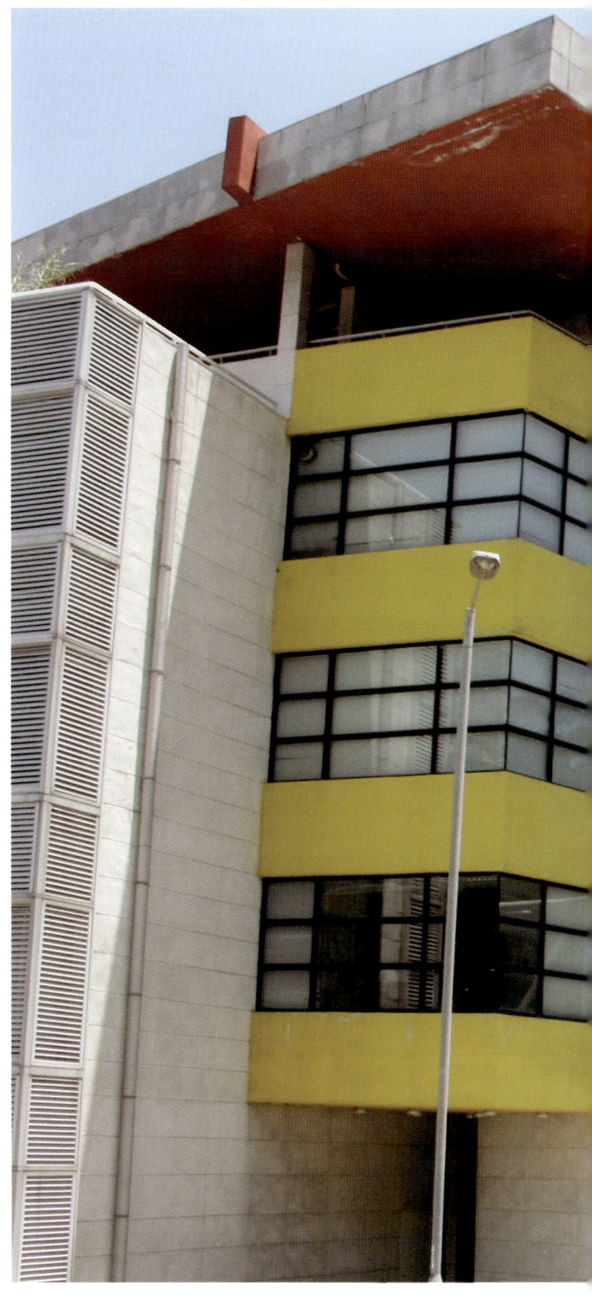

112. Kindergarten Dom José da Costa Nunes

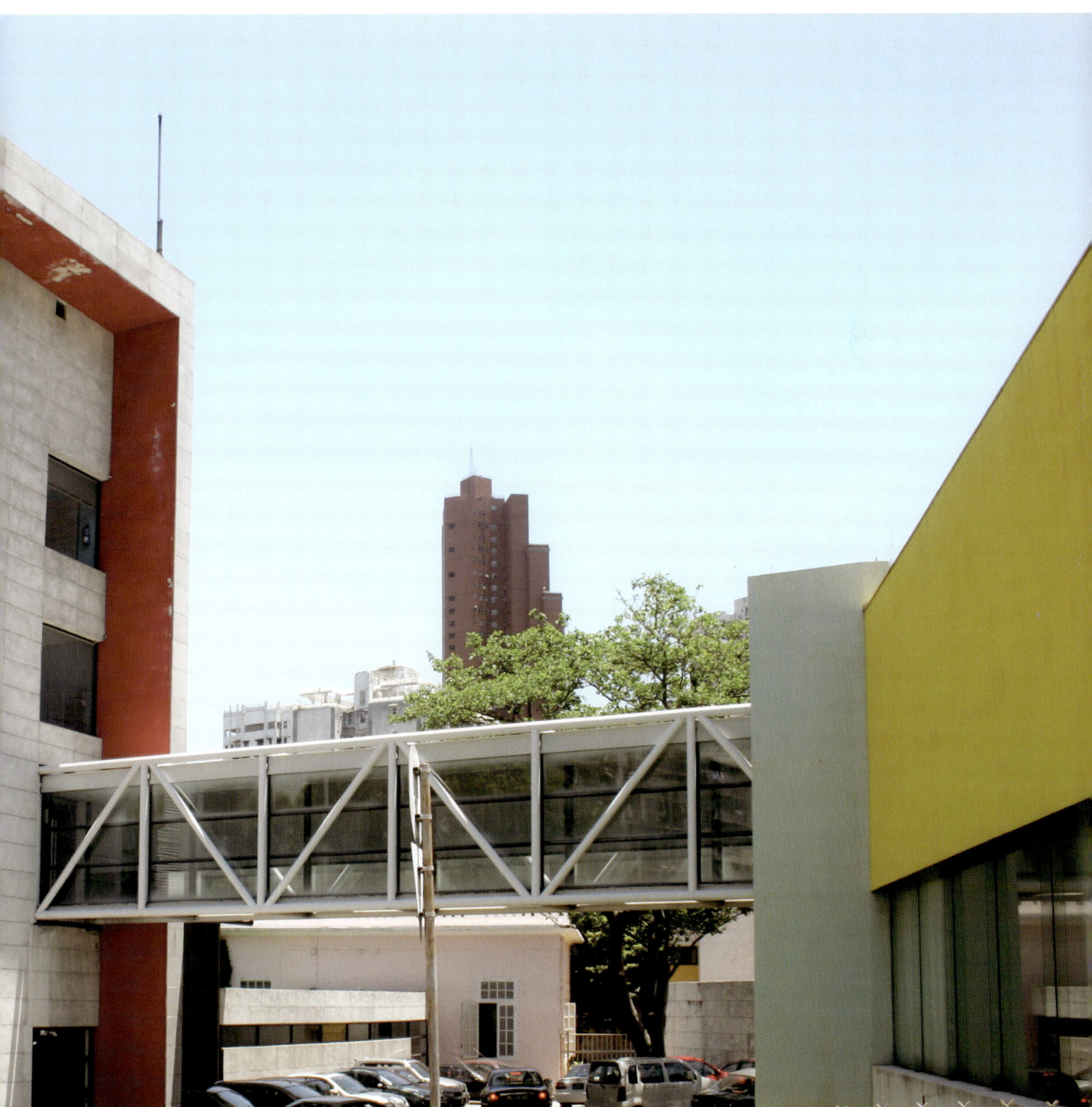

The taller left-hand building is painted with bright colours — the bright yellow carries primary, naïve associations with children's perception and their need to explore space. Traffic also becomes a dominant motif of the layout: there is heavy traffic running across the school, and a car park from where access is gained is under the footbridge connecting the two buildings — a passageway whose structure is repeated in the Final Court. This is playful architecture, whose irregularities take children away from conceptions of uniformity, and provide them with an interior long slope to run up and down, guiding them within a safe space; but in the case of the Supreme Court, the irregularities seem contrived, or forced. The baroque was defined as a 'guided culture' which suggests that it may be dirigiste, the language of the state, but, as with the Lou Kau mansion, that architecture (if tentatively seen as baroque) decentres power and sanctions no single position. But the buildings of the Legislative Assembly and the Supreme Court, however much the architecture attempts to decentre, do not decentre at all. Architecture here decentres the person before the law, but the institution itself remains what Deleuze and Guattari would call a 'molar', single structure.[2] The additions to the buildings that prevent them appearing mere rectangular block, though they seem like baroque folds, are add-ons; details only seem to disavow the regularity of the law.

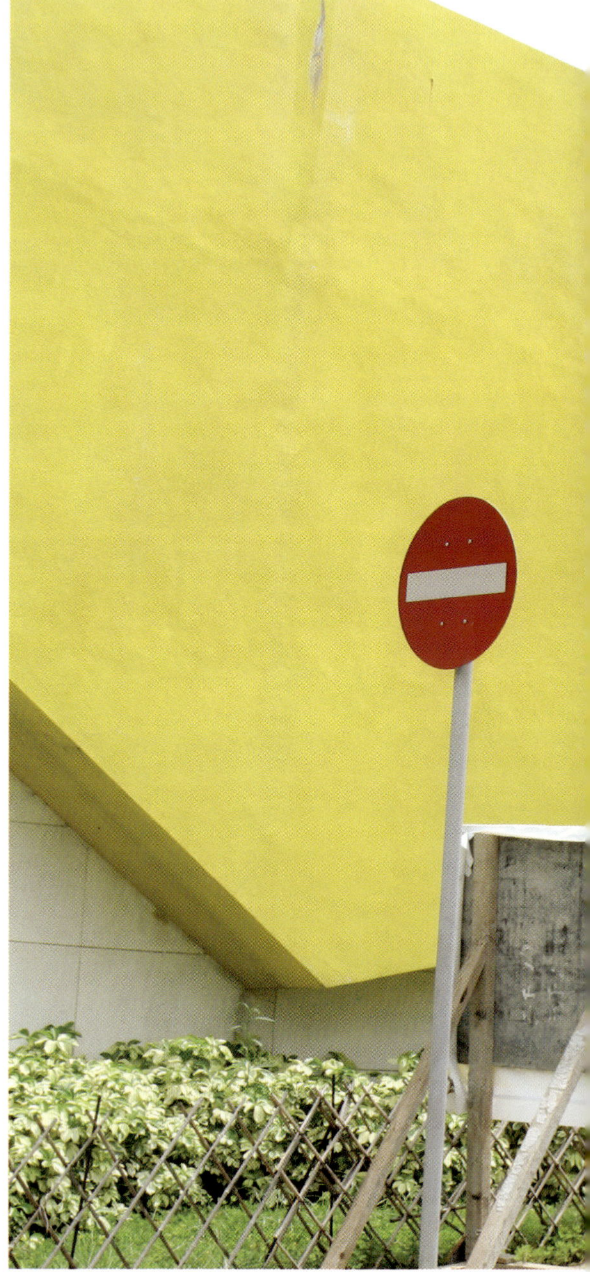

113. Kindergarten Dom José da Costa Nunes

204

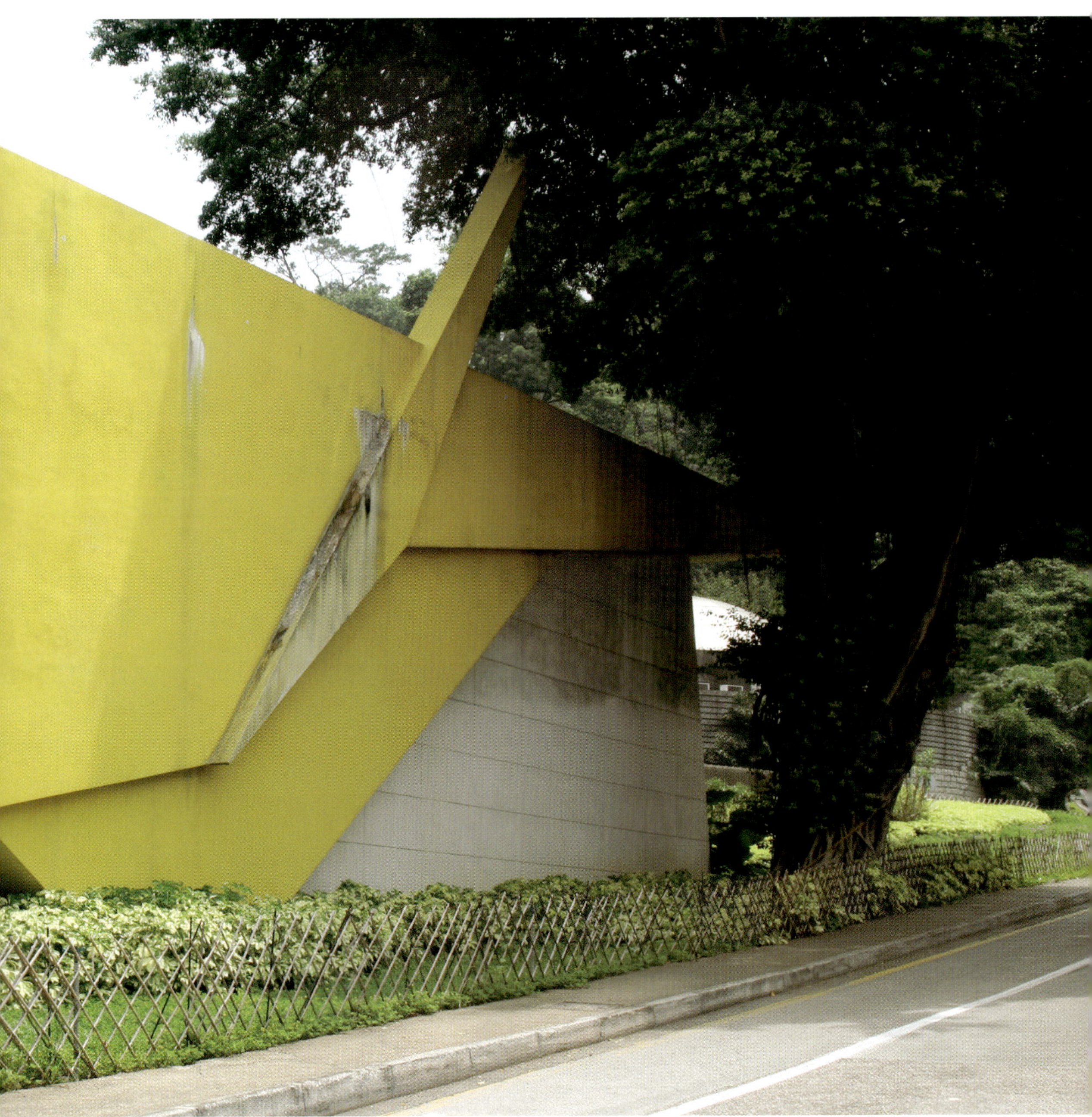

Fire Station: Taipa Island

Many of the modern buildings in Macao are postmodern principally in the sense that they add on details to disguise the functional (modernist) aspects of the building. A good example is the fire station on Taipa, designed by Adalberto Tenreiro (Adalberto Tenreiro ATeliers, 1995). (Equally interesting is the fire station headquarters on Macao, designed by Manuel Vicente, 1996.) Nothing could be more functional than a fire station, and one feature that it must include, in the context of Macao's high-rise buildings, is a practice tower: this one is forty metres in height, ten floors altogether.

This photograph was taken from behind the fire station, and captures the tower surrounded by waste ground about to be built on. On the other side of the fire station is the CTM building, and it is interesting to compare the two. The practice tower is a quadrant whose circular exterior disguises a rectangular structure, and the building has been put together as much as possible to look like a child's model. It is as if the school and the fire station had the same inspiration, perhaps to suggest that the work of the fire station (always celebrated in books read in kindergarten) is child's play. The exterior rounded wall is full of tongues protruding, or of pieces cut out of it, as if suggesting the fragment. While its shape is there to defeat the dominance of the rectangle, it also plays with the rectangular form, in that some of its balconies deliberately jut out in a rectangular manner. It is not that the building is being made to look as if it has suffered some kind of violence, it is rather making fun of the idea of wholeness, playing with fragments, ruins. The CTM building opposite, much more modernist in style due to its being simpler, more functional in appearance, looks as if its face, its façade, has been cut across and scarred: that effect can just be seen in the photograph, on the right; in that way, the modernism of the building is, as it were, cancelled out, or put under erasure; the scar being, it seems, playful, not serious. Just the same playfulness is exhibited in the fire station, whose brown, soil-like colour (the opposite of fire) contrasts both with the bright red of the sheds where the fire-engines are kept, and with the gleaming silver of the CTM building. The postmodernism of this plays with the fragment, as the baroque does, but this building is not a fragment, rather, a whole disguised as fragmentary, whereas baroque is the art of the fragment itself. This distinction seems to hold good for many of Macao's new buildings; decoration of the surface of the building disguises, or attempts to nullify, the actual modernism of the rectangular structures built into the air. The symbolism of the tower may suggest the idea of broken floors, and protruding gaps that have been gutted by fire. If so, this playfulness, which is also perhaps a warning in a minor sense, implies that the fire station exists after the fire, for the city in ruins, the 'invisible city'.

114. Taipa fire station

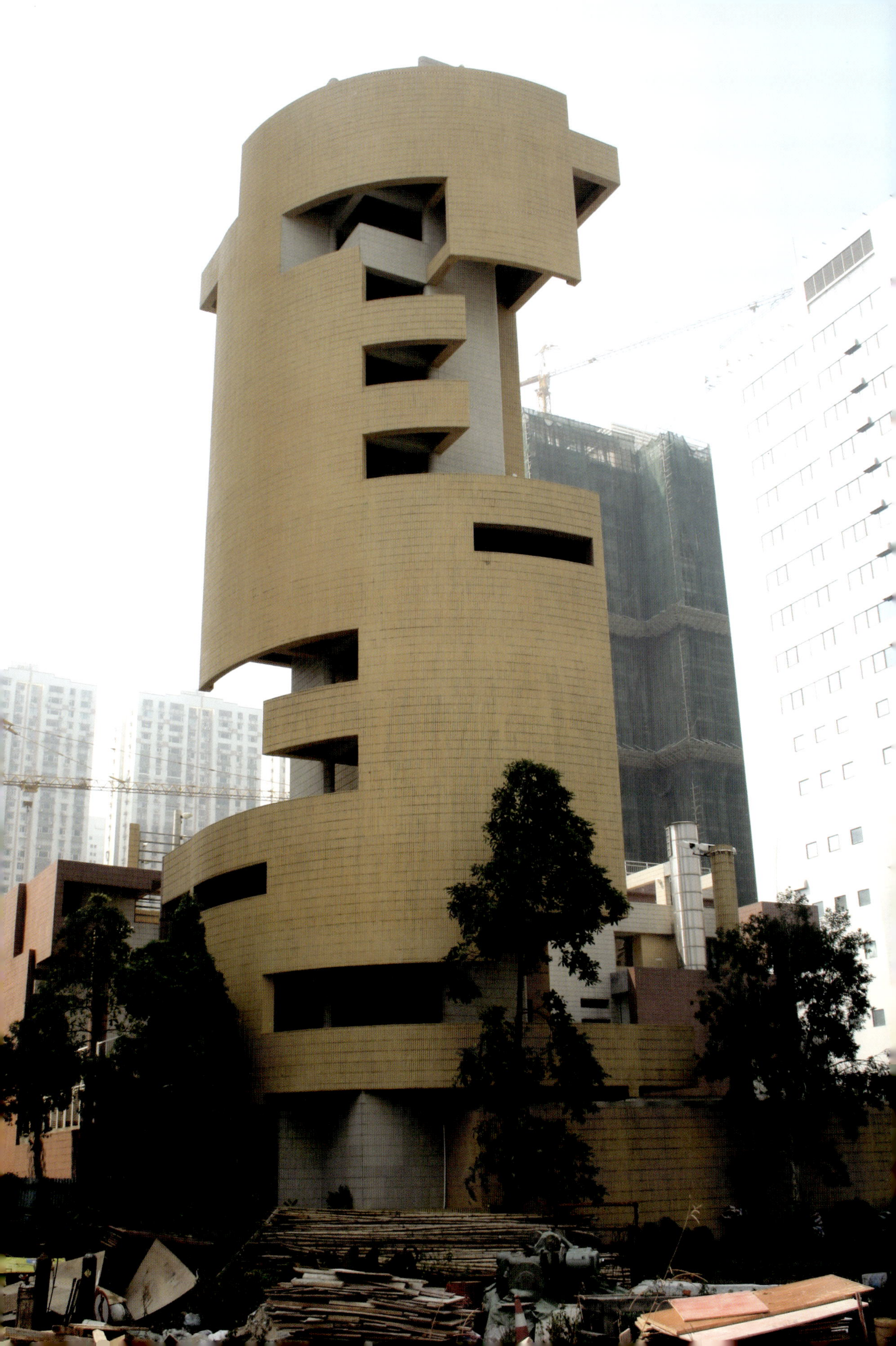

But the ruins here are deliberate, and all around the tower are huge high-rises. The tower stands out amongst these, and seen against the sky, as it is possible to view it, there seems to be a new creation of space in the way the walls jag out and recede as it climbs upward.

It must also be added that the buildings described here are all particular to Macao: they could hardly be imagined in Hong Kong in their playfulness, use of colour and creation of space.

The Institute for Tourism Studies

An interesting combination of older and newer style, as well as older and newer sites, appears in the Institute for Tourism Studies (Instituto de Formação Turística), opened in 1995. The Institute is located in the northern part of Macao, on the Mong-Ha Hill ('Watchout for Xiamen' i.e. the city in Guandong; or, literally, 'watching out for a building'). The hill is some sixty metres above sea level. The visitor approaches this past Avenida do Coronel Mesquita and Macao's radio station, and goes up a road which passes, on the left, the new Inspiration Building (designed by Mimi Cheung (New Design Company Limited)), which comprises classrooms and lecture halls for the students, and squash courts as well (these jut out over the road as rectangular shapes whose function cannot be guessed from the outside). The centre of this building is a courtyard, and all round it are balconies on three storeys onto which the classrooms give. The road turns to the left after this building, and the visitor continuing the climb upwards finds a hotel on the left, run by members of the Institute as a part of their training. The hotel, the Pousada of Mong-Ha, is an old barracks. The road continues up beyond this point to reach a plateau, with fountains playing. To the left appears the 'Educational Restaurant', part of the Institute, designed by Chan Meng (New Design Company Ltd). To the viewer's right, there is a semi-circle of arches which frames the fountains, and partially behind these, there is a slope down to another space, leading down to a grotto, and an area for children and the new Ecological Center and greenhouse.

But if the visitor continues on upwards, the Mong-Ha Fortress is reached, built after 1849, overlooking the China border. (Another choice of route is an exercise path which contours the hill and provides access to some old military structures.) The colonial forces in the nineteenth century were waiting for an attack from the mainland which never materialised. The building was continued under the orders of the Governor Coelho do Almaral, and abandoned in 1962. The date over the entrance reads 1866, and one of the buildings inside the fort, which had an ammunition store, an observatory and platforms with Armstrong guns, reads 1887.

If the visitor now returns downhill to Inspiration Building, and gets access past the concierge, something very interesting happens. Climbing up the three storeys of the building gives onto a roof garden.

Photograph 115 shows the view down from the roof, into the well of the Inspiration Building. The stairs in the photograph are what the person sees first upon entering the building from the side, to the right corner of the photograph. The abyssal effect will recall the Lou Kou mansion, discussed in chapter 8. The garden contains a herb garden, growing all specimens of European and Asian spices and herbs. It is also a space for leisure itself.

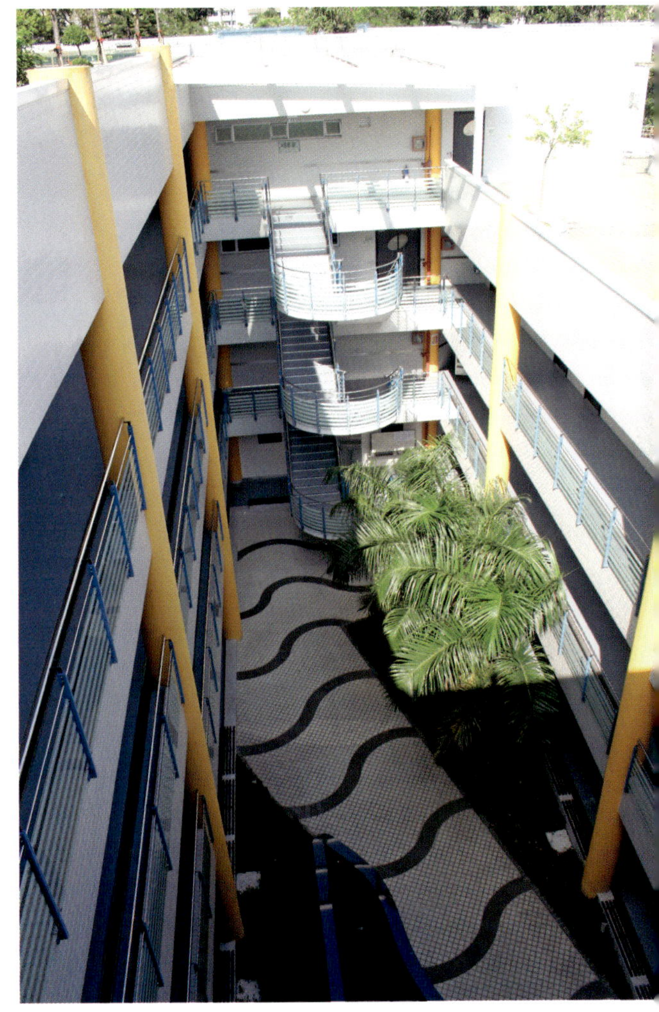

115. Courtyard of the Inspiration Building

The photograph here looks across to the roof of the Inspiration Building, which can be seen to the right. The abyssal space in the middle, which divides the building, can also be seen. Behind the building itself, sunken as it seems into the earth, may be seen the top of the radio building. The high-rises of Macao are all around. This is an alternative space whose existence could never be guessed at from the road, the line of which can be traced on the left, as it corresponds to the white L-shaped parapet of the roof. The curve of the footpath above echoes the wavelike curves of the floor of the Inspiration Building (photograph 115), which replicate so many wavelike curves in the city's pavements.

And beyond this roof-garden is a door which leads into the top part of the hotel. The lower building at the foot of Mong-Ha, and the hotel half-way up the hill are connected both by road, but also, more interestingly, from above. Just as the barracks can only be understood, as to their old function, when the fort is seen, so the journey over the top links the various new parts of this site.

At this point, it is worth looking in more detail at the Educational Restaurant further up. As the viewer stands where the road flattens out into a plateau, there is the arcade of columns to the right, but to the left, a building oddly decentred.

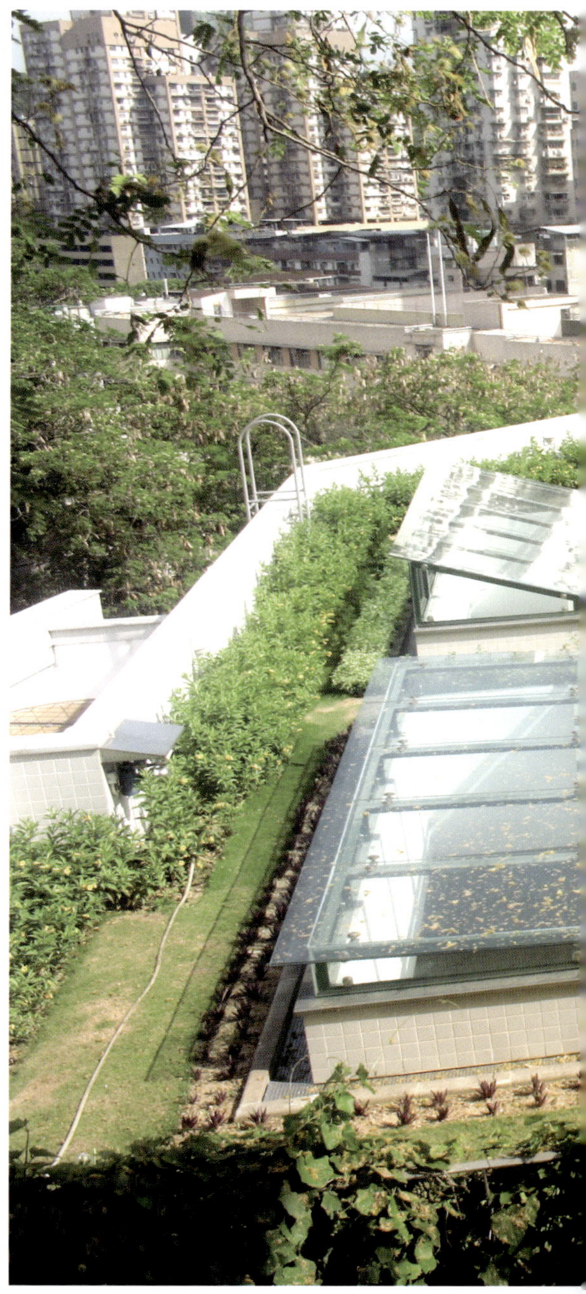

116. Roof-garden

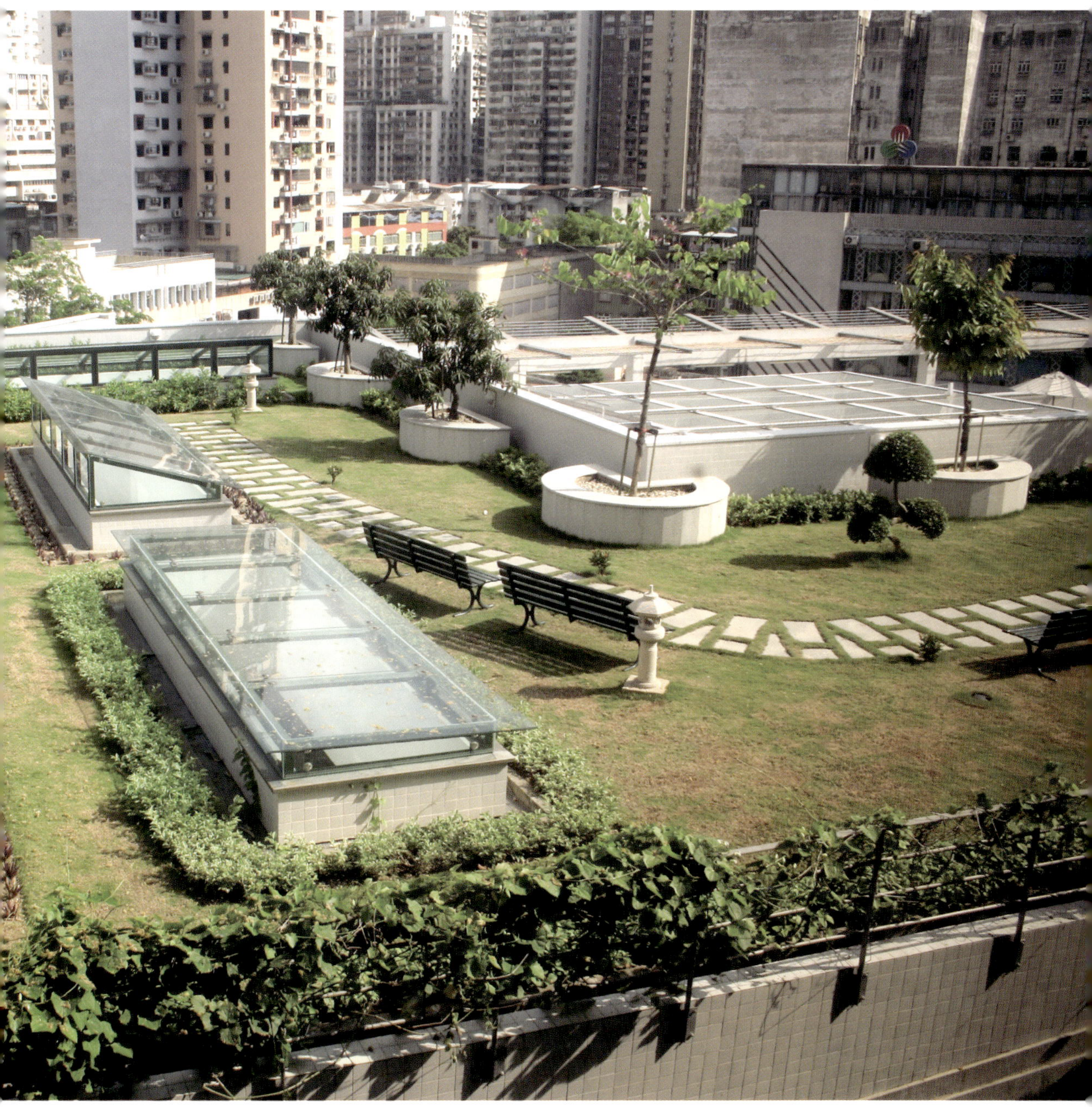

The restaurant is flanked by two wings that come out, and which have ochre colonnades fronting them. The back wall has an asymmetrically placed portico of five columns standing on a low platform. The interior of this portico is bisected by a wall, and if entering, via the left of the wall, the visitor walks through a door, while to the right, entry is into a blue metallic tower — or funnel, or even cage — whose floor-plan is ovaloid. On entering this funnel, spiral-like steps are discovered, leading up to the first-floor dining rooms. The steps are not rounded like a spiral, but squashed by the oval dimensions which funnel the visitor upwards: this space seems baroque indeed. The portico was thus designed because it was built in two different stages, but the effect from the outside is a more extreme de-centring than the entrance to the Legislative Assembly, and it baffles vision. The photograph was taken at a distance from the building to the right of the approach road, now seen on the left, and concluded by the bollards. To the right may be seen the central space of the plateau and just the lip for the fountains.

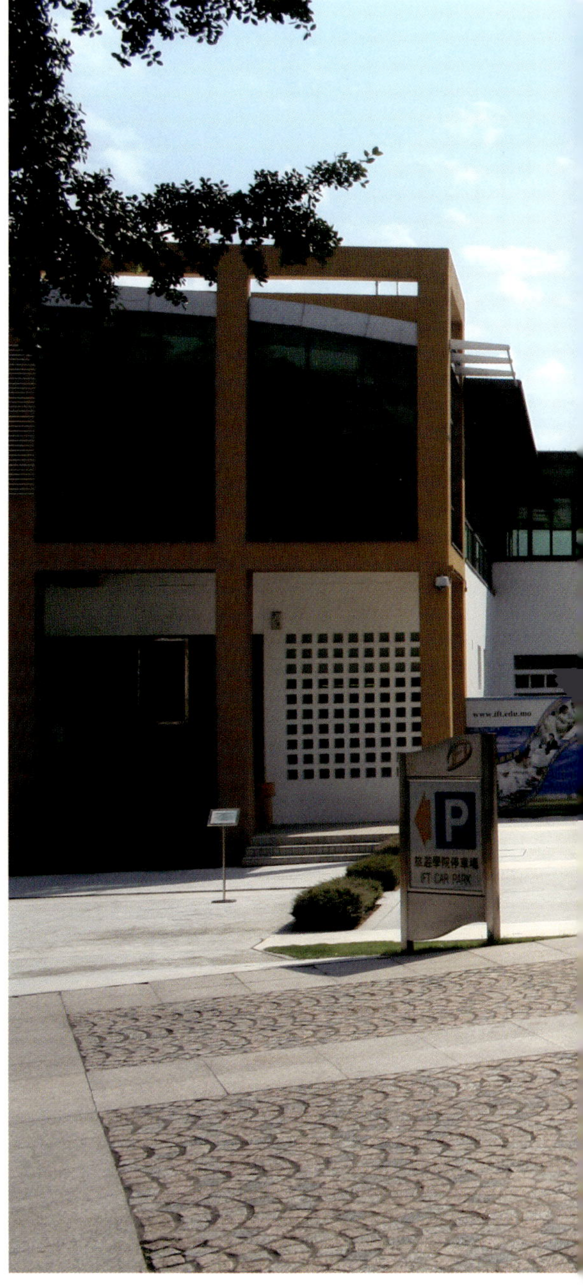

117. The Educational Restaurant

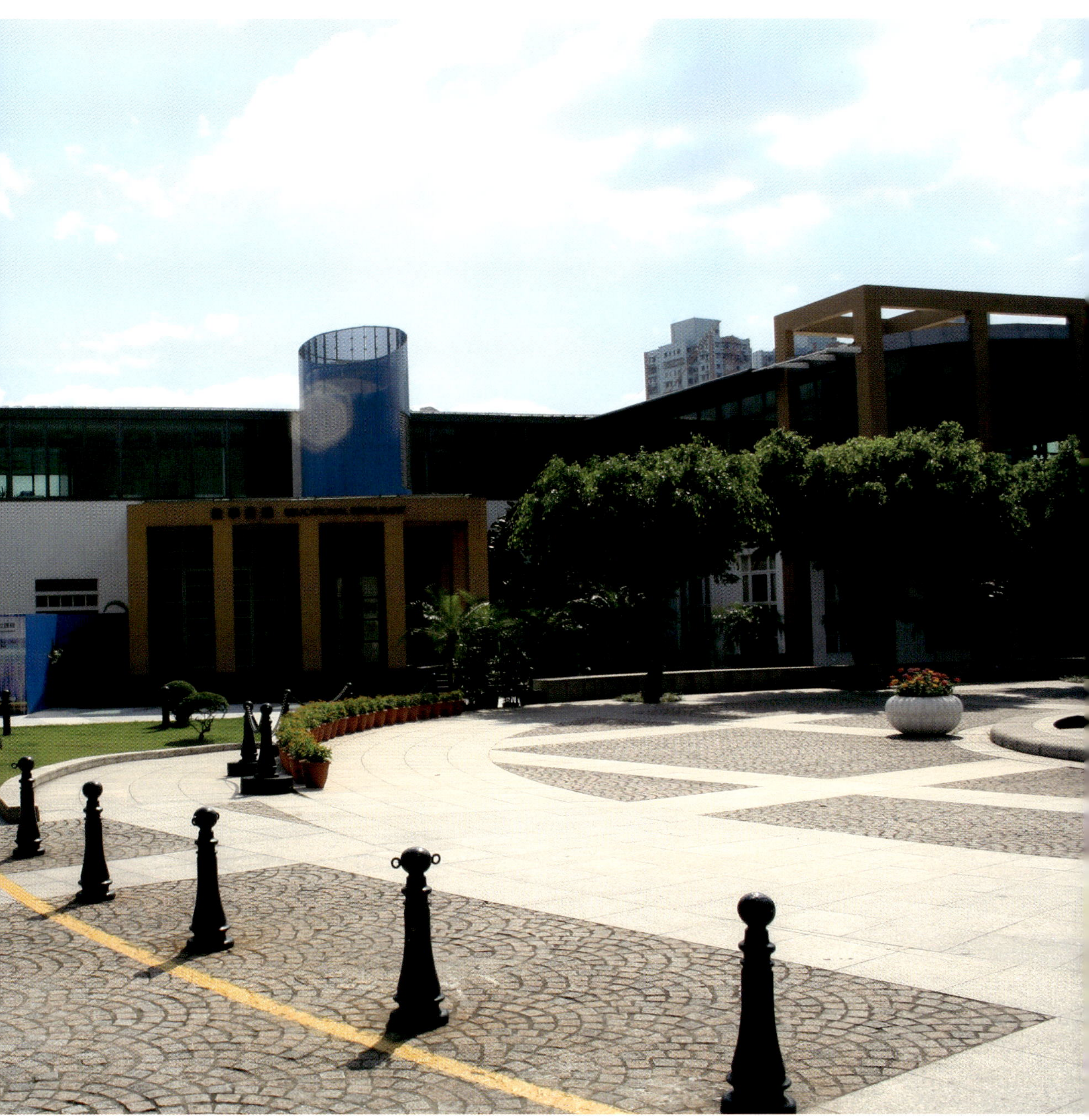

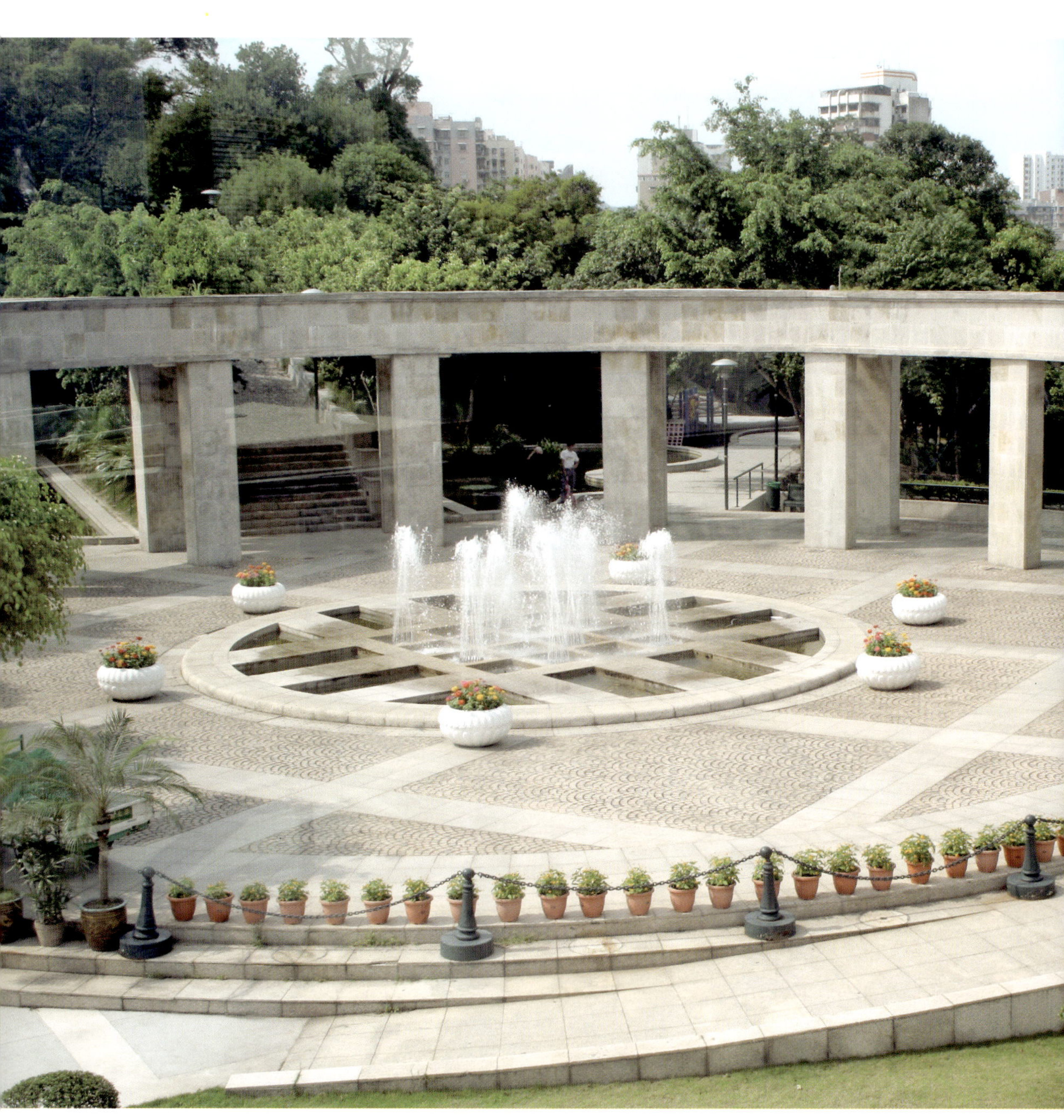

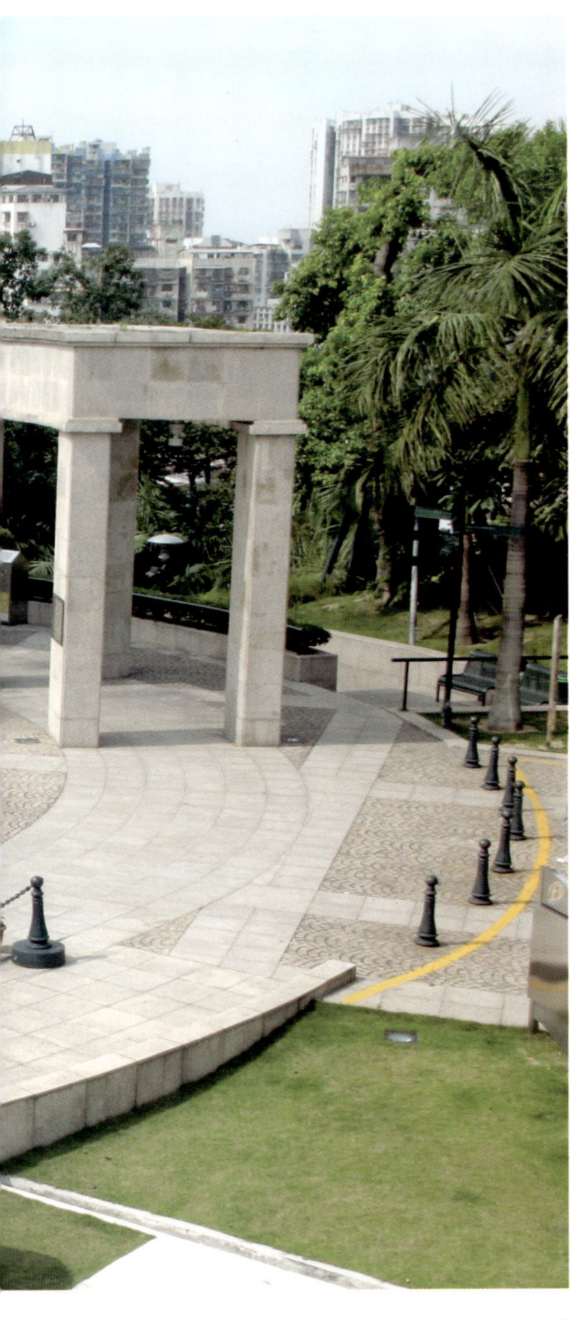

118. Colonnade

This photograph, taken from the first floor of the Education Restaurant, shows where the previous photograph (117) was taken: standing at the far right of the picture. (The bollards may be clearly seen.) The fountains are shown in the middle of the picture as is a concrete colonnade behind, which is, however, a broken segment, on the circumference of a slightly raised circular platform. The straight lines crossing the plan of the fountains make no alignment with either the vertical lines of the colonnade or those on the pavements. This park was designed by another Portuguese woman architect practising in Macao, Maria José de Freitas, who also renovated the Dom Pedro V Theatre. If this colonnade, which contrasts with the colonnade of the Educational Restaurant, is considered, it will be thought that the inspiration, however remote, is Bernini's front to St. Peter's in Rome, the ultimate classical and baroque grand design, inaugurated after 1656. Anthony Blunt discusses the oval shape of this as like a 'teatro' [theatre], clearly meant to reflect the shape of a Roman amphitheatre, so again recalling the theatrical, illusionistic nature of the baroque.[3]

In comparison to Bernini's wholly symmetrical enclosure, complete with fountains, this space is fractured by the irregularity of both the building and the concrete colonnade, which deliberately disturbs the spectator's sense of alignment, and is also short of being a perfect semicircle. Space has been distorted, the eye unsettled, by something which is subtly heterogeneous to the order of the place. The plan of the colonnade has also been cut to allow for the trees to continue the circling, on the viewer's near side. Everything, from the subtle changes in floor level to the colonnade-like trees (trees as pillars), is there to disorientate a sure sense of place.

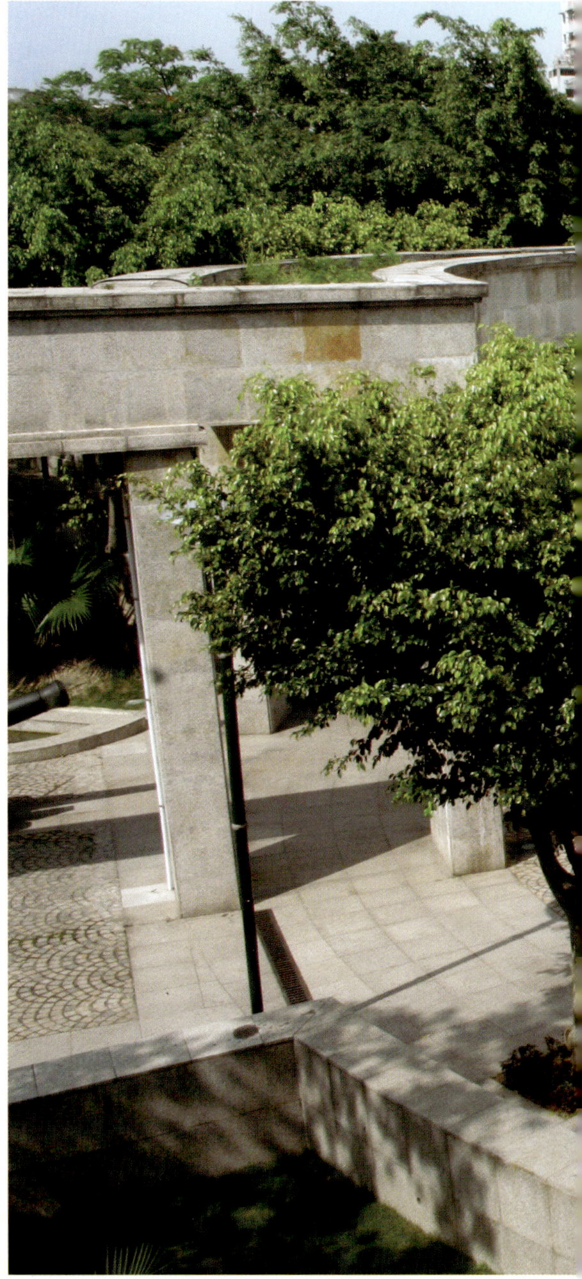

119. Colonnade and trees

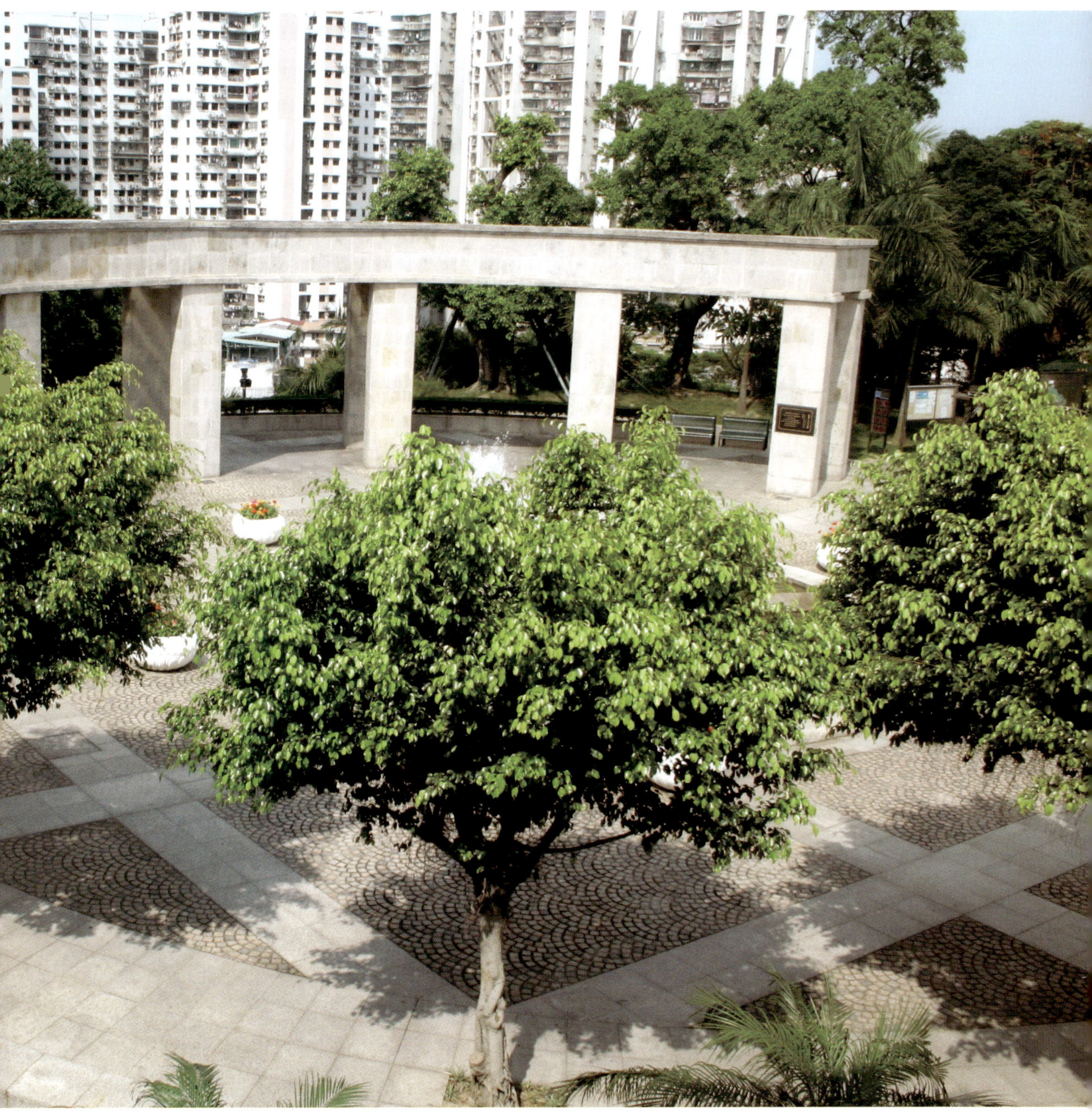

Church of St Joseph the Worker

The northern, working-class area of Macao, Iau Hon, near the border with Zhouhai, contains a church, designed by the Portuguese architect Luís Tomás Pineiro Nagy, which opened in 1998. It is dedicated to St Joseph the Worker as the patron of the Chinese mission: its façade, indeed, gives out straight onto an avenue leading down to the water's edge, beyond which China can be seen. As the viewer looks at this façade, there may be seen a white rectangular outline, broken by a cross mounted above it, its arms parallel with the top of the rectangular shape of the façade wall. However, the façade is also broken half-way down by a balcony, which means that the entrance to the church is on a first floor. To emerge from the church is to stand on a balcony looking towards the mainland. Steps up to this balcony from the street level are, unlike St Joseph's seminary, to the right and left, and are concealed behind rough brown brick walls. The space between these walls underneath is for classrooms. When the church was built it stood by itself; now it is surrounded by a parish of high-rises. The interior is rectangular, with triangular wings extended on both sides of the church, whose shapes can be seen from the outside. The central aisle runs from the west end to the east and the altar, behind which is a fake brick wall, repeats that wall on either side of the west entrance. In front of the wall at the east end hangs a huge picture with blue background and a

Christ with the cross behind him, with outstretched arms welcoming the Chinese from the mainland. The north and south walls are recessed outwards into a triangular shape as if stretching out an extra welcome.

The most remarkable feature of the church is its pictures, fourteen in all, which are hung on the balconies. Their prominence means that windows in this church are reduced to narrow horizontal strips above the pictures: the windows in this church are the paintings themselves, by an Italian artist, Giuseppe Francavilla, who was apparently brought to Hong Kong and Macao by the Pope in 2000 as a priest. Those to the left are of the Old Testament: 'The Call of Abraham', 'The Divine Promises and Covenant made to Abraham', 'Jacob's Dream', 'The Burning Bush', 'The Table of the Law Committed to Moses', and 'Elijah is Taken Up into Heaven'. The last in the series is 'The Call of Isaiah'. On the right, the seven from the New Testament are in symmetry with these, though perhaps the exact relationship is not always clear, and gives the sense (as with allegory) that anything could be compared to anything else. They comprise 'The Birth of Jesus', 'The Visit of the Magi', 'Jesus is Baptised', 'The Transfiguration', 'Jesus and his Mother' — referring to the Crucifixion — and 'The Resurrection', followed by 'Pentecost'. The pairing of these as they run from east to west suggests 'The Birth of the History of Salvation', 'The Revelation of the History of Salvation', 'The Way of the

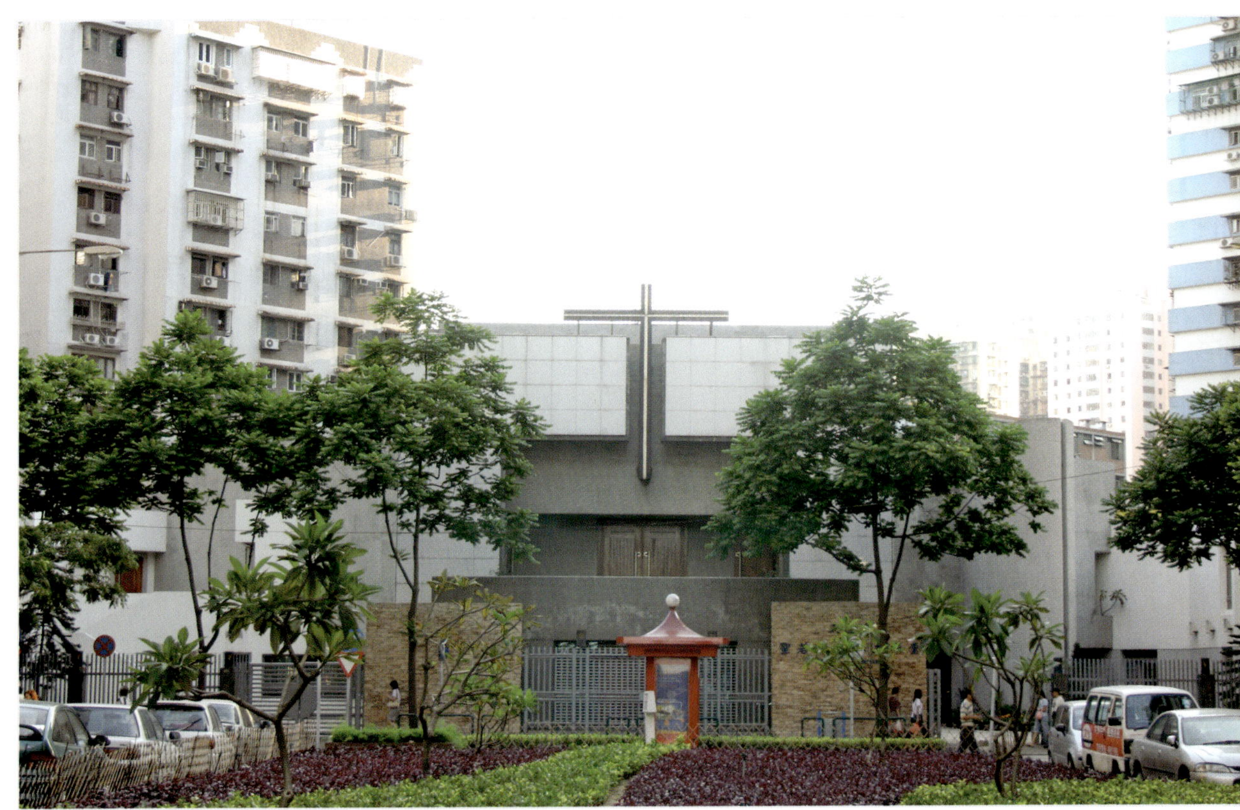

120. Front view of church

History …', 'the Centre of the History …', 'The Fulfillment …' and 'The Ultimate Purpose …', and last, 'The Actuality of the History of Salvation'. They are suggestive of Giotto's frescoes in Padua, Assisi and Florence, most significantly in the presentation of the mountains, and in the attention to narrative; they also evoke Byzantine art, with elongated figures in hieratic poses.

In keeping with the thought that these pictures are acting as windows, it will be noticed how many give visions of the open heavens: the point applies to virtually all of the Old Testament series, and the third and fourth of the New Testament, with in addition the first and the sixth and last, all of which add in angels. Deliberately, the choice has been made to paint in relation to the beginnings of modern European art, when Cimabue (1240–1302) and Giotto (1267–1337) moved away from older Byzantine styles, which froze figures into stiff, unmoving figures (so that they did not appear to take part in narrative painting). The paintings, which look like a recreation of the early period of Italian art, are rendered in childlike colours and show a childlike naivety in design, evidenced throughout, and in that sense, typical of all the postmodern art and architecture discussed in this chapter. Especial features of the childlike appear, for example, in the schematic skull and crossbones at the foot of the cross, in the comparative absence of perspective, and in the readiness to put two separated scenes together into one painting, with no sense of the incongruity of associating them. (For example, the scene on the mountain when Moses is given the law, and the scene in the valley below when the people make the golden calf, are presented adjacent to each other.) The reader who wants to see how Francavilla has followed Giotto may compare the horse taking up the chariot of fire on which Elijah sits with the horse in Giotto's *The Vision of the Chariot* in the upper Church of St

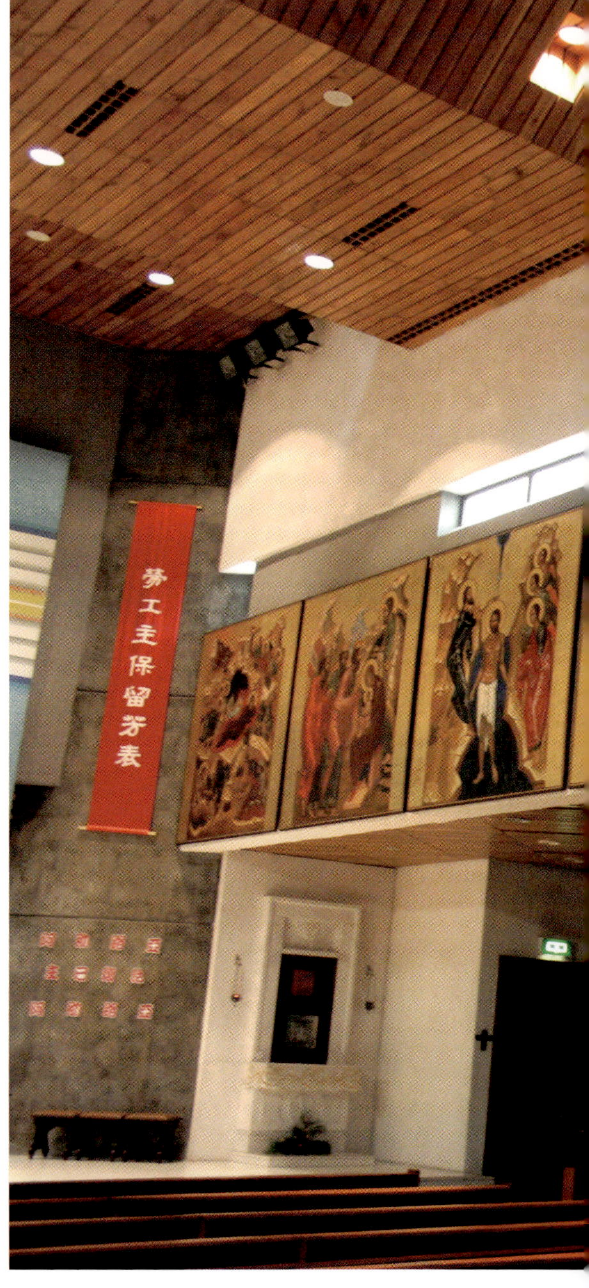

121. Paintings of New Testament scenes

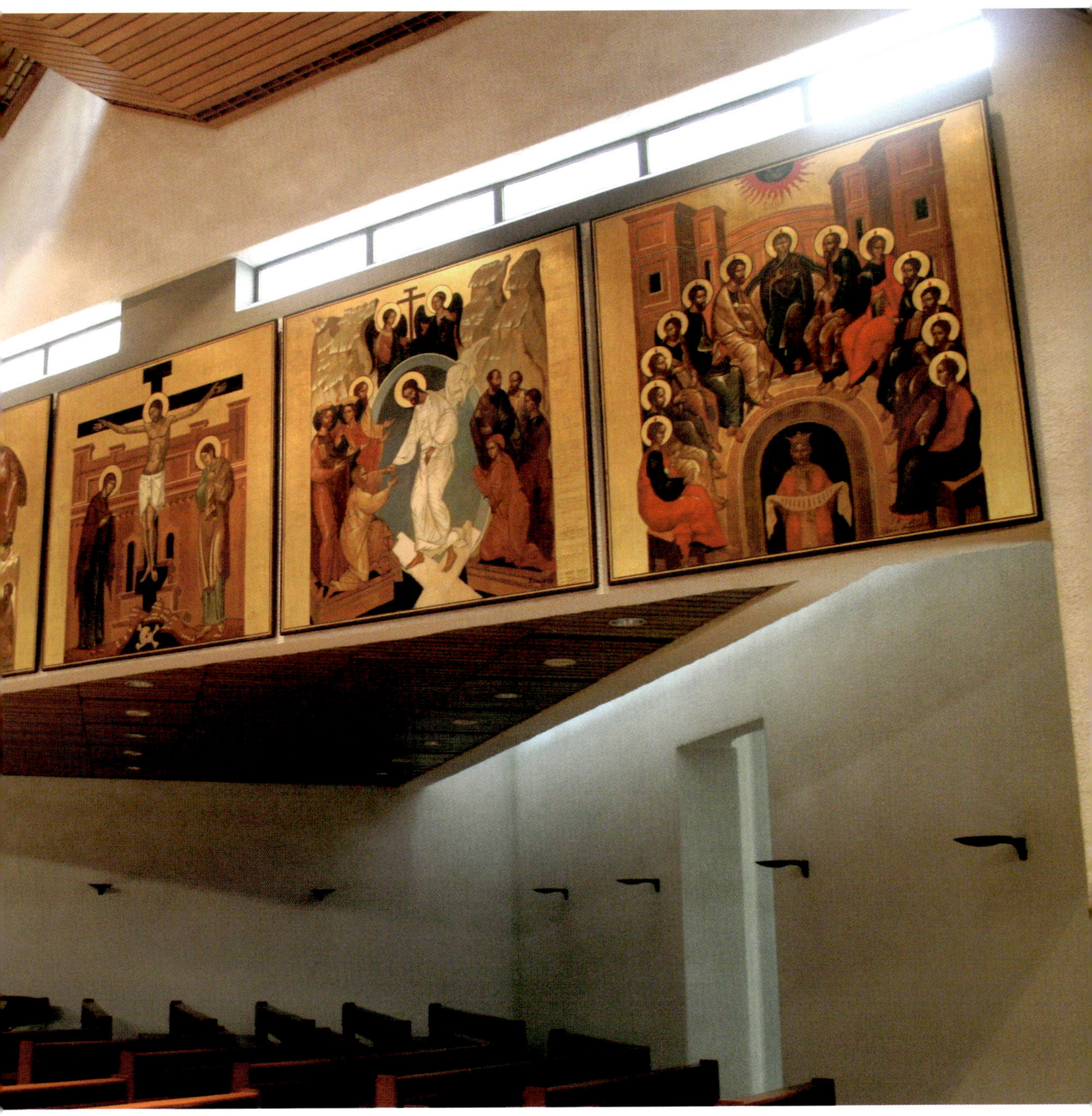

Francis in Assisi. Here, Francis, as though he was Elijah, is being taken up by horses and a chariot, while his disciples watch from below, and Alastair Smart says that the bronze-red colouring given to the figure of St Francis and to the chariot and horses denotes the fiery heat which according to the *Legenda maior* (the Life of St Francis) emanated from the visionary forms. The horses in the picture of Elijah are bright red, though Elijah is not, but he is wrapped in what looks like a huge tongue of fire.[4] These pictures are narrative art, and of course there is narrative both in the individual paintings, and in their presentation as a sequence.

The Baptism of Christ, the third along in the photograph, contrasts with the one discussed in chapter 3 (see photograph 20). That was dark; this one is in the brightest possible colours. Christ stands at the front in the middle: there is no de-centring here. His white loincloth contrasts with the royal blue of the River Jordan on which he stands and which reaches behind him up to the top of the shoulder. Water falls from above as part of the tail of the Holy Spirit who is in a dove-form. St John the Baptist stands to the left, on a ledge of mountain, his right hand suspended over the head of Christ. To the right of the picture are three angels, the most prominent in red. Whereas the older picture emphasised the affective and emotional aspect of religion, and may be described as 'heavy' in feeling, this one is light and bright and childlike, and has no emphasis on feeling or on the desire

of the picture to create affect. It is religion which has nothing to do with the nineteenth century but which instead evokes a world of play. It has avoided the realism which sabotaged Christianity in the nineteenth century through the power of science. Biblical events now are seen in the atmosphere of the medieval world and in the light of imagination which has nothing to do with realistic foundations. This is postmodern art for postmodern religion, reacting against nineteenth-century pieties, which are heavy and dark, and by the same token, reacting against melancholic aspects of the baroque.

Elsewhere in the church are representations of Christ, looking not European but Chinese. In this representation of St John's Gospel chapter 4, a Daoist Christ, looking older than the woman, sits teaching her, while she, looking prosperous, with a bucket and a rope, is about to lower the bucket into the well. The picture is Chinese — the way trees, grass and the mountain at the far background are represented — apart from the halo, which makes the painting more kitsch than rococo. If the picture is trying to attract converts by making Jesus and the woman Chinese, it nonetheless becomes more problematic in playing on Chinese clichés, and even suggests a romance rather than a scene of conversion. The Giottoesque pictures avoid the problems of trying to situate sacred events in a recognisable landscape: that is their postmodernism.

122. Jesus and the Woman of Samaria

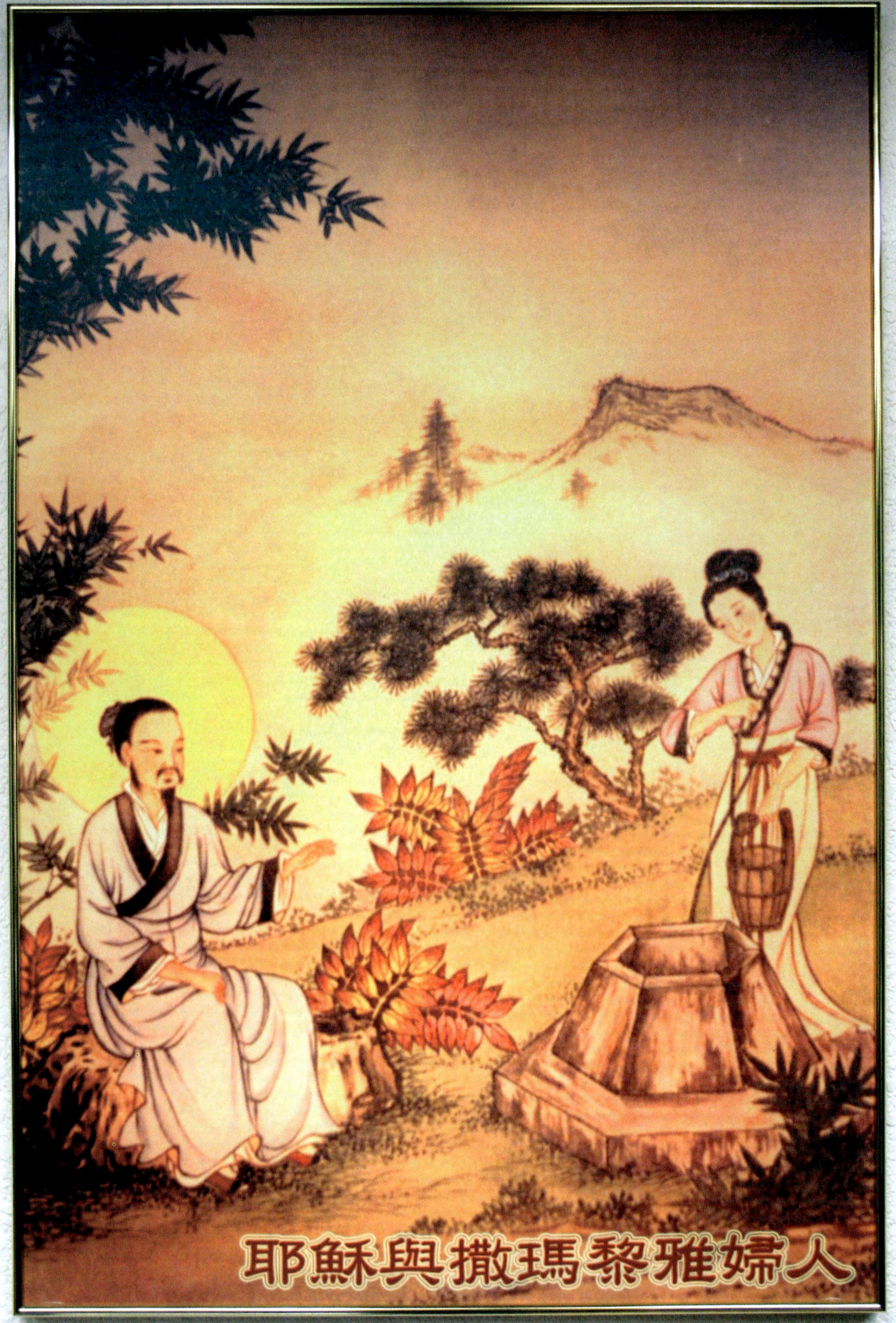

耶穌與撒瑪黎雅婦人

Death in Macao

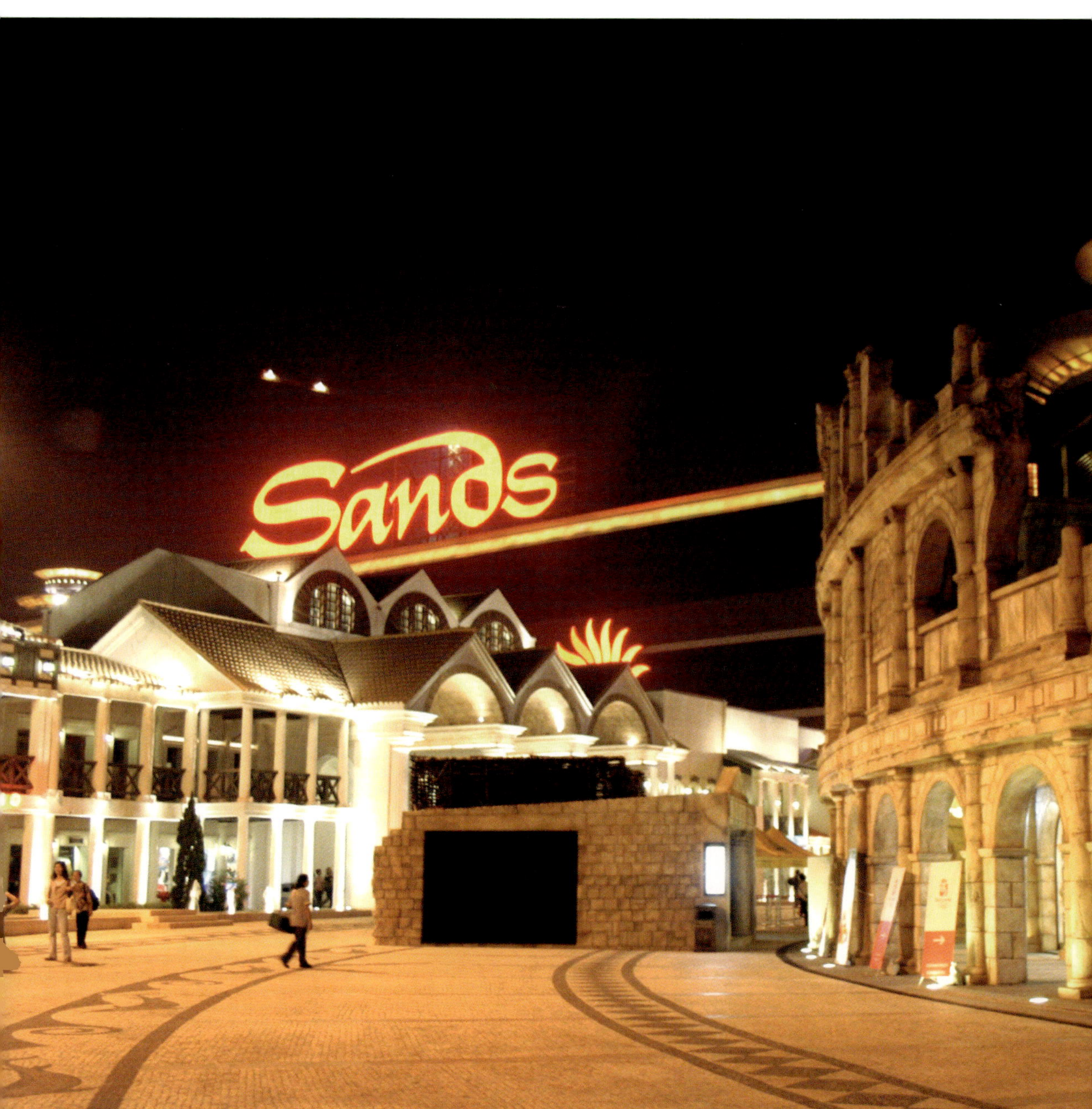

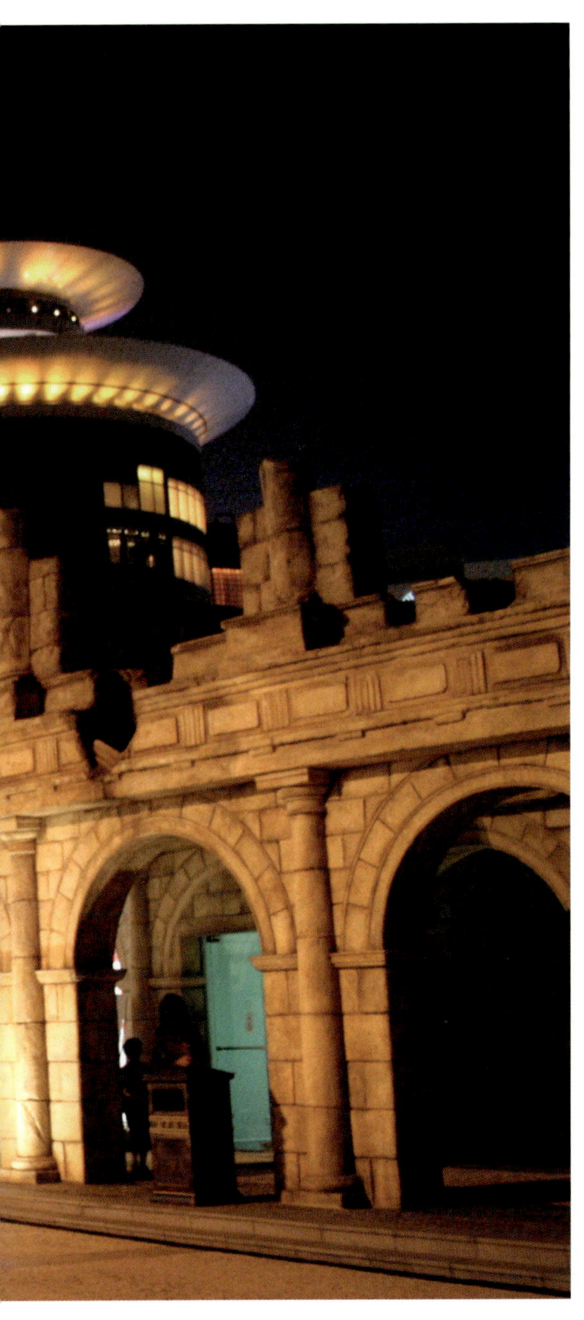

123. Colosseum

It is a question how much analysis of baroque Macao applies to the new city-space, much of which has been created out of reclaiming land, threatening to make Taipa and Coloane disappear as separate islands, as it has also profoundly changed the Praya Grande and bulldozed so many of Macao's earlier buildings.

Fisherman's Wharf, copying America (San Francisco) in the name, is no wharf, though it is on a newly built waterfront. It opened at the end of 2005, for casinos, shops, restaurants and theme-parks. These include a series of pastiche sites of interest: a T'ang dynasty palace; a mock mountain called Vulcania, which includes a 'River of Fire' ride; a Dragon Quest; an Aladdin's Fort, which includes much pseudo-Islamic building and advertises minaret jumping, and which is accessed by an Imperial gate, the Roman Colosseum, and a mock Trajan column complete with what is called a statue of Caesar. There are old English medieval houses where the wood is rendered in concrete disguised to look like old wood, and a main street. This has a series of old Dutch houses, a New Orleans area, an Afrikana section of native huts, a casino, and adjacent to it, going back, returning up the main street, a Miami art deco–style restaurant, and some other sites, including what looks like a pastiche of Macao itself, where there are mock Portuguese buildings. The hero of *The Lusiads* has given his name to a Da Gama waterworld. All these are shops, and bars and restaurants, and there is the inevitable conference and centre. The Colosseum, built as a ruin, is nevertheless a practical working space for stage shows, and its ovaloid shape unconsciously aligns it with the baroque, as with other examples in Macao. The photograph shows the oval shape of the amphitheatre, which seems here to be enclosing the tower of the Sands Casino. The amphitheatre is deliberately fragmented, like the fire station. Where the cutting out of elements that would give completeness was a feature of that building, and was for artistic reasons, to give wholeness, here it makes the building look like a cliché representation.

At the end of the street is the Babylon Casino. It has kitsch art deco features like the entrance to a 1930s cinema; it means to conjure up thoughts of the exotic and non-European. The bright blues of the façade disguise the absence of windows, which means that there is no mutuality in the exchange of looks given by the person outside the building, and by the building. The building looks but does not return the look. Perhaps the name's intention is to suggest that the power of the primitive takes over in this casino: perhaps that is implied in the bearded heads that are to be seen as mock-capitals high up in the decoration; these are the heads of those who have lost fortune and life together in the casino, and have their heads held up as trophies.

In Fisherman's Wharf, the buildings are fake, like stage scenery: no one lives here, there are not even outside staircases to take people from the ground level where shops would be expected to the upper regions where people would live. The modern shopping mall divorces work from lives as the older city did not, but more to the point is the miniaturisation of the architecture — the 'colossal' nature of the Colosseum becomes scenery like that for a Broadway musical. No one could live in these toy-like spaces which evoke historical architecture only to mock it by making impractical its spaces which were designed for practicality. A restaurant occupies, as to street façade, two different 'Dutch' houses (it is one house, disguised as two), and on inspection, the ground-floor ceiling is located half-way up the windows of the first floor. Projecting cranes, a feature of Dutch houses, appear under the gables here, as they should, but have no practical use. The left-hand façade of the two even pretends to have a cellar, but in the prevailing flatness of architecture here, could not have. Nothing, least of all a cellar, which suggests intimacy, could be folded into its platitudinousness. The baroque fold and this flatness represent two opposites.

Fisherman's Wharf is not a parody of the copy; it would be impossible to parody it in its turn. As simulacral, it makes any kind of criticism more difficult, because a pastiche could be included amongst the existing buildings. Some of the postmodern buildings discussed in this chapter may be articulated with the baroque, but the cynicism which underlies Fisherman's Wharf does not relate to what is baroque in Macao, but opposes it. There, the buildings were trying to be something different; here, in this other modern Macao, they are in the service of the same: predictable brand names and commodities which can be bought anywhere. There, the buildings have a memory; here, the memory that is allowed is a cliché, which is abolition of the past. However exciting Macao may be, these parts of it have the power to dull. They reflect not an exciting postmodernism, but that the territory is coming under the power of global culture, which parodies each local form of architecture, more fully than colonialism in Macao did, and adds to the difficulties of photography: that images of one city look exactly the same as images of another on the other side of the world.

In Macao, the colonial power added something strange to the territory, and something beautiful emerged, perhaps against the odds, and certainly in dialogue with Chinese culture. The folds of the baroque, and its awareness of the power of feeling, remain as a challenge to the universalising power of globalisation.

The Venetian Resort

Chapter 11 noted a tendency to make Macao look a little like Venice, by making buildings rest on water, and by giving as much prominence to the sea as possible, as if compensating for the erosion of the Praya Grande which brought sea and land into closer contact. But that effect is outdone by the Venice-ising of Macao which is outstandingly obvious in the new Venetian resort on the Cotai strip (the new name for the land-filled area which connects Taipa and Coloane by more than a bridge and makes them a single space) with Estrada da Baía de Nossa Senhora da Esperança to the north, and Istmo Causeway Taipa-Coloane to the east. Not 'Venice', but 'The Venetian': this new character type is, perhaps, supposed to be the new Marco Polo; if Thomas Mann thought of death in Venice, the art of the Venetian offers a second death: death in Macao.

The Venetian, part of the Sands group of casinos, run by Steve Wynn who set up the Bellagio casino in Las Vegas, represents neo-colonialism in an ex-colony: showing neither Portuguese nor Chinese influence, but American. America presents itself in Macao with all the cultural capital of Europe, not Portugal. So the Venetian is dissimilar from the Lisboa casinos: it is Italy, and specifically Venice, the home of merchant adventurers, those who preceded the various East India Companies. The Venetian is a massive casino plus shopping malls plus hotels, leisure centre and conference centre. Inside, real Italians, but whose previous post, one told us, was in Las Vegas, work computerised gondolas and sing snatches of Puccini. One exterior wall, photographed here, shows the façadal wall of the Ducal Palace of which Ruskin writes in *The Stones of Venice* that, 'though very sparing in colour [it], is yet, as an example of finished masonry, in a vast building, one of the finest things, not only in Venice, but in the world' (*Stones of Venice* 3.32). Ruskin gives great detail to the sculpture of Adam and Eve, analysing the forbidden fruit from the fig-tree (*Stones of Venice* 2.358–9). This sculpture has been put in the wrong position, at the other end of the façade, an example of Casino architecture, which copies not from Venice but from Las Vegas. The architecture and ornaments are the copy of an indifferent American copy. The mainland visitor is not being sold Venice but a consumerist model originally made for Americans who would never visit Europe. The model therefore is for mainland tourists who will never go to America.

The images of the exterior of the Doge's Palace and the Grand Canal reappear as framed pictures inside the casino (copies of *vedute* of Venice by Guardi (1712–1793) and Canaletto (1697–1768)). These are copies of copies, where the eighteenth-

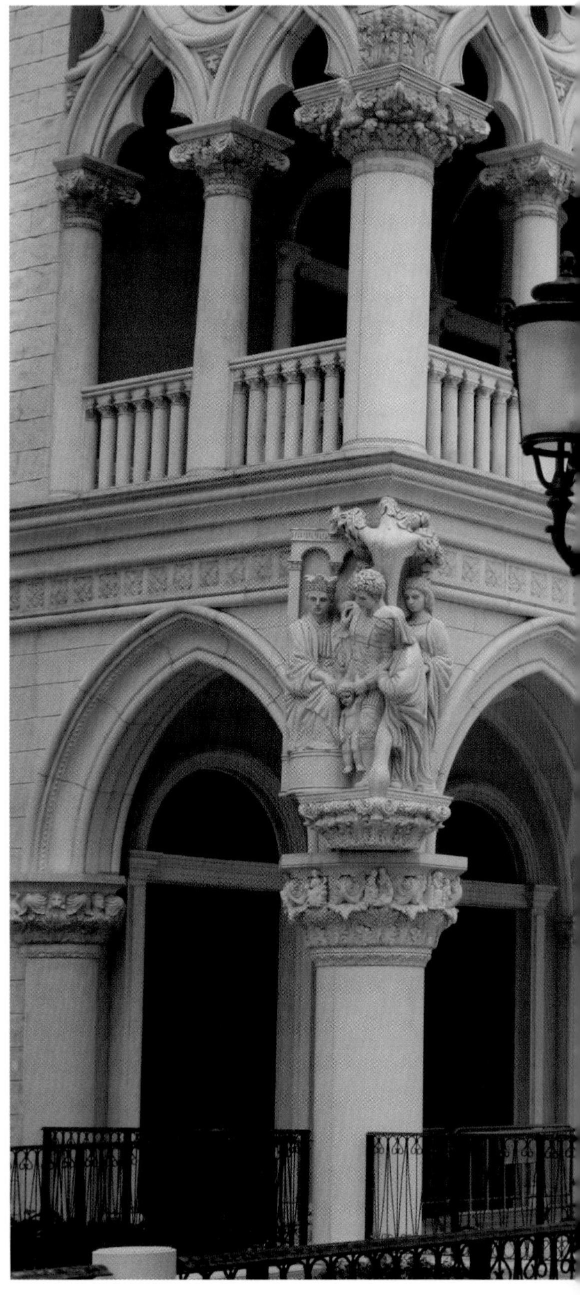

124. Doge's Palace, Macao

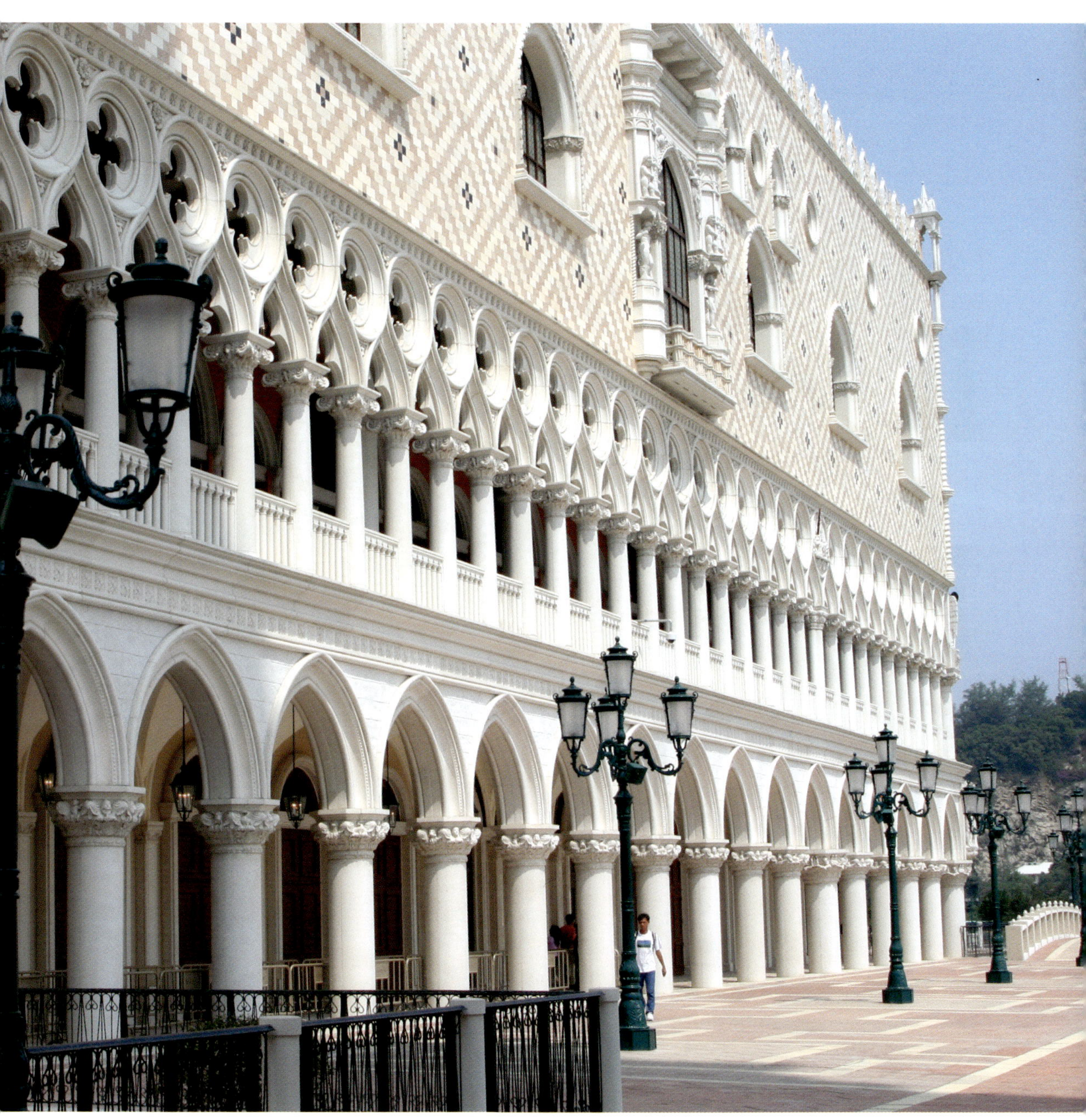

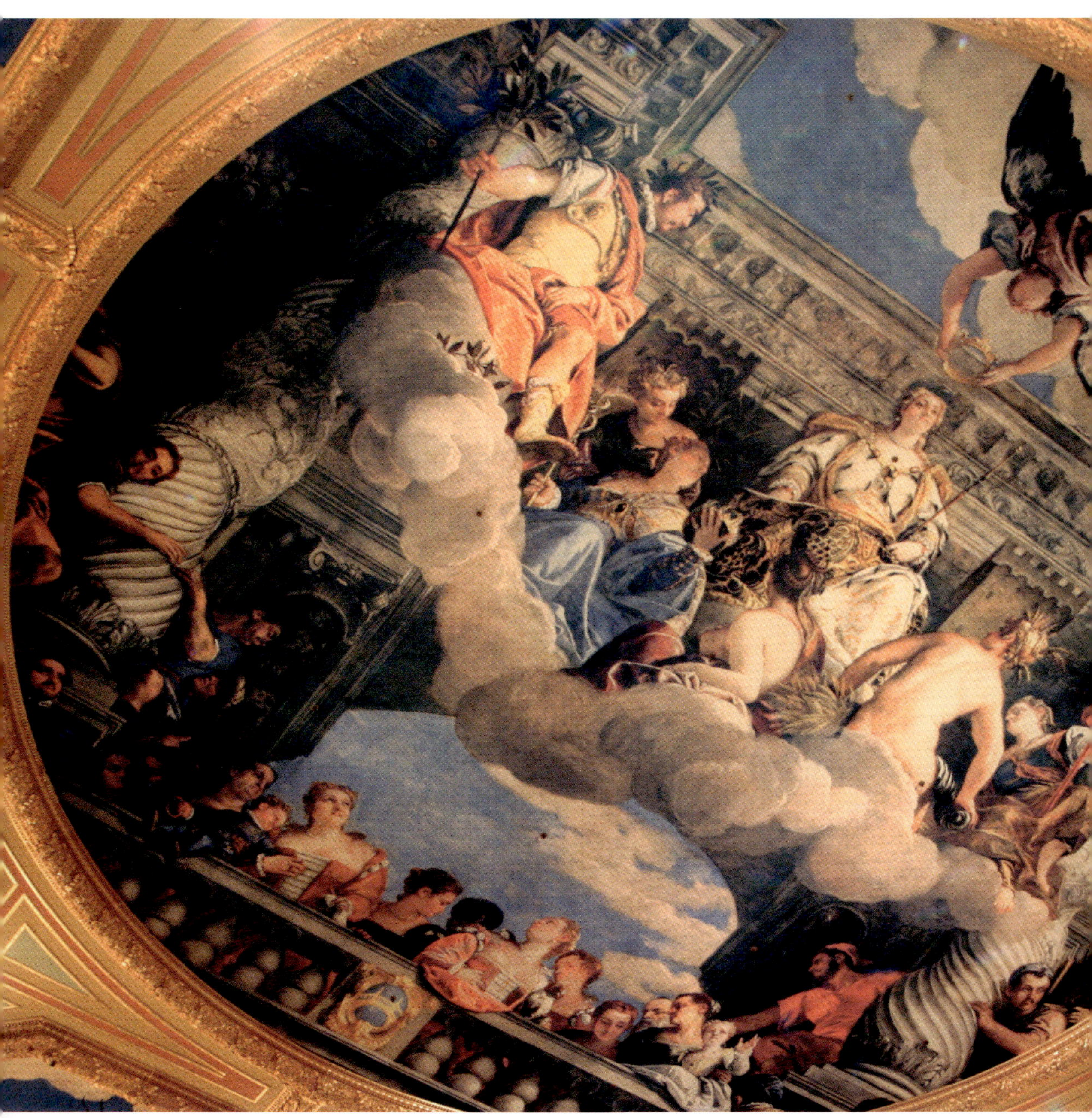

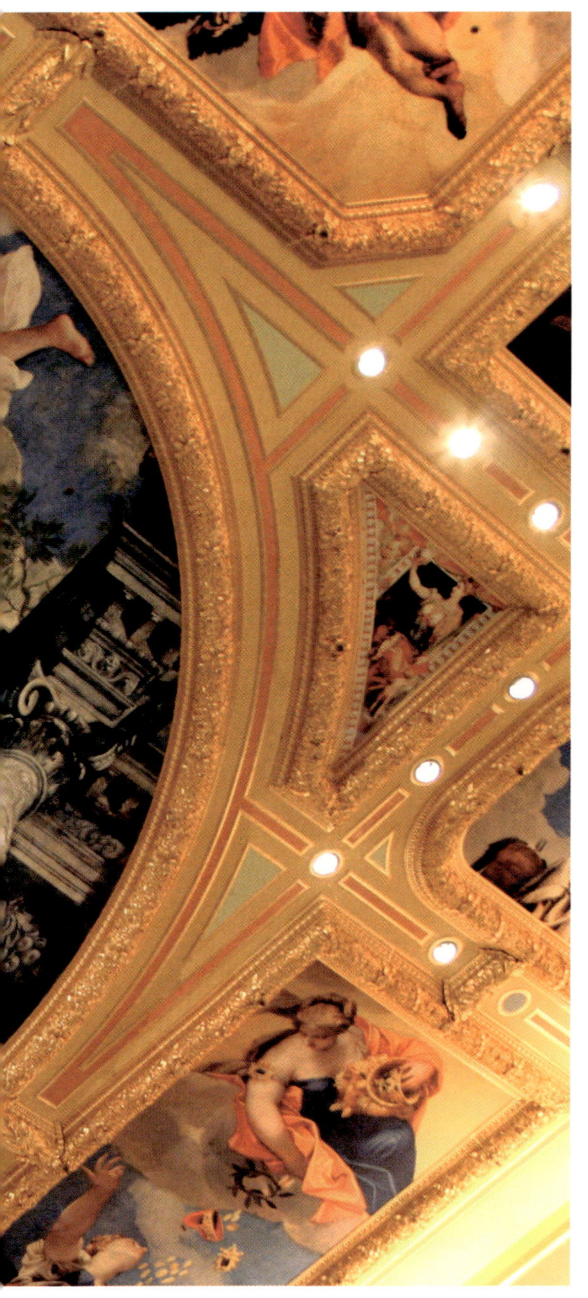

125. Ceiling at the
Venetian Resort

century painters were themselves yielding to a cliché sense of Venice. The copy of Borget in the A-Ma temple (photograph 88) is quite different: there the representation is side by side with the original temple. Inside the Casino massive semi-circular escalators lead up to a first floor and then stairs go higher to the second, underneath a mock baroque ceiling, a 'reproduction' of Paolo Veronese's mannerist work *Venice Triumphant* (1584) housed in the Sala del Gran Consiglio in the Ducal Palace under the throne of the Doge.[1] It is no fresco, however, but produced by digital technology, and shows the crowning of Venice by an angel, Fame. As a then modern version of Rome, Venice is ascending to heaven past a building with a double loggia and twisting Solomonic columns (but every human shape in this picture is twisting, turning, in a state of torsion). On the loggia below her are admiring Venetian women and female allegories of Venice, and priests. The viewer has come up escalators and sees more of an ascent taking place, as a female Venice rises from the earth.

Readers of the baroque will be aware of the *trompe l'oeil* effect, but also should be aware that the oval original has been truncated, turned into a circular shape. Veronese was given an awkward, elliptical frame to work with by Cristoforo Sorte, who designed the ceiling of the Sala del Gran Consiglio, as an architectural feat in itself, full of difficult frameworks in which the artist had to paint. The elliptical framework may be thought of as characteristically baroque. The design in the Venetian has turned an ellipse into a circle, cropping the top goddess above Fame, and leaving out entirely the ground floor where captive soldiers and armed men on horses are found: those masculine figures who bring out the point that Venice, already weakened by the success of Portugal and Spain's seaborne empires, was beginning to lose power, which it had to fight for at the naval battle of Lepanto against the Turks (1571). The battle was won but the danger did not recede. A plague of 1576 also brought out Venice's weakness. By truncating the ellipse, the reproduction leaves out three horses, two rearing, and a huge dog, and, as part of the repression of animal motifs, which are also provocatively sexual, it perforce represses the winged lion of St Mark, which has become the logo for the Venetian resort. The casinos are on the ground floor of the Venetian, the shopping malls upstairs. But this dual world has not been represented. Anything visualising the violent or visceral character of gambling has been repressed; in the women on the balconies may be glimpsed the satisfaction of the shopper.

The circularity of the design makes the art kitsch for the benefit of Americans visiting Las Vegas, and now has been imported into Macao, the place of the copy of the copy. This circularity centres the art and turns the design back to something more comfortably triumphalist, and changes the perspective. Whereas in the original the Solomonic columns converge as they rise upwards, because they are presented in perspective (but there is no single perspective: the painting tricks the eye), here, because of the regularising, the two columns seem to point in the same direction, thus making the vision not upwards, but gazing out as it were on the same level, horizontally. They have taken a picture for a ceiling and made it like a picture on the wall. The *trompe l'oeil* effect, which makes the picture seem to hold the gaze, has been negated. Lacan suggests that the painter 'gives something for the eye to feed on, but he invites the person to whom this picture is presented to lay down his gaze there as one lays down one's weapons. This is the pacifying, Apollonian effect of painting' (*Four Fundamental Concepts* 101).

It is as if the gaze is the Dionysiac, terrifying aspect of reality which threatens the subject's individuality, tearing him to pieces (Lacan certainly has Nietzsche's treatise, *The Birth of Tragedy*, in mind). The picture, according to Lacan, concedes that the wild Dionysiac element is there, but it also gives something calmer, more serene, more pacifying, with the element which corresponds to Apollo as the god of individuality. Pictures contain a dialectic in them between what destroys subjectivity, and what sustains it. The reproduction of Veronese leaves out the threatening Dionysiac, which

like the 'stain' that Lacan talks about, threatens
death to the individual subject (see above, pp. 95,
150). All forms of conflict have been turned into
something homogenous. Illusion has been rejected,
as though casino architecture was the art of honesty
and consistency. While this cheating actually fits
casino culture, the removal of the lower third of
the painting especially excludes the 'otherness'
which sustains the central image of the triumph
of Venice. The city in triumph now no longer
contains anything conflictual within it to question
its achievement. Consumerism smoothes out and
flattens contradiction. The artwork, hanging over
the heads of gamblers, excludes death, which the
baroque did not do, but is dead in its flatness.[2]

Notes

Chapter One

[1] This material is taken from Mao Sihui, 'Desire for the (Hyper) Real: New Challenges for Macao Tourism in the Age of Simulation', *Chinese Cross Currents* 3.1 (2006) 66–82, specifically 66–7.

[2] See on Macao, César Guillén Nuñez, *Macao* (Hong Kong: Oxford University Press, 1984) and César Guillén Nuñez and Leong Ka Tai, *Macao Streets* (Hong Kong: Oxford University Press, 1999). On Portuguese baroque, see James Lee-Milne, *Baroque in Spain and Portugal* (London: B.T. Batsford, 1960); see also Carl A. Hanson, *Economy and Society in Baroque Portugal, 1668–1703* (London: Macmillan, 1981). For an introduction to the architecture of Portugal, see José Manuel Fernandes, *Synthesis of Portuguese Culture: Architecture* (Lisbon, Imprensa Nacional – Casa da Moeda, 1991). See also Christina Miu Bing Cheng, *Macao: A Cultural Janus* (Hong Kong: Hong Kong University Press, 1999), and Jonathan Porter, *Macao, the Imaginary City: Culture and Society, 1557 to the Present* (Boulder: Westview Press, 1996). David Clarke, 'Illuminating Facades: Looking at Post-Colonial Macau', *Journal of Visual Culture*, vol. 6, issue 3, 2007, 395–419.

[3] On Hong Kong architecture see Ackbar Abbas, *Hong Kong: Culture and the Politics of Disappearance* (Hong Kong: Hong Kong University Press, 1997) 63–90, and *The Heritage of Hong Kong: Its History, Architecture and Culture*, ed. Norman Owen (Hong Kong: FormAsia Books Ltd., 1999) 30–57. David Clarke, *Reclaimed Land: Hong Kong in Transition* (Hong Kong University Press, 2002) and *HONG KONG x 24 x 365: A Year in the Life of a City* (Hong Kong University Press, 2006), and more informally, Jason Wordie, *Streets: Exploring Hong Kong Island* (Hong Kong University Press, 2002).

[4] Stephanie Hemelryk Donald, 'The Idea of Hong Kong: Structures of Attention in the City of Life', *Urban Space and Cityscapes: Perspectives from Modern and Contemporary Culture*, ed. Christoph Lindner (New York: Routledge, 2006) 63–76, and for colonial architecture generally, see Mark Crinson, *Modern Architecture and the End of Empire* (Aldershot: Ashgate, 2003).

[5] For this reason, Walter Benjamin's essay 'The Work of Art in the Age of Mechanical Reproduction', *Illuminations*, trans. Harry Zohn (London: Jonathan Cape, 1970) is often seen as a founding text of postmodern theory. See also Charles Jencks' books, starting with *Post-modernism: The New Classicism in Art and Architecture* (New York: Rizzoli, 1987), Robert Venturi, *Learning from Las Vegas: The Forgotten Symbolism of Architectural Form* (Cambridge: MIT Press, 1977). Jencks dates the ending of modernism with the destruction of the Puitt-Igoe high-rise modernist buildings in St Louis, Missouri in 1972.

[6] *Postmodern Culture*, ed. Hal Foster (London: Pluto Press, 1985) xv. The theorist who has discussed this most fully is Jean-Francois Lyotard, *The Postmodern Condition: A Report on Knowledge*, trans. Geoff Bennington and Brian Massumi (Minneapolis: University of Minnesota Press, 1984). Lyotard says, 'simplifying to the utmost, I define postmodernism as incredulity towards meta-narratives' (xiii). Postmodernism works with micro-narratives, not grand-narratives.

[7] See Fredric Jameson, *Postmodernism, or, The Cultural Logic of Late Capitalism* (London: Verso, 1991).

[8] Alain Badiou, *Deleuze, the Clamour of Being*, trans. Louise Burchill (Minneapolis: University of Minnesota Press, 2000) 10.

[9] *Baroque Poetry*, ed. J.P. Hill and E. Caracciolo-Trejo (London: Dent, 1975) xv.

[10] For Macao's gardens, see Francisco M. Caldeira Cabral, Annabel Jackson and Leong Ka Tai, *Macao Gardens and Landscape Art* (Hong Kong: Fundação Macau & Asia 2000 Ltd., 1999).

[11] For medieval gargoyles, see Michael Camille, *Image on the Edge: The Margins of Medieval Art* (Cambridge: Harvard University Press, 1992).

[12] *Cinematic City*, ed. David B. Clarke (London: Routledge, 1997).

[13] See *Jean Baudrillard: Selected Writings*, ed. Mark Poster (Stanford: Stanford University Press, 1988).

[14] Walter Benjamin, 'The Work of Art in the Age of Mechanical Reproduction', *Illuminations* 240.

[15] On Wölfflin, see Michael Ann Holly, 'Imagining the Baroque', *Past Looking: Historical Imagination and the Rhetoric of the Image* (Ithaca: Cornell University Press, 1996) 90–111.

[16] Anthony Blunt, *Guide to Baroque Rome* (London: Granada, 1982) 43.

[17] Heinrich Wölfflin, *Renaissance and Baroque*, trans. Kathyrn Simon (Ithaca: Cornell University Press, 1964) 29–30.

[18] Roland Barthes, *Sade, Fourier, Loyola*, trans. Richard Miller (New York: Hill and Wang, 1976). By discussing the Jesuits as the 'heirs and propagators of Latin rhetoric' (39), Barthes draws attention to the baroque as a form of rhetoric, an art of persuasion.

[19] Michel Foucault, *The Order of Things: An Archaeology of the Human Sciences*, trans. Alan Sheridan (London: Tavistock, 1970) 11.

[20] See Alejo Carpentier's novel *Concierto barroco* (Mexico City: Siglo Veintiuno Editores, 1974), and Roberto González Echevarría, *Alejo Carpentier: The Pilgrim at Home* (Austin: University of Texas Press, 1977) 266–71.

[21] Octavio Paz, *Children of the Mire*, trans. Rachel Phillips (Cambridge, Mass.: Harvard University Press, 1974) 2.

[22] See Mario Perniola, *Enigmas: The Egyptian Moment in Society and Art*, trans. Christopher Woodall (London: Verso, 1995); Robert Harbison, *Reflections on Baroque* (London: Reaktion Books, 2000) 164–91.

[23] For discussion of the baroque and the postmodern, see Gregg Lambert, *The Return of the Baroque in Modern Culture* (London: Continuum, 2004). For its use in French literature of the seventeenth century, see 'Baroque Topographies: Literature, History, Philosophy', *Yale French Studies* 80 (1991). This includes a translation of part of Deleuze's *The Fold*, where the translator comments on the difference between 'pli' (for organic matter) and 'repli' for inorganic. He translates 'pli' as 'fold' and 'repli' as 'coil', since the latter 'invokes the movements of a reptile [...], the idea of folding in on oneself and the springs ... which Deleuze says underlie Leibnizian matter' (227).

Chapter Two

[1] Walter Benjamin, *The Origin of German Tragic Drama*, trans. John Osborne (London: Verso, 1977) 140.

[2] On Goa, see José Pereira, *Baroque Goa: The Architecture of Portuguese India* (New Delhi: Books and Books, 1995); José Pereira, *Churches of Goa* (New Delhi: Oxford University Press, 2002); Helder Carita, *Palaces of Goa: Models and Types of Indo-Portuguese Civil Architecture* (London: Cartago, 1999).

[3] Walter Benjamin, *The Arcades Project*, trans. Howard Eiland and Kevin McLaughlin, ed. Rolf Tiedemann (Cambridge: Belknap Press, 1999) 522.

[4] The building of this convent is the subject of José Saramago's magic realist novel, *Baltasar & Blimunda* (1982), trans. Giovanni Pontiero (London: Harvill, 1998).

[5] Yves Bottineau, *Living Architecture: Iberian-American Baroque* (London: Macdonald, 1971) 16.

[6] Decentring is an aspect of the baroque and described by Ruskin in his account of *Christ Bearing His Cross* by Tintoretto (1518–1594): 'The power of the picture is chiefly in effect, the figure of Christ being too far off to be very interesting, and only the malefactors being seen on the nearer path; but for

this very reason it seems to me more impressive, as if one had been truly present at the scene, though not exactly in the right place for seeing it' (428). See John Ruskin, *The Works of John Ruskin vol. 11: The Stones of Venice Part 3*, ed. E.T. Cook and Alexander Wedderburn (London: George Allen, 1904).

[7] Fernando R. de la Flor, *Barroco: Representacion e Ideologia en el Mundo Hispanico (1580–1680)* (Catedra: Madrid, 2000). We owe this reference to Jonathan Hall.

[8] Dalibor Vesely, *Architecture in the Age of Divided Representation: The Question of Creativity in the Shadow of Production* (Cambridge, Mass.: MIT Press, 2004) 438, associates rocaille (discussed 223–4) with the cult of the grotesque: we shall return to this through discussion of the Camões grotto in chapter 10.

[9] Jacques Derrida, *Of Grammatology*, trans. Gayatri Chakravorty Spivak (Baltimore: Johns Hopkins University Press, 1976) 65.

[10] Gilles Deleuze, *The Fold: Leibniz and the Baroque*, trans. Tom Conley (Minneapolis: University of Minnesota Press, 1993).

[11] 'Paris taught me this art of straying; it fulfilled a dream that had shown its first traces in the labyrinths on the blotting pages of my school exercise books' — Walter Benjamin, 'A Berlin Chronicle', *Reflections: Essays, Aphorisms, Autobiographical Writings*, trans. Edmund Jephcott (New York: Schocken Books, 1978) 9.

[12] Jorge Luis Borges, 'Death and the Compass', *Collected Fictions*, trans. Andrew Hurley (Harmondsworth: Penguin, 1998) 147–56, at 156.

[13] *Baroque Garden Cultures: Emulation, Sublimation, Subversion*, ed. Michel Conan (Washington, D.C.: Dumbarton Oaks, 2005) 7.

Chapter Three

[1] See Patrick Conner, *George Chinnery 1774–1852: Artist of India and the China Coast* (Woodbridge, Suffolk: Antique Collectors' Club, 1993) plate 112, p. 114.

[2] See Edgar Wind, *Pagan Mysteries in the Renaissance* (Harmondsworth: Penguin, 1967) 128–41.

[3] José Antonio Maravall, *Culture of the Baroque: Analysis of a Historical Structure*, trans. Terry Cochran (Minneapolis: University of Minnesota Press, 1986), quoting Jean Rousset, *La littérature de l'âge baroque en France: Circé et le paon* (Paris: Corti, 1954) 168.

[4] The parergon, as that which disturbs the sense of the borders of the artwork, is the theme of Jacques Derrida, *The Truth in Painting*, trans. Geoff

Bennington and Ian McLeod (Chicago: University of Chicago Press, 1987) 37–82; see also Derrida's chapter 'Cartouches', 183–284.

[5] These do not form the symmetry implied in Roland Barthes's critical study of Balzac's novella *Sarrasine*, which is called *S/Z* (and which is a commentary on baroque culture through its discussion of the Italian opera castrato: opera itself is a baroque form). Instead, it creates a pattern of Z/S, and so plays even more with sexual difference than Barthes's title does (Sarrasine is the naive male hero, Zambinella is the castrato with whom he falls in love, thinking she is a woman). Z/S makes gender even more unstable, sexual difference completely interchangeable, just as Deleuze argues that the baroque is the world of 'incompossibilities', a point which he illustrates from Borges' short story 'The Garden of Forking Paths' (a fantasia where a Chinese who must kill an Englishman is confronted with a garden which is also a book) and which presents what Deleuze calls 'a baroque labyrinth whose infinite series converge or diverge, forming a web of time embracing all possibilities' (*The Fold* 62). In Deleuze's version of Borges' baroque, everything happens, and everything also reverses; so that an action done may be undone at the same moment. See chapter 8, above.

[6] Jacques Derrida, *Spurs: Nietzsche's Styles*, trans. Barbara Harlow (Chicago: University of Chicago Press, 1978) 115.

[7] Quotation from the Norton Shakespeare, ed. Stephen Greenblatt (New York: W. W. Norton, 1997).

[8] Jorge Luis Borges, *Collected Fictions*, trans. Andrew Hurley (Harmondsworth: Penguin, 1999) 4.

[9] For a study of the significance of the Escorial and Simancas, see Roberto González Echevarría, *Myth and Archive: A Theory of Latin-American Narrative* (Cambridge: Cambridge University Press, 1990), and Louis Lo, *Male Jealousy: Literature and Film* (London: Continuum, 2008) 58–62.

[10] Maravall, *Culture of the Baroque: Analysis of a Historical Structure* 78.

[11] Octavio Paz, *Children of the Mire: Modern Poetry from Romanticism to the Avant-Garde* 2.

[12] Lacan calls the Symbolic Order, which is language, the Law of the Father; and its first activity is to gender the child, creating the norms of sexual difference. The dead writing in the grave suggests the dead character of the law.

[13] Walter Benjamin, *The Origin of German Tragic Drama* 218. Freud thinks of a dream as a 'picture-puzzle', which he calls a 'rebus': making a link between allegory and the idea of a dream as writing, as allegorical inscription. See Freud, *The Interpretation of Dreams: Penguin Freud 4* (Harmondsworth: Penguin, 1976) 382.

14 Benjamin, *The Origin of German Tragic Drama* 166.

Chapter Four

[1] For the symbolism of the burning heart, see Jeremy Tambling, 'Thinking Melancholy: Allegory and the Vita Nuova', *Romanic Review* 96 (2005) 85–105, at 100, fn37.

[2] Gilles Deleuze, *Cinema I*, trans. Hugh Tomlinson and Barbara Habberjam (Minneapolis: University of Minnesota Press, 1996) 109.

[3] Lacan refers to the body in pieces in Jacques Lacan, 'The Mirror Stage', *Écrits*, trans. Alan Sheridan (London: Tavistock, 1977) 4. Compare this image with the French artist Géricault's studies of dissected limbs, between 1818 and 1819. See Lorenz E.A. Eitner, *Géricault: His Life and Work* (London: Orbis, 1983) 181–2. Géricault and these relics both contemplate psychic and bodily fragmentation, and this could be seen as a baroque drive to fragment reality.

[4] Nikolaus Pevsner, *An Outline of European Architecture* (Harmondsworth: Penguin, 1963) 254–5.

[5] Saint Teresa of Avila, *The Life of Saint Teresa of Avila*, trans. J.M. Cohen (Harmondsworth: Penguin, 1958) 210.

[6] Jacques Lacan, 'God and the *Jouissance* of The Woman: A Love Letter' (*Seminar* XX (1972–73)) in *Feminine Sexuality: Jacques Lacan and the* École Freudienne, ed. Juliet Mitchell and Jacqueline Rose (London: Macmillan, 1982) 137–48, at 147.

[7] Jacques Derrida, 'Force and Signification', *Writing and Difference*, trans. Alan Bass (London: Routledge, 1978) 3–30, at 6. Derrida is reviewing Jean Rousset's *Forme et signification: essais sur les structures littéraires de Corneille à Claudel*. He quotes Jean Rousset, 'Hell is a world in pieces, a pillage that the poem imitates closely through its disordered shouts, bristling with scattered tortures in a torrent of exclamations. The sentence is reduced to its disordered elements, the framework of the sonnet is broken: the lines are too short or too long, the quatrains unbalanced; the poem bursts' (302). See Jean Rousset, *La littérature de l'âge baroque en France, vol. 1: Circe et le paon* (Paris José Corti, 1954) 194.

Chapter Five

[1] For a detailed study, see Manuel Teixeira, *The Church of St Paul in Macao* (Lisboa: Centro de Estudos Históricos Ultramarinos da Junta de Investigações Científicas do Ultramar, 1979). See also Gonçalo Couceiro and Luís Sales Marques, *St. Paul's Church Fortress of the Monte* (Macao: Gabinete de Comunicação Social, 1990). For early Macao, see C.R. Boxer, *Seventeenth Century*

Macau, in Contemporary Documents and Illustrations (Hong Kong: Heinemann Asia, 1984). See also César Guillén Nuñez, *Macao's Church of St. Paul: A Glimmer of the Baroque in China* (Hong Kong: Hong Kong University Press, 2008).

2 On a discussion of staircases, see Nikolaus Pevsner, *An Outline of European Architecture* (Harmondsworth: Penguin, 1972) 278–84, 335–6.

3 See Jacques Lacan, *The Ethics of Psychoanalysis 1959–1960, Seminar VII*, trans. Dennis Porter (London: Routledge, 1992) 135 and Denis Hollier, *Against Architecture: The Writings of Georges Bataille*, trans. Betsy Wing (Cambridge, Mass.: MIT Press, 1992).

4 See Millard Meiss, *Painting in Florence and Siena after the Black Death: The Arts, Religion, and Society in the Mid-Fourteenth Century* (Princeton: Princeton University Press, 1978).

5 Jacques Derrida, *Aporias*, tran. Thomas Dutoit (Stanford: Stanford University Press, 1993) 43.

6 Su Shi's poem 《食荔枝二首（其二）》：「羅浮山下四時春，盧桔楊梅次第新。日啖荔枝三百顆，不辭長作嶺南人。」 [It is always Spring at the foot of Mount Law Fo, Lou Chee's cherry is always fresh. Eating lychees three hundred per day, do not want to quit and stay at Lingnan.] (trans. Lo)

7 Roberto González Echevarría, *Celestina's Brood: Continuities of the Baroque in Spanish and Latin American Literature* (Durham: Duke University Press, 1993) 198.

8 Xu Zhonglin, *Creation of the Gods* (2 vols.) (1567–1619), trans. Gu Zhizhong (Beijing: New World Press, 1992). See the birth and reincarnation of Na Tcha (or Nezha) in chapters 12–14. Na Tcha is also a figure of the Monkey King in Wu Cheng'en, *The Journey to the West* (4 vols.), trans. Anthony C. Yu (Chicago: University of Chicago, 1977).

9 Lacan, *The Ethics of Psychoanalysis* 140.

10 For the martyrdoms of Jesuits in Japan, see C.R. Boxer, *The Christian Century in Japan, 1549–1650* (Berkeley: University of California Press, 1951) 334–5 and 358, for the 1597 incident, see 163–7 and 416–24. Boxer shows illustrations of Japanese crucifixions, which compare interestingly with the painting here.

11 Sir Thomas Browne, 'Urn-Burial', *Religio Medici Hydriotaphia, and The Garden of Cyrus*, ed. Robin Robbins (Oxford: Oxford University Press, 1972) 127.

12 Jacques Lacan, *The Four Fundamental Concepts of Psychoanalysis*, trans. Alan Sheridan (Harmondsworth: Penguin, 1977) 88–9.

[13] Christine Buci-Glucksmann, *La folie du voir: De l'esthétique baroque* (Paris: Galilée, 1986) 41.

Chapter Six

[1] For this history, see *China and Macao*, ed. Clive Willis (Aldershot: Ashgate, 2002) xiii–xxviii. This book gives excellent excerpts of early writings about China and Macao in the years 1513–1557, and of the Jesuit missions in China: it goes up to the end of the 1660s in scope.

[2] On Macao history, see César Guillén Nuñez, *Macao* (Hong Kong: Oxford University Press, 1984). We have used colonial names because of the nineteenth-century context.

[3] The point is made by R.D. Cremer, 'Macao's Place in the History of World Trade', in R.D. Cremer, *Macao: City of Commerce and Culture* (Hong Kong: UEA Press, 1987) 35.

[4] Jonathan Spence, *The Memory Palace of Matteo Ricci* (London: Faber, 1984) 173.

[5] *China in the Sixteenth Century: The Journals of Matthew Ricci: 1583–1610*, trans. Louis J. Gallagher (New York: Random House, 1953) 129.

[6] Jorge Graça, *Fortifications of Macao: Their Design and History* (2nd edition, Macao: Direcção dos Serviços de Turismo de Macao, 1984) 20.

[7] The reference is to Walter Benjamin's 'angel of history', who seems to be in a state of trauma. See Benjamin, 'Theses on the Philosophy of History', *Illuminations*, trans. Harry Zohn (London: Fontana Press, 1922) 249.

[8] See Jaime Lara, 'A Vulcanological Joachim of Fiore and an Aerodynamic Francis of Assisi in Colonial Latin America', *Signs, Wonders, Miracles: Representations of Divine Power in the Life of the Church*, ed. Kate Cooper and Jeremy Gregory (Woodbridge: Boydell and Brewer, 2005) 249–72.

[9] Kristeva writes, 'For abjection, when all is said and done, is the other facet of religious, moral, and ideological codes on which rest the sleep of individuals and the breathing spells of societies. Such codes are abjection's purification and repression. But the return of their repressed make up our "apocalypse", and that is why we cannot escape the dramatic convulsions of religious crises'. See Julia Kristeva, *Powers of Horror*, trans. Leon S. Roudiez (New York: Columbia University Press, 1982) 209.

[10] Jacques Derrida, 'On a Newly Arisen Apocalyptic Tone in Philosophy', *Raising the Tone of Philosophy: Late Essays by Immanuel Kant, Transformative Critique by Jacques Derrida*, ed. Peter Fenves (Baltimore: Johns Hopkins University Press, 1993) 117–71.

[11] *Impressions of the East: The Art of George Chinnery* (Hong Kong: Hong Kong Museum of History and Hong Kong Museum of Art, 2005) 157.

Chapter Seven

[1] C.R. Boxer, *The Dutch Seaborne Empire, 1600–1800* (London: Hutchinson, 1977) 27.

[2] Michel Foucault, 'Different Spaces', *Aesthetics, Method, and Epistemology*, trans. Robert Hurley et al., ed. James D. Faubion (Harmondsworth, Penguin, 1994) 175–85.

[3] For the lighthouse, see César Guillén Nuñez, 'Macao's Heritage: The Guia Lighthouse', *Arts of Asia* 22 (July–August 1992) 92–103.

[4] John Ruskin, *The Stones of Venice* (1853), *The Works of John Ruskin vol. 11: The Stones of Venice* Part 2 vol. 10, 202–3.

Chapter Eight

[1] William Blake: *Collected Writings*, ed. Geoffrey Keynes (Oxford: Oxford University Press, 1966) 152.

[2] Jorge Luis Borges, *Collected Fictions*, trans. Andrew Hurley (Harmondsworth: Penguin, 1999) 124.

[3] The only extant picture of a Shakespearean theatre, the De Witt picture of the Swan, shows the audience in galleries behind the stage, looking down onto the actors who are on stage. It is also surmised that the people in these galleries may also be actors. Benjamin describes how the baroque plays used improvised stages, whereas the classical and Renaissance theatre assigned fixed positions to the actor and audience. In this way, the baroque confuses roles and disallows the single vision of the audience.

[4] Michel Foucault, *The Order of Things: An Archaeology of the Human Sciences* (London: Tavistock, 1970) 14.

[5] Maurice Merleau-Ponty, *Maurice Merleau-Ponty Basic Writings*, ed. Thomas Baldwin (London: Routledge, 2004) 297.

[6] For the implications of this formulation in 'New Historicist' readings of Shakespeare, see Leonard Tennenhouse, *Power on Display: The Politics of Shakespeare's Genres* (New York: Methuen, 1986).

[7] Gilles Deleuze, *Cinema II: The Time-Image*, trans. Hugh Tomlinson and Robert Galeta (Minneapolis: University of Minnesota Press, 1989) 117.

[8] Jacques Lacan, *Four Fundamental Concepts of Psychoanalysis* 97.

[9] See Louis Lo, *Male Jealousy: Literature and Film* (London: Continuum, 2008) chapter 1.

Chapter Nine

[1] See César Guillén Nuñez, 'Macao through the Eyes of Nineteenth Century Painters' in *Macao: City of Commerce and Culture*, ed. R.D. Cremer (Hong Kong: UEA Press, 1987) 55–6, John Webber's (1751–1793) illustration of the Mage temple from the sea (1788) is reproduced in Cremer (36); see also no. 15, 80 of *Views of the Pearl River Delta: Macao, Canton and Hong Kong* (Hong Kong Museum of Art and Peabody Essex Museum, 1996). For Webber, and George Carter, both associated with Captain Cook, see Bernard Smith, *Imagining the Pacific: In the Wake of the Cook Voyages* (New Haven: Yale University Press, 1992) 225–40. The catalogue *Views of the Pearl River Delta* reproduces two works by Borget: a hand-coloured lithograph, *The Square outside the Ma Kok [A Ma] Temple* (no. 14, 78) and a pencil sketch, *Chinese Figures and Boat Dwellings* (no. 17, 84).

[2] On the diorama, see William H. Galperin, *The Return of the Visible in British Romanticism* (Baltimore: John Hopkins University Press, 1993).

[3] Linda Nochlin, *The Body in Pieces: The Fragment as a Metaphor of Modernity* (London: Thames and Hudson, 1994).

[4] Charles Baudelaire, *Selected Writings on Art and Artists*, trans. P.E. Charvet (Harmondsworth: Penguin, 1972) 403.

[5] See *Views of the Pearl River Delta: Macao, Canton and Hong Kong*, no. 10, 70; see also *Impressions of the East: The Art of George Chinnery* (Hong Kong: Hong Kong Museum of History and Hong Kong Museum of Art, 2005) plate 43, 124. See Patrick Conner, *George Chinnery 1774–1852: Artist of India and the China Coast* (Woodbridge: Antique Collectors' Club, 1993) plate 127, 199 and colour plate 71, 200 (henceforward, referred to in the text as Conner 1993) and *Views of the Pearl River Delta: Macao, Canton and Hong Kong*, colour plate C48, 128. Note the exception, in Conner 1993 (plate 128, 200), of a pencil sketch, *Tanka Boatwoman Rowing* in plate 128. For renderings of ships and port scenes, see Patrick Conner, *Chinese Views: Western Perspectives 1770–1870: The Sze Yuan Tang Collection of China Coast Paintings and The Wallem Collection of China Coast Ship Portraits* (London: Asia House, 1996). See also for Chinnery collections in Henry Berry-Hill and Sidney Berry-Hill, *George Chinnery, 1774–1852, Artist of the China Coast* (Leigh on Sea, F. Lewis, 1963), Ernest S. Dodge, *George Chinnery, 1774–1852, and Other Artists of the Chinese Scene* (Peabody Museum, Salem, Massachusetts, 1967), Robin Hutcheon, *Chinnery* (Hong Kong: FormAsia, 1989), Conner, *Chinese Views: Western Perspectives 1770–1870* and *Impressions of the East: The Art of George Chinnery*.

[6] Charles Baudelaire, *Les Fleurs du Mal* (London: Picador, 1987) 269.

[7] Charles Baudelaire, *Art in Paris 1845–1862: Salons and Other Exhibition*, trans. & ed. Jonathan Mayne (New York: Phaidon, 1965) 26.

[8] Robin Hutcheon, *Souvenirs of Auguste Borget* (Hong Kong: SCMP, 1979) 7, reprints another version of a parallel scene, thus indicating how the picture is not the rendering of a single moment, but more generic.

[9] Conner, *George Chinnery 1774–1852: Artist of India and the China Coast* plate 113, 184.

[10] William J. Hunter, *Bits of Old China* (Shanghai: Kelly and Walsh, 1911) 149, 156. See the pictures of Canton in the catalogue for the exhibition in *Views of the Pearl River Delta* 138–200: In this volume, Conner (19) locates the source for the panorama in no. 54 (170), which is a panoramic view of Canton across the rooftops of the foreign factories. Dated 1810, it comes from the Chinese export trade, possibly from the artist Tonequa. See also no. 59 (180).

[11] Dodge, *George Chinnery, 1774–1852, and Other Artists of the Chinese Scene* vii.

[12] Harriett Low Hillard, *My Mother's Journal: A Young Lady's Diary of Five Years Spent in Manila, Macao and the Cape of Good Hope from 1829–1834*, ed. Katharine Hillard (Boston: George H. Ellis, 1900). See Rosemarie W.N. Lamas, *Everything in Style: Harriett Low's Macau* (Hong Kong: Hong Kong University Press, 2006) for a very thorough reading of Harriett Low's Diaries, and of the Macao culture they reveal.

[13] Conner, *George Chinnery 1774–1852: Artist of India and the China Coast*, colour plate 53, 172; Hutcheon, *Chinnery* (Hong Kong: FormAsia, 1989) 78, and *Impressions of the East*, 100.

[14] In another, his wife is shown playing the harp. This is not extant, but one survives of the husband and wife, where she plays the harp, and he sits across the picture; behind is a classical pillar and red draperies, and no association with China. (Conner 1993, colour plate 95, 229) On the use of music in portraiture, with special reference to Johan Zoffany (1733–1810), in India between 1783–1789, see Richard Leppert, 'Music, Domestic Life and Cultural Chauvinism: Images of British Subjects at Home in India', *Music and Society: The Politics of Composition, Performance and Reception*, ed. Richard Leppert and Susan McClary (Cambridge: Cambridge University Press, 1987) 63–104. In 1844, Chinnery sent 'Portrait of Assor', 'A "Tanka" boat-girl of Macao in China'. See Henry and Sidney Berry-Hill, *George Chinnery, 1774–1852, Artist of the China Coast*.

¹⁵ For these two paintings, see Conner, *George Chinnery 1774–1852: Artist of India and the China Coast* colour plate 96, 232; *Impressions of the East* 100, and colour plate C20 and plate C21, 108. For Chinnery's self-portrait, see Conner, *George Chinnery 1774–1852: Artist of India and the China Coast* colour plate 102, 242 and *Impressions of the East* colour plate B14, 61.

¹⁶ For the association of the fingers and blindness, especially in representations of blindness in the Bible, see Jacques Derrida, *Memoirs of the Blind: The Self-Portrait and Other Ruins*, trans. Pascale-Anne Brault and Michael Nasse (Chicago: University of Chicago Press, 1993) 4–15.

¹⁷ See Conner, *George Chinnery 1774–1852: Artist of India and the China Coast* (1993) colour plates 86 and 87, 214–5 and Hutcheon, *Chinnery* 52 for William Jardine; and Conner, *George Chinnery 1774–1852*, colour plate 88, 218 for Henry Wright.

¹⁸ Derrida, *Memoirs of the Blind: The Self-Portrait and Other Ruins* 70.

¹⁹ Conner, *George Chinnery 1774–1852: Artist of India and the China Coast* 272; see also Marcia Pointon, *Hanging the Head: Portraiture and Social Formation in Eighteenth-Century England* (New Haven: Yale University Press, 1993) 204–5 for a comparison with Sir Thomas Lawrence.

²⁰ See Jacques Lacan, *The Four Fundamental Concepts of Psychoanalysis* 74 for the stain, 88 for the anamorphosis as the stain within the picture, 95–7 for the subject in the picture as a stain, 207–8 for aphanisis.

²¹ Derrida, *Memoirs of the Blind* 68–9. Derrida's point about the ruin is relevant, yet he critiques Benjamin for seeing the ruin as a theme of baroque culture only. 'It is precisely not a theme, for it ruins the theme, the position, the presentation or representation of anything and everything'. The point is valid, if — as is not shown or proved by Derrida — Benjamin uses the word 'theme'. But it is unfortunate, because it essentialises the ruin, and so erases the historical reference which is essential to this book.

²² Jacques Derrida, *Acts of Religion*, ed. Gil Anidjar (London: Routledge, 2002) 278.

²³ *Impressions of the East* plate 72, 147 and plate 58, 136.

²⁴ *Views of the Pearl River Delta* plate 20, 90.

²⁵ Walter Benjamin, *Charles Baudelaire: A Lyric Poet in the Age of High Capitalism*, trans. Harry Zohn (London: Verso, 1973) 176.

²⁶ Walter Benjamin, *The Origin of German Tragic Drama* 178.

Chapter Ten

[1] Patrick Conner, *George Chinnery 1774–1852: Artist of India and the China Coast* plate 150, 231.

[2] Conner, *George Chinnery 1774–1852: Artist of India and the China Coast* plate 151, 223, and plate 70, 145.

[3] Charlotte Brontë, *Jane Eyre* chapter 4, ed. Michael Mason (Harmondsworth: Penguin, 2003) 40.

[4] For detail of this cemetery, see Lindsay and May Ride, *An East India Company Cemetery: Protestant Burials in Macao*, ed. Bernard Mellor (Hong Kong: Hong University Press, 1996).

[5] See John Prendergast's 1843 pencil-on-paper, *Protestant Cemetery and Macao*, in *Views of the Pearl River Delta: Macao, Canton and Hong Kong* (Hong Kong Museum of Art and Peabody Essex Museum, 1996) no. 16, 82.

[6] Malcolm Andrews, *The Search for the Picturesque: Landscape Aesthetics and Tourism in Britain 1760–1800* (Aldershot: Scolar Press, 1989).

[7] Views of this grotto, by Thomas and William Daniell, appear in *Views of the Pearl River Delta* 66, no. 8, and Conner, *George Chinnery 1774–1852: Artist of India and the China Coast* colour plate 65, 186.

[8] The Portuguese name of the poem is itself puzzling: it can be a masculine or feminine plural, it does not appear in the poem, save in the title, and it seems to have been created in the sixteenth century to mean 'the sons of Lusus', a name relating to the Latin name for present-day Portugal, Lusitania. The humanist André de Resende (1500–1573) gave the title to Camões, saying that 'from Lusus, whence Lusitania gets its name, we call the Lusitanians Lusíadas ...'. Harold V. Livermore, 'On the Title of *The Lusiads*', in *Empire in Transition: The Portuguese World in the Time of Camões*, ed. Alfred Hower and Richard A. Preto-Rodas (Gainesville: University of Florida Press, 1985) 164.

[9] Lawrence Lipking, 'The Genius of the Shore: Lycidas, Adamastor and the Poetics of Nationalism', *PMLA* 111 (1996) 215.

[10] For discussion of Adamastor, see David Quint, *Epic and Empire: Politics and Generic Form from Virgil to Milton* (Princeton: Princeton University Press, 1993) 113–30. See also Jonathan Crewe, 'Recalling Adamastor: Literature as Cultural Memory in "White" South Africa', in Mieke Bal, Jonathan Crewe and Leo Spitzer, *Acts of Memory: Cultural Recall in the Present* (Hanover, University Press of New England, 1999) 75–86.

[11] William C. Atkinson, translating *The Lusiads* (Harmondsworth: Penguin, 1952) 8–9. The history is described in C.R. Boxer, *The Portuguese Seaborne Empire 1415–1825* (Harmondsworth: Penguin, 1973).

[12] Jack E. Tomlins, 'Gil Vicente's Vision of India and Its Ironic Echo in Camões' "Velho do Restelo"', *Empire in Transition: The Portuguese World in the Time of Camões* 175.

[13] Luís de Camões, *The Lusiads*, trans. Landeg White (Oxford: Oxford University Press, 1997) 194–5. Atkinson's translation is in prose; a free verse translation of Camões' *ottava rima* appears in the version by Landeg White, *The Lusiads* (Oxford: Oxford University Press, 1997).

[14] Bernhard Klein, '"We are not Pirates": Piracy and Navigation in *The Lusiads*', in *Pirates? The Politics of Plunder 1550–1650*, ed. Claire Jowitt (London: Palgrave Macmillan, 1997) 105–17.

[15] See Hans Turley, *Rum, Sodomy, and the Lash: Piracy, Sexuality and Masculine Identity* (New York: New York University Press, 1999) for a suggestive bibliography here.

Chapter Eleven

[1] For Mário Duarte Duque, Adalberto Tenreiro, Luís Tomás Pineiro Nagy, Maria José de Freitas, Joy Tin Tin Choi, Manuel Vicente, Carlos Moreno and Carlos Baracho (architects of the Museum of Macao, referred to in chapter 7), see *Macao Contemporary Architecture*, ed. Yan Chang (Macao: China Architecture and Building Press, 1999). There are many more architects and buildings in modern Macao than we can discuss here. See also special issue of *Dialogue: Architecture + Design + Culture*, ed. Weijen Wang (October 1999).

[2] For the distinction between molar and molecular, see Gilles Deleuze and Félix Guattari, *Anti-Oedipus: Capitalism and Schizophrenia*, trans. Robert Hurley (London: Athlone Press, 1983) 181.

[3] Anthony Blunt, *Guide to Baroque Rome* (London: Granada, 1982) 137.

[4] See for a reproduction of the latter, Alastair Smart, *The Assisi Problem and the Art of Giotto* (New York: Hacker Art Books, 1983) plate 55, see also pp. 176–7.

Chapter Twelve

[1] Paolo Veronese, *Venice Triumphant* (1584), 904 x 580 cm, Sala del Gran Consiglio, Doge's Palace, Venice. See, for a reproduction, Filippo Pedrocco, *Veronese* (Florence: Scala, 1998) 66.

[2] Roland Barthes, *Camera Lucida: Reflections on Photography*, trans. Richard Howard (New York: Vintage, 1982) discusses the modern age of the photography as giving 'flat Death'. 'One day, leaving one of my classes, someone said to me with disdain: "You talk about Death very flatly." — As if the horror of Death were not precisely its platitudinousness!' (93). He sees the modern as marked by the problem that there is nothing to say about death, that it produces indifference.

Glossary of Terms

The glossary here applies to terms as they are used in this book and therefore does not pretend to give complete definitions.

Allegory

Artworks where one subject is represented by another. A literary or artistic device where an abstract idea is turned into a character (this is called personification allegory). For example, in classical art, Fame is always represented as a female (in baroque art, with a trumpet). Since there is no reason why Fame=Woman, the Romantic poets and critics (Goethe, Coleridge) criticised allegory as presenting an arbitrary system of relationships. (Walter Benjamin contests this view, and the place given to symbolism [*q.v.*] by the Romantics.)

Anamorphosis

A distorted picture, which is designed to seem regular when seen from a particular perspective, when it is 'eyed awry' (Shakespeare, *Richard II* Act 2 scene 2 line 19, which explains how these 'perspective paintings' work.)

Architrave

The lintel (horizontal piece of timber or stone) extending from the capital of one column to another.

Art deco

In French, *art décoratif*, literally 'decorative art': modernist art style of the 1920s–30s with geometrical shapes and harsh colours.

Baldacchino

A canopy over a throne or an altar. Baroque art used twisted columns and fringed canopies.

Cartouche

A framed, ornamental space for an inscription, set in an architectural wall, often in the form of a scroll.

Chiaroscuro

'Light-dark': term in art criticism expressing the arrangement of light and shadow in a painting.

Classical art

The art of Greece and of Rome, up to the destruction of Rome in 410 CE; revived in Europe in Romanesque art, and more fully in the Renaissance, through such architects as Palladio (1508–1580), working with Vitruvius (c.75 BCE–25 BCE)'s designs in *De architectura* (which was rediscovered in 1414). Classical architecture was revived in the seventeenth century as neo-classicism, in opposition to the baroque, which may be seen as an art form distorting classicism. Classical art insists on formality, symmetry, 'taste' and restraint.

Classical orders

The 'order' in architecture refers to the base of a column, the shaft, the capital and the entablature. The capital, at the head of the pillar, may be undecorated (Doric), as with Santo Agostinho's double columns flanking the door (photograph 3). Capitals may be shaped like rams' horns, i.e. with volutes (Ionic), as at the lowest level of São Paulo (photograph 45); these volutes begin to look like sea-shells. They may have elaborate plant-like decorations (Corinthian), as at the third level of São Paulo.

Colonnade

A series of columns carrying an entablature.

Corbel

Stone or woodwork that projects out of the wall as the end of a beam which is bearing the weight of the structure above.

Cornice

The ornamental surmounting on a piece of architecture; any moulding which runs along the top of a building, completing it or crowning it.

Coulisse

In landscape painting, what appears to either side of the picture; the term derives from the flats placed at the sides in the theatre to prevent audiences seeing into the wings; coulisses give to the painting the appearance of depth.

Cupola

A dome which in a church is placed above the crossing (see Transept).

Entablature

In a building, that which is supported by a column. It includes the architrave, the frieze and the cornice.

Façade

The front or face of a building usually emphasised as separate from the structure of the rest of the building.

Fresco

Term used for painting on walls or ceilings, specifically where pigments are applied to fresh (hence fresco), still wet lime plaster.

Frieze

Usually decorated, the band between the architrave and the cornice, above a row of columns.

Gable

The triangular upper part of a wall under a pitched roof, sometimes specially shaped.

The Gaze

The essence of baroque, in theory. Synonyms for it are 'the real' and 'the *objet a*', or perhaps what Merleau-Ponty calls 'visibility'. Lacan suggests that something outside what can be symbolised is within the field of vision. This, because it seems to look at the viewer (but what 'it' is can never be identified) makes the viewer see himself as a single identity, which is an illusion. Outstandingly, this happens in the 'Mirror Stage'. Since what it is cannot be known, all attempts to symbolise it entail decentring, creating spaces which are strange and non-symmetrical, and they give to the baroque the sense of something awry.

Globalisation

Term of the 1990s; the process by which in the modern world, separate states and nationalities are brought into increasing contact and rendered similar to each other. The term may be seen as a development from postmodernism, or as a challenge to the activities taking place within countries which are postcolonial.

Gothic

The architecture prevalent in France, which pioneered it, c.1150, and marked by three attributes in cathedrals: the pointed arch, as opposed to the rounded arch of classical architecture, the flying buttress, and stained glass. Gothic architecture was seen as primitive in comparison with the classical, but was 'revived' several times in the seventeenth, eighteenth and nineteenth centuries. Gothic art is praised by Ruskin for the place it gave to the individual artist.

Iconography

Study of symbolism: an icon is an image, or portrait, or statue, or other likeness.

Manueline style

Named after King Manuel the Fortunate (1495–1521). It was the distinctive architecture of the Portuguese Renaissance, marked out by incrustation of surfaces and twisting of columns decorating the surrounds of doorways. Some of the decorations are inspired by tropical vegetation and plants.

Mannerism

Refers to an art style of the sixteenth century, often associated with Michelangelo, which reacts from the serenity of Renaissance styles, emphasising, exaggerating and distorting shapes and bodies in movement.

Mise en abîme

Refers to a picture placed within a picture, where the inner picture illuminates or illustrates, or copies, something in the outer, framing picture.

Modernism

In literature and architecture, this refers to art which reacts against nineteenth-century realism, replacing its heaviness by lack of ornamentation and stressing that art is functional. Often criticised for its failure to communicate itself to a wide audience.

Parergon

Decorative work surrounding another work of art (e.g. a painting); in deconstruction, the *parergon* questions what is the inside and what is the outside of the work of art.

Pediment

The gable above a portico. It may have straight sides or be curved, and may be open or broken at the apex.

Pilaster

Properly, a rectangular column protruding only slightly from the wall of a building, usually decorated at the capital with one of the three orders of architecture: Doric, Ionic, Corinthian.

Portico

Doorway in the façade of a temple or public building, usually with detached or attached columns and a pediment above.

Postcolonialism

Refers to the period after the removing of the colonial power from a country, and to the political and cultural situation thereafter. Sometimes used for the period after colonialisation has taken place.

Postmodernism

As used in this book, this term has two meanings: 1. Art which is playful and decorative as a reaction against modernism and which is intended to be popular and for consumption. 2. In philosophical terms, it refers to thinking which is 'anti-foundational', which does not believe in thought and language being based necessarily on self-evident truths, but considers thought as a play of language.

Realism

In the nineteenth century applies to art forms which accept an empiricist, 'common-sense' or scientific view of reality. Often associated with use of great detail and presenting its world-view as authoritative, giving middle-class values, which may be taken for granted.

Reredos/Retable

Decorated wall or screen behind an altar, either on the altar or standing behind it.

Rocaille

Rock-like or shell-like material used in gardens, often derived from Chinese models, associated with the rococo.

Rococo

Usually refers to eighteenth-century styles, which are aristocratic, decorative, sweet and playful, and stress delicate movement. Often uses light colours in contrast to the dark colours of the baroque.

Solomonic Columns

Associated with Bernini's baladacchino in St Peter's in Rome (1624–1633), twisted columns that were supposed to have been associated with Solomon's Temple in the Old Testament; appearing in the reproduction by Veronese (photograph 125) in the context of earthly glory.

Symbolism

Where a concept or an idea is represented by an object or person. The term has been seen as identical to allegory, but the Romantic poets downplayed allegory because they said that the comparisons it made were arbitrarily chosen, whereas the symbol implied a special relationship or identity between the idea and the object, the symbolised and the symbol.

Transept

In Gothic churches particularly (but not classical, and sometimes not baroque) the floor plan of the church is a cross: the west-to-east nave, and side-aisles, chancel and altar form the shaft of the cross, while the north and the south transepts project outwards to form two arms. The middle space is the crossing. (The church's alignment does not necessarily follow the points of the compass, but the basic point remains: you enter from the 'west' and look 'east' to the altar.)

Triglyph

The three markers often appearing on a lintel or architrave, in groups: signs of where rafters had been pushed through to support the roof; often placed simply for decoration: see photograph 61.

Trompe l'oeil

French, literally, 'deceives the eye': used here to refer to baroque tricks which make a picture or a part of an architectural design seem real; an illusion. For Lacan, the gaze tricks the eye in that it makes the eye see the world as a picture.

Tympanum

The area above the lintel of a door and the arch above it, or the triangular space inside the mouldings of the pediment.

Vedute

Italian, 'views', landscape paintings of cities, especially Venice, in the rococo period of the eighteenth century, concentrating on realism, in contrast to picturesque paintings, like those of Chinnery, these are of landscape, and less objective in character.

Index of Macao Places

Numbers in *italics* refer to photographs, numbers in **bold** refer to detailed discussion of places which we hope will help the visitor at each site. Numbers in italics and bold refer to both.

The Index of place-names suffers from the problem of knowing whether to reference names in Portuguese or English (and how accurately to Romanise Chinese names). We have tried to index names on the basis of what is most familiar to people, but there are bound to be inconsistencies here, not least because of different nationalities visiting or living in Macao, and places where the authors' judgment will differ from that of the reader. We know that Praya Grande should be Praia Grande, but decided eventually to use the more common spelling. Even the choice 'Macao' or 'Macau' is not free from controversy.

General Index